The Vikings Reimagined

The Northern Medieval World

On the Margins of Europe

The Vikings Reimagined

Reception, Recovery, Engagement

Edited by
Tom Birkett and Roderick Dale

DE GRUYTER

WESTERN MICHIGAN UNIVERSITY

MEDIEVAL INSTITUTE PUBLICATIONS

ISBN 978-1-5015-1815-7
e-ISBN (PDF) 978-1-5015-1388-6
e-ISBN (EPUB) 978-1-5015-1364-0

Library of Congress Control Number: 2019947710

Bibliographic information published by the Deutsche Nationalbibliothek
The Deutsche Nationalbibliothek lists this publication in the Deutsche Nationalbibliografie;
detailed bibliographic data are available on the Internet at http://dnb.dnb.de.

MIX
Papier aus verantwor-
tungsvollen Quellen
FSC® C083411

Acknowledgements

The editors would like to thank the Irish Research Council, who funded the "Rediscovering the Vikings Conference" from which this collection arose through a New Horizons Starter Grant (2015–2017), and who recognized the value of engaging the community in research on the Viking past. We are also grateful to the School of English at University College Cork for hosting the project, to Dr. Sarah Baccianti for keeping Old Norse going at UCC during Tom's research leave, to Kevin Crossley-Holland for his unfailing generosity, and to all the contributors, presenters, and exhibitors who took part in the conference or submitted material to the World-Tree Project archive. A big debt of thanks is also due to the *comitatus* at UCC (and particularly Alison, Niamh, Trisha, and Laura) for helping everything to run smoothly. It is not practicable to name everyone here, but this edited collection would not have been possible without the good will of many people. Finally, we'd like to thank Anne Schoerner and Karen for their support.

https://doi.org/10.1515/9781501513886-202

Contents

Acknowledgements —— V

List of figures —— IX

Tom Birkett
Introduction —— 1

M. J. Driscoll
1　Vikings! —— 19

Neil Price
2　My Vikings and *Real Vikings*: Drama, Documentary, and Historical
　Consultancy —— 28

Leszek Gardeła
3　(Re)discovering the Vikings in Poland: From Nineteenth-Century
　Romantics to Contemporary Warriors —— 44

Klaudia Karpińska
4　Women in Viking Reenactment —— 69

Jessica Clare Hancock
5　Who's Afraid of an Electric Torch? Reimagining Gender
　and the Viking World in Contemporary Picturebooks —— 89

Thomas Spray
6　The Terrible *Njorl's Saga:* Comedic Reimaginings of the
　Íslendingasögur from the Victorians to the Present Day —— 107

Heather O'Donoghue
7　The One that Got Away in Old Norse Myth, *Moby-Dick,*
　and the Work of Hugh MacDiarmid —— 129

Richard North
8　Death ere the Afternoon: *Jómsvíkinga saga* and a Scene
　in Hemingway's *For Whom the Bell Tolls* —— 145

Carolyne Larrington

9   "(No More) Reaving, Roving, Raiding, or Raping": The Ironborn in George R. R. Martin's *A Song of Ice and Fire* and HBO's *Game of Thrones* —— 162

Kendra Willson

10   A Saga King in a Finnish Beijing Opera —— 180

Maja Bäckvall

11   "Pick up Rune": The Use of Runes in Digital Games —— 201

Roderick Dale

12   From Barbarian to Brand: The Vikings as a Marketing Tool —— 214

Rebecca Boyd

13   Raiding the Vikings: How Does Ireland Consume Its Viking Heritage? —— 232

Eleanor Rosamund Barraclough

14   The Great Viking Fake-Off: The Cultural Legacy of Norse Voyages to North America —— 250

Kevin Crossley-Holland

Afterword: Tell These Stories Yourself —— 267

Index —— 273

List of Figures

Figure 3.1 1 – Thor's hammer from the vicinity of Wolin in Western Pomerania; 2 – Fragment of a cross-shaped pendant from Kąty in Greater Poland; 3 – Fragment of a cross-shaped pendant from Gralewo in Greater Poland; 4 – A small plaque with a triquetra motif from Ostrów Lednicki in Greater Poland. Reproduced after Gardeła, *Scandinavian Amulets in Viking Age Poland*, pp. 70, 118 and Żurowski, "Z ostatnich odkryć na Ostrowie Lednickim," p. 108 —— **47**

Figure 3.2 Selection of objects from a Viking Age cremation grave discovered at Świelubie in Pomerania: 1 – Oval brooch; 2 – Fragmented catch-plate of the oval brooch; 3 – Indeterminate iron object; 4 – Copper alloy tubes; 5 – Fragment of a clay vessel; 6 – Gaming pieces made of bone; 7 – Melted glass beads; 8 – Amber fragment. Reproduced after Kostrzewski, *Obrządek ciałopalny u plemion polskich*, p. 68 —— **48**

Figure 3.3 Selection of finds from an early medieval cemetery at Łubowo in Greater Poland, including a spear, an axe, an iron knife, and iron hoops of a bucket. Reproduced after Gardeła, *Scandinavian Amulets in Viking Age Poland*, p. 28 —— **50**

Figure 3.4 Excavations in Wolin under the Nazi banner (1936). Reproduced after Kazimierz Błahij, *Ostatnia tajemnica zatopionych bogów* —— **52**

Figure 3.5 Grave 10 from the early medieval cemetery at Lutomiersk in central Poland. 1 – Two copper alloy cheek pieces with a decorative motif probably representing two flying serpents, supernatural creatures well-known from Slavic beliefs; 2 – Decorated bridle mounts; 3 – Two copper alloy spurs with zoomorphic motifs. Artistic reconstruction by Mirosław Kuźma. Finds redrawn after Grygiel, "Cmentarzysko wareskich drużynników w Lutomiersku," p. 715 and Nadolski, Abramowicz, Poklewski, *Cmentarzysko z XI wieku w Lutomiersku pod Łodzią*, plates XLIV and LIV —— **54**

Figure 4.1 Recreation of a battle during the 22nd Festival of Slavs and Vikings, Wolin, Poland. Photograph: Klaudia Karpińska —— **72**

https://doi.org/10.1515/9781501513886-204

Figure 4.2   Women taking part in the recreation of a cremation burial during the Rękawka Fest in Cracow, Poland in 2014. Photograph: Klaudia Karpińska —— **73**

Figure 4.3   A modern *vǫlva* with a magic staff based on her own design. Photograph: Klaudia Karpińska —— **78**

Figure 4.4   Replica of a Viking Age staff made by Robert Pustelak. Photograph: Klaudia Karpińska —— **78**

Figure 4.5   The only warrior woman (among over 500 warriors) who took part in battles at the 22th Festival of Slavs and Vikings. Photograph: Klaudia Karpińska —— **80**

Figure 10.1   Elias Edström as Sigurd Ring (image used in production poster) —— **185**

Figure 10.2   Sigurd Ring (Elias Edström) holds the dying Hilma (Talvikki Eerola) —— **188**

Figure 13.1   A tour guide at the Viking Splash Tour. Image © Viking Splash Tours —— **235**

Figure 13.2   Déise Medieval at Gallows Hill in Co. Waterford, 2017. Image © John Foley Images —— **241**

Figure 13.3   The race medals and T-shirts for the 2018 Waterford Viking Marathon. Image © Waterford Viking Marathon —— **243**

Tom Birkett
Introduction

Vikings in the Public Eye

The question "who were the Vikings?" is one that scholarship is well equipped to address. We may argue (a great deal) about when the Viking Age began and ended, what drove the exodus from Scandinavia, and what exactly constituted Viking activity in the various areas of what is sometimes called the "Viking world" (a loosely defined area stretching from Greenland in the west to the Black Sea river routes in the east). New finds and new approaches to existing sources continually refine or challenge our picture of those seafarers who, as one Byzantine patriarch memorably put it (talking of the Rus' raid on Constantinople in 860 rather than localized Scandinavian piracy), "have been stirred up from the ends of the earth, holding bow and spear" their voices "as the roaring sea."[1] But as Driscoll demonstrates in the opening chapter of this collection, whilst there are many cases where the label "Viking" is used in a potentially misleading way, there is a broad scholarly consensus about the historical meaning of the term (if not its etymology), the contexts in which it is appropriate to use the designation in an unqualified way in academic discourse (referring to a particular group of people involved in a particular activity), and the period in which seaborne raiding was a prominent feature of Scandinavian affairs. We are also well equipped to reassess the tangible impact of the Vikings and the wider Norse expansion, in terms of the effect on settled societies, linguistic, literary, and cultural cross-fertilization, and the discovery and settling of new lands. The historical Vikings, and indeed the "Viking phenomenon" itself, are in no danger of being neglected.[2]

The questions "what does the term 'Viking' mean today?" and "what role do the Vikings play in contemporary culture?" are, on the other hand, ones that scholarship has in the past sometimes found easier to avoid, preferring to prescribe or clarify usage rather than interrogate new meanings. It is clear that the term "Viking" is used in public discourse in a much broader sense than that of "a pirate of Scandinavian origin engaged in raiding and extortion in the early medieval period": it has become a shortcut to a historical period (the Viking Age) as well as a broad cultural designation, as indispensable to academics engaged in a public-facing discourse as it is to the tourist industry, commerce,

Tom Birkett, University College Cork

https://doi.org/10.1515/9781501513886-001

and the cultural economy. Many of us have become adept at a kind of medievalist double-think, using the term "Viking" precisely in one situation, and as a useful catch-all in another, as descriptors such as "the Viking world," "Viking studies," and the various Viking museums, publications, conferences, and exhibitions (few of which focus exclusively on raiding) suggest. This malleability is as necessary as it is sometimes confusing: as Judith Jesch puts it in her introduction to *The Viking Diaspora*, "Viking seems to be a word ... that has expanded and developed to fill a gap, to give a name to a phenomenon which previously had no name but needed one."[3] This "inclusive meaning" is developing all the time as the Viking brand is marketed in different ways and new interpretations of the Vikings are disseminated in the public domain, and it varies depending on perspective: to put it crudely, a Dane living in Roskilde and surrounded by tangible heritage, Viking festivals, and glorious reconstructed longships – and in a country where the Vikings are heavily promoted as a national brand – is likely to have a different baseline for imagining the Vikings than someone who grew up in Berwick-upon-Tweed raised on stories of the sacking of nearby Lindisfarne and with bloodthirsty Norsemen on the curriculum, or a resident of Viking, Minnesota (population 100) supporting her state's NFL team. Different sub-cultures and interest groups – from local-history societies to gamers, neo-pagans to navy personnel – also reimagine the Norse past in a guise that reflects their particular interest in the period. Rather than trying to move us back towards the "real Viking," this book is about some of the ways through which the popular image of Viking and Old Norse culture has been channeled and disseminated in the public domain as well as the central place that reimagined Viking history plays in our cultural world.

As Rebecca Boyd points out in her chapter on the branding of the Viking Age in Ireland "the Vikings are an easy concept for people to grasp and accept," and this ease of recognition, along with the malleability that Wawn highlights in his *BBC History* article on the subject,[4] are perhaps two of the main reasons that the Viking past is invoked so frequently in both popular and scholarly discourse. If we refer to an Anglo-Saxon seafarer, or a Vendel warrior, there are limited points of reference. If we refer to a Viking, there are thousands of cultural reference points, from the branding of multinational companies to the friendly Vikings of children's TV series and the cultural antagonists of Hollywood films: it is no exaggeration to say that there's an image of the Vikings to suit all tastes and all agendas. Of course, many of these re-imaginings of the Vikings replicate unhelpful stereotypes or falsehoods, the continuing ubiquity of the horned helmet in popular culture (regularly, and perhaps unnecessarily, debunked by academics) being a case in point. But even the remarkable endurance of certain stereotypes, when viewed alongside the myriad ways in which the Vikings are invoked in popular culture, can tell us a great deal about the re-uses of the past and the wider impact of Old Norse language, literature, and culture that has been mediated through the Viking brand. As Neil Price points out in his contribution to this collection, sometimes contemporary (and popular) reimaginings of the Vikings present scholars with a new way of seeing and engaging with the period: not only through push-back against misuse, but through the challenge of responding to and further nuancing a vividly reimagined history. Even a hoax such as the Kensington runestone can be useful, "an effective catalyst of scientific and scholarly debate," as Eleanor Barraclough, quoting Henrik Williams, argues in her chapter on the role of the Vikings in the American foundation myth.[5] Misappropriations should not go unchallenged of course: the growing confidence of far-right groups to parade their manufactured Viking heritage underscores the need for scholarship to respond to and actively resist pernicious misuses of the past. However, it is not enough for experts to dismiss popular responses to the Vikings and the role that the Vikings play in our wider culture as illegitimate, inaccurate, or unworthy of scholarly attention. Reimaginings with the reach of the series *Vikings*, the video game *God of War*, or national tourism campaigns are establishing a baseline for public understanding of the Viking past and Norse culture, and their impact on the discipline – for good and for bad – has been profound. If scholarship will not engage with reception, it has lost its prerogative to inform reception.

The cultural legacy of the Vikings has received increasing prominence in recent years, though usually with reference to reception history rather than the reimagining of Vikings in the present. The influence of Norse myth and literature on different literary and artistic traditions has been a particularly rich area of enquiry,[6] whilst other studies have focused on the reception and exploitation of Norse and Viking cultures in particular historical periods:[7] occasionally attempts have been made to sketch out the reception landscape as a whole,[8] though usually with a focus on the influence of Old Norse literature on different cultural products and political movements, rather than taking up the question of the role that the "imagined" Viking plays in contemporary culture at large. Andrew Wawn's collection *Northern Antiquity* is one exception, but its focus is again on reception history rather than contemporary Vikings, and the reception landscape has changed a great deal in the two decades since it was published. Every now and again it is important to pause and take stock of where we are, how we reached this point, and where the fault lines exist between the scholarly and public discourse.

As several of the essays in this collection serve to illustrate, the reimagining of the Vikings is by no means a recent phenomenon: indeed, every iteration of Norse culture in the popular imagination is the product of a long history of reception, "an accumulation of texts, images, sounds, and ideas that reverberate through the fabric of various cultures at various times" as Helgason has recently described it.[9] Localized periods of intense national interest in the Viking past, combined with what is sometimes called the "Viking revival" of the eighteenth and nineteenth centuries should make us wary of ascribing too much significance to the vogue for Vikings that we've seen in recent years: indeed, certain preconceptions about the Viking past are remarkably persistent, having changed little from the image presented to us by Wagner or the Victorian translations of George Webbe Dasent. In a study of popular Vikings some twenty years ago, Alexandra Service claimed that "Vikings are everywhere" and that 1997 "could well be called the Year of the Viking Festival,"[10] whilst in a more recent article I argued that 2014 could be considered the "Year of the Vikings."[11] Neither of us was entirely wrong: and yet the public appetite for the Vikings shows no sign of abating. Indeed, it is hard to avoid the impression that we are currently witnessing a twenty-first-century "Viking revival," perhaps distinguished from previous periods of intense interest in the Norse past only by the prominence of different media, and by the increasingly international reach of Vikings disseminated online and through productions aimed at a large global audience. Marvel's reimagining of the Norse god Thor reaches many millions of cinema goers; adaptations of Viking Age history are being streamed across the globe, from History's hit series *Vikings*, to the BBC adaptation of Bernard Cornwell's *Saxon* series (*The Last Kingdom*) and the medieval-themed phenomenon that is *Game of Thrones*. Video games such as the critically acclaimed *Skyrim* (2011) and *God of War* (2018), have immersed gamers in vivid reimaginings of Norse myth and legend, replete with runes and snippets of Old Norse; new versions of the myth cycle – including Neil Gaiman's acclaimed retelling, Kevin Crossley-Holland's "fast-moving and ice bright" rendition, beautifully illustrated by Jeffrey Alan Love, and my own *Norse Myths* for Quercus – have appeared in the space of a few years[12]; whilst the 2017 series remake of Gaiman's beloved *American Gods* has seen Odin driving a Cadillac across our screens to join the ranks of increasingly high-budget forays into the world of the Norse gods. Viking tourism is flourishing, as witnessed by new international tourism concepts such as Destination Viking,[13] the newly opened Thor's Rike theme park in Norway,[14] and the proposed Viking Coast tour in Ireland, whilst established Viking experiences such as the recently re-opened Jorvik, Dublinia and the Ribe VikingCenter continue to innovate in their presentation of the Viking past to new audiences. Several high-profile discoveries including the possible Norse settlement at Point Rosee in Newfoundland have garnered huge attention in the media and served to underscore the fact that the Viking legacy is not confined to areas of permanent Norse settlement, whilst collaborations such as the blockbuster *Vikings: Life and Legend* exhibition organized by Denmark's Nationalmuseet, the British Museum, and the Staatliche Museen zu Berlin, and festivals such as Ireland's 2014 Battle of Clontarf anniversary celebrations (bringing together reenactors from across Europe), as well as Viking heritage projects such as "Languages, Myths and Finds,"[15] have further highlighted the transnational appeal of the Viking past. Viking branding also draws heavily on the international appeal of Vikings as pioneers and global travelers, as well as targeting specific audiences. Viking-branded companies, Vikings in advertisements, and new Viking-themed products are entering the market at a bewildering rate – in Connecticut you might have Viking windows and appliances from Viking Range Corporation installed by Viking Construction Inc. and protected by a Viking sprinkler system: you can have Mobile Viking as your network provider in Belgium, office supplies delivered by Viking Direct, and embark on a Viking cruise to the Caribbean safe in the knowledge that your ship is equipped with Viking Life Saving Equipment. It remains to be seen whether or not we have reached "peak Viking," but the cultural and commercial exploitation of the Viking brand shows little sign of slowing down.

The World-Tree Project, which was based at University College Cork and funded by a 15-month Irish Research Council "New Horizons" grant (2015–2017), aimed to make sense of this rapidly evolving legacy and to collaborate with the public in the creation of a new online resource on the Vikings.[16] The Project used international community collection – a form of cultural heritage crowdsourcing – to create a digital archive of material relating to the Vikings for use in research and teaching (www.worldtreeproject.org). Targeted groups such as academics and reenactors as well as the wider public were approached and asked to contribute materials such as photographs, text, language aids, and video clips to the archive, which the researchers then described, collated, and made available on the project website, using these resources to create a series of educational exhibits aimed at different audiences.[17] Many of the contributions that the public made to the archive fell into the category of modern Vikings: examples of branding, expressions of heritage and identity, and local responses to the Viking past including information about events. In all, over 4,000 individual items were collected from contributors in some thirty countries, giving a tantalizing glimpse into the different ways in which the Viking past is used and perceived across Europe, and revealing much about what a twenty-first-century public expects from its Vikings.

As several of the essays in this collection caution, the increasingly global profile of the Vikings and the targeting of large international audiences (whether through major brands, popular series, or projects with an international focus) perhaps in itself privileges certain ways of representing the past.

It is easy to laugh at the Vikings of the Victorian era with their steely eyes, spirit of "derring-do," and imperial ambitions, or even at the bloodthirsty two-dimensional characters from the text-books of a previous generation, but recent focus on the outward-looking, internationalist Vikings, a welcome emphasis on cultural contact and exchange, and fascination with certain aspects of appearance (including the tattoos, eye-shadow, and elaborate hairstyles that seem to be obligatory in recent on-screen representations) may be equally contingent: these are twenty-first-century Vikings. The "Rediscovering the Vikings" conference from which the present collection arose was held in November 2016 under the auspices of the World-Tree Project and recognized the need to interrogate this rapidly evolving legacy in collaboration with the wider community and to give some context for the Vikings' extraordinary appeal in the present day. It sought to bring together different people with a stake in this shared past – heritage experts, living history enthusiasts, and the wider public, as well as scholars from different disciplines – in order to discuss the impact of the popular discourse on the study of the Viking Age and to rethink the ways in which the academy engages with the Viking past in the public domain. The current collection is presented in the same spirit of interdisciplinarity and collaboration: highlights from the conference have been included as short exploratory essays supplemented by chapters commissioned from experts in particular aspects of the reception of Viking and Norse cultures. Diverse in their individual approaches, these essays collectively move us closer to an understanding of the twenty-first-century image of the Viking, and to an appreciation of reception not simply as ancillary to Viking and Old Norse Studies, but at the heart of the subject and its value in the modern world.

Opening the collection, M. J. Driscoll queries the validity of the term "Viking," outlines its origins, meaning, and the period which it has come to define, and asks whether it is ever applicable outside reference to a particular group of people (male warriors) engaged in a particular activity (seaborne raiding): perhaps as representative of Scandinavian society at large as polo players are representative of Western culture today. Several of the individual contributions that follow allow for a wider definition than suggested by Driscoll, and the collection as a whole recognizes the utility of the term "Viking" outside the strict definition that needs to be upheld within certain scholarly arenas. But the fact that the term "Viking" has taken on a life of its own (a legacy that this collection tries to account for) perhaps makes it even more imperative to begin with a study such as Driscoll's: a solid launching point for a journey into less charted territory.

Slippages in the use of the term "Viking" are just one facet of the shifting perception of the Viking Age, which Neil Price, in the second chapter of the collection, argues is always a "curiously personal" matter, even (and perhaps especially) for scholars who are acutely aware that our own knowledge of the Viking Age does not remain static. Indeed, Price cautions against mistaking our scholarly reconstruction of history for the rich reality of the period itself: one of the things that the recent TV series *Vikings* gets right is portraying "a world that sings and breathes": a complex, curious culture open to change and not in the least bit self-conscious about the fact they are "Vikings," "Norsemen," "pagans," or whatever other labels they have been given by posterity. It is easy to quibble with the chronology of events or the many oversights in the material culture portrayed, and Price doesn't shy away from critiquing other aspects of the series (to the clichéd Orientalism of the Mediterranean cultures noted by Price, I would add the portrayal of the uniformed and hierarchical Anglo-Saxon English as another lazy stereotype of the period). However, scholarly nit-picking risks missing the potential that series with such a vast reach and imaginative depth have to alter public perceptions of the Vikings for the better. Price's involvement in *Real Vikings*, a rare example of a documentary intended to "academically engage with and nuance an imagined reconstruction" gives him the opportunity – increasingly absent from academia – to take stock of the discipline and how his own perceptions have changed, and also to recognize the potential of the screen to let us imagine and reimagine the period.

A history of recent archaeological developments across the Norse world and how they have changed our perception of the Vikings would require a multi-volume work. However, Gardeła, through his survey of the major developments in the archaeology of the Vikings in Poland, provides a microcosm for the subject at large. By tracing the trends in thinking about the Vikings in this particular (and until recently, largely overlooked) context, Gardeła draws attention to the fact that scholarly as well as public responses to Viking archaeology have been profoundly influenced by the politics and priorities of the receiving culture, coming "to reflect the difficult cultural and political transformations in this part of Europe, as well as the spirit of its people." Today's trending image of the Viking as international, outward-looking Europeans perhaps still motivates certain kinds of research and causes us to overstate the evidence in favor of particular interpretations: Gardeła's survey reminds us that our own reimagining of the Vikings is likely to be provisional, just like those of previous generations that we are now in a position to critique.

The reenactment scene, both in Poland and further afield, has developed in tandem with the changing archaeological landscape, and recent years have seen greater collaboration between academics and living history enthusiasts, as well as an increased focus on the roles of women within a traditionally male-dominated arena. Klaudia Karpińska, as a scholar who bridges the academic and reenactment worlds, is well placed to comment on these developments. Female participants have diverse reasons for their involvement in reenactment beyond a fascination with the period – many of which are closely linked with identity, belonging, and perceptions of Viking women as models of strength and independence. Indeed, the appeal of two particular "roles," that of *vǫlva* and female warrior, is probably more a reflection of the agency of these figures in Norse society and the traditional focus of reenactment on displays of combat and ritual than it is on recent finds and debate about the existence of the shieldmaiden figure: indeed, many of the reenactors surveyed by Karpińska are understandably less concerned about authenticity than visibility. Increasing focus on displays of handicrafts and domestic life at Viking events is, Karpińska suggests, in part a legacy of important reappraisals of Norse women in the 1990s and early 2000s. Reenactment responds to new finds, developments, and reimaginings of the Vikings in the academic discourse, and is itself an important means through which public perceptions of the Viking past, and the public understanding of the role of women in Norse culture, are mediated.

Gendered constructions of the Vikings reach us in many ways, from the particular roles assigned in reenactment, to the recent scholarly reinterpretation of Viking Age graves that sparked off a debate not only about women in Norse society, but about contemporary gender politics and the risk of projecting modern sensibilities onto past cultures. One hugely influential, but largely overlooked, way in which preconceptions about the period are formed is through early exposure to Viking characters in children's picturebooks. Taking a sample of recent offerings, Jessica Clare Hancock identifies the different roles that female Vikings are assigned, from bit-characters in a world of burly men and raider-masculinities to protagonists who bring intelligence to the activities of raiding and adventuring and who control their own narratives. The varied portrayal of the Vikings found in this formative genre create a baseline for later responses to the past which "will only ever be modified, rather than erased": that different ideas about Viking gender identity are promoted at such an early stage should make us reconsider whether such preconceptions are embedded in our own responses to the Viking past, particularly if these responses are as personal as Price suggests.

Children's books usually present a light-hearted image of the Norse past, with potential for poking fun at the brawny and not-so-bright caricature of the Viking warrior. But the re-imagining of the Vikings as comic figures is not by any means limited to the meat-headed compatriots of Wickie the Viking, or the skull-sipping warriors of *Asterix and the Vikings* (on a search for the meaning of fear). The stereotypical image of the Viking – particularly the humorless portrayal of the winged-helmeted warrior feasting in Valhalla beloved by the Victorians – has become a site of humor of a more sophisticated kind: a humor that can tell us a great deal both about the popular understanding of the Vikings, and also about the willingness of popular culture to interrogate these same stereotypes. From amongst the myriad comic responses to Norse literature and culture (ranging from comics poking fun at Thor's macho image, to the tongue-in-cheek "Norse Power" scent range developed by York tourist board)[18] Thomas Spray's chapter takes on the less-studied example of the Icelandic Family Saga. Whilst the irreverent, knowing (and thoroughly postmodern) take on "Njorl's saga" by *Monty Python's Flying Circus* may have seemed like a thoroughly new departure for comic reimaginings of the Norse past, Spray demonstrates that there is precedent for mocking of both the "hardy northerners" on display in the sagas, and the eccentricities of Norse scholars that can be traced to the era of the first translations of the sagas in Victorian England. Whilst the Victorians get the blame for many of the most egregious myths laid down about the Viking past (from winged helmets and skull quaffing, to solemn admiration of the noble northern spirit), Spray demonstrates that such stereotypes were under interrogation even at the time they were most prevalent in the public imagination, through mock travel accounts such as that by Charles Cavendish Clifford and even in such unexpected places as the novels of Charles Dickens. The gap between reality and the weight a past culture is expected to bear perhaps lies at the source of such irreverent humor as found to the present day in such diverse forms as children's cartoons, the poetry of Ian Duhig, and feminist stand-up comedy. Comic reimaginings of the Vikings, rather than taking us further away from that illusive concept of the "real Vikings," perhaps show us a culture that is fully aware of our capacities to remake history and to reflect the "absurdities of our own time."

As Spray points out, "no one writes a parody of an unknown genre": for such humor to work effectively, the object of parody must be known and the debt must be made explicit. But there are other responses to Norse and Viking cultures where the reimagining does not depend on acknowledgement of any source, and in which the literary inspiration may be hard to recognize without specialist knowledge, mediated by other popular forms, or even actively concealed. Heather O'Donoghue's essay focuses on a largely overlooked correspondence between the main plotline of one of the great American novels, Melville's *Moby-Dick*, and the story of Thor's unsuccessful attempt to land the Midgard Serpent on his fishing trip with the giant Hymir. O'Donoghue demonstrates that Melville owes a clear debt to the Norse narrative of "the One that Got Away," from descriptions of the White Whale itself, to the repeated cutting of the taut line, to comparisons between Captain Ahab and Thor. The links are strengthened by the fact that Hugh MacDiarmid makes clear reference to both the frustrations of Ahab and the near landing of the Miðgarðsormr as an "allegory of literary creativity" in his poetry and like Melville even appropriates the narrative of the one that got away as "ostensible autobiography." Where Melville obtained his knowledge of the Norse myth of Thor and the World Serpent is a question left for others to answer, though O'Donoghue suggests that the influence of Old Norse literature may be more extensive than his knowledge of this one myth. What this essay makes clear is that our cultural debt to Norse mythology is not limited to wholesale reworkings, direct borrowing, or even subtle poetic allusions to the Norse gods: Old Norse literature has been so thoroughly imbibed into our culture that authors often write "under the influence" of the sources without ever making the debt explicit.[19] Perhaps such unacknowledged replication is one reason that certain tropes and images concerning the Viking past are so deeply embedded and resistant to change: we feel we *know* these narratives. Every student who has read *Moby-Dick* and internalized the failure of Ahab's single-minded quest to land the white whale is perhaps conditioned to find Thor losing the Midgard Serpent somehow appropriate (as O'Donoghue points out, he was not foiled in every version of the myth). As anyone teaching Norse myth knows, exposure to later reimaginings of mythical narratives (such as the pop-culture image of Thor) impacts on the way we encounter and interpret the originals. Recognizing the true extent of this pre-conditioning can perhaps help us to navigate assumptions about the literature and rethink the role of reception in our teaching of the Viking past.

In the following chapter Richard North looks at the question of influence on another of the greats of the American literary canon, Ernest Hemingway, and here the chain of connections, if anything, stretches even deeper. North argues that a memorable scene in *For Whom the Bell Tolls* (an episode of cold-blooded violence that Hemingway himself expresses surprise in having "invented") is a reflection of an episode of Viking bravado recounted in *Jómsvíkinga saga*. Through careful study of Hemingway's library, North suggests it wasn't the saga itself that Hemingway knew, but most likely a twentieth-century novel, itself based on a romanticized retelling of the episode. In tracing these correspondences across texts and literary genres – and Hemingway's projection of "Viking" values onto the fascist *guardias civiles* in Spain's civil war – North's essay raises another important point about the image of the Vikings in the popular imagination and the way this image is continually repurposed as a literary touchstone. For Hemingway to have – perhaps unconsciously – turned to the Jómsvíkings for an example of insouciance in the face of death "for an enemy he admired" shows how deeply embedded such cultural reference points are. It is worth remembering that *Jómsvíkinga saga* itself is a fiction, and may bear only a cursory resemblance to the historical Jómsvíkings (if, indeed, this brotherhood of pirates existed at all). When a writer recalls an episode from Old Norse literature, as Hemingway seems to have done here, it is already a fiction in process at several removes from what we might call the historical realities of the Vikings: as North argues, such examples suggest "influence of a wider kind" than we often credit, being used to stylize not only modern literature, but "modern history."

Carolyne Larrington refers to such refracted knowledge of the sources, mediated via other popular genres that may themselves have strayed quite far from the originals, as a key component of "neomedievalism," and nowhere is it more prominent than in the modern fantasy genre. There are few novels with as wide a reach as George R. R. Martin's *A Song of Ice and Fire*, with the *Game of Thrones* series based on his books reaching many millions of viewers. That Martin would draw on Norse and Viking cultures in the creation of his medieval-themed fantasy is perhaps not as surprising as the use of Norse myth by literary greats such as Hemingway and Melville: what is notable are the aspects of this culture that he chose to draw on, outlined by Larrington in the next essay in the collection. Like the other authors taken up in this collection, Martin draws "primarily on popular knowledge and second-order reimaginings about the Vikings" (including Tolkien's fiction) to create his composite neomedieval world, but also demonstrates knowledge of the sources themselves: such a fluid "postmodernist" approach, melding real and fictional Viking cultures with modern sensibilities, complicates the reception narrative. The Viking mindset is most conspicuous in the "Old Way" of the Ironborn culture in Martin's novels, but also manifests itself in the choices facing these "reavers" about whether, like the Norse settlers, to abandon the piratical life and focus on an existence and livelihood more in line with the cultures with whom they interact. The fact that the heroine Yara champions the future that medieval Scandinavians actually took, against the determination of the patriarchy to drag the Ironborn back to more stereotypically "Viking" ways, signals Martin's desire to use the medieval past "to signal ways in which our present may also be reconfigured."

The influence of Norse literature, and depictions of legendary Vikings, has traveled a long way, and not only informs adaptations for the page and screen, but has also melded with the traditional art forms of various cultures, ranging from Japanese manga to Beijing capital-city theatre. Kendra Willson's essay considers *Sigurd Ring*, a 2016 Beijing opera-style theatrical performance produced in Finland and based around a legendary eighth-century Norse king whose exploits are alluded to in various kings' sagas and the *Gesta Danorum*, reworked in a seventeenth-century Latin retelling of a lost *Skjöldunga saga*, and brought together in a nineteenth-century Swedish play: the ultimate source for the 2016 performance under discussion. Willson considers the aspects of the heroic life of Sigurd that make it appropriate source material for the genre, conventions, and character types of "capital-city-theatre," as well as the new perspective on the past afforded by the Finnish director Edström's attempts "to connect the Chinese theatrical tradition he had studied to his own Nordic heritage." Stories of a warrior-elite dictated by an "honor system" are favored in both medieval kings' sagas and *jingju* performance, and the effect of adapting the romantic Swedish play *Sigurd Ring* to this traditional Chinese form actually had the effect of bringing it closer to the ethos of the original, allowing for "renewal through synthesis."

Edström's unusual cross-fertilization sees the Vikings reimagined across language, culture and media: perhaps the most influential of these mediated Vikings (both in terms of reach and immersion) occur in video games. Maja Bäckvall's contribution to the collection focuses on one specific "semiotic resource", in the wider reimagining of the Vikings in digital games: the use of the runic script. Runes are often used in popular culture as a shorthand for Viking textual culture, even if the script used is sometimes the older futhark and the forms of literacy represented (particularly lengthy communicative utterances and rune-staves) are more representative of the later medieval evidence. However, because runes, like the Vikings themselves, have certain deeply ingrained cultural associations, game developers can draw on these connotations to realize specific semiotic effects, from hinting at a deep past, to evoking magic and sorcery. Through surveying several high-profile examples of the genre, Bäckvall demonstrates not only how digital games reflect semiotic modes, but also how they now play a central role in reimagining aspects of Norse and Viking culture and disseminating these ideas to the mass audience who interact with and consume these cultural products.

The final three chapters of this collection put the marketing and consumption of the Vikings center stage, moving from a consideration of the various ways in which the Vikings are reimagined and mediated through popular art forms, to a consideration of the role that Viking branding plays in creating the popular image of the Viking past: whether that be the marketing of a business or product, the promotion of Viking tourism, or the use of the Viking brand in the construction of regional and national identities. As Roderick Dale points out in his chapter on "Marketing the Vikings," examples of the exploitation of the Vikings in the commercial sphere are not hard to spot, and range from well-known advertisements and brands (such as Marvel's *Thor* or Viking Life Saving Equipment) to local iterations of this global brand. Using examples of branding crowdsourced from across Europe by the World-Tree community-collection project, Dale surveys the changing nature of the Viking brand and identifies several common tropes – endurance, adventurousness, joviality, and feasting – that appear to make the Vikings particularly useful in the promotion of certain products and services. What is perhaps most surprising is the way the brand is applied to products that have no discernible connection with the Vikings: to the Wickie Chicken nuggets and salami, we might add the German-branded "Wikinger waffeln," or the Indian underwear manufacturer Viking (one of their adverts carries the rather disconcerting slogan "feel alive, with Viking inside").[20] What these uses demonstrate is that the Viking brand itself is so strong it can add commercial value even when the public knows there is no connection to a historical period or indeed to Norse culture. Rather than decrying such uses and engaging in condescending "mythbusting" activities, Dale suggests that we regard it as a play activity and acknowledge that "people can accommodate both meanings in their lives": far better that scholars direct their energies towards countering those toxic myths of the Vikings that are deployed in order to exclude and marginalize people from a shared past.

As Dale points out, whilst the Viking brand is a global one, particular constructions of the Vikings can also be important markers of identity at an individual and local level. Rebecca Boyd's discussion of the way the Vikings have been presented to the public in Ireland, and the very different role the Viking past plays in the civic identities of cities such as Dublin and Waterford, draws attention to the fact that whilst some images of the Vikings have remained static, other aspects of this past are continually being reimagined in the public domain, sometimes outpacing the dissemination of new research on the period and certainly reaching a wider audience. This constant process of repackaging and repurposing of the Vikings for both civic identity and tourist consumption – made explicit through the prominence of the Vikings in the development of new "destination brands" such as Waterford's Viking Triangle and Ireland's Ancient East – is driven by commercial exploitation of a brand that is both popular and easily recognizable. However, it also provides scholars, heritage organizations, and living history enthusiasts an opportunity for the presentation of progressively richer and more complex visions of the Vikings to the wider public, ones that move us away from the image of the bearded barbarian (the Viking that a previous generation in Ireland was introduced to at school) and towards a fuller range of Norse activities including the roles of women, children, the elderly, and the infirm. As the term "Viking" has come to refer in public parlance to Norse culture at large, why not seek, as Boyd suggests, to broaden the public view of "Viking" culture rather than to correct the way in which the term is applied? Engagement with living history events – and the immediate connection with the past that it affords – is one way in which academics could help shape the public discourse.

The popular image of the Vikings that has developed in North America has perhaps the most tenuous connection to history, but as Eleanor Rosamund Barraclough argues in her chapter on "The Cultural Legacy of Norse Voyages to North America," "this largely faux-history continues to occupy an unusually prominent place in the national consciousness," connected as it is with belonging and identity. Barraclough first outlines the evidence for Norse contact with the "New World," before suggesting how the Vinland sagas have provided the opening for a myth that fits well with America's vision of itself as a nation of pioneers and adventurers. It is undoubtedly this image of the powerful and daring Viking explorer that has the most currency in the United States (as witnessed by evocation of "Viking pride" in the mottos and iconography of schools and military units across the country)[21] and is particularly prominent in areas with high levels of Scandinavian immigration. This has led to some enduring myths about the extent of Norse contact with and influence on America, to the great spectacles of pseudo-heritage performed at Minnesota Vikings NFL games, and even to elaborate fakes such as the Kensington rune stone. It is easy to dismiss such examples of modern Vikings as "fake news" or a nostalgia for origins, yet Barraclough also asks the provocative question: "how often does historical enquiry have less to do with establishing past facts, and more to do with the establishing of present identity?" As the essays in this collection make clear, the history of what we have come to call the Vikings – with all its slippages and shades of meaning – will always be a dialogue between the present and the past, verifiable history and contemporary perceptions.

To give us a personal take on this dialogue with history, the collection closes with an afterword from the master of reimagining medieval worlds: author, translator, and poet, Kevin Crossley-Holland. Many of the contributors to this collection (as well as its intended readers) will have been introduced to medieval literature and Norse mythology through Crossley-Holland's supple reworkings. His *Norse Myths* has not been out of print since its publication in 1980,[22] something that looks even more extraordinary against the backdrop of the shifting reception landscape that this collection explores: this is an author who managed to avoid writing to prevailing fashions, and instead tapped into something timeless. But Crossley-Holland has also returned to reimagine the Vikings again and again throughout a long career, writing for different audiences, through translations, retellings, and historical novels such as the Viking Sagas trilogy.[23] There was no better way to end a conference on the reception of the Vikings than with a reading from the greatest reimaginer of all; there is no better way to end this collection than with his words.

Bibliography

Arnold, Martin. *Thor: Myth to Marvel*. London: Continuum, 2011.

Birkett, Tom. "The Clontarf Effect: Teaching Old Norse in the Year of the Vikings." *Studies in Medieval and Renaissance Teaching* 25, no. 1 (2018): 15–33.

Birkett, Tom. *The Norse Myths: Stories of the Norse Gods and Heroes Vividly Retold*. London: Quercus, 2018.

Bödl, Klaus. *Der Mythos der Edda: Nordische Mythologie zwischen europäischer Aufklärung und nationaler Romantik*. Tübingen: Francke, 2000.

Clark, David and Carl Phelpstead, eds. *Old Norse Made New: Essays on the Post-Medieval Reception of Old Norse Literature and Culture*. Exeter: Viking Society for Northern Research, 2007.

Clunies Ross, Margaret. *The Norse Muse in Britain, 1750–1820*. Trieste: Parnasso, 1998.

Crossley-Holland, Kevin. *Norse Myths: Tales of Odin, Thor and Loki*. London: Walker Studio, 2017.

Crossley-Holland, Kevin. *The Penguin Book of Norse Myths: Gods of the Vikings*. London: Penguin, 2018.

"Destination Viking: The Legacy of the Vikings." https://www.destinationviking.com/.

Gaiman, Neil. *Norse Mythology*. New York: W. W. Norton, 2017.

Griggs, Mary Beth. "You Could Smell Like a Viking." *Smithsonian Mag*, May 28, 2014. https://www.smithsonianmag.com/smart-news/you-could-smell-viking-180951575/.

Hafner, Tina. *Peter Madsens Valhalla: Studien zur Rezeption altwestnordischer Mythen im modernen Comic*. Munich: GRIN Verlag, 2008.

Jesch, Judith. *The Viking Diaspora*. London: Routledge, 2015.

Jón Karl Helgason. *Echoes of Valhalla: The Afterlife of the Eddas and Sagas*. Translated by Jane Victoria Appleton. London: Reaktion Books, 2017.

Kipper, Rainer. *Der Germanenmythos im Deutschen Kaiserreich*. Göttingen: Vandenhoeck & Ruprecht, 2000.

"Languages, Myths and Finds: Translating Norse and Viking Cultures for the Twenty-first Century." https://languagesmythsfinds.ac.uk/.

O'Donoghue, Heather. *From Asgard to Valhalla: The Remarkable History of the Norse Myths*. New York: I. B. Tauris, 2007.

O'Donoghue, Heather. *English Poetry and Old Norse Myth: A History*. Oxford: Oxford University Press, 2014.

O'Donoghue, Heather. "From Heroic Lay to Victorian Novel: Old Norse Poetry about Brynhild and Thomas Hardy's *The Return of the Native*." In *Translating Early Medieval Poetry: Transformation, Reception, Interpretation*, edited by Tom Birkett and Kirsty March-Lyons, pp. 183–98. Cambridge: D. S. Brewer, 2017.

Photius. *The Homilies of Photius, Patriarch of Constantinople*. Translated by Cyril Mango. Cambridge, MA: Harvard University Press, 1958.

Price, Neil. "The Viking Phenomenon." http://www.arkeologi.uu.se/Research/Projects/viking-phenomenon/.

Quinn, J. and M. A. Cipolla, eds. *Studies in the Transmission and Reception of Old Norse Literature: The Hyperborean Muse in European Culture*. Turnhout: Brepols, 2016.

Roesdahl, Else and Preben Meulengracht Sørensen, eds. *The Waking of Angantyr: The Scandinavian Past in European Culture*. Århus: Århus University Press, 1996.

Schulz, Katja, ed. *Eddische Götter und Helden: Milueus und Medien ihrer Rezeption.* Heidelberg: Winter, 2011.
Service, Alexandra. "Popular Vikings: Constructions of Viking Identity in Twentieth Century Britain." Unpublished D.Phil. thesis, University of York, 1998.
Thor's Rike Adventure Park. "Homepage." https://thorsrike.no/en/.
Viking [Clothing]. "Homepage." http://vikinginside.com/.
Wawn, Andrew, ed. *Northern Antiquity: The Post-Medieval Reception of Edda and Saga.* Enfield Lock: Hisarlik, 1994.
Wawn, Andrew. *The Vikings and the Victorians: Inventing the Old North in Nineteenth-Century Britain.* Cambridge: D. S. Brewer, 2000.
Wawn, Andrew. "The Post-Medieval Reception of Old Norse and Old Icelandic Literature." In *A Companion to Old Norse-Icelandic Literature and Culture*, edited by Rory McTurk, pp. 320–37. Oxford: Blackwell, 2005.
Wawn, A. "The Viking Revival." *BBC History*, February 2, 2011. http://www.bbc.co.uk/history/ancient/vikings/revival_01.shtml.
Williams, Henrik. "The Kensington Runestone: Fact and Fiction." *The Swedish-American Historical Quarterly* 63, no. 1 (2012): 3–20.
Wilson, David. *Vikings and Gods in European Art.* Højbjerg: Mosegård Museum, 1992.
The World-Tree Project. http://www.worldtreeproject.org.

Notes

1. *The Homilies of Photius, Patriarch of Constantinople*, trans. Cyril Mango (Cambridge, MA: Harvard University Press, 1958), p. 84.
2. This is the title of a 10-year project at Uppsala University led by Neil Price, investigating the beginnings of the Viking trajectory, who the Vikings were, and the reasons for this violent expansion, "The Viking Phenomenon," http://www.arkeologi.uu.se/Research/Projects/viking-phenomenon/.
3. Judith Jesch, *The Viking Diaspora* (London: Routledge, 2015), p. 5.
4. A. Wawn, "The Viking Revival," *BBC History*, February 2, 2011, http://www.bbc.co.uk/history/ancient/vikings/revival_01.shtml.
5. Henrik Williams, "The Kensington Runestone: Fact and Fiction," *The Swedish-American Historical Quarterly* 63, no. 1 (2012): 3–20 at 20.
6. For recent studies of the reception of Old Norse literature and mythology see, for example, Heather O'Donoghue, *From Asgard to Valhalla: The Remarkable History of the Norse Myths* (New York: I. B. Tauris, 2007); Martin Arnold, *Thor: Myth to Marvel* (London: Continuum, 2011); Jón Karl Helgason, *Echoes of Valhalla: The Afterlife of the Eddas and Sagas*, trans. Jane Victoria Appleton (London: Reaktion Books, 2017); Andrew Wawn's chapter on "The Post-Medieval Reception of Old Norse and Old Icelandic Literature," in *A Companion to Old Norse-Icelandic Literature and Culture*, ed. Rory McTurk (Oxford: Blackwell, 2005), pp. 320–37; and the six-volume series on "Edda Rezeption" published by Universitätsverlag Winter, including Katja Schulz, ed., *Eddische Götter und Helden: Milueus und Medien ihrer Rezeption* (Heidelberg: Winter, 2011). On the influence of Norse myth on the visual arts see David Wilson's catalogue, *Vikings and Gods in European Art* (Højbjerg: Mosegård Museum: 1992); for an overview of the English literary tradition see

Heather O'Donoghue, *English Poetry and Old Norse Myth: A History* (Oxford: Oxford University Press, 2014); on its use in comic books see Tina Hafner, *Peter Madsens Valhalla: Studien zur Rezeption altwestnordischer Mythen im modernen Comic* (Munich: GRIN Verlag, 2008), esp. Chap. 3.

7. Such as Margaret Clunies Ross, *The Norse Muse in Britain, 1750–1820* (Trieste: Parnasso, 1998) and Andrew Wawn, *The Vikings and the Victorians: Inventing the Old North in Nineteenth-Century Britain* (Cambridge: D. S. Brewer, 2000); there are many titles dealing with the reception of Norse mythology in various periods of Germany's history, including Klaus Bödl, *Der Mythos der Edda: Nordische Mythologie zwischen europäischer Aufklärung und nationaler Romantik* (Tübingen: Francke, 2000) and Rainer Kipper, *Der Germanenmythos im Deutschen Kaiserreich* (Göttingen: Vandenhoeck & Ruprecht, 2000).

8. See the collected essays in Else Roesdahl and Preben Meulengracht Sørensen, eds., *The Waking of Angantyr: The Scandinavian Past in European Culture* (Århus: Århus University Press, 1996); Andrew Wawn, ed., *Northern Antiquity: The Post-Medieval Reception of Edda and Saga* (Enfield Lock: Hisarlik, 1994); David Clark and Carl Phelpstead, eds., *Old Norse Made New: Essays on the Post-Medieval Reception of Old Norse Literature and Culture* (Exeter: Viking Society for Northern Research, 2007); and most recently J. Quinn and M. A. Cipolla, eds., *Studies in the Transmission and Reception of Old Norse Literature: The Hyperborean Muse in European Culture* (Turnhout: Brepols, 2016) which includes essays on the contemporary reception of Old Norse literature in the third section of the book.

9. Helgason, *Echoes of Valhalla*, p. 12.

10. Alexandra Service, "Popular Vikings: Constructions of Viking Identity in Twentieth Century Britain" (Unpublished D.Phil. thesis, University of York, 1998), p. 223.

11. Tom Birkett, "The Clontarf Effect: Teaching Old Norse in the Year of the Vikings," *Studies in Medieval and Renaissance Teaching* 25, no. 1 (2018): 15–33.

12. Neil Gaiman, *Norse Mythology* (New York: W. W. Norton, 2017); Kevin Crossley-Holland, *Norse Myths: Tales of Odin, Thor and Loki* (London: Walker Studio, 2017); Tom Birkett, *The Norse Myths: Stories of the Norse Gods and Heroes Vividly Retold* (London: Quercus, 2018).

13. See the homepage of the project "Destination Viking: The Legacy of the Vikings," https://www.destinationviking.com/.

14. Thor's Rike Adventure Park, "Homepage," https://thorsrike.no/en/.

15. The project "Languages, Myths and Finds: Translating Norse and Viking Cultures for the Twenty-first Century," which ran in 2013–2014, involved academics working with local partners in five communities with Norse heritage, https://languagesmythsfinds.ac.uk/.

16. The World-Tree Project, "About," http://www.worldtreeproject.org/about.

17. The World-Tree Project, "Exhibits," http://www.worldtreeproject.org/exhibits.

18. Mary Beth Griggs, "You Could Smell Like a Viking," *Smithsonian Mag*, May 28, 2014, https://www.smithsonianmag.com/smart-news/you-could-smell-viking-180951575/.

19. This is a phrase used elsewhere by O'Donoghue to characterize Thomas Hardy's unacknowledged debt to Old Norse poetry, "From Heroic Lay to Victorian Novel: Old Norse Poetry about Brynhildr and Thomas Hardy's *The Return of the Native*," in *Translating Early Medieval Poetry: Transformation, Reception, Interpretation*, ed. Tom Birkett and Kirsty March-Lyons (Cambridge: D. S. Brewer, 2017), pp. 183–98 at p. 185.

20. Viking, "Homepage," http://vikinginside.com/.

21. The World-Tree Project, "Insignia [search term]," http://www.worldtreeproject.org/items/browse?tags=Insignia.

22. The most recent edition is Kevin Crossley-Holland, *The Penguin Book of Norse Myths: Gods of the Vikings* (London: Penguin, 2018).

23. His most recent retelling is *Norse Myths: Tales of Odin, Thor and Loki*, wonderfully illustrated by Jeffrey Alan Love.

M. J. Driscoll
1 Vikings!

Nearly 40 years ago, in 1980, the British-Icelandic television personality Magnus Magnusson scripted and presented a series for the BBC called *Vikings!*, which was accompanied by a large coffee-table-style book of the same name. The exclamation point was telling: Vikings were exciting in a way that few other actors in history could be: one somehow cannot imagine a major BBC series called *Monks!* or *Ironmongers!*

The series and accompanying book were typical of a new trend in the popular perception of the Vikings, a trend which had begun perhaps a decade earlier. On the very first page of *Vikings!*, Magnusson states that the received image of the Vikings as "merciless barbarians who plundered and burned their way across the known world" was in the process of being replaced by "a fuller and rounder" one, where there was "less emphasis on the raiding, more on trading; less on the pillage, more on the poetry and artistry; less on the terror, more on the technology of these determined and dynamic people from the northlands of Denmark, Norway and Sweden and the positive impact they had on the countries they affected."[1]

Interest in the Vikings continued, with publication after publication, and major exhibitions such as "Vikings: The North Atlantic Saga" at the National Museum of Natural History in Washington D.C. in 2000 and another, a collaboration between Denmark's Nationalmuseet, the British Museum in London, and the Museum für Vor- und Frühgeschichte in Berlin, held sequentially in all three cities in the years 2013–2014. This Viking frenzy has perhaps now reached its culmination with another TV series with almost the same name as Magnusson's, History channel's *Vikings*, which began in 2013 and at time of writing is in its fifth season. Vikings are everywhere.

The Word "Viking"

Although the word "Viking" is attested in early written sources, both Old Norse and Old English, its origin is disputed.[2] A word's etymology is of course not the same as its meaning. The origin of the word "dog" (*canis familiaris*) is also unknown, and, in the words of the OED, "all attempted etymological explanations

M. J. Driscoll, University of Copenhagen

https://doi.org/10.1515/9781501513886-002

are extremely speculative,"[3] but there is no uncertainty whatsoever as to what it means.

So it is with "Viking." Its attestations in Old Norse (and Old English, on which see below) indicate clearly that it refers almost exclusively to men, predominantly Scandinavians, who practiced piracy at sea. It is also clear that it was primarily something one did, rather than something one was.

There are two separate words. One, a feminine abstract noun, *víking*, was used to refer to the practice of voyaging to foreign parts to engage in plundering there, "að fara í víking(u)" (to go a-viking) or "að vera í víking(u)" (to be a-viking).[4] Those who went west, to the British Isles, Ireland, and Northern France, "fóru í vestrvíking," while those who went east, to the Baltic and into the land of the Rus, "fóru í víking í austrveg." As explained in Cleasby-Vigfusson: "In heathen days it was usual for young men of distinction, before settling down, to make a warlike expedition to foreign parts; this voyage was called 'víking,' and was part of a man's education like the grand tour in modern times."[5]

The other word, *víkingr* (pl. *víkingar*), a masculine noun, is simply one who engaged in such activities, a pirate, in short. It is used principally in the plural to refer to bands of pirates, but is certainly not unknown in the singular – phrases such as "hann var víkingr mikill" (he was a great Viking) abound in the sagas – and is even found as a personal name or cognomen on rune-stones from the early eleventh century. Its use in the sources indicates that it was not an occupational designation, however. While a shoemaker might be so described even when not actively engaged in making shoes, a Viking was only a Viking when out a-Viking. So Ragnar's wife Áslaug, in response to the question "What does your husband do for living, Mrs. Loðbrók?" is unlikely to have replied "He's a Viking." Though if asked "Where is your husband, Mrs. Loðbrók? she might well have replied, "He's gone Viking."

There is no consensus regarding the origin of either of these words, although it is assumed that they are related – that is, that one derives from the other. Although most attempts at determining their origin focus on the masculine noun *víkingr*, it is for various linguistic reasons the feminine noun which is more likely to have come first.[6]

One of the most popular theories, or at least one of the most persistent, for the word's origin derives it from *vík* (a bay, creek, or inlet), allegedly owing to the Vikings' predilection for using such bays and creeks as places from which to launch their attacks. Some would even have it refer specifically to Vík – used generally with the definite article, Víkin – the name for the large fjord in southern Norway on which the city of Oslo now lies. There are various problems with this explanation, however. Firstly, Vikings do not in fact seem to have frequented bays and inlets, preferring small islands or headlands, where they could more easily defend themselves from attack by land. Nor did a particularly significant proportion of Vikings come from Víkin. Secondly, although the masculine noun *víkingr* (*víkingur* in modern Icelandic) is the ordinary term for inhabitants of settlements whose names end in –*vík*, such as Reykjavík or Húsavík, the inhabitants of which are known to this day as Reykvíkingar and Húsvíkingar respectively, there are no instances of its use other than in cases of such composite place names – and indeed, the inhabitants of Vík(in) are known as *víkverjar* (sing. *víkverji*), not *víkingar*. Given all of this, derivation from *vík* would not seem to have much going for it. It is, however, corroborated, seemingly, in the Irish (Gaelic) name for Scandinavia, and specifically Norway, *Lochlann* (place of lochs – that is, fjords), an inhabitant of which is referred to as *Lochlannach*, a word also used of marauders generally.[7]

A rival theory derives the word *víkingr* from the Old English *wīc* (a camp or temporary settlement),[8] itself a loanword from Latin *vicus*, the formation of such temporary encampments being a feature of Viking raids. Instances of the word *wīcing* (pl. *wīcingas*) are found in a variety of Old English sources, sometimes glossed with the Latin *pirata*. A derived verb, *wīcian*, to make such a camp, would be the origin of the feminine noun *víking*.[9] According to this theory the Old Norse words are in fact borrowings from Old English, or, given their apparent age, from Anglo-Frisian. It is interesting, and undeniable, that these Old English attestations predate the earliest instances in Old Norse by several centuries, and indeed predate the so-called Viking Age.

Old English *wīc* can also have the sense "harbor, trading place, or town." Derivation from this began to be stressed in connection with the rebranding of the Vikings as merchants and traders. This is in no way supported in the actual sources, unfortunately, where a clear distinction is maintained between *víking* and *kaupferðir*; the following sentence, from *Egils saga Skallagrímssonar*, is typical: "Bjǫrn var farmaðr mikill; var stundum í víking en stundum í kaupferðum" (Bjǫrn was a great seaman, sometimes raiding, sometimes on trading voyages).[10]

Other possibilities have been proposed – for example, that the term derives from *víkja*, a verb meaning "to turn (away) or move," according to some at least with reference to the way in which the Vikings, cat-like, turned suddenly to pounce upon their prey, and/or having so pounced, were quickly gone again. A slightly less fanciful explanation takes *víkja* in the sense of "departing, leaving home." This is obviously something anyone going on a Viking voyage would have had to do, but then so would almost everyone else at some point in their lives. It is thus difficult to see why this term, if this is its origin, should have been applied so narrowly and specifically to persons traveling abroad by sea for purposes of plunder. Another theory, linking it to the word *víg* (OE *wīg*) (a fight, battle), or, as a legal term (a slaying, homicide), despite its "semantic appropriateness," does not have many adherents.[11]

Yet another theory, one which seems to be gaining ground, relates the word to *vika*, a feminine noun derived from *víkja* (older forms *víkva* or *víka*), and refers to the shift of oarsmen or the distance covered between these shifts (as in the term *vika sjávar*, "a sea-mile"). This theory would have the word *víking* refer to this practice of rowing in stints, which by extension means that it must predate the so-called Viking Age, by which time sails were used (in addition to rowing). The Old English word *wīcing*, as mentioned, corroborates this, being found in sources from at least the eighth century. The Old English word would then be a loan from Old Norse, rather than the other way round, as those who favor derivation from *wīc* would have it. As far-fetched as all this may appear, the rowing-stint theory does seem to be the current favorite.[12] On the whole, though, the jury is still out regarding this question, and is likely to remain so for some time to come.

Whatever its origin, the meaning of these words, as was said, is clear enough. The OED's definition of Viking will suffice: "One of those Scandinavian adventurers who practised piracy at sea, and committed depredations on land, in northern and western Europe from the eighth to the eleventh century; sometimes in general use, a warlike pirate or sea-rover."[13]

Among the Scandinavian languages the words survived in everyday usage, it seems, only in Icelandic,[14] but were reintroduced from Old Norse by the antiquarians of the late seventeenth century. The words are not found in Otto Kalkar's *Ordbog til det ældre danske Sprog* (1881–1907; 2nd ed. 1976), which covers written Danish in the period 1300–1700, but both are found in Matthias Moth's *Ordbog*, compiled in the period 1680–1709. "Viking," he writes, "Er en Sørøver. *Pirata*" (is a pirate [lit. "sea-robber"]), while "Vikinge," representing the abstract feminine noun, "Er Sørøveri. *Piratica*" (is piracy ["sea-robbery"]).[15] The earliest example given in *Ordbog over den danske Sprog* is from Ludvig Holberg's *Danmarks og Norges Søe-Historie*, published in 1747.[16] The word in fact appears six times in that work, glossed each time with the Danish "Søerøver" (pirate) or "Fribyttere" (freebooter). *Holberg-Ordbog* has a somewhat earlier example, however, from Holberg's *Dannemarks Riges Historie*, vol. 1, published in 1732; here Holberg also glosses the word with the equivalent Danish word, referring to "Vikinger eller Søerøvere."[17]

In English the word Viking is not found in seventeenth- or eighteenth-century sources – despite the keen interest in things northern and relatively close connections to antiquarian circles in especially Denmark.[18] The earliest examples cited in the OED are from the beginning of the nineteenth century, the first reference being to George Chalmers (d. 1825), who uses the form "vikingr," with the Old Norse nominative singular ending, although curiously for both singular and plural, in the first volume of his book *Caledonia; or, An Account, Historical and Topographic, of North Britain*, published in 1807. It caught on quickly, however, in keeping with the growing fascination for the Vikings in Victorian-era Britain, when the modern concept of the Viking came into being.[19]

The term "Viking Age" first appears in English in 1889 as the title of a book by Paul Beloni Du Chaillu, subtitled "The early history, manners, and customs of the ancestors of the English-speaking nations." Du Chaillu affirms that "we must come to the conclusion that the 'Viking Age' lasted from about the second century of our era to about the middle of the twelfth without interruption, hence the title given to our work which deals with the history and customs of our English forefathers during that period."[20] It is presumably this same understanding of the extent of the Viking Age that lies behind the 1967 Hammer film *The Viking Queen*, which is set in Roman Britain. For most scholars, however, the Viking Age extends from the late-eighth century to the mid-eleventh, specifically from the attack on Lindisfarne in 793 to the Battle at Stamford Bridge in 1066. A "more generous definition," as Judith Jesch puts it, "would stretch from ca. 750 to 1100"[21]; the "long Viking age" project based at the University of York would push the start date back to 700.[22]

The Danish term "vikingetid" was first used by archaeologist and historian J. A. A. Worsaae (1821–1885) in the title of his book *De Danskes Kultur i Vikingetiden*, published in 1873. Worsaae had been a student of Christian Jürgensen Thomsen (1788–1865), who developed the archaeological system of the three main ages – stone, bronze, and iron. Worsaae proposed subdivisions for each of these, calling the last part of the iron age (*jernalderen*), the period from 800 to 1000, *vikingetiden*, "det Tidspukt, hvor det danske Folk for første Gang optræder paa den verdenshistoriske Skueplads" (that point in time when the Danish people make their début on the stage of world history).[23]

The appropriateness or otherwise of applying the term "Viking" to an entire historical period has been much discussed, and some scholars, such as the Norwegian historian Hans Jacob Orning, prefer to talk about the "late Iron Age."[24] The period in question was undeniably characterized by raids on the British Isles and the continent beginning in the late eighth century and ending some three centuries later. The people doing the raiding can with justification be referred to as "Vikings" – indeed, as we have seen, this was their own term for themselves, and for the activity in which they engaged. But as Guðbrandur Vigfússon's gloss on the word *víking*, cited above, makes clear, "going Viking" was an activity engaged in by a relatively small, and select, percentage of the population, the equivalent today to playing polo, say. There are vastly more people who don't play polo than do, and even those who do, don't do so all the time. So it was with the Vikings.

Kristján Eldjárn, archaeologist and director of the National Museum in Reykjavík and Iceland's president from 1968 to 1980, complains in an essay from 1982 that "in modern usage the term 'Viking' tends to be applied to the entire population of the Norse countries in the so-called Viking Age." "It is a handy use of the word," he goes on, "but it is far from corresponding to the concept it expresses in the language of the Viking Age itself. At that time a Viking was a pirate, but if he abandoned that occupation and returned home, or settled down as a farmer in a hitherto unsettled country, he was no longer a Viking. He was a Viking only as long as he was on board a Viking ship, not at any other time."[25]

So while one can perhaps justify the use of the term "Viking Age," what cannot be justified are statements such as "Iceland was settled by Vikings in the ninth century" (which gets over 3,000 hits on Google). Among Iceland's first settlers there were doubtless those who had participated in Viking raids at some point in their lives, but they traveled to Iceland in order to settle there, not to raid, and thus were not Vikings. Nor can terms like "Viking culture," "Viking religion," "Viking art," "Viking civilization," be said to be in any way meaningful. Just try substituting "Pirate."

The prize for meaninglessness must surely go to "Viking language," the title of a recent introduction to Old Norse.[26] There is no such thing as "the Viking language," and a book purporting to teach it can be taken no more seriously than can "International Talk Like a Pirate Day" (September 19, for those interested in participating).[27]

Back in the 1980s, Ray Page of Cambridge University, never one to mince his words, began a review of R. T. Farrell's essay collection *The Vikings* (in which the article by Kristján Eldján mentioned above appeared) with the following: "Enough is enough. Something really must be done to stop publishers putting the word 'Viking' in the titles of all books that have vaguely medieval and faintly Germanic subjects."[28]

Alas, there's no sign that this is happening. A friend of mine recently published a well-researched and well-received book on Snorri Sturluson, which I read pre-publication. When it appeared, I was surprised to see that it had acquired the title *Song of the Vikings*.[29] How could this be, I asked the author; Snorri wasn't a Viking. No, she admitted, he wasn't, but the publisher had insisted that the book had to have the word Viking in the title.

Probably there is nothing to be done. In the hope that prayer may help, I offer the following litany of despair: *A disputationibus de Viccingis, Domine, libera nos!*[30]

Bibliography

Andersson, Th. "Wikinger: Sprachlich." *Reallexikon der germanischen Altertumskunde* 35: 687–97. Berlin: de Gruyter, 2007.

An Anglo-Saxon Dictionary. Edited by Joseph Bosworth and T. Northcote Toller. Oxford: Oxford University Press, 1898.

Askeberg, Fritz. *Norden och kontinenten i gammal tid: Studier i forngermansk kulturhistorie.* Uppsala: Almqvist & Wiksell, 1944.

Brown, Nancy Marie. *Song of the Vikings: Snorri and the Making of Norse Myths.* New York: Palgrave Macmillan, 2012.

Byock, Jesse L. *Viking Language 1: Learn Old Norse, Runes, and Icelandic Sagas; Viking Language 2: The Old Norse Reader.* Pacific Palisades, CA: Jules William Press, 2013.

Chalmers, George. *Caledonia; or, An Account, Historical and Topographic, of North Britain.* 3 vols. London: Cadell, 1807–1824.

Du Chaillu, Paul B. *The Viking Age: The Early History, Manners, and Customs of the Ancestors of the English-Speaking Nations.* New York: Scribners, 1889.

Egils saga Skalla-Grímssonar. Edited by Sigurður Nordal. Reykjavík: Hið íslenzka fornritafélag, 1933.

Eldjárn, Kristján. "The Viking Myth." In *The Vikings*, edited by R. T. Farrell, pp. 262–73. London: Phillimore, 1982.

Fell, Christine, E. "Modern English Viking." *Leeds Studies in English* 18 (1987): 111–23.

Heide, Eldar. "Víking – Rower Shifting? An Etymological Contribution." *Arkiv för nordisk filologi* 120 (2005): 41–54.

Hødnebø, Finn. "Who Were the First Vikings?" In *Proceedings of the Tenth Viking Congress*, pp. 43–54. Oslo: Universitetets Oldsaksamling, 1987.

Holberg, Ludvig. *Dannemarks Riges Historie.* 3 vols. Copenhagen: Høpffner, 1732–1735.

Holberg, Ludvig. "Danmarks og Norges Søe-Historie." In *Skrifter, som udi det Kiøbenhavnske Selskab af Lærdoms og Videnskabers Elskere ere fremlagte og oplæste* 3, 15: 255–71. Copenhagen: Videnskabernes Selskab, 1747.

Holberg-Ordbog: Ordbog over Ludvig Holbergs Sprog. Edited by Aage Hansen et al. Copenhagen: Det danske Sprog- og Litteraturselskab, 1981–1988.

An Icelandic–English Dictionary. Edited by Richard Cleasby and Gudbrand Vigfusson; 2nd ed., edited by William A. Craigie. Oxford: Clarendon Press, 1957.

Jesch, Judith. *The Viking Diaspora.* London: Routledge, 2015.

Krüger, Jana. *Wikinger im Mittelalter: Die Rezeption von "víkingr" m. und "víking" f. in der altnordischen Literatur.* Berlin: de Gruyter, 2008.

"The Long Viking Age." https://thelongvikingage.wordpress.com/.

Magnusson, Magnus. *Vikings!* London: Dutton, 1980.

Ó Dónall, Niall. *Foclóir Gaeilge-Béarla.* Baile Átha Cliath: An Gúm, 1977.

Ordbog over den danske Sprog. Edited by Verner Dahlerup et al. 28 vols. Copenhagen: Det danske Sprog- og Litteraturselskab, 1918–1956.

Ordbog til det ældre danske Sprog. Edited by Otto Kalkar. 6 vols. Copenhagen: Thiele, 1881–1907.

Orning, Hans Jacob. *Norvegr – Norges historie 1: Frem til 1400.* Oslo: Aschehoug, 2011.

The Oxford English Dictionary. 2nd ed. Edited by John Simpson and Edmund Weiner. 20 vols. Oxford: Clarendon Press, 1989.

Page, R. I. "*The Vikings* [review]." *Saga-Book* 21 (1982–1985): 308–11.
Thorson, Per. "A New Interpretation of Viking." In *Proceedings of the Sixth Viking Congress*,
    pp. 101–4. Uppsala: Almqvist & Wiksell, 1971.
Wawn, Andrew. *The Vikings and the Victorians: Inventing the Old North in Nineteenth-Century
    Britain*. Cambridge: D. S. Brewer, 2000.
Worsaae, J. A. A. *De Danskes Kultur i Vikingetiden*. Copenhagen: Gad, 1873.

Notes

1. Magnus Magnusson, *Vikings!* (London: Dutton, 1980), p. 7.
2. The literature on the subject is vast and the arguments are often complex. Good
    summaries can be found in, e.g., Fritz Askeberg, *Norden och kontinenten i gammal tid:
    Studier i forngermansk kulturhistorie* (Uppsala: Almqvist & Wiksell, 1944); Finn
    Hødnebø, "Who Were the First Vikings?," in *Proceedings of the Tenth Viking Congress*
    (Oslo: Universitetets Oldsakssamling, 1987), pp. 43–54; Eldar Heide, "Víking – Rower
    Shifting? An Etymological Contribution," *Arkiv för nordisk filologi* 120 (2005): 41–54;
    Th. Andersson, "Wikinger: Sprachlich," *Reallexikon der germanischen Altertumskunde*
    35 (Berlin: de Gruyter, 2007), pp. 687–97; Jana Krüger, *Wikinger im Mittelalter: Die
    Rezeption von "víkingr" m. und "víking" f. in der altnordischen Literatur* (Berlin:
    de Gruyter, 2008); Judith Jesch, *The Viking Diaspora* (London: Routledge, 2015), pp. 4–10.
3. *OED Online*, Oxford University Press, June 2017, http://www.oed.com/view/Entry/
    56405.
4. Forms both with and without the accusative and dative singular ending -*u* are found;
    those without are more common.
5. *An Icelandic–English Dictionary*, ed. Richard Cleasby and Gudbrand Vigfusson; 2nd ed.,
    ed. William A. Craigie (Oxford: Clarendon Press, 1957), p. 716.
6. The arguments are presented in Heide, "Víking – Rower Shifting?"
7. Niall Ó Dónall, *Foclóir Gaeilge-Béarla* (Baile Átha Cliath: An Gúm, 1977), p. 794; Irish
    also has the loanword *Uigingeach* (Viking).
8. See the entry on *wīc* in *An Anglo-Saxon Dictionary*, ed. Joseph Bosworth and T. Northcote
    Toller (Oxford: Oxford University Press, 1898), pp. 1212–13; the main meaning of *wīc* is
    "a dwelling-place, abode, habitation, residence, lodging, quarters." "A temporary
    abode, a camp" etc. is only the fourth meaning.
9. *Anglo-Saxon Dictionary*, p. 1214.
10. *Egils saga Skalla-Grímssonar*, ed. Sigurður Nordal (Reykjavík: Hið íslenzka fornritafélag,
    1933), p. 83.
11. The case for this is put by, among others, Per Thorson, "A New Interpretation of Viking,"
    in *Proceedings of the Sixth Viking Congress* (Uppsala: Almqvist & Wiksell, 1971),
    pp. 101–4.
12. See, e.g., Heide, "Viking," and Andersson, "Wikinger."
13. sv. "Viking," *The Oxford English Dictionary*, 2nd ed., ed. John Simpson and Edmund
    Weiner (Oxford: Clarendon Press, 1989), vol. 19, p. 628; "Viking, n.," *OED Online*,
    Oxford University Press, June 2017, http://www.oed.com/view/Entry/223373.
14. The Norwegian scholar Finn Hødnebø has said that it "probably" also survived in
    Norwegian but offers no real evidence for this; Hødnebø, "First Vikings," p. 43.

15. http://mothsordbog.dk/ordbog?query=viking; http://mothsordbog.dk/ordbog?query= vikinge.
16. *Ordbog over den danske Sprog*, ed. Verner Dahlerup et al. (Copenhagen: Det danske Sprog- og Litteraturselskab, 1918–1956), vol. 26, cols. 1469–71; and online at http://ordnet.dk/ods/ordbog?query=viking.
17. *Holberg-Ordbog: Ordbog over Ludvig Holbergs Sprog*, ed. Aage Hansen et al. (Copenhagen: Det danske Sprog- og Litteraturselskab, 1981–1988), vol. 5, cols. 1332–33; and online at http://holbergordbog.dk/ordbog?query=viking.
18. On the use of the word "Viking" in English see Christine E. Fell, "Modern English Viking," *Leeds Studies in English* 18 (1987): 111–23.
19. On which see Andrew Wawn, *The Vikings and the Victorians: Inventing the Old North in Nineteenth-Century Britain* (Cambridge: D. S. Brewer, 2000).
20. Paul B. Du Chaillu, *The Viking Age: The Early History, Manners, and Customs of the Ancestors of the English-Speaking Nations* (New York: Scribners, 1889), vol. 1, p. 26.
21. Jesch, *Viking Diaspora*, p. 8.
22. See https://thelongvikingage.wordpress.com/.
23. J. A. A. Worsaae, *De Danskes Kultur i Vikingetiden* (Copenhagen: Gad, 1873), p. 4.
24. Hans Jacob Orning, *Norvegr – Norges historie 1: Frem til 1400* (Oslo: Aschehoug, 2011). Orning uses the term "Vikingtid" but does not treat it as a separate period.
25. Kristján Eldjárn, "The Viking Myth," in *The Vikings*, ed. R. T. Farrell (London: Phillimore, 1982), pp. 262–73 at p. 266.
26. Jesse L. Byock, *Viking Language 1: Learn Old Norse, Runes, and Icelandic Sagas; Viking Language 2: The Old Norse Reader* (Pacific Palisades, CA: Jules William Press, 2013).
27. https://en.wikipedia.org/wiki/International_Talk_Like_a_Pirate_Day.
28. R. I. Page, "The Vikings [review]," *Saga-Book* 21 (1982–1985): 308–11 at 308.
29. Nancy Marie Brown, *Song of the Vikings: Snorri and the Making of Norse Myths* (New York: Palgrave Macmillan, 2012).
30. Lord, deliver us from discussions of the Vikings!

Neil Price

2 My Vikings and *Real Vikings*: Drama, Documentary, and Historical Consultancy

Introduction

The study of the Viking Age is a curiously personal thing. It reflects the (un)conscious biases of the student and the prevailing sensibilities of the times, and there is always a risk that the past will be subtly molded to fit the changing preoccupations of scholarly fashion. The same can be said of the many public faces of the period, reimagined or reenacted according to taste. Today the Vikings are as popular as they have ever been, perhaps even more so in terms of the growing audience for both accessible recreations and academic mediations of their vanished world. This volume, and the conference on which it was based, provide useful but actually quite rare opportunities for reflection, and to review our perceptions of the Vikings, not least on the level of the individual researcher – in this case, myself.

"It matters to me what a person was in the Viking Age."[1] That statement formed part of the very first sentence in my doctoral thesis, published by Uppsala University in 2002 as *The Viking Way*, and all these years later it is still my position. In the course of some three decades of work in this field, I have often been asked to convey my own particular readings of the Viking Age. Curiously, I've also often been informed of my opinions by critics who happily tell me what I apparently "want" in "my" Vikings (it seems invidious to cite them, and they know who they are, but their assertions sometimes reveal a truly heroic lack of self-knowledge). With this in mind, I therefore offer this essay as an explicit attempt to consider what the Vikings really mean to me – all obvious pitfalls notwithstanding.

If one were to try to sum up in a sound-bite the long theoretical convulsions of archaeology during the 1980s and 1990s, the years of post-processualism, it might be to say that never again have we been able to maintain the illusion of objectivity in our interactions with the past. We are in no way neutral observers, omnipotent sorters (or generators) of data that somehow gives of itself. More than a decade ago I found my own views on this unexpectedly reflected

Neil Price, University of Uppsala

https://doi.org/10.1515/9781501513886-003

in an obituary for the classical historian Keith Hopkins, with a useful summary of what I see as our condition:

> History is a conversation with the dead. We have several advantages over our informants. We think we know what happened subsequently; we can take a longer view; we can do all the talking; and with all our prejudices, we are alive. We should not throw away these advantages by pretending to be just collators or interpreters of our sources. We can do more than that. Although, almost inevitably, whatever our ambitions, we finish up by foisting simplifying fictions on the complexities of the past which is largely lost.[2]

For Hopkins, in ground-breaking works such as *A World Full of Gods*, any order that might be discerned in the patterns of prehistory could only be arrived at through a process of negotiation with multi-vocal strands of evidence, obtained from wherever it could be found.[3] In what follows I will try to review a selection of the current trends in Vikings studies and their reception, filtered through my own perspectives and commitment to an interdisciplinary approach.

In so doing, I will also make some lengthy and specific references to what is perhaps an unexpected current work in this context, namely the History drama series *Vikings*. Despite frequent public exhibitions, books, and other popular media, I single this one out as something especially significant because it seems to me that there has never before been such an investment in the communication of the Viking Age to an audience as large as this, over such a long period of time. Quite simply, more people come into contact with the Vikings through this production than through anything that academics will ever produce: constructive engagement is, in my opinion, an imperative. This paper will therefore also explore my reflections on the series and my experience as historical consultant for *Real Vikings*, a documentary commissioned by the same team as a unique experiment in academic commentary on a historical drama.

Parameters, Preconceptions, Principles, and Prejudices

If any exploration of the past inevitably begins in the present, to a degree it is also possible to identify at least some of the parameters that frame such an endeavor (though ultimately, of course, we cannot truly judge our own work, only others can do that). I have had cause to think carefully about this in recent years, being fortunate to have been awarded a major ten-year grant from the Swedish Research Council to study *The Viking Phenomenon*,[4] which necessitated the establishment of a clear platform from which to begin. For what it is worth, then, here are some of my starting points for what I try to do.

Perhaps the most basic of all is to be clear that the very concept of the Viking Age has a testable, empirical reality that can be illuminated by the application of theory and by inter-disciplinary comparative analysis. National Romanticism, Victorian imperialism and its darker European successors all certainly impacted how the Vikings were seen afterwards,[5] but in itself it is important to understand that this says nothing at all about what actually happened between the mid-eighth and eleventh centuries – only about how it was subsequently appropriated and weaponized.

Others argue that the cultures of Viking Age Scandinavia were merely the regional manifestation of pan-European trends in the reorganization of the post-Roman economy, a kind of burgeoning early medieval EU with some particularly aggressive negotiators in the North.[6] In this light, it is also true that raiding and maritime warfare undoubtedly existed around the Baltic and the North Sea for centuries (and probably millennia) before the time of the Vikings, as we see clearly in the great Danish bog deposits of whole armies' worth of equipment. However, there is no doubt that the flow, scale, and range of seaborne piracy gradually but dramatically increased from the 750s onwards, culminating in the full-blown military campaigns of the ninth and tenth centuries that would shatter the political structures of western Europe. At the same time, parallel and intertwined movements of colonialism, trade, and exploration brought the Scandinavians into contact with some thirty-seven present-day countries and documented encounters with at least fifty-two contemporary cultures. Quite simply, no other peoples at this time ranged over the then-known Eurasian and North Atlantic world to the same degree: the "Viking Age," hindsight construct of historians though it undoubtedly is, has genuine validity as a concept.

With this in mind, it may also be time to critically dismantle the boundaries between the Vendel or Merovingian period and the Viking Age itself, and to ask whether this artificial "transition" was simply the outward projection of behavioral patterns that had long been the norm inside what are now the Nordic countries.

As a coda to all this, we need to proactively confront the stereotypes of the period, challenging and elucidating them, but in a way that is also prepared to acknowledge the precise contexts in which they retain some veracity. It should be emphasized that it is not only Viking Age men who have been reduced to cliché in this manner – the tired image of the androcentric raider, maritime and violent – but also women with the notion of the strong "mistress of the hall" and her shield-maiden sisters.[7] As part of this revision, a commitment needs to be made against the ongoing ghettoization of gender.[8] All too often, a supposedly gendered Viking Age in fact exacerbates the androcentric focus on hegemonic masculinity, by relegating the lives of women to some kind of intensively studied but nonetheless discrete category distinct from society in general (the classic example being the exhibition display case on "Viking women," treating them in a manner akin to, say, "metalworking" or "trade," rather than as half of humanity). Our academic works, and our popular communications of all kinds, should instead be populated simply with people – old and young, of all genders and ethnicities, and notably including neglected communities such as the unfree.

This brings me to what I see as an especially vital precondition for studying the Viking Age from the inevitable perspective of the present, namely the impossibility of trying to do so without engaging with the weight of its social impact and implications today. To a degree, we must be selective – the Vikings have infiltrated so many aspects of our cultures in the past century that fully getting to grips with all their manifestations would be a job in itself. There is also a world of difference between the Viking landers exploring the surface of Mars, the Minnesota Vikings football team, and the Wiking division of the Waffen-SS (and so on, and on). But this is precisely why I think the TV drama series *Vikings*, already mentioned above, is so important. If we are looking towards public engagement, outreach and knowledge transfer (an explicit mission of most universities, for example) then it can be instructive to consider the series in a little more detail, in the light of current themes in the research agendas of Viking studies.

Dramatic License? "Accuracy" Contested in the Tales of Ragnarr loðbrók

Readers of my work will know that I have always been fond of reconstruction drawings, something that has followed me since childhood. When visiting ancient monuments, castles, and the like with my parents, what fascinated me most were always the models and illustrations that purported to show how the place we found ourselves in might have *looked* in the past. In the years since, having both bought in and commissioned new reconstructions (particularly of graves) for my publications, of course I have had to wrestle with the myriad assumptions, decisions, guesses, and prejudices that underpin any attempt to visualize the vanished past.[9] All this is doubly true for a filmed, moving image, with such a broader canvas and an infinite depth of detail.

So, is *Vikings* "accurate?" For any historical drama series or movie, this is the question most often asked by members of the public, and usually answered negatively by focused reenactors and academics. Bearing in mind that I write this as a professor of archaeology with a life-long specialism in Viking studies, it may sound odd to say that frankly I'm not really worried. This is not because I am indifferent to careless errors or misrepresentations of history – I am certainly not – but rather because other factors are, for me, more important in this context.

First, we must consider intention. It is vital to understand that *Vikings* is a *show*, an entertainment produced ultimately for profit – not a documentary, in any sense. Material fidelity is a bonus and perhaps an aspiration, but it is not a goal in itself (the same is true for historical dramas on the big screen, which have enjoyed a renaissance since the appearance of Ridley Scott's *Gladiator* in 2000). If academics do not understand this, then they have fallen at the first hurdle of any successful engagement with the public mediation of the past in this particular way. Most or all such productions have historical advisors (for *Vikings* it is Justin Pollard),[10] but advisors advise, they do not decide or direct. There may also be many other constraints, such as weather that abruptly alters filming schedules in ways that do not accord with prop availability, not to mention the sheer cost of ensuring museum-quality replicas for a cast of hundreds and shaping a variety of settled landscapes and other locations (there is a large and interesting literature on consultancy and historical accuracy in drama productions of this kind).[11]

In this light, it is also worth acknowledging what a sensible decision was made by Michael Hirst, the showrunner and writer of every episode, when he chose Ragnarr loðbrók and his family as the central characters. It is really very hard to argue about the "veracity" of people who may never have existed, and even if they did, whose lives and actions are to say the least debatable and embellished over centuries of accumulating narratives.[12]

Nevertheless, we can still ask the question – are there errors in the objects, clothing, and general look of *Vikings*? Yes, of course there are, and we all have our personal bugbears (personally I can't get past the Anglo-Saxon cavalry helmets that appear to have been borrowed from the conquistadors), but this is to miss the point. In general, the characters look *okay*, or better, they look fine to me. They don't look like Romans, or Aztecs, or like something from a Frazetta painting. It is also a tribute to the script that most of the time I'm concentrating on the plot and simply don't notice what someone is wearing or holding. And not least, with the caveat that the following number is a guess, it is worth remembering that perhaps only a few thousand people in the world can really tell the difference at this level of close detail.

We also have to ask what is meant by "accuracy" in the first place, and how comparatively little we actually know about the detailed appearance of Viking Age people and their environment. Even if we take things for which we have clear empirical evidence, in quantity, such as the female jewelry sets of oval brooches, equal-armed brooches and beads – we really have very little idea whether this was everyday wear, or something equating to "Sunday best," or even a kind of special funeral suit. Consider this carefully, and then imagine the challenge to viably expand upon it to fill out the Vikings' visual, aural, living world in all its complexity.

What do we really know of their hairstyles, their music, their fashions? Were their halls carved all over like stave churches, or not? What games did children play? What did those cult buildings really look like, and what actually happened inside them? Can we take single excavated examples of these things, and then just make them a standard across the Viking world? All of this and so much more has to be recreated for the screen, and "we don't know" is not an adequate academic response – unless the intention is really to say that one should never even attempt to make such dramas at all (which I suspect, sadly, is precisely what some Viking specialists think).

I *am* concerned about the clear inaccuracies in the history itself – not so much the conflation of different sieges of Paris into one event, for example, but more in terms of overall trajectories and perspectives. While I'm very pleased indeed about the initial focus on the Baltic and the domestic concerns of the Scandinavians, their apparent ignorance of lands to the west is ... unsettling. Similarly, Uppsala is not a mountainous landscape with waterfalls (I know, I live there!), and nobody suddenly invented ships that could, you know, actually venture onto the open sea – to talk of just the first season. But in the larger picture, these seem to me ultimately minor points, and in any case they may result from the fact that when a showrunner prepares the first episodes of a drama, they have no way of knowing whether the story will end after a single season, or maybe run for years, which can result in tangled plot threads down the line.

In the end, there is one overriding aspect of the *Vikings* series that stands out for me, the reason why I value an engagement with as much of it as I can access: this production is the first time I have seen a consistent, large-scale vision of the Viking Age that depicts a believable world, a world that sings and breathes, populated by people who actually seem real. Within reason, I am *very* much less concerned about whether they got somebody's belt buckle right.

This sense of situated agency seems important to me, the notion of people living in their own, their only, present. To "think ourselves back" to the Viking Age is a delusion, but at the same time we must try to consider the actions of the Vikings and their contemporaries not only on an individual basis, but also in the context of a very different set of world views, customs, notions of morality, and, ultimately, a radically unfamiliar concept of reality itself in the case of the pre-Christian Scandinavians. This is especially crucial with regard to exactly the kinds of behavior that we ourselves most shrink from, the reasons why the Vikings are *not* heroes, and must never be regarded as such. Or as Christopher Hitchens pithily put it in his comments to Alasdair MacIntyre's essay on "How to Write about Lenin – and How Not To": "The one unpardonable sin [in the writing of history] was that of being patronising. If you could not or would not care to imagine what conditions were like in 1905 or 1917, then it might be best if you kept your virginal judgements to yourself."[13]

Rather than asking what *Vikings* gets wrong, isn't it much more interesting to ask what it gets right?

Education without Lectures

In reviewing the series in this light, perhaps inevitably it is here that my own perceptions of the time – "my" Vikings – begin to emerge, since it is obviously these things that tend to catch my attention, or stimulate my imagination. In literature or film it is often said that we respond to the familiar, to opinions that we recognize, and so it is here: my *Vikings*, in fact, even though I have no input into the show itself.

Most obvious, right from the very first episode, is an emphasis on the Scandinavians before others, seen on their own terms and not through the lens of someone else's prejudices. Almost the entire first season is concerned with internecine, civil strife at home, and Scandinavia is seen as the fragmented landscape of petty jarldoms that it undoubtedly was. Similarly, the Viking raids in the classic sense are clearly something that have their origins in the Baltic sphere – their ultimate extension to the west is merely a spatial shift in the structuring of identities that are already established. Although there are errors of detail, consider what a radical set of suggestions that all represents, utterly different from the It-All-Began-At-Lindisfarne of the traditional Viking Age, viewed exclusively through the eyes of foreign, Christian monks.

There is also a focus on the domestic scene. Again and again, characters are encountered at home: cooking, eating, sleeping, loving, quarrelling, and conversing – a long way from the barbarian marauders of stereotype. The main figures also evolve naturally over time (the series has been running since 2013), gaining new hairstyles, gradually accumulating tattoos, and clearly ageing in some cases. Everyone also wears a continually changing variety of clothing: think how often, in historical dramas, a character has their "costume" and sticks with it. And very little of all these transitions is actively depicted while happening, or is explained in exposition: they have simply occurred somewhere in the background of daily life.

Just as the late Eric Christensen once described the period as "the golden age of the pig farmer,"[14] the series never loses sight of the important fact that most of those we think of as "Vikings" never went anywhere or did any harm to anyone. The rural world is a constant backdrop, and it is interesting how much sheer ground-truthed economics is on display as we travel through the different settlements. Ragnar and Lagertha begin as farmers and at times regret they ever became anything else, and agrarian life – the need for land and the almost spiritual bond with it – is a repeated theme over several seasons. Similarly, when Harald Finehair of Norway enters the story in season 4, his northern home has its own particular sources of subsistence, seen to be heavily reliant on whaling and with a general emphasis on deep-sea harvesting – both very up-to-the-minute research topics. In the dockside scenes, one can almost smell the fish, and even Harald's royal hall is decorated with whalebone (and why not?).

The same variety and complication extends to the Vikings' mind-set. Their moral world is entirely contingent, and even "sympathetic" characters perform acts of extreme violence and casual cruelty, to a near psychopathic degree that is shocking to us but not regarded as such in context. This is contrasted in later seasons with individuals such as Ivar the Boneless, whose unhinged sadism frightens even his own brothers.

Similarly, the series goes to great lengths in its discussion of religious tensions, and in its depiction of "paganism" as a far from coordinated or orthodox set of beliefs and practices. Worshippers of the gods are genuinely intrigued by the White Christ, and a developing plot thread of the first three seasons is the near-apostasy of a Christian monk who sees the deeper value systems below the surface of Odin and the others. Most interestingly, in a show about people known for a caricature of violence, an awful lot of time is spent in philosophical conversation about the nature of faith, friendship, power, and what it means to lead in both spiritual and profane terms. In general, intellectual curiosity is a hallmark of the main characters.

Much has been made by critics of the show's supposedly "strong female characters": the lead role of Lagertha, shield-maiden and Ragnar's queen from Saxo's *Gesta Danorum*; the sorceress Aslaug; and a long list of independent-minded women. This is true up to a point, but I think it actually does a disservice to one of the series' real strengths: these are not "strong women," but simply believable ones. In fact, the various seasons are full of female characters from across the entire social spectrum, from slaves to warriors and rulers, and they experience misfortune, oppression, and exploitation just as often as they exert their agency and rise. Above all, they are real.

Another of my personal priorities among the positive qualities of *Vikings* is the consistent presence of children, in all the settlements and environments of the show. They are always treated as fully-rounded individuals, with their own dreams and aspirations, which is a remarkably rare thing in dramas of this kind (and in academia). Ragnar's children with both Lagertha and Aslaug grow up over several seasons, and the later track of their character arcs is laid down early. Similarly, child mortality is a regular feature of the storylines. Almost every major adult figure loses children to either miscarriage, illness, or infanticide, with an emotional impact that continues to resonate over several seasons. On multiple occasions, men return home from abroad to find that their children, and sometimes their partners, are dead; by the same token, women wait on the quayside, but their men are never going to come back. Long ago in my doctoral thesis, I posed the question of what it was like to be married to a Viking – more than a decade later it feels quite surprising to find some answers attempted by a TV series.[15]

From women and children, one can also consider the elderly, and the treatment of disability and difference. Sigurd Snake-in-the-Eye is born with a defect in his iris, interpreted as an omen and a sign, but never as an impairment. Far more prominent is Ivar the Boneless, with an unspecified condition that renders his legs useless. In opting for a literal interpretation of his nickname, the producers place a disabled person in the center of the show's narrative from season 5 onwards, following the death of Ragnar. This includes practicalities of mobility and the implied effects of constant pain, coupled with the consequences of social rejection at the hands of Ivar's brothers and contemporaries. While the treatment of these issues is relatively superficial, the simple fact of a disabled Viking war commander is striking in itself – again, a genuine departure from the stereotypes.

We can also briefly review some of the current research trends that make an appearance in *Vikings*, slipped into the storylines in an unobtrusive way but building to a remarkably nuanced – and in some ways subversive – picture. There are the details of personal appearance, the tattoos and eye make-up (from Ibn Fadlān and al-Turtūshī); startling customs such as the group sex, but even that coming from Ibn Fadlān again[16]; the practice of polygyny and concubinage, and the social complexities resulting from men fathering children with multiple women[17]; the presence of sorcerers of both sexes, even the word *völva* is used[18]; the Viking armies divided into separate bands, led by individual and occasionally quarrelling commanders[19]; the gender ambiguity of several lead characters[20]; and much more, here following only my personal interests.

As an archaeological Viking specialist, it can be a fun exercise to guess exactly which papers the writer and designers have been reading. An especially fruitful seam can be mined in the series' treatment of funerary practice. This phenomenon has already been explored in interesting depth online by Howard Williams,[21] but I was struck in particular by the sequence in which the trickster character Floki is seen digging at a woodland pile of stones, only to be revealed as opening the grave of his father.[22] Having exposed the burial, Floki retrieves a sword, which he then employs in his own marriage ritual. We know little of Viking marriage customs,[23] but there has been extensive recent work on the reopening of burials for reasons that we can only surmise.[24] What an excellent way to communicate a complex subject to a general audience, combining guesswork with empiricism but without cumbersome explication.

To put it mildly, despite the series containing all the raiding and pillaging that viewers will be expecting, the people of the preceding paragraphs are decidedly *not* your usual Vikings (they are certainly not what I first learned about in college, some thirty-odd years ago). In all of this, we see the sheer difference of the Vikings presented for a modern audience – which should not be confused with Othering them. As academics we should never underestimate the impact that these messages have on our publics, nor should we dismiss them on the pedantic grounds that somebody's sword hilt has the "wrong" typology. That said, there are downsides to the series' messages too, and these cannot be ignored just because there is so much to be celebrated. In later seasons especially, there is a distressing Orientalism in the depiction of Arab and Mediterranean culture (the "exotic" East is in full flow), and in some respects the Sámi are atrociously misrepresented. These things matter, a lot. It will be evident that I like *Vikings* and think that its net benefit to our profession is considerable, but it is not a quick fix.[25]

Real Vikings

I began with the parameters of research, and continued through the possible impacts of that academic work on a popular entertainment that reaches a global audience. I can end this article with a brief consideration of a second media series that in a direct sense links the two.

Just over a year after *Vikings* hit the screens for the first time, History Canada and the Toronto production company Take 5 decided to launch a set of companion documentary programs under the title *Real Vikings*. The first batch of four were each to be an hour long, including time for commercials, and would air in North America directly after the drama series episodes with the intention of retaining viewers (essentially, persuading them not to change the channel). Alongside the early seasons of *Vikings*, History had already commissioned a series of web-only short films, 10–15 minutes long and focusing on tightly constrained sites or issues, featuring archaeologists in discussion. Their director, Kenton Vaughan, was picked to expand the format into the new, longer series, and based on my previous work with him I was asked to come on-board as historical consultant.

Of course, there are many, many documentaries on Viking themes, several being produced each year, but what set this one apart was its direct relationship to a dramatized series (as opposed to the docu-drama sequences that are becoming quite common in other documentaries). The key point with *Real Vikings* is that – to the best of my knowledge – it was the first ever on-screen attempt to academically engage with and nuance an imagined reconstruction, produced by the same company with the intention that the two series be shown together. As a professional archaeologist, this seems to me highly significant, a brave choice by the broadcaster, and a considerable challenge.

As a result, a large cast of specialists[26] interacted with the drama series cast members across nine countries, ranging from arctic Norway to Galicia, discussing the actors' experiences on the show in relation to topics of relevance to their characters. In programs covering armies and invasions, pre-Christian religion, and the family history of Ragnar, we were able to deepen the issues that I have already mentioned above. In looking at the objects and visiting the sites, we were of course supporting the series but also taking the opportunity to express uncertainty and caution where appropriate. The distinction between academic interpretation and dramatic inspiration was important, but also at times finer than one might expect. We must have done something right: the episode on Viking Age women was nominated for Best Historical Documentary and won Best Director in the 2018 Canadian Screen Awards (Canada's combined version of the Emmys and Oscars), and the Director of Photography Mark Caswell won Best Photography in 2017, with the series also nominated in other categories.

The documentary was also undeniably fun to make, not least for the chance to work with the actors whose adventures one had watched with close attention and emotional investment through several seasons of Viking mayhem. As professional biographers of long-lost Viking lives, we should not forget all the glorious doors that television can open but which – to the frequent surprise of TV producers – simple academia sometimes cannot. This can be literally the case, as at the site of Charlemagne's court in the Palatine Chapel of Aachen, Germany, when Simon Coupland and I got to physically push through the original bronze double doors that had stood there since the Viking Age, putting our shoulders to the very same gates through which the Scandinavians once entered the building as plunderers. It was likewise a rare experience to handle the only complete copy of *Ragnars saga loðbrókar* in the Royal Library at Copenhagen, turning its wood-bound pages and seeing the familiar names leap from the lines, Ragnarr, Björn, Sigurðr and the rest; to stand beside Rollo's tomb in Rouen cathedral in Normandy; to (very badly) row a replica longship in the fjord at Borg in Lofoten; to take a slow boat ride up the Seine to Paris, following the path of Reginheri's advance in the ninth century, arriving at l'Île de la Cité at dusk as the floodlights burst onto Nôtre Dame; to see the display cases and finds stores open up in museum after museum, as well as visiting again the monuments of Scandinavia – all the way to the final shoot, at previously unexplored sites of possible Viking presence in northern Spain, conducting actual research on film, combined with the wonderful discovery that Galicia's leading Viking specialist also happens to be one of the region's leading food critics to whom no restaurant kitchen is closed . . . One could say that it beats the day job, but in fact – and this is important – it is an essential *part* of it.

Over the years, many specialists have attempted to trace the research trajectory of Viking studies, and to suggest its future. I have tried myself on a few occasions,[27] but sometimes I wonder if in the end we can do no better than the late Patrick Wormald, with his paraphrase of Lady Caroline Lamb's judgement on Byron: "The importance, and the interest, of studying the development of Scandinavia in the Viking Age is in no way diminished if one believes, as in the last resort I do, that though the Vikings may not have been mad, they were probably bad, and certainly dangerous to know."[28]

I can close here with my watchwords for where we might be going, with what I see as key factors in the approaches we need to take. As a basic principle, we must acknowledge the limits of our knowledge, and the uncertainty of our interpretations. Above all, we need to embrace the complexity and variety of lived experience in the Viking Age, inclusively, in the widest sense of that term. We must be willing to see beyond stereotype, of course, but also to view the Vikings simply as people, in all their marvelous ambiguity of outlook and intent, allowing them to be human.

We should pay them the compliment of permitting them to live forever in their own vibrant present, rather than merely in our distant past.

Acknowledgements: Many thanks to Tom Birkett for the invitation to the conference on which this volume is based, and a toast to the World-Tree Project that is making an innovative and important contribution to Viking studies as situated in the contemporary world. I attend a lot of Viking conferences, but this one was different and all the better for it. I would like to especially acknowledge Kevin Crossley-Holland – as Neil Gaiman says, "the Master" – who has been an inspiration to me since I was a teenager. Kevin, it was such a pleasure to meet you, and thanks for the conversation, the books, and the poetry.

The *Real Vikings* series was made for History Canada by Take 5 Productions and Shaw Media in Toronto, later taken up by History US, MGM, and Corus Entertainment. I would like to thank the executives at Take 5, particularly Gina Vanni and her team, for their hospitality and support. Special thanks to the *Real Vikings* series director Kenton Vaughan, whose belief in the value of the finished product harks back to the golden age of historical documentaries. Two episodes were directed by respectively Rebecca Snow and Peter Findlay, consummate professionals and a pleasure to work with. Nothing would have been the same without the regular team of Mark Caswell as director of photography and Mike Fillipov on sound: guys, hope to see you soon again. A resounding *skål* to showrunner Michael Hirst and the cast members of *Vikings* – Katheryn, Clive, Alyssa, and Maude – for being so unintimidating and in all ways very nice indeed to a series of nervous archaeologists, philologists, and historians.

Lastly, grateful thanks to my employers at Uppsala University for their belief in the importance of what is known in Sweden as the "third mission," or knowledge transfer and public outreach, and for making it possible to accommodate the long weeks of filming in my everyday schedule. You recognized from the beginning that not only is this work, but that it is just as important as the teaching and research.

Bibliography

Christensen, Eric. *The Norsemen in the Viking Age*. Oxford: Blackwell, 2002.

Cyrino, Monica S. *Big Screen Rome*. Oxford: Blackwell, 2005.

Cyrino, Monica S. *Rome, Season One: History Makes Television*. Oxford: Blackwell, 2008.

Davison, Brian. *Picturing the Past through the Eyes of Reconstruction Artists*. London: English Heritage, 1997.

Díaz-Andreu, Margarita. "Gender Identity." In *The Archaeology of Identity: Approaches to Gender, Age, Status, Ethnicity and Religion*, edited by Margarita Díaz-Andreu et al., pp. 13–42. London: Routledge, 2005.

Hedenstierna-Jonson, Charlotte et al. "A Female Viking Warrior Confirmed by Genomics." *American Journal of Physical Anthropology* 164, no. 4 (2017): 853–60.

Hitchens, Christopher. *And Yet . . . Essays*. New York: Simon & Schuster, 2015.
Hodges, Richard. *Goodbye to the Vikings? Re-reading Early Medieval Archaeology*. London: Duckworth, 2006.
Hopkins, Keith. *A World Full of Gods: Pagans, Jews and Christians in the Roman Empire*. London: Weidenfeld & Nicolson, 1999.
Kelly, Christopher. "Professor Keith Hopkins, Provocatively Modern Historian." [Obituary] *The Independent*, March 24, 2004. http://www.independent.co.uk/news/obituaries/profes sor-keith-hopkins-549668.html.
Klevnäs, Alision. "'Imbued with the Essence of the Owner': Personhood and Possessions in the Reopening and Reworking of Viking-Age Burials." *European Journal of Archaeology* 19, no. 3 (2016): 456–76.
Lane Fox, Robin. *The Making of Alexander*. Oxford: R&L, 2004.
Lunde, Paul and Caroline Stone. *Ibn Fadlān and the Land of Darkness: Arab Travellers in the Far North*. London: Penguin, 2012.
Molyneux, Brian Leigh. *The Cultural Life of Images: Visual Representation in Archaeology*. London: Routledge, 1997.
Pollard, Justin. *The World of Vikings*. San Francisco: Chronicle, 2015.
Price, Neil. *The Viking Way: Religion and War in Late Iron Age Scandinavia*. Uppsala: Uppsala University Press, 2002.
Price, Neil. "Cognition, Culture and Context: Observations on the 'New' Viking Archaeology." In *Viking and Norse in the North Atlantic*, edited by Símon Arge and Arne Mortensen, pp. 375–82. Tórshavn: Føroya Fróðskaparfelag, 2005.
Price, Neil. "From Ginnungagap to the Ragnarök: Archaeologies of the Viking Worlds." In *Viking Worlds: Things, Spaces and Movement*, edited by Marianne Hem Eriksen et al., pp. 1–10. Oxford: Oxbow Books, 2015.
Price, Neil. "Viking Archaeology in the 21st Century." In *Medieval Archaeology in Scandinavia and Beyond: History, Trends and Tomorrow*, edited by Mette S. Kristiansen et al., pp. 275–94. Aarhus: Aarhus University Press, 2015.
Price, Neil. "De första vikingarna?" *Populär Arkeologi* 2 (2017): 10–15.
Price, Neil. "Vikings on the Volga? Ibn Fadlan and the Rituals of the Rūssiyah." In *Muslims on the Volga in the Viking Age: Diplomacy and Islam in the world of Ibn Fadlan*, edited by Jon Shepard and Luke Treadwell. London: I. B. Tauris, in press.
Raffield, Ben. "Bands of Brothers: A Re-Appraisal of the Viking Great Army and Its Implications for the Scandinavian Colonization of England." *Early Medieval Europe* 24, no. 3 (2016): 308–37.
Raffield, Ben et al. "Male-Biased Operational Sex Ratios and the Viking Phenomenon: An Evolutionary Anthropological Perspective on Late Iron Age Scandinavian Raiding." *Evolution and Human Behavior* 38, no. 3 (2017): 315–24.
Raffield, Ben et al. "Polygyny, Concubinage and the Social Lives of Women in Viking-Age Scandinavia." *Viking and Medieval Scandinavia* 13 (2018): 165–209
Stamp, Jonathan. *Rome*. New York: Melcher, 2007.
Svanberg, Fredrik. *Decolonizing the Viking Age*. Stockholm: Almqvist & Wiksell, 2003.
Tveskov, Mark A. and Jon M. Erlandson. "Vikings, Vixens, and Valhalla: Hollywood Depictions of the Norse." In *Box Office Archaeology: Refining Hollywood's Portrayals of the Past*, edited by Julie M. Schablitsky, pp. 34–50. Walnut Creek: Left Coast Press, 2007.
Williams, Howard. *Archaeodeath* (blog). https://howardwilliamsblog.wordpress.com.
Williams, Howard et al. eds. *The Public Archaeology of Death*. Sheffield: Equinox (2019).
Winkler, Martin M. ed. *Gladiator: Film and History*. Oxford: Blackwell, 2005.

Winkler, Martin M. ed. *Troy: From Homer's Iliad to Hollywood Epic*. Oxford: Blackwell, 2007.
Wormald, Patrick. "Viking Studies: Whence and Whither?" In *The Vikings*, edited by Robert T. Farrell, pp. 128–56. Chichester: Phillimore, 1982.

Notes

1. Neil Price, *The Viking Way: Religion and War in Late Iron Age Scandinavia* (Uppsala: Uppsala University Press, 2002), p. 25.
2. Christopher Kelly, "Professor Keith Hopkins, Provocatively Modern Historian," [Obituary] *The Independent*, March 24, 2004, http://www.independent.co.uk/news/obituaries/pro fessor-keith-hopkins-549668.html.
3. Keith Hopkins, *A World Full of Gods: Pagans, Jews and Christians in the Roman Empire* (London: Weidenfeld & Nicolson, 1999).
4. Neil Price, "De första vikingarna?," *Populär Arkeologi* 2 (2017): 10–15.
5. Fredrik Svanberg, *Decolonizing the Viking Age* (Stockholm: Almqvist & Wiksell, 2003).
6. See Richard Hodges, *Goodbye to the Vikings? Re-reading Early Medieval Archaeology* (London: Duckworth, 2006).
7. Raffield, Ben et al., "Male-Biased Operational Sex Ratios and the Viking Phenomenon: An Evolutionary Anthropological Perspective on Late Iron Age Scandinavian Raiding," *Evolution and Human Behavior* 38, no. 3 (2017): 315–24; Raffield, Ben et al., "Polygyny, Concubinage and the Social Lives of Women in Viking-Age Scandinavia," *Viking and Medieval Scandinavia* 13 (2018): 165–209. Charlotte Hedenstierna-Jonson et al., "A Female Viking Warrior Confirmed by Genomics," *American Journal of Physical Anthropology* 164, no. 4 (2017): 853–60.
8. Margarita Díaz-Andreu, "Gender Identity," in *The Archaeology of Identity: Approaches to Gender, Age, Status, Ethnicity and Religion*, ed. Margarita Díaz-Andreu et al. (London: Routledge, 2005), pp. 13–42 at p. 14.
9. See Brian Leigh Molyneux, *The Cultural Life of Images: Visual Representation in Archaeology* (London: Routledge, 1997); Brian Davison, *Picturing the Past through the Eyes of Reconstruction Artists* (London: English Heritage, 1997); Howard Williams et al. eds., *The Public Archaeology of Death* (Sheffield: Equinox, 2019).
10. Justin Pollard, *The World of* Vikings (San Francisco: Chronicle, 2015).
11. Robin Lane Fox, *The Making of* Alexander (Oxford: R&L, 2004); Monica S. Cyrino, *Big Screen Rome* (Oxford: Blackwell, 2005); Martin M. Winkler, ed., *Gladiator: Film and History* (Oxford: Blackwell, 2005); Mark A. Tveskov and Jon M. Erlandson, "Vikings, Vixens, and Valhalla: Hollywood Depictions of the Norse," in *Box Office Archaeology: Refining Hollywood's Portrayals of the Past*, ed. Julie M. Schablitsky (Walnut Creek: Left Coast Press, 2007), pp. 34–50; Martin M. Winkler, ed., *Troy: From Homer's Iliad to Hollywood Epic* (Oxford: Blackwell, 2007); Jonathan Stamp, *Rome* (New York: Melcher, 2007); Monica S. Cyrino, *Rome, Season One: History Makes Television* (Oxford: Blackwell, 2008).
12. Sources include the Icelandic legendary saga *Ragnars saga loðbrókar*; the short tale *Ragnarssona þáttr*; the account of Ragnar by Danish chronicler Saxo Grammaticus in his *Gesta Danorum*; and the skaldic poem *Krákumál*.

13. Christopher Hitchens, *And Yet . . . Essays* (New York: Simon & Schuster, 2015), pp. 147–53.
14. Eric Christensen, *The Norsemen in the Viking Age* (Oxford: Blackwell, 2002), p. 6.
15. Price, *Viking Way*, p. 393.
16. For both these sources, see Paul Lunde and Caroline Stone, *Ibn Fadlān and the Land of Darkness: Arab Travellers in the Far North* (London: Penguin, 2012).
17. Raffield et al., "Polygyny, Concubinage."
18. Price, *Viking Way*.
19. Ben Raffield, "Bands of Brothers: A Re-Appraisal of the Viking Great Army and Its Implications for the Scandinavian Colonization of England," *Early Medieval Europe* 24, no. 3 (2016): 308–37.
20. There are many sources for this, but it is a consistent theme; even the series title music is by a queer, gender-fluid artist, Fever Ray (Karin Dreijer).
21. Howard Williams, *Archaeodeath* (blog), https://howardwilliamsblog.wordpress.com.
22. Season 2 Episode 7 "Blood Eagle." The scene gains an added dimension in that the only dialogue is the phrase, "Hej, pappa" [Hi, dad], spoken in Swedish by Gustaf Skarsgård as Floki, with an in-joke in that his own father is also a famous actor.
23. For an estimation, see Neil Price, "Vikings on the Volga? Ibn Fadlan and the Rituals of the Rūssiyah," in *Muslims on the Volga in the Viking Age: Diplomacy and Islam in the World of Ibn Fadlan*, ed. Jon Shepard and Luke Treadwell (London: I. B. Tauris, in press).
24. E.g., Alison Klevnäs, "'Imbued with the Essence of the Owner': Personhood and Possessions in the Reopening and Reworking of Viking-Age Burials," *European Journal of Archaeology* 19, no. 3 (2016): 456–76.
25. As an interesting coda, one could also write a similar paper to this around *Vikings*' close contemporary, the Anglo-Saxon/Norse TV saga *The Last Kingdom*, based on the books by Bernard Cornwell. The Vikings of this series are different again, but no more or less "inaccurate" for that.
26. These included Aðalheiður Guðmundsdóttir, Steve Ashby, Simon Coupland, Clare Downham, Terry Gunnell, Charlotte Hedenstierna-Jonson, Cat Jarman, Anna Kjellström, John Ljungkvist, Unn Pedersen, Ben Raffield, Gareth Williams, and others.
27. Neil Price, "Cognition, Culture and Context: Observations on the 'New' Viking Archaeology," in *Viking and Norse in the North Atlantic*, ed. Símon Arge and Arne Mortensen (Tórshavn: Føroya Fróðskaparfelag, 2005), pp. 375–82; Neil Price, "From Ginnungagap to the Ragnarök: Archaeologies of the Viking Worlds," in *Viking Worlds: Things, Spaces and Movement*, ed. Marianne Hem Eriksen et al. (Oxford: Oxbow Books, 2015), pp. 1–10; Neil Price, "Viking Archaeology in the 21st Century," in *Medieval Archaeology in Scandinavia and Beyond: History, Trends and Tomorrow*, ed. Mette S. Kristiansen et al. (Aarhus: Aarhus University Press, 2015), pp. 275–94.
28. Patrick Wormald, "Viking Studies: Whence and Whither?," in *The Vikings*, ed. Robert T. Farrell (Chichester: Phillimore, 1982), pp. 128–56 at p. 156.

Leszek Gardeła
3 (Re)discovering the Vikings in Poland: From Nineteenth-Century Romantics to Contemporary Warriors

Viking studies in Poland has a long history which goes back to the early nineteenth century, but due to various historical and political circumstances, as well as the linguistic barrier, this history remains largely unknown to international audiences.[1] The primary aim of this paper is to shed light on the dynamic, yet sometimes controversial, development of Viking and Old Norse research in Poland and its academic and popular reception over the course of the last 150 years.

The geo-political focus of this paper is the area of Poland within its current borders. However, it is necessary to point out that in the period from the Middle Ages to the end of the Second World War, this part of Europe underwent numerous transformations leading to the shifting of its borders and, at one point, as a result of foreign occupation, even the disappearance of Poland from the map for over 120 years. All these changes had a profound impact on the life of Poles; their deep influence is reflected in the character and tone of some of the artistic and academic endeavors that have been carried out over the course of the last three centuries. In discussing the history and reception of Viking and Old Norse studies in Poland, it is therefore essential to acknowledge and understand the broader socio-political context in which the subject developed.

We may distinguish at least five phases of the development of academic and popular reception of Vikings in Poland:[2] beginning with the national romantic fascination with the northern world, through the difficult time of Nazi occupation followed by the post-war communist period when research was strongly driven by ideology, to the years after the fall of communism but before Poland's accession to the EU, and up to the modern "Viking craze." All of these phases will be discussed in more detail below.

Phase 1: Viking Studies in the Nineteenth Century

Towards the end of the eighteenth century, as a result of the so-called "partitions of Poland," the Polish-Lithuanian Commonwealth disappeared from the

Leszek Gardeła, Department of Scandinavian Languages and Literatures, University of Bonn

https://doi.org/10.1515/9781501513886-004

map of Europe and its territory was divided among three superpowers: the Russian Empire, the Kingdom of Prussia and Habsburg Austria. The partitions deeply affected the everyday life of Poles, but despite these difficult circumstances, Polish language and culture prevailed and continued to be cultivated. At that time, the city of Lviv (Polish Lwów) was among the most prominent centers of Polish cultural life and was also one of the places where the Polish interest in Old Norse and Viking studies was born.

One of the true pioneers of Viking studies in nineteenth-century Poland was Karol Szajnocha, a man of many talents, deeply interested in prehistory and the Middle Ages. He studied at the Philosophical Department of Lviv University and as early as 1834 he founded a society called Towarzystwo Starożytności (The Antiquarian Society), the aim of which was to collect and disseminate knowledge about antiquities. Szajnocha's revolutionist ideas and his involvement in anti-government "conspiracy" had dire consequences and led to his imprisonment in 1835. For almost two years he was kept in chains in a damp and completely dark cell, the conditions of which severely damaged his health and especially his sight. After his release, as former political prisoner, Szajnocha was unable to continue his education at the university, but this did not discourage him from pursuing an academically oriented career – he soon became a prolific writer and author of dozens of publications. Today, Szajnocha is best known for his monograph *Lechickie początki Polski* (*The Lechite Beginnings of Poland*), published in 1858, a highly controversial work in which he argued that the Polish state was founded by Scandinavian immigrants.[3] Szajnocha sought to prove his theory primarily on a linguistic basis, but he approached the sources in an impressionistic way, which often involved manipulating them to fit his own view of history. Looking at his work from today's perspective, it seems that he had no racial or political motivations in trying to argue for the Norse origins of Poland – his ideas were probably driven by the romantic spirit of his time and the fact that the so-called "conquest theory" was very popular among Polish scholars in the nineteenth century.[4] What Szajnocha unconsciously did, however, was to lay the foundations for the more dangerous and politically motivated views on history that were soon to evolve.

Apart from Szajnocha, in the nineteenth century many other scholars, writers, and artists were inspired by the Viking world and Icelandic sagas. One of them was Tadeusz Czacki, a historian, economist, numismatist, and bibliophile, who released a study about the legal system which functioned in Poland and Lithuania in the distant past.[5] In contrast to other authors of his time, who argued for the Roman roots of the legal system, he tried – in vain – to find analogies between Slavic and Baltic laws and those of the Germanic peoples.[6] Czacki's ideas were misunderstood by several prominent scholars of his time who probably only cursorily read his work. As a result, he was considered the first Polish Normanist, a rather derogatory and inappropriate label given the fact that he had never actually subscribed to any politically motivated Normanist theories. Another scholar of the nineteenth century, whom some also wrongly called a Normanist, was Franciszek Piekosiński. His main scholarly specialism was heraldry, and in his book *O dynastycznym pochodzeniu szlachty polskiej* (*On the Dynastic Origin of Polish Nobility*), he suggested that some of the symbols depicted on Polish coats of arms were based on Germanic runes, a rather controversial idea to which no scholars today would subscribe.[7]

Thanks to Joachim Lelewel, rightly regarded as one of the fathers of Polish history, the late nineteenth century also saw the first translations of the Poetic Edda and the Prose Edda into Polish.[8] His pioneering work not only had an effect on academia, but also provided an inexhaustible source of ideas for writers, such as Juliusz Słowacki, whose play *Lilla Weneda* and epic *Król Duch* contained clear references to Eddic poems.[9] Towards the end of the nineteenth century, the celebrated artist Henryk Siemiradzki also created two large-scale paintings showing important episodes from the Viking Age, one being the funeral of a Rus' noble at the Volga (based on the Arabic description by Ibn Fadlān) and the other depicting the dramatic scenes from the famous battle between the Kievan Rus' and the Byzantine army which took place at Dorostolon in 971 (today's Silistra in Bulgaria).[10]

Having now outlined the different origins of fascination with the North among historians and artists, let us turn our attention to the beginnings of Viking archaeology in Poland. In the nineteenth century, a number of Scandinavian-style objects were found in Poland, while others, already well-known (such as the so-called Cammin Casket held at the cathedral in Kamień Pomorski), were for the first time published in a scholarly format.[11] Regrettably, the majority of new finds were not excavated in a professional manner and today relatively little is known about their contexts. Among the most interesting Scandinavian-style finds dated to the Viking Age and discovered in the nineteenth century are two Thor's hammers from Pomeranian hoards – one from Łupawa and one from the vicinity of Wolin (Figure 3.1).

These objects are still important in that they represent the only examples of silver Thor's hammers that have been discovered in the area of Poland to date and as such they provide interesting hints about the pre-Christian beliefs of Scandinavian migrants to these lands.[12] In 1867 and 1896, two other hoards were discovered in Kąty and Gralewo in Greater Poland respectively. Each of them contained small fragments of Scandinavian-style silver pendants in the form of equal-armed crosses, similar to those known from Hiddensee and other localities in the Viking world (Figure 3.1).[13] In addition to these pendants,

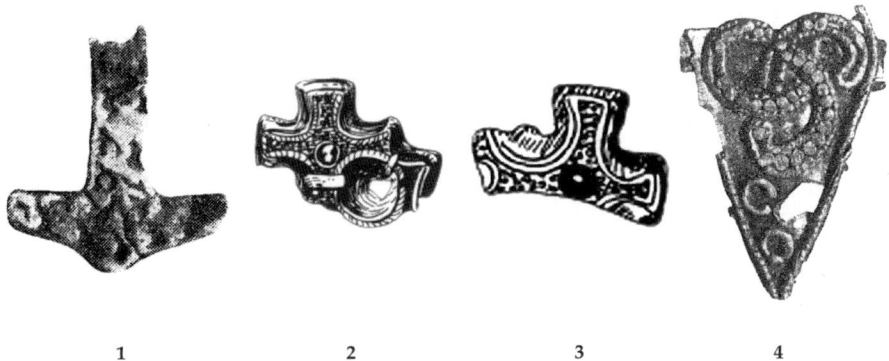

1   2   3   4

Figure 3.1: 1 – Thor's hammer from the vicinity of Wolin in Western Pomerania; 2 – Fragment of a cross-shaped pendant from Kąty in Greater Poland; 3 – Fragment of a cross-shaped pendant from Gralewo in Greater Poland; 4 – A small plaque with a triquetra motif from Ostrów Lednicki in Greater Poland. Reproduced after Gardeła, *Scandinavian Amulets in Viking Age Poland,* pp. 70, 118 and Żurowski, "Z ostatnich odkryć na Ostrowie Lednickim," p. 108.

a number of other hoards containing objects of Scandinavian provenance (mostly coins and occasionally jewelry) were unearthed in Pomerania.[14]

Of particular interest for both German and Polish scholars was the discovery of a Viking Age cremation cemetery at Świelubie in Central Pomerania in 1897.[15] One of the graves excavated there included three gaming pieces made of bone, pottery shards, pieces of amber, a copper alloy tube (possibly a needle case), and a copper alloy oval brooch of Scandinavian type (Figure 3.2). After an interval of several decades, the excavations at Świelubie were resumed by Adolf Stubenrauch in ca. 1900, Carl Schuchhardt in 1923 and in the 1960s by Władysław Łosiński;[16] we will consider these developments in more detail below.

Phase 2: Viking Studies in the Early Twentieth Century

Old Norse and Viking studies in Poland started to take a new form in the early years of the twentieth century. Due to the enduring interest in Scandinavian–Slavic relations in the area of Pomerania, several Polish academics devoted particular attention to the vivid descriptions of the fortress of Jómsborg which, according to *Jómsvíkinga saga* and other written sources, allegedly housed a group of renowned Scandinavian Vikings and was said to be located somewhere on the

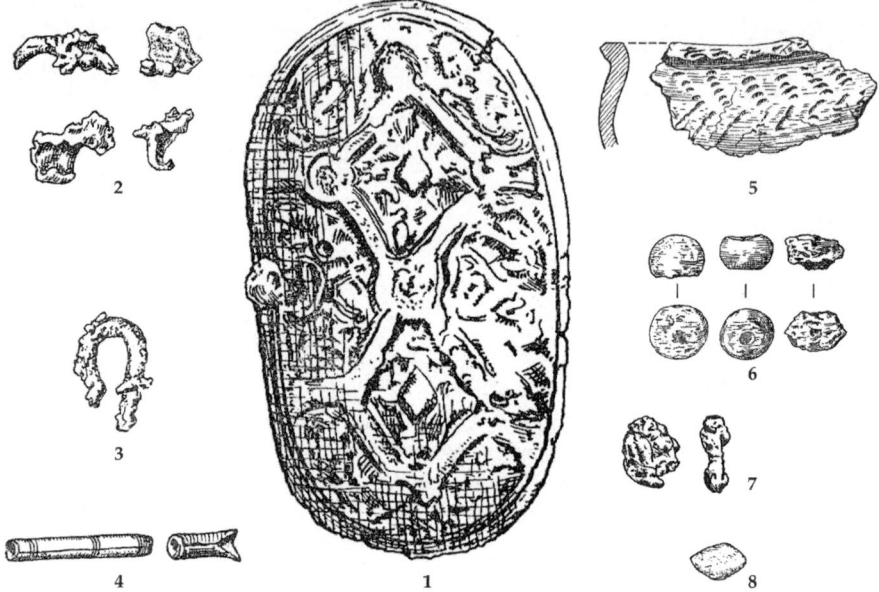

Figure 3.2: Selection of objects from a Viking Age cremation grave discovered at Świelubie in Pomerania: 1 – Oval brooch; 2 – Fragmented catch-plate of the oval brooch; 3 – Indeterminate iron object; 4 – Copper alloy tubes; 5 – Fragment of a clay vessel; 6 – Gaming pieces made of bone; 7 – Melted glass beads; 8 – Amber fragment. Reproduced after Kostrzewski, *Obrządek ciałopalny u plemion polskich*, p. 68.

southern coast of the Baltic.[17] These vivid accounts led some scholars to look for the traces of Jómsborg at the mouth of the Oder River, in particular in Wolin. Although none of them ever found any remains of such a fortress, this did not discourage their successors from continuing the search and spurred other enthusiasts to creatively (re)use stories and legends about Wolin in their various scholarly, literary, and artistic endeavors.[18]

In 1918, the Silesian scholar Robert Holtzmann published an article which, in line with the then popular conquest theory, argued that the first historical ruler of Poland, Duke Mieszko I (the father of Bolesław I Chrobry / Bolesław the Brave), was of Germanic descent and that his original name was Dago or Dagon.[19] Holtzmann's idea was primarily based on the document called *Dagome iudex*, a papal regesta listing the lands which Mieszko I had placed under the protection of the Apostolic See. Holtzmann concluded that the Piasts, who founded their state in the area between the rivers Oder and Vistula, stemmed from Scandinavia just like the Rurik dynasty. Similar views were expressed by Lambert Schulte,[20] who also believed Mieszko to be of Norse origin. These perspectives on Polish history, created on the basis of very problematic source material and equally problematic pseudo-academic arguments, became the cornerstones of a long and heated debate which continued for the next several decades.

The early twentieth century was also the time when the nature of the Scandinavian presence in Poland started to be more seriously and comprehensively examined by archaeologists. One of the first Polish scholars to discuss the discoveries of Scandinavian-style objects was Józef Kostrzewski from the milieu of Poznań University. Kostrzewski was a very prominent academic with a remarkably broad spectrum of interests, but today he is best known for his research on prehistoric societies and his excavations of the Early Iron Age stronghold at Biskupin. Kostrzewski analyzed Scandinavian finds from Poland in a number of studies and expressed very balanced views on the roles that the people from the North played on the southern coast of the Baltic and in the interior of Poland.[21] One of Kostrzewski's most detailed – albeit rather controversial from today's methodological standpoint – contributions to this topic was an article devoted to the extraordinary finds from the early medieval cemetery at Łubowo in Greater Poland (Figure 3.3).[22] The site was discovered in 1912, during the building of a local road, when workers came across a lavishly decorated spearhead and an axe, as well as human bones and clay pottery. Unfortunately, the exact contexts of the discovery were not recorded, and it is unclear whether all these objects came from one or several different graves. At the time when Kostrzewski was writing his article on the finds from Łubowo, relatively little was known about the military equipment used by the Western Slavs, so to him the weapons discovered there seemed to be of foreign provenance. Based on this assumption, he put forward the argument that the cemetery held the remains of Scandinavian immigrants. Today, these simplistic views are no longer maintained, however, and it is acknowledged that the cultural and ethnic provenance of the dead cannot be determined by weapons alone.[23]

In 1925, the Polish historian Kazimierz Krotoski published an article in which he argued for the Scandinavian descent of some of the legendary and semi-legendary rulers of Poland.[24] Interestingly, in his discussions he referred to archaeological finds unearthed, *inter alia*, in the early medieval cemetery at Łubowo in Greater Poland, which at that time was deemed to contain graves of Scandinavians. According to Piotr Boroń, Krotoski's work can be regarded as "the last voice in Polish historiography that spoke for the Normanist theory."[25]

On the other hand, German scholars, especially in the 1930s[26] and in the wake of Nazism, strongly argued for the Scandinavian origins of Poland; such opinions may be found, for example, in the publications of Albert Brackmann[27] and Hermann Aubin,[28] both of whom shared strong sympathies for Nazi ideology.

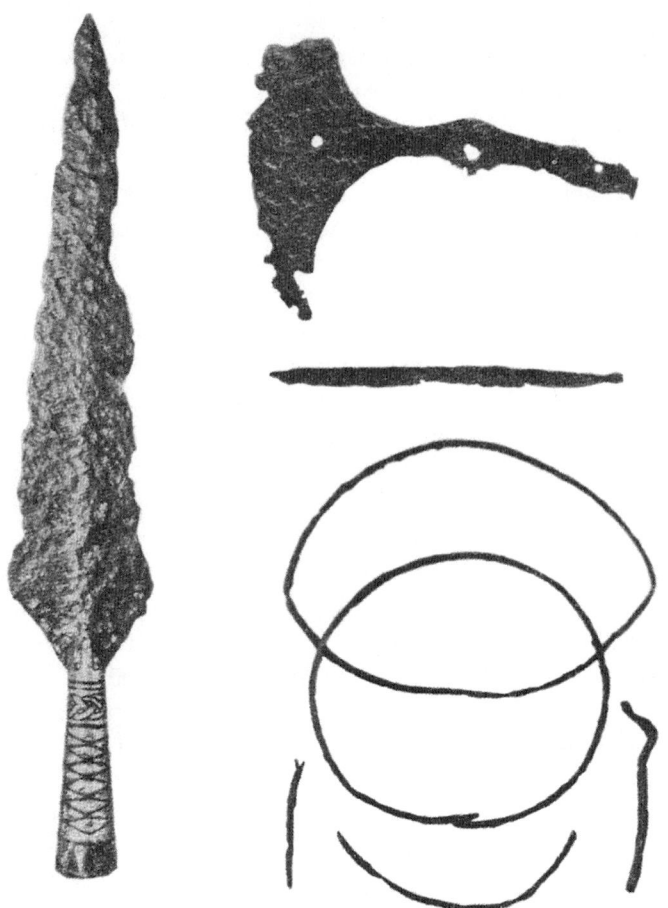

Figure 3.3: Selection of finds from an early medieval cemetery at Łubowo in Greater Poland, including a spear, an axe, an iron knife, and iron hoops of a bucket. Reproduced after Gardeła, *Scandinavian Amulets in Viking Age Poland,* p. 28.

In later years, especially during the Second World War and in the communist period, many Polish scholars made efforts to dismiss their arguments and sought to demonstrate that Viking Age Scandinavians had never played any significant role in founding the Piast state – we will discuss these views below.

The first three decades of the twentieth century also saw increased interest in the Old Norse sagas. It is worthy of note that some Polish scholars and writers considered Iceland to be the perfect society of free and independent farmers. The ideas conveyed by the sagas were very close to their heart, and by romanticizing and glorifying the northern world, they expressed their hopes for

Poland to regain its freedom and independence from oppressors. Such romantic approaches to Old Norse literature can be seen especially in Artur Górski's comments accompanying his saga translations.[29]

After twenty years of independence (1918–1939), a dark shadow once again rose over Poland; in September 1939 the Nazis invaded the country leading to the outbreak of the Second World War. This marked the beginning of yet another stage in the history of the reception of Vikings in central Europe.

Phase 3: Viking Studies in Poland during the Second World War (1939–1945)

During the Second World War, a number of excavations were undertaken in Nazi-occupied Poland. Many of them were politically and ideologically motivated,[30] with the primary objective being to demonstrate that the Polish lands had been settled and dominated by the Germanic population since prehistory and that the early medieval Slavs had been incapable of independent thought and of building a state on their own.

One of the places of particular interest for German scholars was Wolin. The town had been systematically excavated by German archaeologists before the war, leading to the discovery of numerous portable objects and architectural features (houses, ramparts etc.). Now, one of the questions they sought to find answers to was whether Wolin could be identified with Jómsborg, the famous Viking fortress known from *Jómsvíkinga saga*. Despite intensive efforts to prove this theory, they failed to find any solid evidence to support it. It is noteworthy, however, that even though German scholars had been skeptical about strong Scandinavian influences in Wolin before the outbreak of the Second World War and regarded it as a Slavic town, these views changed quite dramatically under the Nazi banner (Figure 3.4). The archaeologist Karl August Wilde even went as far as to call a certain type of high-quality pottery from Wolin "Palnatóki ceramics," the name referring to the jarl of Jómsborg known from *Jómsvíkinga saga*.[31]

The ideologically driven search for Vikings also took place in Central Poland. In 1940, German soldiers destroyed an old Jewish cemetery in the town of Lutomiersk near Łódź, with the intention of using the grave slabs as building material. While conducting their work, they came across a number of early medieval graves with very rich furnishings. One of the most spectacular finds was a richly decorated sword. Because of this remarkable discovery – which was immediately labeled a "Viking sword" – and its importance for Nazi propaganda,

Figure 3.4: Excavations in Wolin under the Nazi banner (1936). Reproduced after Kazimierz Błahij, *Ostatnia tajemnica zatopionych bogów.*

Lutomiersk drew the attention of German archaeologists, who started their excavations there in 1941. Altogether fifteen graves were discovered, but these did not provide any finds of distinctively Scandinavian style; quite the contrary, all the furnishings were typical of Slavic culture. The lack of solid proof for "Viking" presence in Lutomiersk greatly disappointed the excavators to the point that they decided to abandon the dig. The documentation they left behind proved to be extremely sloppy and some of the finds disappeared in the turmoil of the war.

Despite difficult circumstances, Polish historians and archaeologists continued their work. Józef Kostrzewski became an academic particularly hated by the Nazis, since his opinions on the Slavic past were not at all in line with their ideologically motivated view of history. Using false documents and constantly remaining on the move, he managed to survive the war and to complete his famous work *Kultura prapolska* (*Pre-Polish Culture*), a fundamental study of early medieval Poland, which was released in print for the first time in 1947.[32] Several chapters of the book touch upon Scandinavian–Slavic relations in the Viking Age and it is noteworthy that even now, after over sixty years since the first edition of *Kultura prapolska* was released, many of Kostrzewski's arguments still hold true.

Phase 4: Viking Studies after the Second World War and in the Communist Period (1945–1989)

Soon after the war ended, a large-scale research program known as the Millennial Project was initiated in Poland. The project arose in the light of the forthcoming 1000th anniversary of the Polish state. Its primary objectives were to gain in-depth knowledge about the early medieval history and archaeology of Poland and to revise the ideologically driven theories that had been put forward by German scholars before and during the time of Nazi occupation. As part of the Millennial Project, numerous excavation campaigns were initiated at major early medieval sites in Poland – for example, at Giecz, Gniezno, Poznań, Szczecin, Wolin – and the outcomes of these endeavors were published regularly, both in academic and popular formats. New archaeological finds were also exhibited in museums, arousing a lot of interest among the educated public.

In 1949, in line with these new research initiatives, the aforementioned cemetery at Lutomiersk was re-excavated by Konrad Jażdżewski from Łódź University, leading to the discovery of over 130 graves with remarkable furnishings.[33] Many of the graves included weapons, such as spearheads, swords and axes, as well as equestrian equipment. Two graves, labeled 5 and 10, drew particular scholarly attention. Grave 5 was a cremation grave, while grave 10 contained the skeletal remains of an individual probably buried in the supine position. What connected these two graves was the presence of lavishly decorated copper-alloy spurs with zoomorphic motifs (Figure 3.5). Because no parallels were known at the time, scholars were unsure about the cultural provenance of these objects. Some archaeologists had the impression that they were Scandinavian or eastern European (Rus') imports and this led them to the supposition that the dead buried at Lutomiersk had come from northern or eastern Europe. Today, it is clear that the origin of the spurs should rather be sought in West Slavic lands. Moreover, new research has shown that the elaborate iconography of the spurs, as well as the motifs depicted on other types of equestrian equipment from Lutomiersk – for example, the copper alloy bridle mounts from grave 10 – can offer important hints about pre-Christian Slavic beliefs.[34] In the opinion of the author, and contrary to the claims of some contemporary Polish scholars,[35] none of the finds from Lutomiersk bear distinctively Scandinavian traits and there is nothing to suggest that the people buried there had come from the North.

After the war and the shifting of the borders of Poland,[36] archaeological excavations were also resumed in Wolin. They were conducted by Polish scholars under the direction of Władysław Filipowiak whose groundbreaking research

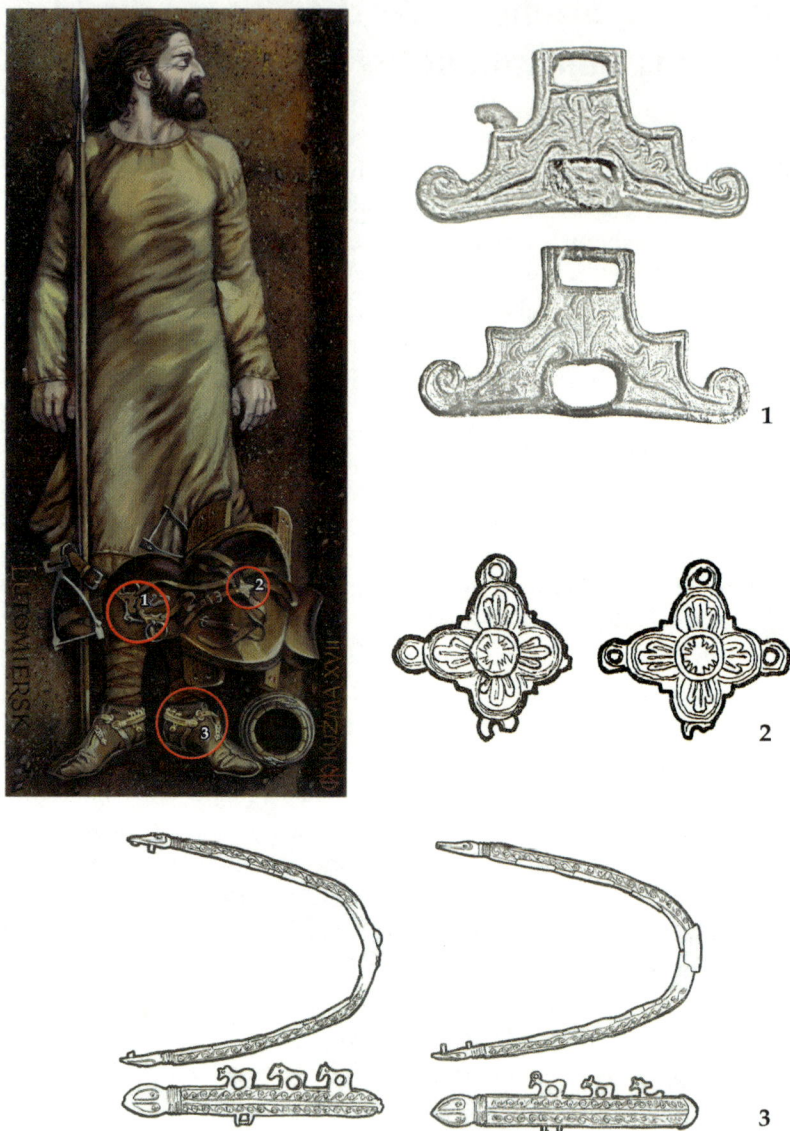

Figure 3.5: Grave 10 from the early medieval cemetery at Lutomiersk in central Poland. 1 – Two copper alloy cheek pieces with a decorative motif probably representing two flying serpents, supernatural creatures well-known from Slavic beliefs; 2 – Decorated bridle mounts; 3 – Two copper alloy spurs with zoomorphic motifs. Artistic reconstruction by Mirosław Kuźma. Finds redrawn after Grygiel, "Cmentarzysko wareskich drużynników w Lutomiersku," p. 715 and Nadolski, Abramowicz, Poklewski, *Cmentarzysko z XI wieku w Lutomiersku pod Łodzią,* plates XLIV and LIV.

led to major revisions of previous, ideologically driven interpretations of the role of this town in the Viking Age.[37] The results of Filipowiak's studies showed unequivocally that Wolin was indeed a prominent port where people from different parts of the world would come to trade. However, judging by the types of artifacts and by the specific features of the town's architecture, Filipowiak demonstrated that the dominant group of people residing there were the Slavs. It is noteworthy that in the post-war period Wolin attracted the interest of many other scholars, including Józef Kostrzewski from Poznań University, who visited the town on several occasions together with his colleagues.[38] Soon, a small exhibition presenting the latest finds from Wolin was organized in one room of the Wolin branch of the Polish Academy of Sciences.[39] Remarkably, over the course of three years, the exhibition had more than thirty thousand visitors, all keen to learn whether there had been any truth behind the legend of Jómsborg.

As a result of the large scale of the Millennial Project, new examples of Scandinavian-style objects were occasionally found during excavations in Poland. Most of them, however, came from the area of Pomerania. In general, Scandinavian-style objects were rarely unearthed in Greater Poland and elsewhere in the interior of the country, but one exception was a small piece of foil with filigree and granulation discovered at Ostrów Lednicki (Figure 3.1). The item is decorated with a triquetra and could be part of a larger object, perhaps a brooch or a pendant.[40]

In the history of Viking archaeology in Poland, the role of the Poznań archaeologist Jan Żak deserves particular attention. Throughout his career, Żak developed a deep interest in various facets of Scandinavian–Slavic interactions and released numerous works on this topic.[41] He is best known for his erudite monograph devoted to Scandinavian "imports" in the West Slavic lands, which he published in three volumes in 1963–1967.[42] Żak was a very diligent scholar, well acquainted with Scandinavian, British, Russian, and German literature on the Viking Age and certainly much more cautious in his claims than many of his predecessors. Several of his students continued his work, although they never made Viking studies the main focus of their careers.[43]

The 1960s were also a time when archaeological excavations in the early medieval cemetery at Świelubie were resumed under the direction of Władysław Łosiński.[44] The site was located on a sandy hill at the Parsęta River and comprised over one hundred mounds. Most of the graves were cremations, although several inhumations were also found. Several graves included objects of Scandinavian provenance, such as jewelry (oval brooches and a trefoil brooch), gaming pieces, a polyhedral weight, fragments of a shield handle (with Borre-style decoration) and a strike-a-light. A number of dirhams were also discovered, dating to the late eighth and ninth centuries. The objects that accompanied the dead in their graves, in particular the polyhedral weight, can give interesting hints about the roles these people had played while living in this area; it is possible that the Scandinavians who came to Świelubie were involved in trade with Slavic communities, and the presence of Slavic pottery in some of the graves could be understood as a signal of exchange of goods. Moreover, the size of the cemetery (with over a hundred mounds) implies that Norse immigrants were not solely transient, but also that some resided in Pomerania on a more permanent basis. We do not know for certain what kind of activities the people buried in Świelubie were engaged in, but it is not unlikely that this area attracted their attention because of the salt springs located nearby.[45]

A real sensation of the early 1980s was the discovery of the Viking Age port of trade known as Truso, which many scholars had been trying to find for decades. Since the 1980s, Marek Jagodziński, the discoverer of the site, has conducted a series of excavations, the results of which have been disseminated internationally and published in a wide range of high-quality articles and monographs.[46] By contrast to Wolin, archaeological work in Truso has provided very solid evidence for Norse presence in the town, as demonstrated by numerous objects of distinctively Scandinavian type, including jewelry, amulets, and weapons.

It is noteworthy that in the communist period, despite limited possibilities for researcher-mobility, contacts between Polish and Scandinavian researchers were maintained through the exchange of publications, as well as international conferences, congresses, and short study visits. The relations between Viking scholars on both sides of the Baltic deserve another detailed paper, but it is worth pointing out a few examples of friendly scholarly collaboration. In 1947, Józef Kostrzewski along with a group of around twenty other researchers spent two months in Sweden by invitation from the Swedish Institute. During his stay, he visited the Swedish History Museum in Stockholm, as well as the museums in Göteborg, Lund, and Uppsala, and the famous Viking Age port of trade at Birka. In his diary, Kostrzewski spoke very highly of his visit to Sweden and the courtesy of his hosts.[47]

The renowned Swedish archaeologist Holger Arbman – author of the famous monograph on Viking Age graves from Birka – also visited Poland on several occasions after the Second World War. In 1949 he came with a group of students and in 1957 he received an invitation from the Polish Academy of Sciences and the Institute of the History of Material Culture to give a series of lectures. According to a brief note published in the magazine *Z Otchłani Wieków*, during his visit Arbman was particularly interested in the ports of trade on the Baltic coast, but also in Scandinavian–Slavic contacts, silver hoards, and glass beads. He stayed in Poland for two weeks and spent time in Warsaw, Poznań, Gniezno, Trzemeszno, Mogilno, Szczecin, Gdańsk, and Łódź where he examined museum collections and visited scientific institutions as well as several archaeological sites. In Poznań, Arbman gave a lecture on *Silver Hoards as Historical Sources* and in Łódź and Warsaw he presented papers on *The Role of the Vikings in Europe.*[48]

It is also worthy of note that in the 1960s and 1970s, several Scandinavian scholars specializing in the Viking Age published their works in Polish archaeological journals – they were probably encouraged to do so by their Polish colleagues. Among them was, for example, Arne Emil Christensen[49] who discussed heritage protection and management in Norway, and Brigitta Hårdh[50] who published an article about Viking Age neckrings and intercultural contacts across the Baltic.

The mutual contacts between early medieval Scandinavians and Slavs were also a theme taken up by a number of writers who used the Viking Age as an attractive setting for their novels and short stories. Wolin often played a prominent part in these works and was described as a melting pot of cultures where the Scandinavians and Slavs engaged in trade and exchange and where many Vikings found refuge and shelter.[51] It should also be mentioned that in the 1980s the Vikings started firing the imagination of the Poles through the extremely successful comic book series *Thorgal*, created by Grzegorz Rosiński and Jean van Hamme.[52] The gripping storyline of the series, with its striking images of warriors, supernatural beings, and even Norse gods, spurred many young enthusiasts to learn more about the North and, in some cases, marked the beginning of a lifetime passion which developed into professional careers in academia and reenactment.

Phase 5: Viking Studies and Their Reception after the Fall of Communism and before the Accession of Poland to the EU (1989–2003)

After the fall of communism in 1989 many new opportunities opened up for academics in Poland. They now had easier access to international literature and could travel more freely than before. All this (and more) surely had an impact on the development of research trajectories in different parts of the country.

The 1990s saw the publication of several articles by Michał Kara who returned to the problem of alleged "Viking" graves in Greater Poland which had been taken up previously by Polish and German scholars in the 1920s and 1930s. Kara argued that among the people buried in several cemeteries in

Greater Poland – for example, Łubowo, Luboń, Ostrowąż, Skokówko, and Sowinki – were Scandinavian immigrants who had served in the retinues of Polish rulers Mieszko I and Bolesław Chrobry.[53] His arguments were mainly based on military equipment that those graves contained which, in his view, was similar to that known from Scandinavia. In his papers, Kara strongly adhered to the problematic conviction (typical of much of central European cultural-historical archaeology at that time) that graves and their contents were "mirrors of life," reflecting social identities, professions, and ethnicity of the dead in an undistorted way. His views about "Viking mercenaries" in the Piast state were applauded and widely accepted by several prominent scholars in Poland and this led to them being repeated numerous times, until they became almost a dogma.

In a sense, Kara's ideas also contributed to a number of misconceptions regarding so-called chamber graves which in the early 2000s started to be found in different parts of Poland. The authors of the first publications on early medieval chamber graves (especially from the cemetery at Kałdus) enthusiastically considered these graves to belong to Scandinavian immigrants.[54] New and more balanced studies, especially by Andrzej Janowski,[55] Jerzy Sikora,[56] Dariusz Błaszczyk,[57] and Leszek Gardeła,[58] have shown the many methodological problems with such one-sided interpretations. It has also been explicitly demonstrated in a series of new studies by Gardeła that none of the inhumation graves from cemeteries in Greater Poland analyzed by Kara can be ascribed to the Scandinavian population.[59] Neither the weapons nor any other objects and features discovered in these sites imply that the dead and/or the mourners responsible for their burials had come from the North.

It is not easy to determine why scholars of the 1990s and early 2000s were so eager and enthusiastic to see traces of Scandinavian presence in Poland, even if the material evidence would not necessarily allow for such claims. Was it an attempt to challenge the views of their predecessors who had argued against any significant role of the Norse population in the Piast state? Or was it because of the social and political changes that were dynamically taking place in Poland – the fall of communism, the rise of capitalism and the desire to make Poland part of the western European civilization which took pride in its Viking heritage? Were some Polish scholars under the influence of Western popular culture, movies and literature? The "Viking craze" is probably a combination of all these different factors. We should also not forget the fact that from the 1990s the popularity of historical reenactment started to rise in Poland.[60] More and more Viking reenactment festivals were organized, leading to the development of a new market for Viking-related themes. Perhaps this broader context also had some influence on how some scholars approached their discoveries. Because the Vikings became so popular in the 1990s and 2000s, having finds originating from Scandinavia at an archaeological site increased the possibility for media coverage and additional funding.

The Vikings in Today's Poland: Conclusions and Perspectives for the Future

As we have seen, over the course of the last three centuries, Old Norse and Viking studies in Poland have come a long way and undergone many changes. From invaders and state builders, through traders and mercenaries in the retinues of the Piasts, to heroes of novels and comic books, as well as role models for contemporary warriors and reenactors, the Vikings in Poland have taken many forms. The history of their reception, both in academia and outside of it, demonstrates that the fluidity in understanding the Vikings in Poland has also come to reflect the difficult cultural and political transformations in this part of Europe, as well as the spirit of its people.

Today, Old Norse and Viking studies are thriving in Poland and there is considerable academic and popular interest in the Early Middle Ages. Over the last fifteen years or so, in addition to several international conferences and museum exhibitions, a number of academic studies have been released which touch upon different aspects of Scandinavian–Slavic interactions in Poland.[61] These studies are devoid of the ideologically motivated arguments which characterized earlier scholarship, especially in the 1930s and 1940s. Nevertheless, some of their authors still have the tendency to overestimate the role which Viking Age Scandinavians played on the southern coast of the Baltic and in the Piast state. One may get the impression that, because the Vikings have become so fashionable and desired in narratives about the European past, archaeological and textual sources (often of very problematic nature) are sometimes stretched to fit certain theories without providing solid arguments.[62] It must be emphasized that these theories (or at least the manner in which they are presented) can strongly influence the way Vikings are shown in popular media and books, leading to misinformation and the embedding of unjustified arguments. With these issues in mind, much more effort should be made to better understand the specificity of West Slavic material culture. Specialist and unprejudiced studies of local art and metalwork can help distinguish objects made in Slavic workshops from those imported from the North, and in the long run contribute to answering much bigger questions regarding migration, settlement, and cross-cultural interaction. The abovementioned reinterpretations of the riding equipment from Lutomiersk are important steps in that direction but further work is certainly necessary.

Although most Polish and international academics today reject the idea that Mieszko I was of Germanic descent and that Poland was founded by Scandinavian immigrants, such opinions tend to resurface time and time again in the works of amateur historians. These dilettante publications, with sensationalist titles like *Czy wikingowie stworzyli Polskę?* (*Did Vikings Create Poland?*),[63] are certainly much easier to read than scholarly works, and they are also printed in much larger numbers and widely distributed in bookshops. Because history does not "belong" to us, as academics, we have to embrace the fact that the Vikings will always be (re)imagined. The key is to find new ways to share our knowledge in an accessible way, but at the same time one which promotes scholarly rigor and nuanced views of the past.

Acknowledgements: I would like to warmly thank Tom Birkett and Roderick Dale for inviting me to the *Rediscovering the Vikings* conference in Cork in 2016. I also thank Howard Williams, Dąbrówka Stępniewska, and Klaudia Karpińska for commenting on earlier drafts of this article.

Bibliography

Armbruster, Barbara and Heidemarie Eilbracht. *Wikingergold auf Hiddensee*. Rostock: Hinstorff Verlag, 2010.

Aubin, Hermann. "Der Weg der Geschichte: Der deutsche Osten bis zum Ende des Ordensstaates." In *Der Deutsche Osten. Seine Geschichte, sein Wesen und seine Aufgabe*, edited by Karl C. Thalheim and Arnold Hillen Ziegfeld, pp. 335–424. Berlin: Propyläen, 1936.

Biermann, Felix. "A Slavic or a Viking Town? The Excavations at Wolin 1934/41 and Their Contemporary Interpretation." In *Scandinavian Culture in Medieval Poland*, edited by Sławomir Moździoch, Błażej Stanisławski and Przemysław Wiszewski, pp. 179–91. Wrocław: Institute of Archaeology and Ethnology of the Polish Academy of Sciences, 2013.

Błahij, Kazimierz. *Ostatnia tajemnica zatopionych bogów*. Warsaw: Iskry, 1971.

Błaszczyk, Dariusz and Dąbrówka Stępniewska, eds. *Pochówki w grobach komorowych na ziemiach polskich w okresie wczesnego średniowiecza*. Warsaw: Instytut Archeologii UW, 2016.

Bogucki, Mateusz. "On Wulfstan's Right Hand: The Viking Age Emporia in West Slav Lands." In *From One Sea to Another*, edited by Sauro Gelichi and Richard Hodges, pp. 81–110. Turnhout: Brepols, 2012.

Boroń, Piotr. "Norsemen and the Polish Territories in the Early Middle Ages: Theories, Ideas and Speculations." In *Scandinavian Culture in Medieval Poland*, edited by Sławomir Moździoch, Błażej Stanisławski and Przemysław Wiszewski, pp. 33–51. Wrocław: Institute of Archaeology and Ethnology of the Polish Academy of Sciences, 2013.

Brackmann, Albert. "Die Anfänge des polnische Stattes." *Sitzungbereiche der preußischen Akademie der Wissenschaften, Philosophisch-Historische Klasse* 29 (1934): 984–1015.

Christensen, Arne Emil. "Kilka uwag o ochronie zabytków w Norwegii." *Materiały Zachodnio-Pomorskie* 8 (1962): 189–206.

Chudziak, Wojciech. "Wikingerzeitliche Spuren des skandinavischen Brauchtums in Kałdus (Ostpommern)." *Archäologisches Korrespondenzblatt* 33, no. 1 (2003): 143–56.

Cnotliwy, Eugeniusz. "Wystawa archeologiczna w Wolinie." *Z Otchłani Wieków* 29, no. 3 (1963): 197.

Czacki, Tadeusz. *O litewskich i polskich prawach, o ich duchu, źrzódłach, związku i o rzeczach zawartych w pierwszem Statucie dla Litwy, 1529 Roku wydanem*. Cracow: Drukarnia J. C. G. Ragoczego, 1800.

Duczko, Władysław. "Obecność skandynawska na Pomorzu i słowiańska w Skandynawii we wczesnym średniowieczu." In *Salsa Cholbergiensis. Kołobrzeg w średniowieczu*, edited by Lech Leciejewicz and Marian Rębkowski, pp. 23–44. Kołobrzeg: Le Petit Café, 2000.

Filipowiak, Władysław and Marek Konopka. "The Identity of a Town: Wolin, Town-State – 9th–12th Centuries." *Quaestiones Medii Aevi Novae* 13 (2008): 243–88.

Gardeła, Leszek. *Scandinavian Amulets in Viking Age Poland*. Rzeszów: Fundacja Rzeszowskiego Ośrodka Archeologicznego/Instytut Archeologii Uniwersytetu Rzeszowskiego, 2014.

Gardeła, Leszek. "Vikings in Poland: A Critical Overview." In *Viking Worlds: Things, Spaces and Movement*, edited by Marianne Hem Eriksen, Unn Pedersen, Bernt Rundberget, Irmelin Axelsen and Heidi Lund Berg, pp. 213–34. Oxford: Oxbow Books, 2015.

Gardeła, Leszek. "Wczesnośredniowieczne groby komorowe – lustra czy miraże życia? Rozważania nad praktykami funeralnymi na ziemiach polskich." In *Pochówki w grobach komorowych na ziemiach polskich w okresie wczesnego średniowiecza*, edited by Dariusz Błaszczyk and Dąbrówka Stępniewska, pp. 154–75. Warsaw: Instytut Archeologii UW, 2016.

Gardeła, Leszek. "Vikings Reborn: The Origins and Development of Early Medieval Re-enactment in Poland." *Sprawozdania Archeologiczne* 68 (2016): 165–82.

Gardeła, Leszek. *Bad Death in the Early Middle Ages: Atypical Burials from Poland in a Comparative Perspective*. Rzeszów: Fundacja Rzeszowskiego Ośrodka Archeologicznego/ Instytut Archeologii Uniwersytetu Rzeszowskiego, 2017.

Gardeła, Leszek. "Lutomiersk Unveiled: The Buried Warriors of Poland." *Medieval Warfare* 8, no. 3 (2018): 42–50.

Gardeła, Leszek. "Death on Canvas: Artistic Reconstructions in Viking Age Mortuary Archaeology." In *The Public Archaeology of Death*, edited by Howard Williams, Jennifer Osborne and Benedict Wills-Eve, pp. 95–112. Sheffield: Equinox, 2019.

Gardeła, Leszek. "Viking Archaeology in Poland: Past, Present and Future." In *Proceedings of the 18th Viking Congress*, edited by Anne Pedersen and Søren Sindbæk. Copenhagen, forthcoming.

Gaumer, Patrick and Piotr Rosiński. *Grzegorz Rosiński. Monografia*. Warsaw: Egmont Polska, 2015.

Górski, Artur. *Saga o Gislim wyjętym spod prawa i inne sagi islandzkie*. Warsaw: Dom Książki Polskiej, Spółka Akcyjna, 1931.

Grygiel, Ryszard. "Cmentarzysko wareskich drużynników w Lutomiersku." In *Początki Łęczycy. Volume 2: Archeologia o początkach Łęczycy*, edited by Ryszard Grygiel and Tomasz Jurek, pp. 681–757. Łódź: Muzeum Archeologiczne i Etnograficzne w Łodzi, 2014.

Holtzmann, Robert. "Böhmen und Polen im 10. Jahrhundert. Eine Untersuchung zur ältesten Geschichte Polens." *Zeitschrift des Vereins für Geschichte Schlesiens* 52 (1918): 1–37.

Hårdh, Brigitta. "Naszyjniki skandynawskie z okresu wikińskiego i kontakty bałtyckie." *Materiały Zachodniopomorskie* 23 (1977): 111–33.

J. G. "Z pobytu w Polsce Prof. Holgera Arbmana." *Z Otchłani Wieków* 23, no. 4 (1957): 226.

Jagodziński, Marek Franciszek. *Truso. Między Weonodlandem a Witlandem / Truso: Between Weonodland and Witland.* Elbląg: Muzeum Archeologiczno-Historyczne w Elblągu, 2010.

Jakimowicz, Roman. "O położeniu słowiańskiego Kołobrzegu w świetle poszukiwań terenowych w r. 1947." *Z Otchłani Wieków* 20, nos. 7–8 (1951): 128–39.

Janowski, Andrzej. *Groby komorowe w Europie Środkowo-Wschodniej. Problemy wybrane.* Szczecin: Instytut Archeologii i Etnologii Polskiej Akademii Nauk, 2015.

Jänichen, Hans. *Die Wikinger in Weichsel- und Odergebiet.* Leipzig: Kabitzsch, 1938.

Kara, Michał. "Z badań nad wczesnośredniowiecznymi grobami z uzbrojeniem z terenu Wielkopolski." In *Od plemienia do państwa. Śląsk na tle wczesnośredniowiecznej Słowiańszczyzny Zachodniej,* edited by Lech Leciejewicz, pp. 99–120. Wrocław and Warsaw: Polska Akademia Nauk/Komitet Nauk Historycznych/Uniwersytet Wrocławski/Centrum Badań Śląskoznawczych i Bohemistycznych, 1991.

Kara, Michał. "Siły zbrojne Mieszka I. Z badań nad składem etnicznym, organizacją i dyslokacją drużyny pierwszych Piastów." *Kronika Wielkopolski* 62, no. 3 (1992): 33–47.

Kostrzewski, Józef. "Cmentarzysko ze śladami wikingów w Łubówku w pow. gnieźnieńskim" *Przegląd Archeologiczny* 1, nos. 3–4 (1921): 140–47.

Kostrzewski, Józef. "Les antiquités vikingues en Pologne." In *Proceedings of the First International Congress of Prehistoric and Protohistoric Sciences.* London: Oxford University Press, 1934.

Kostrzewski, Józef. "Legenda o wikińskim początku Polski." *Kurier Poznański* 492 (1938): 1.

Kostrzewski, Józef. *Kultura prapolska.* Poznań: Instytut Zachodni, 1947.

Kostrzewski, Józef. "Nowe odkrycia w Danii." *Z Otchłani Wieków* 19, nos. 9–10 (1950): 168.

Kostrzewski, Józef. *Obrządek ciałopalny u plemion polskich i Słowian północno-zachodnich.* Warsaw: Państwowe Wydawnictwo Naukowe, 1960.

Kostrzewski, Józef. *Z mego życia. Pamiętnik.* Wrocław, Warsaw and Cracow: Zakład Narodowy im. Ossolińskich, 1970.

Kóčka-Krenz, Hanna. *Złotnictwo skandynawskie IX–XI wieku.* Poznań: Uniwersytet im. Adama Mickiewicza, 1983.

Krotoski, Kazimierz. "Echa historyczne w podaniu o Popielu i Piaście." *Kwartalnik Historyczny* 39 (1925): 33–69.

Łosiński, Władysław. *Początki wczesnośredniowiecznego osadnictwa grodowego w dorzeczu dolnej Parsęty (VII–X/XI w.).* Wrocław, Warsaw, Cracow and Gdańsk: Polska Akademia Nauk, 1972.

Majewska, Renata. *Arkadia Północy. Mity eddaiczne w Lilli Wenedzie i Królu-Duchu Juliusza Słowackiego.* Białystok: Katedra Badań Filologicznych "Wschód-Zachód," Wydział Filologiczny Uniwersytetu w Białymstoku, 2013.

Minta-Tworzowska, Danuta and Włodzimierz Rączkowski eds. *Archeologia-Paradygmat-Pamięć.* Poznań: Wydawnictwo Poznańskie, 2001.

MKP. "Wycieczka naukowa do Wolina i Szczecina." *Z Otchłani Wieków* 22, no. 6 (1953): 245.

Morawiec, Jakub. *Vikings among the Slavs: Jómsborg and the Jómsvikings in Old Norse Tradition.* Vienna: Verlag Fassbaender, 2009.

Morawiec, Jakub. "Old Norse Studies in Poland: History and Perspectives," *Fasciculi Archaeologiae Historicae* 28 (2015): 27–32.

Moździoch, Sławomir, Błażej Stanisławski and Przemysław Wiszewski eds. *Scandinavian Culture in Medieval Poland*. Wrocław: Institute of Archaeology and Ethnology of the Polish Academy of Sciences, 2013.

Nadolski, Andrzej, Andrzej Abramowicz and Tadeusz Poklewski. *Cmentarzysko z XI wieku w Lutomiersku pod Łodzią*. Łódź: Łódzkie Towarzystwo Naukowe, 1959.

Nowowiejski, Feliks Maria. "Legenda Winety." *Z Otchłani Wieków* 21, no. 5 (1952): 158–63.

Piekosiński, Franciszek. *O dynastycznym pochodzeniu szlachty polskiej*. Cracow: Wydawnictwo Akademii Umiejętności w Krakowie, 1888.

Potkański, Karol. "Drużyna Mieszka a Wikingi z Jomsborga." *Sprawozdania z Posiedzeń Polskiej Akademii Umiejętności* 6 (1906): 8–9.

Prosnak, Mieczysław. "Z zagadnień skandynawskiej sztuki korabniczej wczesnego średniowiecza." *Materiały Zachodnio-Pomorskie* 13 (1967): 199–237.

Rohrer, Wiebke. *Wikinger oder Slawen? Die ethnische Interpretation frühpiastischer Bestattungen mit Waffenbeigabe in der deutschen und polnischen Archäologie*. Marburg: Verlag Herder-Institut, 2012.

Schulte, Lambert. "Beiträge zur ältesten Geschichte Polens." *Zeitschrift des Vereins für Geschichte Schlesiens* 52 (1918): 38–57.

Sikora, Jerzy. "Ethnos or Ethos? Some Remarks on Interpretation of Early Medieval Elite Burials in Northern Poland." In *Scandinavian Culture in Medieval Poland*, edited by Sławomir Moździoch, Błażej Stanisławski and Przemysław Wiszewski, pp. 411–36. Wrocław: Institute of Archaeology and Ethnology of the Polish Academy of Sciences, 2013.

Skrok, Zdzisław. *Czy wikingowie stworzyli Polskę?* Warsaw: Iskry, 2013.

Stanisławski, Błażej. *Jómswikingowie z Wolina-Jómsborga – studium archeologiczne przenikania kultury skandynawskiej na ziemie polskie*. Wrocław: Instytut Archeologii i Etnologii Polskiej Akademii Nauk, 2013.

Stanisławski, Błażej and Władysław Filipowiak, eds. *Wolin wczesnośredniowieczny*. 2 vols. Warsaw: Fundacja na rzecz Nauki Polskiej/Instytut Archeologii i Etnologii Polskiej Akademii Nauk, 2013–2014.

Szajnocha, Karol. *Lechicki początek Polski. Szkic historyczny*. Lwów: Nakładem Karola Wilda, 1858.

Szołdrska, Halszka. "Na targowisku." *Z Otchłani Wieków* 20, nos. 11–12 (1951): 199–200.

Szołdrska, Halszka. "Prehistoria w najnowszej naszej beletrystyce." *Z Otchłani Wieków* 20, nos. 7–8 (1951): 143–44.

Wachowski, Kazimierz. *Jomsborg (Normannowie wobec Polski w w. X): studium historyczne*. Warsaw: Towarzystwo Naukowe Warszawskie, 1914.

Zoll-Adamikowa, Helena. *Wczesnośredniowieczne cmentarzyska ciałopalne Słowian na terenie Polski. Cz. I. Źródła*. Wrocław, Warsaw, Cracow and Gdańsk: Polska Akademia Nauk, 1975.

Żak, Jan. *"Importy" skandynawskie na ziemiach zachodniosłowiańskich od IX do XI wieku*. 3 vols. Poznań: Poznańskie Towarzystwo Przyjaciół Nauk, 1963–1967.

Żak, Jan. "Zarys stanu i dziejów badań nad 'importami' skandynawskimi na Słowiańszczyźnie Zachodniej. Część 1." *Materiały Zachodniopomorskie* 11 (1965): 411–60.

Żak, Jan. "Zarys stanu i dziejów badań nad 'importami' skandynawskimi na Słowiańszczyźnie Zachodniej. Część 2." *Materiały Zachodniopomorskie* 12 (1966): 547–607.

Żurowski, Kazimierz. "Z ostatnich odkryć na Ostrowie Lednickim." *Z Otchłani Wieków* 21, no. 3 (1952): 106–9.

Notes

1. For the latest English-language studies on the presence of Viking Age Scandinavians in Poland, including historiographic overviews, see Sławomir Moździoch, Błażej Stanisławski and Przemysław Wiszewski, eds., *Scandinavian Culture in Medieval Poland* (Wrocław: Institute of Archaeology and Ethnology of the Polish Academy of Sciences, 2013); Leszek Gardeła, *Scandinavian Amulets in Viking Age Poland* (Rzeszów: Fundacja Rzeszowskiego Ośrodka Archeologicznego/Instytut Archeologii Uniwersytetu Rzeszowskiego, 2014); Leszek Gardeła, "Vikings in Poland: A Critical Overview," in *Viking Worlds: Things, Spaces and Movement*, ed. Marianne Hem Eriksen, Unn Pedersen, Bernt Rundberget, Irmelin Axelsen and Heidi Lund Berg (Oxford: Oxbow Books, 2015), pp. 213–34.

2. Various scholars distinguish different phases in the development of Old Norse and Viking studies in Poland, but nevertheless the general conclusions they draw are very similar. See, for example, Jan Żak, "Zarys stanu i dziejów badań nad 'importami' skandynawskimi na Słowiańszczyźnie Zachodniej. Część 1," *Materiały Zachodniopomorskie* 11 (1965): 411–60; Jan Żak, "Zarys stanu i dziejów badań nad 'importami' skandynawskimi na Słowiańszczyźnie Zachodniej. Część 2," *Materiały Zachodniopomorskie* 12 (1966): 547–607; Piotr Boroń, "Norsemen and the Polish Territories in the Early Middle Ages: Theories, Ideas and Speculations," in *Scandinavian Culture in Medieval Poland*, ed. Sławomir Moździoch, Błażej Stanisławski and Przemysław Wiszewski (Wrocław: Institute of Archaeology and Ethnology of the Polish Academy of Sciences, 2013), pp. 33–51 at p. 34; Gardeła, *Scandinavian Amulets in Viking Age Poland*, pp. 11–20.

3. Karol Szajnocha, *Lechicki początek Polski. Szkic historyczny* (Lwów: Nakładem Karola Wilda, 1858). For critical commentaries on Szajnocha's work, see Wiebke Rohrer, *Wikinger oder Slawen? Die ethnische Interpretation frühpiastischer Bestattungen mit Waffenbeigabe in der deutschen und polnischen Archäologie* (Marburg: Verlag Herder-Institut, 2012), p. 51; Boroń, "Norsemen and the Polish Territories in the Early Middle Ages," pp. 37–38; Gardeła, *Scandinavian Amulets in Viking Age Poland*, pp. 12–13.

4. Boroń, "Norsemen and the Polish Territories in the Early Middle Ages," pp. 38–39.

5. Tadeusz Czacki, *O litewskich i polskich prawach, o ich duchu, źródłach, związku i o rzeczach zawartych w pierwszem Statucie dla Litwy, 1529 Roku wydanem* (Cracow: Drukarnia J. C. G. Ragoczego, 1800).

6. See a more detailed discussion on Czacki's work in Boroń, "Norsemen and the Polish Territories in the Early Middle Ages," pp. 35–36.

7. Franciszek Piekosiński, *O dynastycznym pochodzeniu szlachty polskiej* (Cracow: Wydawnictwo Akademii Umiejętności w Krakowie, 1888).

8. On Lelewel's work, see Jakub Morawiec, "Old Norse Studies in Poland: History and Perspectives," *Fasciculi Archaeologiae Historicae* 28 (2015): 27–32.

9. For more details on Słowacki's inspirations, see Renata Majewska, *Arkadia Północy. Mity eddaiczne w Lilli Wenedzie i Królu-Duchu Juliusza Słowackiego* (Białystok: Katedra Badań Filologicznych "Wschód-Zachód," Wydział Filologiczny Uniwersytetu w Białymstoku, 2013).

10. On Siemiradzki's artwork related to the Viking Age, see Leszek Gardeła, "Death on Canvas: Artistic Reconstructions in Viking Age Mortuary Archaeology," in *The Public Archaeology of Death*, ed. Howard Williams, Jennifer Osborne and Benedict Wills-Eve (Sheffield: Equinox, 2019), pp. 95–112.

11. See Żak, "Zarys stanu i dziejów badań (1)," p. 432.
12. See discussion in Gardeła, *Scandinavian Amulets in Viking Age Poland*, pp. 69–70.
13. On the Hiddensee find, see Barbara Armbruster and Heidemarie Eilbracht, *Wikingergold auf Hiddensee* (Rostock: Hinstorff Verlag, 2010).
14. See Żak, "Zarys stanu i dziejów badań (1)," pp. 413–14 with references.
15. Józef Kostrzewski, *Obrządek ciałopalny u plemion polskich i Słowian północno-zachodnich* (Warsaw: Państwowe Wydawnictwo Naukowe, 1960), pp. 49, 68.
16. Helena Zoll-Adamikowa, *Wczesnośredniowieczne cmentarzyska ciałopalne Słowian na terenie Polski. Cz. I. Źródła* (Wrocław, Warsaw, Cracow and Gdańsk: Polska Akademia Nauk, 1975), p. 226.
17. See, for example, the work of Karol Potkański, "Drużyna Mieszka a Wikingi z Jomsborga," *Sprawozdania z Posiedzeń Polskiej Akademii Umiejętności* 6 (1906): 8–9; Kazimierz Wachowski, *Jomsborg (Normannowie wobec Polski w w. X): Studium historyczne* (Warsaw: Towarzystwo Naukowe Warszawskie, 1914).
18. On the reception of the legends surrounding Wolin, see Feliks Maria Nowowiejski, "Legenda Winety," *Z Otchłani Wieków* 21, no. 5 (1952): 158–63.
19. Robert Holtzmann, "Böhmen und Polen im 10. Jahrhundert. Eine Untersuchung zur ältesten Geschichte Polens," *Zeitschrift des Vereins für Geschichte Schlesiens* 52 (1918): 1–37. For a modern critique of Holtzmann's views, see Rohrer, *Wikinger oder Slawen?*, pp. 51–52; Boroń, "Norsemen and the Polish Territories in the Early Middle Ages," pp. 39–40.
20. Lambert Schulte, "Beiträge zur ältesten Geschichte Polens," *Zeitschrift des Vereins für Geschichte Schlesiens* 52 (1918): 38–57.
21. Kostrzewski's interest in Viking archaeology can be seen in the following publications: Józef Kostrzewski, "Les antiquités vikingues en Pologne," in *Proceedings of the First International Congress of Prehistoric and Protohistoric Sciences* (London: Oxford University Press, 1934); Józef Kostrzewski, "Legenda o wikińskim początku Polski," *Kurier Poznański* 492 (1938): 1. Occasionally, he also disseminated news about the latest Viking Age discoveries from Scandinavia, one example being a short note about the 1949 excavations of the Viking fortress at Aggersborg in Jutland, Denmark – see Józef Kostrzewski, "Nowe odkrycia w Danii," *Z Otchłani Wieków* 19, nos. 9–10 (1950): 168.
22. Józef Kostrzewski, "Cmentarzysko ze śladami wikingów w Łubówku w pow. gnieźnieńskim," *Przegląd Archeologiczny* 1, nos. 3–4 (1921): 140–47.
23. See critical discussion on Łubowo in Rohrer, *Wikinger oder Slawen?*, pp. 58–69; Gardeła, *Scandinavian Amulets in Viking Age Poland*, pp. 27–29.
24. Kazimierz Krotoski, "Echa historyczne w podaniu o Popielu i Piaście," *Kwartalnik Historyczny* 39 (1925): 33–69.
25. Boroń, "Norsemen and the Polish Territories in the Early Middle Ages," p. 41.
26. Hans Jänichen, *Die Wikinger in Weichsel- und Odergebiet* (Leipzig: Kabitzsch, 1938).
27. Albert Brackmann, "Die Anfänge des polnische Stattes," *Sitzungbereiche der preußischen Akademie der Wissenschaften, Philosophisch-Historische Klasse* 29 (1934): 984–1015.
28. Hermann Aubin, "Der Weg der Geschichte: Der deutsche Osten bis zum Ende des Ordensstaates," in *Der Deutsche Osten. Seine Geschichte, sein Wesen und seine Aufgabe*, ed. Karl C. Thalheim and Arnold Hillen Ziegfeld (Berlin: Propyläen, 1936), pp. 335–424.
29. Artur Górski, *Saga o Gislim wyjętym spod prawa i inne sagi islandzkie* (Warsaw: Dom Książki Polskiej, Spółka Akcyjna, 1931).
30. See critique in Żak, "Zarys stanu i dziejów badań (1)," p. 418 with references.

31. See discussion in Felix Biermann, "A Slavic or a Viking Town? The Excavations at Wolin 1934/41 and Their Contemporary Interpretation," in *Scandinavian Culture in Medieval Poland*, ed. Sławomir Moździoch, Błażej Stanisławski and Przemysław Wiszewski (Wrocław: Institute of Archaeology and Ethnology of the Polish Academy of Sciences, 2013), pp. 179–91 at p. 186.

32. Józef Kostrzewski, *Kultura prapolska* (Poznań: Instytut Zachodni, 1947).

33. Andrzej Nadolski, Andrzej Abramowicz and Tadeusz Poklewski, *Cmentarzysko z XI wieku w Lutomiersku pod Łodzią* (Łódź: Łódzkie Towarzystwo Naukowe, 1959).

34. See discussion in Leszek Gardeła, *Bad Death in the Early Middle Ages: Atypical Burials from Poland in a Comparative Perspective* (Rzeszów: Fundacja Rzeszowskiego Ośrodka Archeologicznego/Instytut Archeologii Uniwersytetu Rzeszowskiego, 2017), pp. 61–64; Leszek Gardeła, "Lutomiersk Unveiled: The Buried Warriors of Poland," *Medieval Warfare* 8, no. 3 (2018): 42–50.

35. For views linking the dead and the finds from Lutomiersk with Scandinavia and the Rus', see Ryszard Grygiel, "Cmentarzysko wareskich drużynników w Lutomiersku," in *Początki Łęczycy. Volume 2: Archeologia o początkach Łęczycy*, ed. Ryszard Grygiel and Tomasz Jurek (Łódź: Muzeum Archeologiczne i Etnograficzne w Łodzi, 2014), pp. 681–757.

36. As the result of the Potsdam Conference in July–August 1945, the borders of Poland shifted to the west. Western Pomerania, Silesia, the southern part of eastern Prussia and the former Free City of Danzig, which had previously been German territory, were annexed into Poland. The provisional western border was defined by the Oder and Neisse rivers.

37. For a detailed English-language summary of Filipowiak's results, see Władysław Filipowiak and Marek Konopka, "The Identity of a Town: Wolin, Town-State – 9th–12th Centuries," *Quaestiones Medii Aevi Novae* 13 (2008): 243–88.

38. MKP, "Wycieczka naukowa do Wolina i Szczecina," *Z Otchłani Wieków* 22, no. 6 (1953): 245.

39. Eugeniusz Cnotliwy, "Wystawa archeologiczna w Wolinie," *Z Otchłani Wieków* 29, no. 3 (1963): 197.

40. Kazimierz Żurowski, "Z ostatnich odkryć na Ostrowie Lednickim," *Z Otchłani Wieków* 21, no. 3 (1952): 106–9 at 109.

41. On Żak's life and work, see Danuta Minta-Tworzowska and Włodzimierz Rączkowski, eds., *Archeologia-Paradygmat-Pamięć* (Poznań: Wydawnictwo Poznańskie, 2001).

42. Jan Żak, *"Importy" skandynawskie na ziemiach zachodniosłowiańskich od IX do XI wieku*, 3 vols. (Poznań: Poznańskie Towarzystwo Przyjaciół Nauk, 1963–1967).

43. For other Viking-related studies published in mid-twentieth century Poland, see for example Mieczysław Prosnak, "Z zagadnień skandynawskiej sztuki korabniczej wczesnego średniowiecza," *Materiały Zachodnio-Pomorskie* 13 (1967): 199–237; Hanna Kóčka-Krenz, *Złotnictwo skandynawskie IX–XI wieku* (Poznań: Uniwersytet im. Adama Mickiewicza, 1983).

44. Władysław Łosiński, *Początki wczesnośredniowiecznego osadnictwa grodowego w dorzeczu dolnej Parsęty (VII–X/XI w.)* (Wrocław, Warsaw, Cracow and Gdańsk: Polska Akademia Nauk, 1972).

45. Roman Jakimowicz, "O położeniu słowiańskiego Kołobrzegu w świetle poszukiwań terenowych w r. 1947," *Z Otchłani Wieków* 20, nos. 7–8 (1951): 128–39; Mateusz Bogucki, "On Wulfstan's Right Hand: The Viking Age Emporia in West Slav Lands," in *From One Sea to Another*, ed. Sauro Gelichi and Richard Hodges (Turnhout: Brepols, 2012), pp. 81–110 at pp. 97–98.

46. See, for example, Marek Franciszek Jagodziński, *Truso. Między Weonodlandem a Witlandem / Truso: Between Weonodland and Witland* (Elbląg: Muzeum Archeologiczno-Historyczne w Elblągu, 2010) and the new series of publications called *Truso Studies*.
47. Józef Kostrzewski, *Z mego życia. Pamiętnik* (Wrocław, Warsaw and Cracow: Zakład Narodowy im. Ossolińskich, 1970), pp. 258–60.
48. J. G., "Z pobytu w Polsce Prof. Holgera Arbmana," *Z Otchłani Wieków* 23, no. 4 (1957): 226.
49. Arne Emil Christensen, "Kilka uwag o ochronie zabytków w Norwegii," *Materiały Zachodnio-Pomorskie* 8 (1962): 189–206.
50. Brigitta Hårdh, "Naszyjniki skandynawskie z okresu wikińskiego i kontakty bałtyckie," *Materiały Zachodniopomorskie* 23 (1977): 111–33.
51. Halszka Szołdrska, "Na targowisku," *Z Otchłani Wieków* 20, nos. 11–12 (1951): 199–200; Halszka Szołdrska, "Prehistoria w najnowszej naszej beletrystyce," *Z Otchłani Wieków* 20, nos. 7–8 (1951): 143–44.
52. Patrick Gaumer and Piotr Rosiński, *Grzegorz Rosiński. Monografia* (Warsaw: Egmont Polska, 2015).
53. Michał Kara, "Z badań nad wczesnośredniowiecznymi grobami z uzbrojeniem z terenu Wielkopolski," in *Od plemienia do państwa. Śląsk na tle wczesnośredniowiecznej Słowiańszczyzny Zachodniej*, ed. Lech Leciejewicz (Wrocław and Warsaw: Polska Akademia Nauk/Komitet Nauk Historycznych/Uniwersytet Wrocławski/Centrum Badań Śląskoznawczych i Bohemistycznych, 1991), pp. 99–120; Michał Kara, "Siły zbrojne Mieszka I. Z badań nad składem etnicznym, organizacją i dyslokacją drużyny pierwszych Piastów," *Kronika Wielkopolski* 62, no. 3 (1992): 33–47.
54. See, for example, Wojciech Chudziak, "Wikingerzeitliche Spuren des skandinavischen Brauchtums in Kałdus (Ostpommern)," *Archäologisches Korrespondenzblatt* 33, no. 1 (2003): 143–56.
55. Andrzej Janowski, *Groby komorowe w Europie Środkowo-Wschodniej. Problemy wybrane* (Szczecin: Instytut Archeologii i Etnologii Polskiej Akademii Nauk, 2015) with references.
56. Jerzy Sikora, "Ethnos or Ethos? Some Remarks on Interpretation of Early Medieval Elite Burials in Northern Poland," in *Scandinavian Culture in Medieval Poland*, ed. Sławomir Moździoch, Błażej Stanisławski and Przemysław Wiszewski (Wrocław: Institute of Archaeology and Ethnology of the Polish Academy of Sciences, 2013), pp. 411–36.
57. Dariusz Błaszczyk and Dąbrówka Stępniewska, eds., *Pochówki w grobach komorowych na ziemiach polskich w okresie wczesnego średniowiecza* (Warsaw: Instytut Archeologii UW, 2016).
58. Leszek Gardeła, "Wczesnośredniowieczne groby komorowe – lustra czy miraże życia? Rozważania nad praktykami funeralnymi na ziemiach polskich," in *Pochówki w grobach komorowych na ziemiach polskich w okresie wczesnego średniowiecza*, ed. Dariusz Błaszczyk and Dąbrówka Stępniewska (Warsaw: Instytut Archeologii UW, 2016), pp. 154–75.
59. Gardeła, *Scandinavian Amulets in Viking Age Poland*, pp. 27–32; Gardeła, *Vikings in Poland: A Critical Overview*, pp. 220–25.
60. On Viking reenactment in Poland, see Leszek Gardeła, "Vikings Reborn: The Origins and Development of Early Medieval Re-enactment in Poland," *Sprawozdania Archeologiczne* 68 (2016): 165–82 with references, and the following essay in this collection.
61. See, for example, Władysław Duczko, "Obecność skandynawska na Pomorzu i słowiańska w Skandynawii we wczesnym średniowieczu," in *Salsa Cholbergiensis. Kołobrzeg w średniowieczu*, ed. Lech Leciejewicz and Marian Rębkowski (Kołobrzeg: Le Petit Café, 2000), pp. 23–44; Jakub Morawiec, *Vikings among the Slavs: Jómsborg and the*

Jómsvikings in Old Norse Tradition (Vienna: Verlag Fassbaender, 2009); Błażej Stanisławski and Władysław Filipowiak, eds., *Wolin wczesnośredniowieczny*, 2 vols. (Warsaw: Fundacja na rzecz Nauki Polskiej/Instytut Archeologii i Etnologii Polskiej Akademii Nauk, 2013–2014); Błażej Stanisławski, *Jómswikingowie z Wolina-Jómsborga – studium archeologiczne przenikania kultury skandynawskiej na ziemie polskie* (Wrocław: Instytut Archeologii i Etnologii Polskiej Akademii Nauk, 2013).

62. To consider these issues would require more space than is available here and therefore they will be taken up elsewhere – see Leszek Gardeła, "Viking Archaeology in Poland: Past, Present and Future," in *Proceedings of the 18th Viking Congress*, ed. Anne Pedersen and Søren Sindbæk (Copenhagen, forthcoming).

63. Zdzisław Skrok, *Czy wikingowie stworzyli Polskę?* (Warsaw: Iskry, 2013).

Klaudia Karpińska
4 Women in Viking Reenactment

The vibrancy of the modern Viking reenactment scene has helped to popularize the archaeology and history of the early medieval period. All over the
world festivals, markets, and performances are organized in open-air museums, castles (or other historical buildings), and on historical battlefields. At
big, established events, such as the Festival of Slavs and Vikings in Wolin
(Poland), the Summer Festival in Hedeby (Germany), or the Moesgaard Viking
Moot (Denmark), thousands of reenactors from different countries meet on a
yearly basis. During these festivals, participants seek to recreate as authentically as possible the living conditions, combat techniques, traditional handicrafts, camp work, and even pre-Christian rituals from the Viking Age (taken
in this essay as the period between the eighth and eleventh centuries). In recent years, women of different ages have started to take part in many of the
above-mentioned activities and performances: by doing so, they may be seeking to experience the distant past and to teach people about life in the early
medieval period, while spending free time away from the pressures of modern
civilization is another motivation. For some female reenactors traveling from
festival to festival has become a form of recreation during their holidays, but
for others it has become a way of life.

In previous studies of Viking reenactment not enough attention has been
paid to the interesting and important category of female Viking reenactors.[1]
This essay attempts to redress this balance by examining different perceptions
of the Viking Age among female reenactors from the Czech Republic, Germany,
Poland, Slovakia, and Sweden, who often interact at large Viking events. In
this essay I will present the results of my first-hand research into female reenactment, conducted at two big international reenactment events: the Festival
of Slavs and Vikings in Wolin and the Carpathian Archaeological Festival
("Two Faces") in Trzcinica. I will discuss how female interaction with the reenactment scene has changed over the years and I will try to explain what, in the
opinion of female reenactors, it means to be a Viking Age woman and what
they think about the current dynamics of Viking reenactment. I will also discuss current tendencies and trends in the female milieu of early medieval reenactment and how these relate to wider developments in Viking and Old Norse
Studies. Finally, I will present two particular case studies concerning the reenactment of warrior women and sorceresses.

Klaudia Karpińska, Institute of Archaeology, University of Rzeszów

https://doi.org/10.1515/9781501513886-005

Women and Viking Reenactment

Archaeology has been influencing Viking reenactment from its very beginnings in the 1960s. Every year during archaeological excavations and field surveys numerous fascinating artifacts, settlements, or graves are found. These different material remains, analyzed and interpreted by archaeologists, provide us with a wealth of information about life in the Viking Age. Reenactors naturally seek to recreate costumes, objects, and rituals from the Viking Age based around the most recent discoveries. Their activities are, in some cases, inspired by "experimental archaeology";[2] however, as the Polish historian Michał Bogacki rightly observed, reenactment is more comprehensively defined as "a set of activities involving visual presentation of various aspects of life in the past by people dressed in costumes and using objects … referring to a chosen time-period, or occasionally even employing original artifacts."[3]

It must be stressed that Viking reenactment in its various forms involves only a selective presentation of different aspects of the past.[4] It can include some features in common with experimental archaeology like the preparation of tool replicas or casting of jewelry.[5] However, unlike experimental archaeology, reenactment never attempts to prove archaeological hypotheses with the use of a full range of scientific methods and long-lasting complex experiments (which must often be repeated several times).[6] The majority of reenactment during festivals is focused on the presentation of traditional handicrafts or combat to a public for whom long "experiments" may not be interesting.

The beginnings of Viking reenactment varied greatly between different European countries, and it is very hard to show exactly when and where this phenomenon started. It is most probable, however, that early medieval reenactment began in the British Isles and Scandinavia simultaneously in the 1960s when the first early medieval festivals were organized – for example, *Olsokdagene* (The Saint Olav Festival) in Stiklestad, Norway. At this time, researchers were convinced that the Viking Age was a period dominated by male travelers, merchants, and above all warriors. Statements to this effect presented in articles, books, and particularly popular works strongly influenced the enthusiast's picture of the past.[7] Therefore, people involved in all such performances tried to demonstrate either combat or experimentally build replicas of ships or boats, reflecting what was considered important in Viking history.[8]

The following years saw the establishment of several new festivals. However reenactors' attitudes towards the presentation of the past remained unchanged in many European countries, and men still dominated living history events focused on combat. This situation in reenactment corresponded to general tendencies in archaeological publications in which the Viking Age was still described as period of male warriors and female mistresses of the house. The biggest Viking reenactment initiative of the 1970s was, however, the first *Moesgård Vikingetræf* (Moesgård Viking Moot) which was organized in 1977 near Århus, Denmark by archaeologist Thomas Geoffrey Bibby and Moesgård Museum curators Egon Hansen and Bjarne Lønborg.[9] Importantly, it was not only warriors who took part in this festival, but also women presenting objects of daily use and traditional handicrafts.[10] Moesgård Viking Moot was most probably the first large-scale early medieval reenactment event in Europe and, moreover, one in which fruitful collaboration between reenactors and experimental archaeologists was initiated and in which a group of women actively took part.

Considerable changes in European Viking reenactment occurred in the 1990s when many new reenactment events were initiated. During this decade researchers "rediscovered" Viking Age women and began to stress their important roles in past societies. Significant monographs like Jenny Jochens' *Old Norse Images of Women* or Judith Jesch's *Women in the Viking Age*, which were published at this time, presented new and different views on the roles of women in this period.[11]

In 1993, the *Festiwal Wikingów* in Wolin, Poland was organized by a group of Danish reenactors and archaeologists.[12] This event was inspired by an important traveling exhibition *WOLIN-JOMSBORG. En Vikingetids-Handelsby i Polen* (Wolin-Jomsborg. The Viking Age Emporium in Poland) which was presented in Denmark, Sweden, and Iceland before coming to Wolin.[13] The Festival in Wolin (currently known as "The Festival of Slavs and Vikings") developed over several years to become one of the most important early medieval events not only in Poland, but also in Europe. Every year this festival is visited by hundreds of early medieval reenactors from all over the world (Figure 4.1). This yearly event has inspired reenactors to improve their combat (or handicraft) skills and even to set up similar historical events in their respective countries.[14]

The beginning of the twenty-first century brought many positive changes to Viking reenactment. First of all, many new festivals were established across Europe, including *Rogar* in the Czech Republic, *Wikingermarkt Jork* (The Viking Market in Jork) and *Sommermarkt im Wikinger-Museum Haithabu* (The Summer Festival at the Viking Museum, Hedeby) in Germany, *Gudvangen Vikingmarked* (The Viking Market in Gudvangen) and *Trondheim vikingmarked* in Norway, *Fotevikens Vikingamarknad* (The Viking Market in Foteviken) in Sweden, and many others. Moreover, since the beginning of the 2000s, reenactors have become increasingly interested in aspects of the past not related to combat, such as traditional handicrafts and the recreation of pre-Christian rituals.[15]

Figure 4.1: Recreation of a battle during the 22nd Festival of Slavs and Vikings, Wolin, Poland. Photograph: Klaudia Karpińska.

It is worth mentioning that in recent years female and male reenactors have also started to collaborate in meaningful ways with academics.[16] They engage in archaeological projects, prepare replicas of finds for scholars, and are active participants in events organized by universities or in the openings of museum exhibitions.[17] For example, in 2015, at the Institute of Archaeology, University of Rzeszów, an event called *Spotkanie z Archeologią* (A Meeting with Archaeology) was organized in which reenactors of different periods from prehistory to the late Middle Ages took part. In 2017, as part of an exhibition *Wikingowie w Polsce? Zabytki skandynawskie z ziem polskich* (Vikings in Poland? Scandinavian Artifacts from Poland) in the Museum of the Origins of the Polish State in Gniezno, photographs of early medieval reenactors from the Czech group *Marobud* were used.[18] In January 2019 this same Museum is set to open the first ever exhibition dedicated to the history and development of Polish early medieval reenactment.[19] Scholars also appeared at reenactment festivals in Poland such as *Ogólnopolski Festiwal Kultury Słowiańskiej i Cysterskiej w Lądzie nad Wartą* (The Nationwide Festival of Slavic and Cistercian Culture in Ląd) or the Festival of Slavs and Vikings in Wolin, where they gave open lectures intended to help enthusiasts to broaden their knowledge of various archaeological or historical topics. It is my opinion that different forms of collaboration between these two groups could have benefits for both sides: reenactors can provide researchers with interesting observations on the manufacture of different finds, whilst reenactment groups can gain scientific input and receive suggestions for improvements to their equipment.

Overall, women were overshadowed by men for many years in the reenactment scene.[20] During the numerous festivals or markets held in the 1990s or the early twenty-first century they tended only to help in camps, preparing meals or feasts and sewing clothing.[21] Moreover, at these events there were no contests in which women could show their skills. A few years ago, this situation changed considerably. Women started to appear not only by hearths in camps or cottages, but also became very important participants within early medieval festivals. They began to take part in many crafting activities – e.g., metalworking and the making of beads – the reconstruction of various rituals (Figure 4.2), archery tournaments, or even battles. It is worth noting that at the majority of Viking events, contests specifically dedicated to female reenactors started to appear – for example, cooking, singing, and poetry competitions, and contests for the most beautiful braid, or for the best mistress of the house. These activities allowed women to demonstrate their impressive reenactment skills and to become more "visible" to the public and other reenactors at festivals or markets.[22]

Figure 4.2: Women taking part in the recreation of a cremation burial during the Rękawka Fest in Cracow, Poland in 2014. Photograph: Klaudia Karpińska.

Current Perceptions of Viking Age Women

As an archaeologist and a Viking reenactor, I have been fascinated by female perceptions of Viking Age women in the reenactment world for many years. In 2016, I decided to examine this topic more closely and to conduct a survey. To achieve this, I visited two major international festivals in Poland: the 22nd Festival of Slavs and Vikings in Wolin (6–7 August) and the 6th Carpathian Archaeological Festival ("Two Faces") in Trzcinica (20 August). During these events, I talked with approximately fifty-three women from various European countries.[23] In my survey, I used a questionnaire with the following nine questions:

1. What is the name of your reenactment group?
2. Are (or were) you a student of archaeology or history (or ethnology) or do you have a person who studies (or studied) these subjects in your reenactment group?
3. What is your current position in the reenactment group?
4. What is your profession in the group?
5. How long have you been involved in Viking reenactment?
   5.1 If involved for more than one year, what has changed since then in Viking reenactment?
6. What is your attitude to the idea of "historicity" in Viking reenactment?
7. On which archaeological finds, iconographical sources, and written sources is your Viking costume based?
8. What does it mean to be a Viking Age woman?
9. What is most important to you in recreating a Viking Age woman?

I collected over one hundred different answers, which in itself indicates that female Viking reenactment in Europe has many diverse facets. However, discussing all of them in detail would exceed the limits of this chapter. Therefore, I have decided to present only the main tendencies and trends which I observed during many discussions with contemporary "Viking women."

First, it must be emphasized that reenactment faces problems connected not only with the quality of costumes, which can be historically inaccurate, but also with the reenactors' attitude to the past they seek to reconstruct.[24] During my research, I asked many women about the kind of sources (iconographical or written) and archaeological artifacts (and from which Scandinavian country) on which their own costumes were based. Most of them answered that their clothing was based on finds from Scandinavia but they could not specify which archaeological site the original artifacts were associated with. Some of them said that they have costumes based on finds from Sweden (Birka), Norway (e.g., Oseberg or Kaupang), Denmark (e.g., Hedeby) or on Rus' artifacts (e.g., from Gnyozdovo). Only five out of fifty women were able to give more detailed answers, including information about the archaeological finds on which their costumes were based. This situation implies that in assembling their costumes, the women I interviewed do not necessarily pay attention to details and mainly rely on the knowledge of the craftspeople from whom they buy reproductions, and that, in general, they do not try to learn more about these objects.

This approach to Viking reenactment often leads to the creation of very low quality reproductions of costumes or to costumes that are completely inappropriate to the past that is being reconstructed.[25] During my numerous visits to early medieval festivals, I observed women wearing different types of dresses and aprons which have corset-like bindings on the sides or are adorned with elaborate embroideries (sometimes based on fantasy patterns) as well as pendants based on Iron or Bronze Age finds and fox pelts with plastic eyes.[26] However, beyond these "ahistorical" or anachronistic uses of clothing and adornments, at some festivals we also encounter well-reconstructed Viking costumes. In the majority of cases, they belong to craftswomen, or to reenactors who are also archaeologists, who pay a lot of attention to the detail and quality of their reconstructions.[27]

My survey showed that current female reenactors have diverse ideas about Viking Age women. The Viking reenactors with whom I talked stressed that for them being a Scandinavian woman does not mean wearing nice clothing or jewelry but rather it means being independent, free, and self-confident. They mentioned also that women in the Viking Age had a high status in society. According to female reenactors, high-status women managed the whole household as well as having authority over men or other women and possessing a wide knowledge concerning many spheres of daily life (such as knowledge of herbs, healing, or handicrafts). In addition – as these reenactors argued – Viking Age women would not only take care of men and children, but also protect the house when the men were on far-flung expeditions and, if need be, they would also use weapons to defend their homes.[28] It is interesting to note that some female reenactors from Poland indicated that it is better to recreate Viking rather than Slavic women. In their opinion, in the early Middle Ages Slavic women were more dependent on men and their only chores involved cooking or taking care of children. This image of Slavic women is probably the result of the fact that we know relatively little about the Slavic way of life and their customs or rituals and so their world does not seem as rich as the world of the Scandinavians, about which we know a lot more.[29]

However, for female reenactors, to be a Viking woman means more than simply being independent. In our discussions, female reenactors often stated that for them being a Viking Age woman is more about "feeling something inside" or "being themselves."[30] Several women emphasized that they consider the process of recreating Viking Age women as an expression of love of and admiration for Viking culture. For other female reenactors, however, being a Viking woman means learning (or improving) various handicrafts or taking care of men during festivals. Several contemporary Viking women also indicated in the survey responses that in recreating the early Middle Ages it is most important to share knowledge concerning the everyday life and beliefs from past cultures.

During my two visits to festivals, I also asked female reenactors what was the most important thing for them in recreating Viking Age women or/and in the concept of Viking reenactment. For the majority of those surveyed, reenactment is a fantastic way to spend free time and to relax without the distractions of modern technology. In addition, it is very important for them to meet people at festivals who have the same interests and with whom they can discuss the period. Female reenactors told me that reenactment allowed them to go "back to their roots" and to "feel closer to nature."[31] For some mature "Viking women" traveling from festival to festival and sharing craftsmanship skills has become a way of life and their main occupation.

At early medieval events, I also met female reenactors who are involved in reenactment of two interesting and increasingly prominent sub-groups of Viking Age women – sorceresses and warrior women – which deserve to be discussed as distinct phenomena.

Vǫlur: The Reenactment of Sorceresses

Inspired mainly by the very detailed description included in chapter 4 of *Eiríks saga rauða* (*The Saga of Erik the Red*), several contemporary female reenactors have decided to recreate Viking Age sorceresses, known as *vǫlur* or *seiðkonur*.[32] According to this account, as well as descriptions in a number of other Old Norse texts, these women dealt with a complex of magic practices known as *seiðr*. These practices allowed them to look into the past and future, engage with the Otherworld, control weather, change their shape into animal form, bring good or bad luck, and even kill people.[33] One of the major accoutrements of these women was a staff. Archaeological excavations in different parts of the Viking world have revealed objects which could be possibly interpreted as staffs associated with Viking Age sorceresses, divided into three main types. The staffs of the first type take the form of long iron rods with basket like "handles" (Price's "staffs with expanded handle construction"); staffs of the second type are metal and have no basket "handles" (Price's "staffs without the expanded handle construction"); and the third type are staffs made of wood: essentially, decorated sticks.[34]

Women recreating the *vǫlur* appear very often at Viking festivals in Europe. When we walk between stalls we can see them sitting at tables and offering to forecast our future using runes. Most of these women use runes from the older *fuþark* burnt on wooden tablets, painted on stones, or carved on bones and cast on a wooden or textile chart with a painted circle. This method of divination is based on modern neo-paganism rather than Viking Age practices; we know nothing about the use of runes for divination in the early medieval period.[35] In addition to rune-casting, modern *vǫlur* often sell runic amulets and small pouches with herbs.

These female reenactors can have different costumes from ordinary women. Some of them wear simple and wild-looking clothing (often including animal pelts, bird feathers, animal bones, fangs, claws) or very fine and rich dresses (with embroidery or silk bands as well as much shining jewelry reflecting their perceived status in Norse society. Some adornments, like pendants (often Thor's hammers), beads, and bracelets, could be interpreted as gifts from persons who had received good prophecies from these women. The modern *vǫlur* have objects – for example, scissors, small bags with herbs – attached to their oval brooches or belts and sometimes hoods or/and coats made of dark wool fabric. Often the different parts of the *vǫlva* costume do not originate from one single region of Scandinavia or archaeological site but from various localities. One of these women maintained that early medieval sorceresses traveled widely from place to place and could collect objects and clothing from wherever they went, and it is noteworthy that in this case justification for a mixed costume was thought to be important.

What is interesting is that not every modern *vǫlva* has a staff. This fact could be the result of personal preferences of female reenactors, or sometimes lack of knowledge concerning artifacts connected with past beliefs. However if they do have a staff, it usually has the shape of a long walking stick and it is often made from a crooked branch or root. Sometimes, all along its length (or only the upper parts), it is covered with runic inscriptions quoting from the *Poetic Edda* or Icelandic sagas. Occasionally, "amulets" (made of animal bones, feathers, fangs, claws, antlers), bags with herbs (or rune tablets) or fox tails are attached to the staffs. To my knowledge, in Polish reenactment there are only two recreations of staffs which resemble archaeological finds from the Viking Age.[36] The first is a pine staff with a small basket handle which belongs to Małgorzata "Gudrun" Dudek. Below its basket handle there is a sentence carved in the older *fuþark: Freyja vígi þessi rúnar* (Freyja blesses these runes) (Figure 4.3). The second staff was manufactured for me by Robert Pustelak.[37] It was made of several steel rods and it has ornamented brass mounts placed above and under the basket "handle" (Figure 4.4).

Figure 4.3: A modern *vǫlva* with a magic staff based on her own design. Photograph: Klaudia Karpińska.

Figure 4.4: Replica of a Viking Age staff made by Robert Pustelak. Photograph: Klaudia Karpińska.

These reenactors using archaeological models for staffs are in the minority, and it seems clear that authenticity is not a priority here either. It is likely that female reenactors often decide to recreate the *vǫlva* because of the mystery surrounding this figure and because this role also allowed them to become important individuals within their reenactment groups.

Armed Women: The Reenactment of Female Warriors

Interest in Viking combat and weaponry is growing among female reenactors, helped by the increasing popularity of the History TV series *Vikings* (created and written by Michael Hirst) where numerous warrior women are depicted, and by recent high-profile archaeological studies.[38] Female reenactors take part in training with men and compete in tournaments and recreations of battles.[39]

Modern "Viking women" who choose the way of a warrior must overcome many difficulties. Not every group allows women to train for combat or fight at festivals. In numerous reenactment groups male warriors, who are usually in the majority, are strongly resistant to this role among female reenactors. They often argue that fighting is not a female "occupation" or that there is no convincing evidence that female warriors existed in the past, and that battles can be both physically draining and very dangerous, causing serious injuries. These clashes usually last more than one hour (for instance at the Festival of Slavs and Vikings every battle – one per day – consists of three clashes) and they are very exhausting even for the most resilient (male) warriors. However, at some festivals, like the Moesgård Viking Moot, where battles are more like performances rather than actual fighting, women are allowed to take an active part.[40]

Tournaments are often safer and take place on different days of the festivals, but there are still too few armed women in reenactment who decide to compete with men. These duels with male Scandinavian or Slavic warriors are not easy and women have not made it to the finals. At several festivals – for example, the *Midgard Battle* in Poland – women can take part in sieges of strongholds, but usually only in the role of archers. In addition to the above, women can compete in archery tournaments at every reenactment event.

During my survey at the 22nd Festival of Slavs and Vikings I met four women who declared that they take part in combat training and in some fights at early medieval events.[41] However, none of them were allowed to fight in large battles at this festival (Figure 4.5).[42] These women fight with swords, spears, and

Figure 4.5: The only warrior woman (among over 500 warriors) who took part in battles at the 22th Festival of Slavs and Vikings. Photograph: Klaudia Karpińska.

langsaxes (battle-knives) and use the same combat techniques as men. It is worth adding that at early medieval festivals they often dress like men, in shirts and trousers, and with battle-knives at their belts. During combat, these warrior women wear helmets and chainmail, which can be very heavy: fighting in them is physically demanding.

Overall, the female warriors I spoke with as part of this survey were satisfied with their own role in their respective reenactment groups. Fighting at festivals allows them to feel equal with men and to eliminate differences between sexes, because in battle all are equal (up to a point).[43] In addition, taking part in these combat situations gives them the opportunity to showcase their strength and skill, and sometimes allows them to feel more important and more "visible" at festivals. In my opinion, however, the presence of female warriors in combat performances is a fascinating but historically problematic phenomenon. It should be mentioned that there is still no convincing evidence that women in the Viking Age actively took part in battles and led the life of warriors.[44] Of those armed recreations involving female reenactors that I witnessed, the majority seemed to be based on puzzling and doubtful information from later medieval written sources – for example, Saxo Grammaticus' *Gesta Danorum*, or accounts in the Sagas of Icelanders – and on the reenactor's own interpretations of archaeological discoveries – for example, several female graves with weapons – as well as iconographical sources – for example, small plates with depictions of armed women).[45] The reenactors in question did not seem to take into account how complex and ambiguous these sources really are and how hard they sometimes are to interpret: for example, weaponry found in a funerary context could be a symbol of status rather than pointing to the occupation of the deceased.[46] I think that those female reenactors who wield swords, axes, or spears during battles should be aware that the "historicity" of their armed recreations is questionable.

The Female World of Viking Reenactment: Conclusions

In this chapter, I set out to demonstrate several different tendencies in female Viking reenactment. To fully understand contemporary Viking women and their "vision" of the past I spent numerous hours at festivals, discussing and listening to female reenactors' interesting stories. Through these meetings, I observed that every woman has her own complex picture of the past she seeks to recreate, and that different aspects of this past are more or less important for the reenactor – for some it is handicrafts, for others combat or the recreation of magic practices. Some women joined the reenactment scene because they wanted to learn how to make reproductions of artifacts; others because they wanted to sell their handmade products; several joined because they were inspired by rock music and fantasy literature and felt like starting a "new adventure." However for a majority of the interviewed participants, to be involved in Viking reenactment means to be a modern, independent, and strong woman and to have the possibility to experience various aspects of the distant past.

It should be mentioned that perceptions of the Viking Age among reenactors are changing very rapidly. Thanks to new archaeological discoveries, often published in accessible formats online as well as in specialist literature, this group of enthusiasts are beginning to discover other fascinating aspects of the past beyond combat. At festivals today we can observe not only warriors preparing for battles, but also craftspeople in workshops, numerous women doing various activities (such as producing traditional handicrafts and selling artifacts) and children playing and running between tents. We can also see different reenactments of rituals – for example, funerals, weddings, prophecies – and the performance of other events known from extant written sources. In addition, we can observe a growing group of female reenactors who are attempting year by year to improve their clothing and handicrafts to correspond more closely with archeological and iconographical sources from the Viking Age.

Bearing in mind the popularity and visibility of reenactment events and festivals, this suggests to me that the versions of the past reimagined by women in reenactment are likely to play an increasingly prominent role in the public imagination of the Viking Age in years to come.

Acknowledgements: I would like to express my sincere thanks to all the Women who took part in my survey and told me their fascinating and unusual stories. I am grateful to Małgorzata "Gudrun" Dudek, Dr. Matthias Toplak, and Tomáš Vlasatý who shared with me their interesting observations on different aspects of Polish, German, and Czech Viking reenactment. I am particularly grateful to the talented craftsman Robert Pustelak who patiently prepared numerous detailed and beautiful replicas of archaeological finds for me.

I should like, in particular, to thank Dr. Leszek Gardeła for his valuable and important comments on drafts of my article and numerous inspiring discussions on Viking Age archaeology and Viking reenactment.

Last but not least, I wish to heartily thank my mother Marzena Karpińska for her help and support during my numerous "time travels."

Bibliography

Bogacki, Michał. "Wybrane problemy odtwórstwa wczesnośredniowiecznego w Polsce: Zagadnienia ogólne i próba charakterystyki środowiska." In *Kultura ludów Morza Bałtyckiego 2: Nowożytność i Współczesność. Materiały z III Międzynarodowej Sesji Naukowej Dziejów Ludów Morza Bałtyckiego. Wolin 20–22 lipca 2007*, Mare Integrans: Studia nad dziejami wybrzeży Morza Bałtyckiego, edited by Michał Bogacki, Maciej Franz and Zbigniew Pilarczyk, pp. 219–69. Toruń: Wydawnictwo Adam Marszałek, 2008.

Bogacki, Michał. "O współczesnym 'ożywianiu' przeszłości – Charakterystyka odtwórstwa historycznego." *Turystyka Kulturowa* 5 (2010): 4–27.

Coles, John. *Experimental Archaeology*. New York: Academic Press, 1979.

Congregalli, Matteo. "Warrior Women of the Viking Reenactment Scene, in Photos." *Broadly*, March 1, 2018. https://broadly.vice.com/en_us/article/437p9b/viking-women-historical-reenactment-larping-photos.

Eiríks saga rauða, Íslenzk fornrit 4. Edited by Ólafur Halldórsson. Reykjavík: Hið Íslenzka Fornritafélag, 1985.

Evans, Gareth Lloyd. "Michael Hirst's *Vikings* and Old Norse Poetry." In *Translating Early Medieval Poetry: Transformation, Reception, Interpretation*, edited by Tom Birkett and Kirsty March-Lyons, pp. 199–212. Cambridge: D. S. Brewer, 2017.

Gardeła, Leszek. "Współcześni wikingowie: Wojownicy, metalowcy i tak zwani poganie." In *Współczesna przeszłość*, edited by Urszula Stępień, pp. 387–403. Poznań: Koło Naukowe Studentów Archeologii and Instytut Prahistorii Uniwersytetu Adama Mickiewicza w Poznaniu, 2009.

Gardeła, Leszek. "'Warrior-women' in Viking Age Scandinavia? A Preliminary Archaeological Study." *Analecta Archaeologica Ressoviensia* 8 (2013): 273–339.

Gardeła, Leszek. "Viking Death Rituals on the Isle of Man." In *Vikings Myths and Rituals on the Isle of Man*, edited by Leszek Gardeła and Carolyne Larrington, pp. 30–37. Nottingham: Centre for the Study of the Viking Age, 2014.

Gardeła, Leszek. "Vikings Reborn: The Origins and Development of Early Medieval Re-Enactment in Poland." *Sprawozdania Archeologiczne* 68 (2016): 165–82.

Gardeła, Leszek. *(Magic) Staffs in the Viking Age*, Studia Medievalia Septentrionalia 27. Vienna: Verlag Fassbaender, 2016.

Gardeła, Leszek. *Bad Death in the Early Middle Ages: Atypical Burials from Poland in a Comparative Perspective*, Collectio Archaeologica Ressoviensis 36. Rzeszów: Fundacja Rzeszowskiego Ośrodka Archeologicznego, Instytut Archaeologii Uniwersytetu Rzeszowskiego, 2017.

Gardeła, Leszek. "Amazons of the North? Armed Females in Viking Archaeology and Medieval Literature." In *Hvanndalir – Beiträge zur europäischen Altertumskunde und mediävistischen Literaturwissenschaft: Festschrift für Wilhelm Heizmann*, edited by Alessia Bauer and Alexandra Pesch, pp. 391–428. Berlin: De Gruyter, 2018.

Hägg, Inga. *Textilien und Tracht in Haithabu und Schleswig*, Die Ausgrabungen in Haithabu 18. Kiel and Hamburg: Wachholtz Murmann Publishers, 2015.

Jensen, Sara H. and Anna Bech Lund, eds. *Moesgaard Viking Moot*. Moesgaard: Moesgaard Museum and Jutland Archaeological Society, 2017.

Jesch, Judith. *Women in the Viking Age*. Woodbridge: Boydell, 1991.

Jochens, Jenny. *Old Norse Images of Women*. Philadelphia: University of Pennsylvania Press, 1996.

Jochens, Jenny. *Women in Old Norse Society*. Ithaca, NY: Cornell University Press, 1998.

Karpińska, Klaudia. "Women in Viking Re-Enactment in Poland: A Survey." Rzeszów: Unpublished results of a survey, 2016.

Konzack, Lars. "Viking Re-enactment." In *Participatory Heritage*, edited by Henriette Roued-Cunliffe and Andrea Copeland, pp. 37–46. London: Facet Publishing, 2017.

Lund Bech, Anna. "'Are You One of the Valkyries, Then?'" In *Moesgaard Viking Moot*, edited by Sara H. Jensen and Anna Bech Lund, pp. 121–33. Moesgaard: Moesgaard Museum and Jutland Archaeological Society, 2017.

Magelssen, Scott. *Living History Museums: Undoing History through Performance*. Lanham, MD: The Scarecrow Press, 2007.

McCalman, Iain and Paul A. Pickering, eds. *Historical Reenactment: From Realism to the Affective Turn*. Basingstoke: Palgrave Macmillian, 2010.

McKinnell, John, Rudolf Simek and Klaus Düwel, eds. *Runes, Magic and Religion: A Sourcebook*, Studia Medievalia Septentrionalia 10. Vienna: Verlag Fassbaender, 2004.

Nowiński, Jacek. "Instytucjonalizacja zabawy: O kulturotwórczym i kooperacyjnym potencjale ruchu rekonstrukcyjnego." In *Dziedzictwo w akcji: Rekonstrukcja historyczna jako sposób uczestnictwa w kulturze*, edited by Tomasz Szlendak, Jacek Nowiński, Krzysztof Olechnicki, Arkadiusz Karwacki and Wojciech Józef Buszta, pp. 73–108. Warsaw: Narodowe Centrum Kultury, 2012.

Olechnicki, Krzysztof. "Muszkieterowie na transporterze: Rekonstrukcje historyczne w pogoni za wiernością i spektaklem." In *Dziedzictwo w akcji: Rekonstrukcja historyczna jako sposób uczestnictwa w kulturze*, edited by Tomasz Szlendak, Jacek Nowiński, Krzysztof Olechnicki, Arkadiusz Karwacki, Wojciech Józef Buszta, pp. 161–205. Warsaw: Narodowe Centrum Kultury, 2012.

Olechnicki, Krzysztof, Tomasz Szlendak and Arkadiusz Karwacki, eds. *Grupy rekonstrukcji historycznej: Edukacja i konsumowanie przeszłości*. Toruń: Wydawnictwo Naukowe Uniwersytetu Mikołaja Kopernika w Toruniu, 2016.

Petersson, Bodil and Cornelius Holtorf, eds. *The Archaeology of Time Travel: Experiencing the Past in the 21st Century*. Oxford: Archaeopress Publishing, 2017.

Petersson, Bodil and Lars E. Narmo. "A Journey in Time." In *Experimental Archaeology: Between Enlightenment and Experience*, Acta Archaeologica Lundensia Series in 8° 62, edited by Bodil Petersson and Lars Erik Narmo, pp. 27–48. Lund: Lund University, Department of Archeology and Ancient History and Lofotr Viking Museum, 2011.

Price, Neil. *The Viking Way: Religion and War in Late Iron Age Scandinavia*. AUN 31. Uppsala: Department of Archaeology and Ancient History, 2002.

Puchalska, Katarzyna J. "Vikings Television Series: When History and Myth Intermingle." *The Polish Journal of the Arts and Culture* 15, no. 3 (2015): 89–105.

Stanisławski, Błażej and Władysław Filipowiak. *Wolin wczesnośredniowieczny: Część 1*. Warsaw: Fundacja na Rzecz Nauki Polskiej, 2013.

Szlendak, Tomasz. "Wehrmacht nie macha: Rekonstrukcyjna codzienność jako sposób zanurzenia w kulturze." In *Dziedzictwo w akcji: Rekonstrukcja historyczna jako sposób uczestnictwa w kulturze*, edited by Tomasz Szlendak, Jacek Nowiński, Krzysztof Olechnicki, Arkadiusz Karwacki and Wojciech J. Buszta, pp. 9–70. Warsaw: Narodowe Centrum Kultury, 2012.

Szlendak, Tomasz, Jacek Nowiński, Krzysztof Olechnicki, Arkadiusz Karwacki and Wojciech J. Buszta, eds. *Dziedzictwo w akcji: Rekonstrukcja historyczna jako sposób uczestnictwa w kulturze*. Warsaw: Narodowe Centrum Kultury, 2012.

"Uwaga Historia! Odtwórstwo historyczne wczesnego średniowiecza w Polsce." Muzeum Początków Państwa Polskiego w Gnieźnie. http://muzeumgniezno.pl/pl/aktualnosci/932.

"Viking Women: The Crying Bones." https://www.vikingwomen.film/.

"Wikingowie w Polsce? Zabytki skandynawskie z ziem polskich." Muzeum Początków Państwa Polskiego w Gnieźnie. http://muzeumgniezno.pl/pl/czasowe/549.

Notes

1. Recent studies include Scott Magelssen, *Living History Museums: Undoing History through Performance* (Lanham, MD: The Scarecrow Press, 2007); Iain McCalman and Paul A. Pickering, eds., *Historical Reenactment: From Realism to the Affective Turn* (Basingstoke: Palgrave Macmillian, 2010); Krzysztof Olechnicki, Tomasz Szlendak and Arkadiusz Karwacki, eds., *Grupy rekonstrukcji historycznej: Edukacja i konsumowanie przeszłości* (Toruń: Wydawnictwo Naukowe Uniwersytetu Mikołaja Kopernika w Toruniu, 2016); and Tomasz Szlendak, Jacek Nowiński, Krzysztof Olechnicki, Arkadiusz Karwacki and Wojciech J. Buszta, eds., *Dziedzictwo w akcji: Rekonstrukcja historyczna jako sposób uczestnictwa w kulturze* (Warsaw: Narodowe Centrum Kultury, 2012).
2. For an introduction to experimental archaeology, see John Coles, *Experimental Archaeology* (New York: Academic Press, 1979); and Bodil Petersson and Cornelius Holtorf, eds., *The Archaeology of Time Travel: Experiencing the Past in the 21st Century* (Oxford: Archaeopress Publishing, 2017).
3. Michał Bogacki "Wybrane Problemy odtwórstwa wczesnośredniowiecznego w Polsce: Zagadnienia ogólne i próba charakterystyki środowiska," in *Kultura ludów Morza Bałtyckiego 2: Nowożytność i współczesność. Materiały z III Międzynarodowej Sesji Naukowej Dziejów Ludów Morza Bałtyckiego. Wolin 20–22 lipca 2007*, ed. Michał Bogacki, Maciej Franz and Zbigniew Pilarczyk (Toruń: Wydawnictwo Adam Marszałek, 2008), pp. 219–69 at p. 222. Translation after Leszek Gardeła, "Vikings Reborn: The Origins and Development of Early Medieval Re-Enactment in Poland," *Sprawozdania Archeologiczne* 68 (2016): 165–82 at 167.
4. On the different aspects of reenactment, see for example Leszek Gardeła, "Współcześni wikingowie: Wojownicy, metalowcy i tak zwani poganie," in *Współczesna przeszłość*, ed. Urszula Stępień (Poznań: Koło Naukowe Studentów Archeologii and Instytut Prahistorii Uniwersytetu Adama Mickiewicza w Poznaniu, 2009), pp. 387–403.
5. See also the explanation the aims of experimental archaeology in Bodil Petersson and Lars E. Narmo, "A Journey in Time," in *Experimental Archaeology: Between Enlightenment and Experience*, ed. Bodil Petersson and Lars Erik Narmo (Lund: Lund University, Department of Archeology and Ancient History and Lofotr Viking Museum, 2011), pp. 27–48 at p. 28.
6. Michał Bogacki, "O współczesnym 'ożywianiu' przeszłości – Charakterystyka odtwórstwa historycznego," *Turystyka Kulturowa* 5 (2010): 4–27 at 12.
7. On the changing perception of Viking Age society in academia see, for example, Leszek Gardeła, "'Warrior-women' in Viking Age Scandinavia? A Preliminary Archaeological Study," *Analecta Archaeologica Ressoviensia* 8 (2013): 273–339 at 273–75; Judith Jesch, *Women in the Viking Age* (Woodbridge: Boydell, 1991), pp. 1–8; Neil Price, *The Viking Way: Religion and War in Late Iron Age Scandinavia* (Uppsala: Department of Archaeology and Ancient History, 2002), p. 26.
8. On experimentally built replicas of Viking ships see Coles, *Experimental Archaeology*, pp. 75–77.
9. Sara H. Jensen and Anna Bech Lund, eds., *Moesgaard Viking Moot* (Moesgaard: Moesgaard Museum and Jutland Archaeological Society, 2017); Lars Konzack, "Viking Re-enactment," in *Participatory Heritage*, ed. Henriette Roued-Cunliffe and Andrea Copeland (London: Facet Publishing, 2017), pp. 37–46.

10. Konzack, "Viking Re-enactment," p. 40.
11. Jesch, *Women in the Viking Age*; Jenny Jochens, *Old Norse Images of Women* (Philadelphia: University of Pennsylvania Press, 1996). See also Jenny Jochens, *Women in Old Norse Society* (Ithaca, NY: Cornell University Press, 1998).
12. Bogacki, "Wybrane problemy odtwórstwa wczesnośredniowiecznego w Polsce," pp. 257–58. On research concerning the emporium in Wolin, see Błażej Stanisławski and Władysław Filipowiak, *Wolin wczesnośredniowieczny: Część 1* (Warsaw: Fundacja na Rzecz Nauki Polskiej, 2013).
13. Bogacki, "Wybrane problemy odtwórstwa wczesnośredniowiecznego w Polsce," p. 258; Gardeła, "Vikings Reborn," p. 171.
14. See Gardeła, "Vikings Reborn," p. 171.
15. Ibid., p. 172.
16. Jacek Nowiński, "Instytucjonalizacja zabawy: O kulturotwórczym i kooperacyjnym potencjale ruchu rekonstrukcyjnego," in *Dziedzictwo w akcji: Rekonstrukcja historyczna jako sposób uczestnictwa w kulturze*, ed. Tomasz Szlendak, Jacek Nowiński, Krzysztof Olechnicki, Arkadiusz Karwacki and Wojciech Józef Buszta (Warsaw: Narodowe Centrum Kultury, 2012), pp. 73–108 at pp. 103–5.
17. In 2014, as part of the project "Languages, Myths and Finds," the jeweler Grzegorz "Greg" Pilarczyk prepared a full-sized replica of ringed-pin from Ballateare; see Leszek Gardeła, "Viking Death Rituals on the Isle of Man," in *Vikings Myths and Rituals on the Isle of Man*, ed. Leszek Gardeła and Carolyne Larrington (Nottingham: Centre for the Study of the Viking Age, 2014), fig. 12. In 2016, the craftsman Robert Pustelak manufactured several replicas of Bronze Age and Iron Age artifacts for archaeology students from the Institute of Archaeology, University of Rzeszów. In the same year Krystyna "Mojmira" Łopata made replicas of the spurs discovered in inhumation grave 10 in Lutomiersk (Poland). see Leszek Gardeła, *Bad Death in the Early Middle Ages* (Rzeszów: Fundacja Rzeszowskiego Ośrodka Archeologicznego, Instytut Archaeologii Uniwersytetu Rzeszowskiego, 2017), fig. 2.24:4. The 2016 "Rediscovering the Vikings" conference at UCC also engaged reenactors and living history enthusiasts in the conference, as well as the Guerilla Archaeology collective, in an effort to promote collaboration.
18. "Wikingowie w Polsce? Zabytki skandynawskie z ziem polskich," Muzeum Początków Państwa Polskiego w Gnieźnie, http://muzeumgniezno.pl/pl/czasowe/549.
19. "Uwaga Historia! Odtwórstwo historyczne wczesnego średniowiecza w Polsce," Muzeum Początków Państwa Polskiego w Gnieźnie, http://muzeumgniezno.pl/pl/aktualnosci/ 932.
20. On the role of women in different reenactment groups, see Krzysztof Olechnicki, "Muszkieterowie na transporterze: Rekonstrukcje historyczne w pogoni za wiernością i spektaklem," in *Dziedzictwo w akcji: Rekonstrukcja historyczna jako sposób uczestnictwa w kulturze*, ed. Tomasz Szlendak, Jacek Nowiński, Krzysztof Olechnicki, Arkadiusz Karwacki and Wojciech Józef Buszta (Warsaw: Narodowe Centrum Kultury, 2012), pp. 161–205 at pp. 175–76 and Tomasz Szlendak, "Wehrmacht nie macha: Rekonstrukcyjna codzienność jako sposób zanurzenia w kulturze," in *Dziedzictwo w akcji*, ed. Szlendak et al., pp. 9–70 at pp. 42–43.
21. Olechnicki, "Muszkieterowie na transporterze," p. 175.
22. It is worth noting that "markets" could be classed as a different type of event to festivals. They are sometimes smaller, lasting for a shorter time than festivals, and often more

focused on the commercial presentation of the past. During these events we may encounter people selling modern "folk" products and plastic souvenirs. Some markets also involve folk concerts and other activities which have little or nothing to do with the reenactment of medieval history.

23. Women from reenactment groups from Belarus, Czech Republic, Denmark, France, Germany, Hungary, Poland, Russia, Slovakia and Sweden took part in my survey. They belong to the following groups: Arcanoa, Bielska Drużyna Najemna "Svantevit," Bractwo Wojników Wataha, Bractwo Ziem Górnej Wisły, Drengowie znad Górnej Odry, Drużyna Grodu Horodna, Drużyna Grodu Piotrówka, Drużyna Grodu Trzygłowa, Drużyna Nidhogg, Drużyna Słowian i wikingów "Nordelag," Drużyna Wczesnośredniowieczna "Grom," Drużyna Wczesnośredniowieczna "Wytędze," Drużyna Wojów Wiślańskich "KRAK," Grupa Rekonstrukcji Historycznych "Wiwern," Gunnar, HERJAN, Jantar, Kram Savastiana, Kruki Południa, Les Gardiens du Temps, Lindholmhøje Vikingegruppe, Mazowiecka Drużyna Wojów "Weles," Midgard, Občanské sdružení Velkomoravané, Okořská Garda, Stockholm Free Vikings (former Birka Boys), Torualds Leather Workshop, TYR Hird, Újszkitia, Usadba, Völvart, and Wotan Hird.

24. See the very detailed analysis of problems in Viking reenactment in Bogacki, "Wybrane problemy odtwórstwa wczesnośredniowiecznego w Polsce," pp. 236–42; Gardeła, "Współcześni wikingowie," pp. 392–99; and Gardeła, "Vikings Reborn," pp. 174–77.

25. In Polish early medieval reenactment the term *historyczność* (historicity) is used to describe the level of archaeological or historical correctness of recreated objects; see also Gardeła "Vikings Reborn," pp. 174–75.

26. See the description of Viking Age clothing in Inga Hägg, *Textilien und Tracht in Haithabu und Schleswig* (Kiel and Hamburg: Wachholtz Murmann Publishers, 2015).

27. See, for instance, recreations of costumes made by reenactors Natália Barboriaková from Nornir – Early Medieval Crafts (Slovakia) or Angelika Strycka from Othala Craft – Viking and Slavic Clothing (Poland) and the costumes of members of the Czech reenactment group Marobud. See also replicas of metal objects made by craftspeople from Ludosza Montanus – Historical Jewellery, and Pustelak Brothers' Art Workshop. See also costumes and jewelry made by archaeologist Adam Parsons from Blueaxe Reproductions. On the level of recreated costumes see Gardeła "Vikings Reborn," p. 176.

28. See the description of Viking Age women in Jesch, *Women in the Viking Age.*

29. See the discussion of early medieval Slavic beliefs and rituals in Gardeła, *Bad Death in the Early Middle Ages*, pp. 15–21.

30. Klaudia Karpińska, "Women in Viking Re-Enactment in Poland: A Survey" (Rzeszów: Unpublished results of a survey, 2016), pp. 1–10.

31. Ibid., p. 11, and pp. 13–14.

32. *Eiríks saga rauða*, Íslenzk fornrit 4, ed. Ólafur Halldórsson (Reykjavík: Hið Íslenzka Fornritafélag, 1985); Leszek Gardeła, *(Magic) Staffs in the Viking Age* (Vienna: Verlag Fassbaender, 2016), pp. 21–24. See discussion on *vǫlur* and *seiðkonur* in Neil Price, *The Viking Way*, pp. 112–19.

33. Neil Price, *The Viking Way*, p. 64.

34. See the typology of staffs in Gardeła, *(Magic) Staffs*, pp. 219–23.

35. On runes and their meaning in early Middle Ages see for instance John McKinnell, Rudolf Simek and Klaus Düwel, eds., *Runes, Magic and Religion: A Sourcebook* (Vienna: Verlag Fassbaender, 2004).

36. As part of my research into modern staffs in 2016, I talked with neo-pagans and reenactors who have their own recreations of these artifacts. During my research, I noted that (besides the staffs mentioned in this chapter) there are only four modern staffs manufactured solely for reenactment purposes which were inspired by finds from Fuldby (Bjernede, Sorø, Sjælland, Denmark) and Gävle (Gastrikland, Sweden).

37. In March 2016, Robert Pustelak manufactured two full-sized replicas of the staff/spear/arrow from grave A505 from Trekroner-Grydehøj (Denmark) which were commissioned by the author.

38. On the *Vikings* History TV series see Katarzyna J. Puchalska, "Vikings Television Series: When History and Myth Intermingle," *The Polish Journal of the Arts and Culture* 15, no. 3 (2015): 89–105; Gareth Lloyd Evans, "Michael Hirst's *Vikings* and Old Norse Poetry," in *Translating Early Medieval Poetry: Transformation, Reception, Interpretation*, ed. Tom Birkett and Kirsty March-Lyons (Cambridge: D. S. Brewer, 2017), pp. 199–212; and Neil Price, "My Vikings and Real Vikings" in this volume. For a very detailed study of warrior women see Gardeła, "'Warrior-women'," pp. 273–339.

39. Women fighting in festivals can be seen in a photo documentary on Broadly (Matteo Congregalli, "Warrior Women of the Viking Reenactment Scene, in Photos," *Broadly*, March 1, 2018, https://broadly.vice.com/en_us/article/437p9b/viking-women-historical-reenactment-larping-photos). It should also be mentioned that in 2018 a crowdfunding project was started the aim of which is to create a documentary on modern Viking women (see "Viking Women: The Crying Bones," https://www.vikingwomen.film/).

40. See, for example, a description of warrior women who took part in Moesgaard Viking Moot in Anna Bech Lund, "'Are You One of the Valkyries, Then?'," in *Moesgaard Viking Moot*, ed. Sara H. Jensen and Anna Bech Lund (Moesgaard: Moesgaard Museum and Jutland Archaeological Society, 2017), pp. 121–33.

41. The female combat reenactors with whom I talked were from Poland (two reenactors), Sweden, and the Czech Republic.

42. It is generally accepted that women cannot take part in battles at Festivals of Slavs and Vikings. The fact that this woman took part in these fights is something unusual and seldom happens at this event.

43. See Lund, "'Are You One of the Valkyries, Then?'," p. 128.

44. Compare for example with studies in Gardeła, "'Warrior-women'," pp. 305–7; Leszek Gardeła, "Amazons of the North? Armed Females in Viking Archaeology and Medieval Literature," in *Hvanndalir – Beiträge zur europäischen Altertumskunde und mediävistischen Literaturwissenschaft*, ed. Alessia Bauer and Alexandra Pesch (Berlin and Boston: De Gruyter, 2018), pp. 391–428.

45. See the discussion of these plates in Gardeła, "Amazons of the North?," pp. 402–8.

46. Ibid., pp. 400–401.

Jessica Clare Hancock
5 Who's Afraid of an Electric Torch? Reimagining Gender and the Viking World in Contemporary Picturebooks

Examining representations of Vikings in children's literature is crucial, because these first impressions will shape later readings of the Old Norse-Icelandic world, contributing to what James Phelan describes as the "entrance," which constructs an "audience's hypothesis, implicit or explicit, about the direction and purpose of the whole narrative."[1] Twenty-first-century children in the UK frequently encounter Vikings, especially due to the recent success of the Marvel Universe;[2] motifs and characters, often clearly gendered, appear on children's clothing, toys, films, TV programs, and books. Peter Hunt contends that "children's literature. . .reflects – must reflect – the culture that surrounds or permeates it. Gender is a central example."[3] Yet books do more than reproduce their contexts; they also contribute to them, demarcating the possibilities for gender. Björn Sundmark argues that in British fictional picturebooks, a Viking is reducible to "a helmet with horns. . .attachable to almost any tribe of muscular, bearded and bold men": emphasizing the gendered use of this signifier as well as echoing David Clark's concerns about "Norse-ploitation."[4] In contrast, I will use Linda Hutcheon's stance of rejecting fidelity as the sole measure of adaptations, as texts that employ Viking themes and characters can be considered rewritings of the Old Norse-Icelandic world as much as those which directly retell a particular saga.[5] As she maintains: "there are manifestly many different possible intentions behind the act of adaptation: the urge to consume and erase the memory of the adapted text or to call it into question is as likely as the desire to pay tribute by copying."[6] Instead of measuring historical or narrative accuracy, my focus in this chapter will be on examining representations of Vikings in picturebooks, which are likely to be a child's earliest encounters, to understand how these portray and construct masculinities and femininities.

Note: There is disagreement about the form of the word picturebook. As the definition I am using suggests the intertwinement of words and illustrations, I follow David Lewis by using a compound word which reflects this; see *Reading Contemporary Picturebooks: Picturing Text* (London: Routledge/Falmer, 2001), p. xiv.

Jessica Clare Hancock, City, University of London

https://doi.org/10.1515/9781501513886-006

It is not always easy to define picturebooks. Some books, consisting of few or no words and spreads of unbordered illustrations, can be straightforwardly classified as picturebooks, and those with many pages of text with a small number of artworks as illustrated books, but many occupy a middle ground. Barbara Bader's much-quoted definition characterizes picturebooks as involving the "interdependence of pictures and words,"[7] and Robyn McCallum similarly proposes that the "visual and verbal texts are given equal emphasis."[8] David Lewis thus concludes that "the form [is] to some extent unbounded. . .[so] all manner of variations on the formula might be included."[9] I have chosen books where the text and pictures "interact to produce meaning," excluding comics, aimed at primary-school-age readers (as I am examining formative experiences), with fewer than forty pages (most are the standard thirty-two).[10] With the exception of *Edda*, a US picturebook (available from UK booksellers) which offers a different focus (on a Valkyrie rather than a Viking), the picturebooks were also selected because they are widely available to British children, through public libraries as well as bookshops.[11] This chapter will begin by examining picturebooks which take a historical approach, and then analyze picturebooks which are more focused on a fictional narrative, although, as with the sagas themselves, there is often an overlap between these distinctions.

Historical Picturebooks

Title	Author / Illustrator	Summary	Year: Publication/ Edition	Pages
How to Be a Viking in 13 Easy Stages[12]	Scoular Anderson	Describes different aspects of Viking life: farming, ships, clothing, pastimes, crafts, weapons, religion, travel, raiding, trading, law, writing, and stories.	2007	32
The Story of the Vikings Picturebook[13]	Megan Cullis / Giorgio Bacchin	Describes different aspects of Viking life: ships, battle, home, ornaments crafts and trade, religion, pastimes, and stories.	2016	24
Men, Women and Children in Viking Times[14]	Colin Hynson / Photographs and reproduced map	Describes different aspects of Viking life: gender, authority, family, education, jobs, clothing, pastimes, and religion.	2007	30

(continued)

Title	Author / Illustrator	Summary	Year: Publication/ Edition	Pages
Children in History: Vikings[15]	Kate Jackson Bedford / Photographs and reproduced pictures	Describes different aspects of Viking life: family, homes, girls, boys, meals, clothing, travel, health, toys, fun, stories, and religion.	2009/ 2011	32
You Wouldn't Want to Be a Viking Explorer![16]	Andrew Langley / David Antram	Describes Leif Ericsson's expedition from Greenland to Newfoundland.	2000/ 2004	32
Viking Longship[17]	Mick Manning / Brita Granström	Grim and Uggla, two Vikings, buy a longship and invade England on behalf of an earl. Grim becomes a farmer and marries Ylva. Their village is attacked by raiders and Uggla dies.	2006/ 2007; 2015 (reprinted with new cover)	40
What a Viking![18]	Mick Manning / Brita Granström	Bjorn leaves Birka, Sweden to travel and raid, then marries Thora and settles as a farmer.	2000/ 2006	40

These picturebooks demonstrate a range of approaches to historical information about the Vikings, both in their choice of illustrations (cartoon, realism, photos) and text (narrative, factual, first, second or third-person narration).

Historical Picturebooks: Raider-Masculinity

Maria Nikolajeva and Carole Scott argue that "the cover of a picturebook is often an integral part of the narrative."[19] Of the seven historical picturebooks examined, *Viking Explorer, Viking Longship, What A Viking* and *How To Be A Viking* use cartoon-style illustrations on their front covers which exclusively feature male warriors or voyagers. This frequently asserted male identity becomes, to use Raewyn Connell's term, the hegemonic masculinity of these picturebooks, or the type of manhood that is endorsed by this particular setting; it will be referred to in this chapter as raider-masculinity, as it involves exploration and leadership as well as bravery, aggression, and physical prowess.[20] Of the remainder, *Vikings Picturebook* features illustrations of armed men and a ship, and larger photographs of artifacts associated with adventure and battle, as well as a coin and game-playing pieces. *Men, Women and Children*'s largest cover photograph is of a Lewis chessmen king, thereby emphasizing maleness (James Robinson comments that this piece has a "particularly heavy beard"[21]) but not combat (the photograph cuts off the sword held in his lap), whereas none of the photographs for *Children In History* depict clearly-gendered figures, although some images appear warfare-related. The covers display a clear variation between picturebooks which present the Viking world as centered around raider-masculinity (*Viking Explorer, Viking Longship, What A Viking* and *How To Be A Viking*), and those that offer a less gendered depiction (*Vikings Picturebook, Men, Women* and *Children* and *Children In History*); this divide is also reflected in the amount of narrative provided in the picturebooks, with the former being more story based. The historical picturebooks which appear more concerned with entertainment demonstrate a greater interest in a masculinity centered around violence and voyaging.

Thus, in *Viking Explorer, Viking Longship, What A Viking* and *How To Be A Viking*, an emphasis on raider-masculinity is constructed from the outset. The Viking on *Viking Explorer*'s cover exudes anger through red cheeks and bared teeth, and his twisted stance creates a sense of imminent attack. Yet the gaps in his teeth are childlike, enabling a young viewer to identify with him through a shared (albeit male) physicality; indeed, Perry Nodelman argues that children are encouraged to see themselves in illustrations as "picturebooks offer a replication of...[Lacan's] mirror stage."[22] The exaggerated artwork also somewhat reduces the Viking's menace. Nevertheless, *How To Be A Viking*'s cover Viking is much less belligerent, with goofy sticky-out teeth, although this humorous presentation may "make [the] violence more palatable" rather than remove it altogether, something Sandra Beckett notes is common in picturebooks.[23] Similarly, *Viking Longship*'s smiling warrior appears defensive rather than aggressive and the cover of *What A Viking* emphasizes travel;[24] but the covers of all four picturebooks establish the importance of raider-masculinity with men prepared for physical combat.

In *What A Viking* raider-masculinity is lauded, albeit by the first-person narrator. Although Bjorn acknowledges that he "didn't know any better" (p. 11), violence will produce "sweet memories" (p. 14). Physical prowess is repeatedly demonstrated by male characters in *Viking Explorer*, whether this is through battle (pp. 16–17, 20, 21, 22–23, 28, 31), manual labor (pp. 3, 7, 8–9, 10–11, 16–17, 18–19, 24, 25, 26–27, 29, 30), or rowing (pp. 5, 12, 13, 15, 25). However, pessimistic feelings are foregrounded in the morose figure of Ragnar Lodbrok on the first spread (pp. 6–7) and unhappiness is portrayed throughout, with an emphasis on the drawbacks of sea-travel (p. 12) and conflict (pp. 27–28). The male warriors in *How To Be A Viking* are not universally aggressive either: two look afraid and distance themselves from a belligerent, chain-mailed figure (p. 15). Similarly, in *Viking Longship* the text comments that "years of war and bloodshed…can't go on like this. Peace must follow!" (p. 23). Raider-masculinity is not, therefore admired in *Viking Explorer*, *Viking Longship* or *How To Be A Viking* as it is in *What A Viking*. Yet in *Viking Explorer* and *Viking Longship*, despite the downsides, raider-masculinity is the only identity available to male characters. In *How To Be A Viking*, farming, shipbuilding, and peaceful pastimes such as singing are described, and, in *What A Viking*, Bjorn eventually settles down and prioritizes his family; there are different possibilities for men in these texts.

Historical Picturebooks: Women and Warfare

If male roles are constrained in *Viking Explorer*, female characters are absent, apart from a carving of a Valkyrie (p. 20) and one woman alienated within a small frame (p. 27), whose hair is recommended for use as a bow-string by the text: a female body becomes a commodity. Nikolajeva and Scott argue that "frames normally create a sense of detachment between the picture and the reader":[25] in this case, distancing the implied viewer/reader from empathizing with the woman and finding her objectification disturbing. Indeed, although *Viking Explorer* relates Leif Ericsson's expeditions, it does not include his sister Freyðis (whose role is recorded in the sources such as *The Saga of Erik the Red* and *The Saga of the Greenlanders*). She does appear in *Men, Women and Children*'s more equal presentation of male and female characters. Yet the narrator mentions her "cruelty" and that "she beheaded some female prisoners that the Viking men refused to harm" (p. 17). This negative depiction of her actions in combat contrasts with male characters. In *Children In History*, Freydis's motivation is given as defending "her family and possessions" (p. 11), thus lessening her warrior identity.

    Children In History also mentions that "some women went to war to care for ill and hurt soldiers" (p. 9); women are only associated with conflict in a protective role. Similarly, in *Viking Longship*, Hilda (the priestess character) appears on the battlefield "try[ing] a magic charm" (p. 23) to heal the wounded. She is distanced from the action and differentiated from the men through clothing. In the penultimate spread on narratives in *Vikings Picturebook*, most tales feature men associated with raider-masculinity (pp. 20–21). The description of manuscript production reinforces this connection between literature and men, which is further emphasized by a picture from the Codex Uppsaliensis of the

Prose Edda depicting a horse-riding man (identified in the manuscript as Jón).[26] Stories are shown to endorse and construct raider-masculinity, and men have narrative control, perhaps indicating why female characters appear to be side-lined. An illustration of a "princess" trapped within the body of a "monstrous snake" who is "rescued" (p. 21) by Ragnar suggests she embodies opposite characteristics to raider-masculinity: impotency and powerlessness. Brynhild, the only female protagonist, is described as "staggeringly beautiful, and admired for her skill and aggression in battle" (p. 21); she exhibits stereotypically feminine characteristics as well as raider-masculinity, perhaps reflecting the confusion in *The Saga of the Völsungs* where she is initially mistaken for a man. In *Men, Women and Children, Children In History, Viking Longship* and *Vikings Picturebook*, female characters can be linked to raider-masculinity, but not straightforwardly. Indeed, in *Children In History* boys "had to learn to fight" (p. 12) whereas "some girls were taught how to fight so they could defend their homes whilst the men were away" (p. 11): associating them with domesticity as well as raider-masculinity.

Historical Picturebooks: Domesticity and Beyond

In *Vikings Picturebook* (pp. 10–11) and *How To Be A Viking* (pp. 4–5), household life involves men and women in distinct roles. *Children In History* more closely connects women with the home (p. 10) and *Viking Longship*'s spread on women illustrates them in a solely domestic setting (pp. 26–27). Indeed, in *What A Viking*, Bjorn is uncomfortable in a female-dominated home environment; the text describes him as "bored" (p. 6) and he is depicted as miserable, facing away from his female relatives (pp. 5–6). Women in *What A Viking*, such as the Byzantine characters (pp. 13–14), are also sexualized: in a market scene, a woman even holds two melons in front of her chest (p. 23). Although there is a possibly similar, in Barbara Wall's phrase, double address (because it is aimed solely at an adult reader/viewer) earlier in the picturebook, with phallic objects positioned near men's crotches (pp. 5–6), this innuendo is much less obvious.[27] Yet Bjorn eventually relinquishes his bachelor existence when he has "met [his] match" (p. 25) in Thora, "the village stone lifting champion" (p. 25), who is pictured carrying her husband in a display of female dominance. Likewise, in *Viking Longship* the main female character, Ylva, is described as "a clever woman...[who] rules the roost" (p. 27). Her daughter, Thora, is shown outwitting her brother, Thorkell, in the first and final spreads (pp. 2–3; pp. 38–39). The final text states that Ylva "is going to pay for a memorial stone for Uggla" (p. 37). This suggests that veneration, and thus the control of narrative, is in this text another potential area for female mastery, in contrast to *Vikings Picturebook*-albeit one which is not fully explored.

Historical Picturebooks: From Both Sides Now

In picturebooks, the narrative cannot be restricted by either pictures or texts alone; as Mo Grenby observes, there are picturebooks "in which words and images compete against each other, each subverting what the other is putting forward, and struggling for supremacy":[28] meaning that, as Lewis argues, words and pictures "can only offer 'the same information' in the loosest possible sense" (p. 302).[29] In *Vikings Picturebook*, the text broadens the definition of Vikings to "merchants, farmers and craft workers" (p. 3), in gender-neutral language. Yet the illustrations depict five male figures wielding swords. Similarly, the spreads on "ships" (pp. 4–5), "battle gear" (pp. 6–7), and "the Viking world" (pp. 8–9) are constructed as male by the pictures alone. *Children In History* juxtaposes the real and imaginary, with photographs of artifacts, of human and model reconstructions, and reproductions of Victorian art. Its color photographs offer greater realism, but the text reveals that the subjects are merely "dressed up as Vikings" (p. 9). Tensions between reality and fiction are enhanced when the text states that a "wooden carving shows a blacksmith mending a boy's sword" (p. 8) but does not identify them as Reginn and Sigurðr, fantastical characters from the Völsung legend. *Men, Women and Children* also provides photographs of "reconstructed" (p. 16) scenes, yet only uses male subjects, thereby electing to marginalize women and girls. The commingling of fictional and factual elements not only reflects saga literature but also emphasizes unreality, indicating the performative and non-real nature of gender and therefore undermining any attempt to essentialize raider-masculinity.

In the historical picturebooks, female raider-masculinity is present in both Freydis and Brynhild. Yet whilst femininity is often tightly constrained (both within the domestic realm and the picturebooks themselves – many confine women or girls to their eponymous pages) there are some representations of a variety of masculinities. Indeed, raider-masculinity is not always revered. These picturebooks all oscillate in some way between fact and fiction which indicates a potential for the expansion of gender roles, something that becomes even more viable in picturebooks that are more focused on fictional narratives.

Fictional Picturebooks

Title	Author / Illustrator	Summary	Year: publication/ edition	Pages
Edda: A Little Valkyrie's First Day of School[30]	Adam Auerbach	A young valkyrie is flown to an Earth school and makes friends by sharing stories of Valhalla.	2014	40
Hiccup: The Viking Who Was Seasick[31]	Cressida Cowell	Timid Hiccup discovers that Vikings can get seasick and overcomes his own travel-nausea to take control of a longship.	1999/ 2001; 2014/ 2016	32
Eric Bloodaxe the Viking[32]	Damian Harvey / Ross Collins	A shepherd boy delivers a helmet to Eric, but is allowed to borrow it during the battle, which ends in Eric's death.	2009	32
Viking Adventure[33]	Roderick Hunt / Alex Brychta	The children use a magic key to transport them to Viking times, where Biff scares off raiders with an electric torch.	1990/ 2011	32
Vikings in the Supermarket[34]	Nick Sharratt	In the first poem (4 pages) of this collection, six Vikings go to the supermarket to get produce to be used as helmet horns.	2016	32
Dragon Stew[35]	Steve Smallman / Lee Wildish	Five Vikings try to catch and kill a dragon but end up getting their bottoms burnt.	2011	32

Fictional Picturebooks: War and Sea

Eric Bloodaxe's cover – like that of *Viking Explorer, Viking Longship, What A Viking* and *How To Be A Viking* – accentuates raider-masculinity. The implied viewer's perspective is from the Viking's feet, so the head of his axe looms at the focal point, increasing his intimidating appearance. Yet on the first page, only his head and torso are visible, floating freely above a fully drawn child, establishing him as fantastical and indicating that his raider-masculinity is inimitable. The narrator is never referred to by name or pronoun and is dressed differently from other male and female characters. Without reading the blurb which identifies him as a "shepherd boy," he is ungendered. He is further distanced from raider-masculinity through his responsibility for animals, rather than physical tasks like his brother or father, and by being "too young" (p. 15) to fight, even when his side is outnumbered (p. 22). When Eric lends the narrator his helmet (p. 24) this connotes entry into raider-masculinity, although as it is worn whilst tending a lamb and watching the battle from a distance, he remains marginalized, demonstrating that this identity cannot be conferred merely by symbols.

In contrast to the historical picturebooks, the narrator's home environment is entirely male. Gunnhild, the only female character, is described as "the scariest woman that I'd ever seen" (p. 6) and snarls and leans forward in an intimidating manner. Whereas male speech is described throughout the text with non-descriptive verbs such as reply (p. 7), tell (p. 11), or said (pp. 14, 15), Gunnhild screeches (p. 7) and shouts (p. 8). Although later in the text, Ulrik cries (p. 21) and Eric booms (p. 24), these are in the context of a rowdy combat scene; Gunnhild is disrupting a household. Nevertheless, if, as she requested, Eric had been given his helmet before the battle, he may not have died, demonstrating her wisdom. In her aggression, Gunnhild exhibits some aspects of raider-masculinity but her performance of this identity is presented as unsettling.

Whilst *Eric Bloodaxe* inverts the historical-picturebooks' association of women with the home, in *Vikings in the Supermarket*, three male and two female Vikings are fully domesticated as they shop for helmet horns. The gender diversity may be possible only because their raider-masculinity is undermined by humor, as with How *To Be A Viking*'s cover, perhaps understandably given Jackie E. Stallcup's observation that modern picturebooks construct a childhood which requires protection from fear.[36] Yet the women make some of the worst choices shape-wise to recreate Viking horns, with their non-curved items insinuating a female inability to occupy this role.[37] Cora and Ida are also positioned in the least eye-catching positions on the ship. As with Gunnhild, a female raider-masculinity is not endorsed, although here it is marginalized rather than presented as troubling.

Despite the new edition including a dedication to Cowell's father where she identifies herself with the protagonist, *Hiccup: The Viking* is focalized around a boy, and includes no female characters. Nodelman argues that reminders of an author's identity ensure "that children realize, not just that a book describes childhood, but that it is an adult – i.e., an authorized, culturally sanctioned, desirable – depiction of childhood."[38] This approved reality is even more of a male domain than *Eric Bloodaxe*'s. However, unlike Eric, Hiccup is small and terrified on the cover, contrasting with the other Vikings who are "enormous roaring burglars" (p. 2). Even the setting is an inhospitable, outdoor, "fierce and frosty land" (p. 1), the opposite of *Eric Bloodaxe*'s male domesticity. This landscape is dominated by Hiccup's father, Stoick, whose presence is physically intimidating (even his name and speech loom large on the page) and has a destructive effect: "wherever Stoick walked the ground trembled, flowers wilted, and bunnies fainted" (p. 4). Nature only provokes terror in Hiccup who "was frightened of spiders...thunder...[and] sudden loud noises" (p. 2), leading him to be unsure "if he was a Viking at all" (p. 3).

However, the other Vikings' raider-masculinity is eventually destabilized during a sea voyage as they do not have the control over nature they boasted about, and become seasick. Once Hiccup observes this alternative form of masculinity he recovers from his own nausea. He takes control of the longship, establishing a harmonious relationship with the sea-creatures which now accompany it (pp. 22–23): an alternative to the destructiveness of raider-masculinity. Hiccup's confidence in his identity is restored by the revelation of weakness present in others. Yet, an ability to deal with seasickness is classified as evidence of bravery, thus reestablishing this characteristic as innate and essential. Stoick cuddles Hiccup in the penultimate pages (pp. 24, 25), indicating approval of his son. Katie Sciurba argues that "male gender variance is fraught with shame and alienation."[39] Indeed, in *Hiccup: The Viking*, raider-masculinity may include vulnerability but its protagonist is only accepted once he demonstrates sailing prowess. The one Viking who does not exhibit physical dominance is Hiccup's grandfather who is also marginalized and excluded from the family reconciliation. The final page depicts a sign reading "Vikings ~~never~~ sometimes get seasick" with Hiccup holding a paintbrush (p. 26). He is now in control of his own narrative – perhaps this mastery is more valuable than recognition.

Fictional Picturebooks: Female Leadership

Dragon Stew features three bearded men (Grim, Bushi, Harald), Yop (whose clothes suggest he is a boy), and one female character in pink clothing (Loggi Longsocks) whose description as "little" (p. 5) implies she is a girl. On the back cover, Loggi's mouth is open widest, suggesting that she is the most aggressive and verbally controlling the situation. Within the main narrative, she is the last to speak, but has the idea to:

> Go and catch a dragon, then tie it to a wagon.
> Then take it home and chop it up and make a dragon stew (p. 5).

The others immediately approve of her idea. On this spread, not only is she depicted as more prominent in size but also the others mimic her stance (pp. 5–6).

Whereas the male characters just have buckles, Loggi's belt bears a human skull, connecting her most closely to a destructive and dangerous raider-masculinity.

Loggi is often in charge and carries the "pointy dragon poking thing" (p. 7) which is another indication of domination and violence. The mission ends in failure and burned bottoms (pp. 20–21), yet no-one chastises her. She is also the only character who appears to notice the irony in the final line, which echoes the opening. She face-palms, declaring "here we go again" (p. 23), indicating her greater sophistication. Like Gunnhild in *Eric Bloodaxe*, she adds intelligence to a raider-masculinity, yet a reader/ viewer also, as Perry Nodelman argues, "learn[s] how dangerous adventurousness and spontaneity are"[40]; female raider-masculinity becomes viable but ultimately this kind of identity is undermined – in this text by the supremacy of a male dragon. The dragon's effortless defeat of the Vikings is accentuated by his attire: a bowtie and hat, more suitable for cocktails than combat. *Dragon Stew* explores the potential for a girl to take charge but a larger character, signifying an adult, easily dominates, and here that authority is gendered as male.

In *Viking Adventure*, present-day children learn about the Vikings at school. The main female character, Biff, is side-lined in these scenes, and when they are "all dressed up as Vikings and pretend to row" (p. 7) a longship she is at the back, the only person without a helmet, complaining that "it's hard work being a Viking" (p. 7). Yet once at home, Biff initiates the magic key transport to a Viking longship. The Vikings that the children encounter are "very fierce" (p. 15), displaying raider-masculinity as they face the children with teeth bared, brandishing their oars. Yet Viking travel is depicted as "not much fun" (p. 17), denigrating this identity in a similar way to *Viking Explorer* or *Viking Longship*.

Once in the Vikings' home, also as in many of the historical picturebooks, there is a clear gendered divide: men eat (p. 22) or carry goods (p. 23) whilst the women serve food (p. 23). However, when the village is under attack, Biff joins male Vikings to investigate:

> Biff had an idea. She shone her torch.
> The raiders and the villagers had never seen a light like this before. They were frightened and they all fell to the ground (p. 27).

The implied viewer is encouraged to focus on Biff, the only character in full color. The torch's beam centers on an axe, and the text's description of characters' collapse also associates her act with violence, despite her actually utilizing ingenuity. Nevertheless, although Biff wishes to leave the Vikings with this technology, "Wilf told her not to" (p. 31) without justification, suggesting that he anticipates Biff's unquestioning compliance.[41] However, a Viking is holding the torch in the last image it appears in (p. 31). Biff has leadership skills, defeats enemies, and demonstrates intelligence, whilst male authority is not visibly obeyed.

One Viking's physical similarity to the school caretaker is reinforced by both carrying heavy goods (pp. 2, 4, 6, 18, 23, 31, 32). As in *Children In History* and *Men, Women and Children* the lines between magic and actuality are blurred. The Viking world is a fantasy space where Biff can explore an alternative identity, but this does not appear fully transferrable to reality. In the final scene, Biff's teacher insists that "Viking shields didn't look like this" (p. 32) as she shows him her present. The final line, however, positions her as powerful: "Biff looked at Wilf and smiled" (p. 32). Indeed, the back cover proposes that children should carefully consider this moment. In *Viking Adventure*, Biff controls key narrative events, in contrast to Sue Wharton's argument that in the Oxford Reading Tree, the series of which *Viking Adventure* is part, "males are dominant."[42] The focus of both *Dragon Stew* and *Viking Adventure* are girls who add imagination and creativity to the characteristics of raider-masculinity, creating a new identity of raider-femininity.

Edda: A Little Valkyrie is the only picturebook focused on a female character: Edda, a Valkyrie who starts school on Earth. The cover and first pages show Edda in a series of defiant postures. Yet in the next spreads (pp. 3–4, 5–6), Edda is small and distanced from her family. She is an outsider, like *Eric Bloodaxe*'s narrator or Hiccup. Indeed, just as in Cowell's picturebook, courage is emphasized: this time in a reassuring manner as Edda is told that "Valkyries are very brave…even little valkyries" (p. 8). Here, fearlessness is constructed as an innate female trait, and fathers encourage rather than intimidate.[43] Yet Edda is also marginalized at school, lingering in the doorway, distanced physically (pp. 9–10) and by her clothing, like Hilda in *Viking Longship*. The picturebook contrasts the freedom available to Edda in Asgard where she can "do what she wants, and go where she pleases" (p. 11) and an ordered school setting where she does not fit in. This is quite different from the autonomy available in *Dragon Stew*, although Edda herself is unhappy with her original lifestyle; *Edda: A Little Valkyrie, Viking Adventure*, and *Dragon Stew* all appear to posit Viking culture as more amenable to female raider-masculinity than an implied reader/viewer's contemporary setting.

Connections with other pupils are only formed when "she tells a tale of danger, bravery, victory and forgiveness" (pp. 22–23). The pictures reveal that this story concerns her relationship with a dragon, both conquering and befriending it. Even more strongly than Loggi and Biff, she demonstrates an alternative to raider-masculinity: conciliation and co-operation. Like Hiccup, she controls her own narrative, and constructs a unique identity, albeit one that conforms to the values of her new setting, confirmed by her tale being "a big hit" (p. 24). When Edda entered the school, one of the shelves showed a book titled "Myth" with a cover depiction of her father's face (p. 9); her story replaces him with a female figure as protagonist, and also transforms the status of a narrative about Valhalla from fantasy into reality. Finally, she adopts an adult role and brings the dragon to school, echoing her father's words as she reassures it that "dragons are very brave" (p. 30). Instead of relying on an adult to solve her problem, which, as Stallcup notes, is most common in similar texts, Edda exhibits autonomy.[44] Indeed, she also acts counter to Crisp and Hiller's analysis of picturebooks which indicates that even "active females often ultimately rel[y] on males to satisfy the conflict."[45] Edda thus offers a different perspective on gender in picturebooks, within and outwith the Viking world.

Conclusion

Fictional picturebooks such as *Dragon Stew, Viking Adventure*, and *Edda: A Little Valkyrie* provide an alternative portrayal of Viking gender identity. Even *Hiccup: The Viking* and *Vikings in the Supermarket* undermine raider-masculinity. Jo Sutliff Sanders argues that "picture books are so prone to nostalgia because [they] rely on a specific way of fixing meaning."[46] Yet the proliferation of picturebooks about Vikings, and their varied representations of gender, indicate that childhood understandings of the Old Norse world will always retain possibilities for alternative identities. In the loss of specificity that Sundmark mourns in his complaint that "today we have only the horns," there is a power in remaking gender, especially for children, thereby providing a more accurate representation of the absence of a fixed gender identity in the Viking past.[47] In their study of folktales, Ann Trousdale and Sally McMillan argue that patriarchal literature cannot be avoided, but it can be countered by a critical reception.[48] A child's response to the picturebooks analyzed is outside the scope of this chapter, but the gender identities presented within some of these picturebooks are likely to provide material for just such a counter-reading/viewing of picturebooks which offer a more straightforward representation of gender expressed through raider-masculinity.

Questioning British primary-aged children I know revealed common notions of Vikings: big, scary, vicious, hairy, and horned warriors who raided and invaded. Adults asked to define Vikings are likely to respond similarly by starting from Cowell's image of "enormous roaring burglars"[49] even if they then go on to reject, qualify, or add to it. Our formative experiences of the Viking world, encountered in picturebooks like these, therefore will only ever be modified, rather than erased. It is thus imperative to foreground and understand these perceptions, particularly in the endeavor to explore contemporary reinterpretations of Viking Age texts and materials. Giuliana Adamo argues that "the beginning of a text indicates to us the beginning of a possible world";[50] picturebooks similarly suggest the potential roles for Norse culture in the present day. Information and impressions gained from picturebooks are, therefore, likely to unconsciously shape our reactions to contemporary meanings of material and textual remains, such as the controversial "Viking female warrior" evidence declared by Charlotte Hedenstierna-Jonson et al. in September 2017:[51] the gender identities found in early childhood encounters with Vikings influencing our later responses to gender in this context. It has long been argued that researchers should use a personal-subjectivity audit to expose facets of their own identities that may influence their interpretation of data.[52] An examination of picturebooks can likewise make explicit our embedded constructions of Vikings.

Bibliography

Primary Sources

Anderson, Scoular. *How to Be a Viking in 13 Easy Stages*. London: Collins, 2007.
Auerbach, Adam. *Edda: A Little Valkyrie's First Day of School*. New York: Henry Holt, 2014.
Cowell, Cressida. *Hiccup: The Viking Who Was Seasick*. London: Hodder, 2001.
Cowell, Cressida. *How to Be a Viking*. London: Hodder, 2016.
Cullis, Megan. *The Story of the Vikings Picturebook*. London: Usborne, 2013.
Harvey, Damian. *Eric Bloodaxe the Viking King*. London: Franklin Watts, 2009.
Hunt, Roderick. *Viking Adventure*. Oxford: Oxford University Press, 2011.
Hynson, Colin. *Men, Women and Children in Viking Times*. London: Wayland, 2007.
Jackson Bedford, Kate. *Children in History: Vikings*. London: Franklin Watts, 2011.
Langley, Andrew. *You Wouldn't Want to Be a Viking Explorer!* London: Hodder, 2004.
Manning, Mick and Brita Granström. *Viking Longship*. London: Frances Lincoln, 2007.
Manning, Mick and Brita Granström. *What a Viking!* London: Franklin Watts, 2006.
Sharratt, Nick. *Vikings in the Supermarket*. Oxford: David Fickling, 2016.
Smallman, Steve. *Dragon Stew*. London: Little Tiger, 2011.

Secondary Sources

Adamo, Guiliana. "Beginnings and Endings in Novels." *New Readings* 1 (1995): 83–104.
Bader, Barbara. *American Picturebooks from Noah's Ark to the Beast Within*. New York: Macmillan, 1976.
Beckett, Sandra L. *Crossover Picturebooks: A Genre for All Ages*. London: Routledge, 2012.

Clark, David. "Old Norse Made New: Past and Present in Modern Children's Literature." In *Old Norse Made New*, edited by David Clark and Carl Phelpstead, pp. 133–51. Exeter: Viking Society for Northern Research, 2007.

Connell, Raewyn. *Masculinities*. Cambridge: Polity, 2005.

Crisp, Thomas and Brittany Hiller. "'Is This a Boy or a Girl?': Rethinking Sex-Role Representation in Caldecott Medal-Winning Picturebooks, 1938–2011." *Children's Literature in Education* 42 (2011): 196–212.

Frank, Roberta. "The Invention of the Viking Horned Helmet." In *International Scandinavian and Medieval Studies in Memory of Gerd Wolfgang Weber*, edited by Michael Dallapiazza, pp. 199–208. Trieste: Parnasso, 2000.

Grenby, Mo. *Children's Literature*. Edinburgh: Edinburgh University Press, 2014.

Hedenstierna-Jonson, Charlotte et al. "A Female Viking Warrior Confirmed by Genomics." *American Journal of Physical Anthropology* 164, no. 4 (2017): 853–60.

Hunt, Peter. *Children's Literature*. Oxford: Blackwell, 2001.

Hutcheon, Linda. *A Theory of Adaptation*. New York: Routledge, 2006.

Lewis, David. *Reading Contemporary Picturebooks: Picturing Text*. London: Routledge/Falmer, 2001.

Lewis, David. "The Interaction of Word and Image in Picturebooks: A Critical Survey." In *Children's Literature*, edited by Peter Hunt, pp. 294–309. London: Routledge, 2006.

McCallum, Robyn. "Cultural Solipsism, National Identities and the Discourse of Multiculturalism in Australian Picture Books." *Ariel* 28, no. 1 (1997): 101–16.

Nikolajeva, Maria and Carole Scott. *How Picturebooks Work*. New York and London: Garland, 2001.

Nodelman, Perry. "The Implied Viewer: Some Speculations about What Children's Picture Books Invite Readers to Do and Be." In *Children's Literature*, edited by Peter Hunt, pp. 264–81. London: Routledge, 2006.

Nodelman, Perry. "Words Claimed: Picturebook Narratives and the Project of Children's Literature." In *New Directions in Picturebook Research*, edited by Teresa Colomer, Bettina Kümmerling-Meibauer and Cecilia Silva-Díaz, pp. 11–26. New York: Routledge, 2010.

Page, Thelma. "Viking Adventure Teaching Notes." https://www.oupjapan.co.jp/sites/de fault/files/contents/eduk/ort/media/ort/ort_bck_viking_tns.pdf.

Peshkin, Alan. "In Search of Subjectivity – One's Own." *Educational Researcher* 17, no. 7 (1988): 17–21.

Phelan, James. *Experiencing Fiction: Judgments, Progressions and the Rhetorical Theory of Narrative*. Columbus: Ohio State University Press, 2007.

Robinson, James. *The Lewis Chessmen*. London: British Museum Press, 2004.

Sanders, Joe Sutliff. "Chaperoning Words: Meaning-Making in Comics and Picture Books." *Children's Literature* 41 (2013): 57–90.

Sciurba, Katie. "Flowers, Dancing, Dresses, and Dolls: Picture Book Representations of Gender-Variant Males." *Children's Literature in Education* 48 (2017): 276–93.

Stallcup, Jackie E. "Power, Fear, and Children's Picture Books." *Children's Literature* 30 (2002):125–58.

Sundmark, Björn. "Wayward Warriors: The Viking Motif in Swedish and English Children's Literature." *Children's Literature in Education* 45, no. 3 (2014): 197–210.

Trousdale, Ann M. and Sally McMillan. "'Cinderella Was a Wuss': A Young Girl's Response to Feminist and Patriarchal Folktales." In *Children's Literature*, edited by Peter Hunt, pp. 261–87. London: Routledge, 2006.

Wall, Barbara. *The Narrator's Voice: The Dilemma of Children's Fiction*. London: Macmillan, 1991.

Wharton, Sue. "Invisible Females, Incapable Males: Gender Construction in a Children's Reading Scheme." *Language and Education* 19, no. 3 (2005): 238–51.

Notes

1. James Phelan, *Experiencing Fiction: Judgments, Progressions and the Rhetorical Theory of Narrative* (Columbus: Ohio State University Press, 2007), p. 19.
2. In wider society, and often in the picturebooks that are the subject of this chapter, "Viking" is employed as an all-encompassing term to describe medieval Scandinavia, Iceland, and their literature and culture; although I am aware of the problematic nature of employing the term in this way (see Driscoll's essay in this collection), I shall replicate the picturebooks' use. I will also reproduce each picturebook's form of names, so, for example, Freydis rather than Freydís.
3. Peter Hunt, *Children's Literature* (Oxford: Blackwell, 2001), p. 18.
4. Björn Sundmark, "Wayward Warriors: The Viking Motif in Swedish and English Children's Literature," *Children's Literature in Education* 45, no. 3 (2014): 197–210 at 197; David Clark, "Old Norse Made New: Past and Present in Modern Children's Literature," in *Old Norse Made New*, ed. David Clark and Carl Phelpstead (Exeter: Viking Society for Northern Research, 2007), pp. 133–51 at p. 135.
5. Linda Hutcheon, *A Theory of Adaptation* (New York: Routledge, 2006), pp. 6–7.
6. Ibid., p. 7.
7. Bader, Barbara, *American Picturebooks from Noah's Ark to the Beast Within* (New York: Macmillan, 1976).
8. Robyn McCallum, "Cultural Solipsism, National Identities and the Discourse of Multiculturalism in Australian Picture Books," *Ariel* 28, no. 1 (1997): 101–16 at 103.
9. Lewis, *Contemporary Picturebooks*, p. 28.
10. McCallum, "Cultural Solipsism," 103.
11. Adam Auerbach, *Edda: A Little Valkyrie's First Day of School* (New York: Henry Holt, 2014).
12. Scoular Anderson, *How to Be a Viking in 13 Easy Stages* (London: Collins, 2007). Due to similarities in titles, these books will be referred to by author in the remaining text.
13. Megan Cullis, *The Story of the Vikings Picturebook* (London: Usborne, 2013).
14. Colin Hynson, *Men, Women and Children in Viking Times* (London: Wayland, 2007).
15. Kate Jackson Bedford, *Children in History: Vikings* (London: Franklin Watts, 2011).
16. Andrew Langley, *You Wouldn't Want to Be a Viking Explorer!* (London: Hodder, 2004).
17. Mick Manning and Brita Granström, *Viking Longship* (London: Frances Lincoln, 2007).
18. Mick Manning and Brita Granström, *What a Viking!* (London: Franklin Watts, 2006).
19. Maria Nikolajeva and Carole Scott, *How Picturebooks Work* (New York: Garland, 2001), p. 241.
20. Raewyn Connell, *Masculinities* (Cambridge: Polity, 2005).
21. James Robinson, *The Lewis Chessmen* (London: British Museum Press, 2004), p. 13.
22. Perry Nodelman, "The Implied Viewer: Some Speculations about What Children's Picture Books Invite Readers to Do and Be," in *Children's Literature*, ed. Peter Hunt (London: Routledge, 2006), pp. 264–81 at p. 278.

23. Sandra L. Beckett, *Crossover Picturebooks: A Genre for All Ages* (London: Routledge, 2012), p. 243.
24. The 2015 reprint has an alternative cover which is slightly more aggressive, with the biggest figure holding up a sword and shield.
25. Nikolajeva and Scott, *How Picturebooks Work*, p. 62.
26. Of course, few reader/viewers would be able to recognize the figure, but the previous pictorial emphasis on raider-masculinity is likely to mean that they would interpret this character as male.
27. Barbara Wall, *The Narrator's Voice: The Dilemma of Children's Fiction* (London: Macmillan, 1991).
28. Mo Grenby, *Children's Literature* (Edinburgh: Edinburgh University Press, 2014), p. 215.
29. David Lewis, "The Interaction of Word and Image in Picturebooks: A Critical Survey," in *Children's Literature*, ed. Peter Hunt (London: Routledge, 2006), pp. 294–309 at p. 302.
30. Shortened titles will be used from this point on.
31. Cressida Cowell, *Hiccup: The Viking Who Was Seasick* (London: Hodder, 2001); Cressida Cowell, *How to Be a Viking* (London: Hodder, 2016).
32. Damian Harvey, *Eric Bloodaxe the Viking King* (London: Franklin Watts, 2009).
33. Roderick Hunt, *Viking Adventure* (Oxford: Oxford University Press, 2011).
34. Nick Sharratt, *Vikings in the Supermarket* (Oxford: David Fickling, 2016).
35. Steve Smallman, *Dragon Stew* (London: Little Tiger, 2011).
36. Jackie E. Stallcup, "Power, Fear, and Children's Picture Books," *Children's Literature* 30 (2002): 125–58.
37. Of course, the curved horns on a Viking's helmet are traditional only from the 1876 performance of Wagner's Ring des Nibelungen in Bayreuth; see Roberta Frank, "The Invention of the Viking Horned Helmet," in *International Scandinavian and Medieval Studies in Memory of Gerd Wolfgang Weber*, ed. Michael Dallapiazza (Trieste: Parnasso, 2000), pp. 199–208 at p. 199. Curved horns are rarely seen in the more historical picture books, but frequently in the fictional works.
38. Perry Nodelman, "Words Claimed: Picturebook Narratives and the Project of Children's Literature," in *New Directions in Picturebook Research*, ed. Teresa Colomer, Bettina Kümmerling-Meibauer and Cecilia Silva-Díaz (New York: Routledge, 2010), pp. 11–26 at p. 19.
39. Katie Sciurba, "Flowers, Dancing, Dresses, and Dolls: Picture Book Representations of Gender-Variant Males," *Children's Literature in Education* 48 (2017): 276–93 at 291.
40. Nodelman, "Implied Viewer," p. 272.
41. The accompanying activities suggest that children are asked why Wilf may have said this, signifying he is making a valid point that Biff has not considered; see Thelma Page, "Viking Adventure Teaching Notes," https://www.oupjapan.co.jp/sites/default/files/con tents/eduk/ort/media/ort/ort_bck_viking_tns.pdf.
42. Sue Wharton, "Invisible Females, Incapable Males: Gender Construction in a Children's Reading Scheme," *Language and Education* 19, no. 3 (2005): 238–51 at 248.
43. Mothers are absent from all of the fictional picturebooks.
44. Stallcup, "Power, Fear."
45. Thomas Crisp and Brittany Hiller, "'Is This a Boy or a Girl?': Rethinking Sex-Role Representation in Caldecott Medal-Winning Picturebooks, 1938–2011," *Children's Literature in Education* 42 (2011): 196–212 at 203.
46. Joe Sutliff Sanders, "Chaperoning Words: Meaning-Making in Comics and Picture Books," *Children's Literature* 41 (2013): 57–90 at 66.

47. Sundmark, "Wayward Warriors," p. 209.
48. Ann M. Trousdale and Sally McMillan, "'Cinderella Was a Wuss': A Young Girl's Response to Feminist and Patriarchal Folktales," in *Children's Literature*, ed. Peter Hunt (London: Routledge, 2006), pp. 261–87.
49. Cowell, *Hiccup: The Viking Who Was Seasick*, p. 2.
50. Guiliana Adamo, "Beginnings and Endings in Novels," *New Readings* 1 (1995): 83–104 at 85.
51. Charlotte Hedenstierna-Jonson et al., "A Female Viking Warrior Confirmed by Genomics," *American Journal of Physical Anthropology* 164, no. 4 (2017): 853–60.
52. See, for example, Alan Peshkin's concept of the multiple I which instructs researchers to reveal aspects such as class, gender, or race; "In Search of Subjectivity – One's Own," *Educational Researcher* 17, no. 7 (1988): 17–21 at 17.

Thomas Spray
6 The Terrible *Njorl's Saga*: Comedic Reimaginings of the *Íslendingasögur* from the Victorians to the Present Day

Comedy and the Icelandic Saga

Think of a purposefully humorous reimagining of the Icelandic sagas. In all probability, what you have in mind is a construct of recognizable elements of medievalism. Perhaps it involves long ships with dragon-headed prows. Perhaps the characters (almost certainly men) are wearing horned helmets.

The figure of the "Viking" – the chief cultural legacy of the saga corpus – is found across the spectrum of comedy. From hen-pecked Hägar the Horrible's unheroic home-life to the many incarnations of the god Thor as the slow-witted butt of jokes, comic Norsemen are prevalent in contemporary culture. The Norse gods of Eddic literature are particularly common to comedic works, whether they are immolating airport check-in desks, consigned to retirement homes, or depicted as a bunch of unruly children.[1]

Yet what of the sagas themselves? On January 14, 1972, television viewers across Britain sat down to watch a scene of stirring music playing over a desolate landscape. The words "Iceland 1126" appeared on the screen, and then a voice:

> CLEESE: (*As announcer*) This little-known Icelandic saga, written by an unknown hand of the late thirteenth century, has remained undiscovered until today. Now it comes to your screens for the first time, fresh from the leaves of Iceland's history, the terrible N-Jorl's Saga!
>
> PALIN: (*Dressed as a stereotypical Viking*) It's not that terrible.
>
> CLEESE: No, I meant terribly violent.
>
> PALIN: Oh, yeah![2]

So begins the third season of *Monty Python's Flying Circus* (1972), with the episode "Whicker's World," also called "Njorl's Saga." Emerging from a low heath-dwelling, a fur-clad warrior, Erik Njorl, the priest, strides slowly towards his horse and makes to mount it. Unfortunately, he is hindered by his interminable introductory genealogy, and subsequently cannot get on with the saga and ride

Thomas Spray, Durham University

https://doi.org/10.1515/9781501513886-007

off: "Well I'm afraid we're having a bit of trouble getting this very exciting Icelandic saga started," apologizes the narrator.[3] Luckily for viewers and the BBC, the North Malden Icelandic Saga Society come to the rescue by providing their own copy of the floundering saga. Yet this just leads to further problems. After finally being allowed to ride away on his horse, Erik finds himself lost on the present-day high street of North Malden. Here he is met by the mayor who subsequently launches into a speech on the economic benefits for independent business leaders who might want to relocate to the area. After some harsh words with the society, the BBC resume the program with a more genuine version of the saga. Yet this too leads to further problems, as a dramatic battle scene is obscured by a growing number of warriors holding signs promoting investment opportunities in North Malden. Eventually the saga is scrapped, and the show continues without it.

In the realm of comedy, Monty Python's episode seems a rare example of knowledgeable engagement with the Icelandic sagas. While comedy involving Norsemen is abundant across children's literature, films, satirical journalism, cartoon strips, and football commentary, at first glance few of these instances demonstrate anything deeper than a superficial resemblance to the characters of the *Íslendingasögur* or a superficial understanding of the sagas themselves.[4] Even in cases where the word "saga" is employed, the implication is more often a long-winded tale than anything drawing on medieval narrative elements.[5] Intriguingly, much of the remaining material ("Njorl's Saga" excepted) focuses on a small selection of texts, and the reason for this may lie with the earliest reception of the sagas in translation in Britain, and, in particular, with Njorl's (near) namesake.

Comic reflection on sagas in English began in the late nineteenth century, as new translations were published in increasingly reliable volumes, and the public's thirst for details of Britain's ancestral relations to its Scandinavian neighbors grew concurrently. These nineteenth-century comic narratives lampooned various aspects of Britain's fascination with the north – from northern stereotypes to the eccentricities of the scholars who studied them, from the "golden age" of northern independence to the wild and snow-covered landscapes where it supposedly took place. In doing so, they unwittingly set the tone for the next one hundred and fifty years of comic interaction with the sagas. Accordingly, one contention of this chapter is that while there have been surprisingly few comic treatments of the Icelandic Family Sagas in the English language, Victorian literature has had a demonstrable influence on the extant examples.

By examining the rare comic reimaginings of the sagas as a genre, object of study, supporter of stereotypes, and source of narrative inspiration, one can gauge something of the academic and public atmosphere whence they were created. Or, as the writer Adam Gopnik phrases it, "by entering into a weird book as an empirical document, as something that reports on the world, it allows us to isolate and better understand the act of imagination peculiar to the poet."[6] As jokes force the audience or readers to analyze given social perceptions (in this case our stereotypes of the past and of other cultures) so jokes about the sagas and more widely about Norsemen should assist in reevaluating the present and historical "given" readings of these phenomena.[7] With these points in mind, the chapter will consider the enduring comedic potential of scholars, scenes, and stereotypes of the Icelandic sagas.

"It Was *Burnt Njal* That Was at the Bottom of It"

The increasing interest in Icelandic literature in the latter half of the nineteenth century was encouraged by the publication of George Webbe Dasent's influential translation of *Njáls saga* in 1861.[8] The influence of this translation on the reception of Old Norse literature cannot be overstated: wherever there was a British expedition to Iceland in the late nineteenth century, "it was *Burnt Njal* that was at the bottom of it."[9] Dasent's work remained the only translation of *Njáls saga* for almost a century, and continues to find devotees today. The year before Njorl came to British television screens, *Burnt Njal* was reissued with a foreword by E. O. G. Turville-Petre, who remarked that Dasent had done "more than any other scholar of the nineteenth century to spread the knowledge of old northern literature among English-speaking peoples."[10] The translation's legacy stretched to influencing concepts of academia, ethnic-nationalism, northern stereotypes, translation practice, and Scandinavian travel literature.

It also prompted one of the earliest examples of humor at the expense of the sagas, drawn from the notes of Dasent's own tour of Iceland. These notes were compiled by Charles Cavendish Clifford, MP, under the alias "Umbra," and initially published as *A Tour Twenty Years Ago* and later as part of his *Travels by "Umbra."*[11] The title alone provides some indication of the nature of the work. In English, Clifford's chosen pseudonym "umbra" denotes a "shade," "ghost," or "spirit" (often unwanted) and is derived from the Latin word for "shadow." This coupled with the fact that the tour occurred in 1861, a mere two years earlier, rather than twenty, should convey the untrustworthy nature of the narrator, despite his own claims of rigorous truthfulness.[12]

The fictionalized cast for Umbra's voyage comprised Mr. Archibald McDiarmid (John Francis Campbell), Ragner, Lord Lodbrog (Lord Newry, a student and Irish peer), Mr. X. (invented, although clearly also based on Clifford), Mr. Digwell (John Roche Daykins, Dasent's nephew), and Mr. Darwin, with the last on the list being a barely-disguised Dasent.[13] Of "Darwin" Dasent, Clifford wrote that he had "written a learned book on Northern Antiquities, in recompense of which a Scandinavian potentate created him a Knight of the second class order of the Walrus, the ribbon of which illustrious Order was suspended across his brawny shoulders."[14] In addition to such honors, Darwin's physical and mental constitution matched his chosen subject matter admirably:

> Of Herculean height and strength, with his long black beard descending to his waist, he resembled a Viking of old, and such I conceive he at times supposed himself to be. In fact, so deeply was he imbued with the spirit of antiquity, that a continual antagonism between the past and the present, or rather, I should say, between the imaginary and the real, existed in his breast. He was two gentlemen at once. Though a sincerely religious man, still I cannot help suspecting that in his heart of hearts he looked on Christianity as a somewhat parvenu creed, and deemed that Thor, Odin, Freya, etc., were the proper objects of worship. In dull fact he was an excellent citizen, a householder, paying rates and taxes, an affectionate husband, and the good father of a family; but in the dream, the fancy – "the spirit, Master Shallow" – he was a Berserker, a Norse pirate, ploughing the seas in his dragon-beaked barque, making his trusty falchion ring on the casques of his enemies, slaying, pillaging, burning, ravishing, and thus gratifying a laudable taste for adventure.[15]

The key element to this comic portrait was the perceived conflict between the Viking Age past and the Victorian present. Darwin appeared to be locked in a constant struggle against himself, with a Hyde-like Norseman continually trying to break out from the respectable scholar. "I fear he preferred the glorious dream to the sober reality," remarked Clifford, "I think that he inwardly pined at his own respectability, that he considered himself misplaced in the narrow sphere of duties."[16]

The cartoonish Darwin–Dasent of the narrative is clearly a humorous depiction of the stereotypical northern scholar. This is not unusual for comedy, which frequently targets academics, know-it-alls, and nitpickers. Hot-blooded, hairy, and prone to over-enthusiastic poetic recitals, Darwin proves a tenacious tour-guide. The land of sagas arrived in the late nineteenth century with a considerable deal of sublime literary baggage. Darwin could survey a landscape made famous by Sir Walter Scott and imbued with semi-mythic settlement narratives.[17] Umbra was an unappreciative tourist. At the often-described Þingvellir he refused to play the saga-loving traveler.[18] Darwin, by contrast, was in his element:

> "See that sandy isle in the river. Did two noble chiefs unhappily quarrel, there they met in duel, while their friends and retainers stood on either bank as spectators. There they decided the quarrel with their good broadswords, till one was hailed as conqueror, and the soul of the other flitted towards the halls of Odin, happy even in his fall; for him to

meet the Warrior Maids, him they welcomed to Valhalla, for him poured they the sparkling mead; at least such was the ignorant superstition of these poor men," concluded Darwin, suddenly pulling up, and remembering he was a nineteenth-century man.[19]

His status as a Victorian gentleman proves a grave annoyance to Darwin, frequently interrupting his romantic sensibilities.

During his recital of the dying chant of Ragnar, his companions complain that, "It all seems to have been about killing."[20] After concluding the tale he is once again dragged back to the present:

"Ah, he was a glorious fellow! You will be happy to hear that his sons did avenge his death. They sailed over to Northumberland, and made Ella a spread eagle. Let us hope that our Ragner will tread in the steps of his heroic ancestor."

"God forbid, Mr. Darwin," said I. "Lodbrog, though I doubt not as brave as his namesake, is a most gentle youth. Surely you do not wish him to kill eight Irish barons, and kiss their widows, in one day?"

Darwin cleared his eyes like one awaking from a dream. At last he said, "What a matter-of-fact fellow you are, Umbra! What I meant to express was a hope that Lodbrog would prove a shining example as well as a useful ornament to society."[21]

Darwin is caught in the act, embarrassingly forced to confront his own alter ego.

This occurs with increasing frequency, particularly in his attempts to reconcile the misogyny of his own reimagined Norsemen with the more progressive opinions of his traveling companions. Darwin appears unable to function in proximity to the other sex, possessing all of the chauvinist rhetoric but none of the sexual vigor of his saga heroes.[22] After explaining the use of Þingvellir's infamous "Pool of the Wicked Women" Darwin was asked why there was not a similar pool for wicked men: "he was not aware of any such, and when we inquired if this was fair play for the other sex, and how he reconciled such one-handed justice with the boasted chivalry of the Norse race, he could only reply that women were sometimes very provoking!"[23] This failure to match up to women is a running theme. At Hitardal he gets into a skaldic battle with a local female poet and loses. Darwin offers her the choice of a brooch as a victory prize from a selection he has purchased.[24] The lady takes them all and Darwin curses the evils of women:

"And then there was poor Gunnar."

"What of him?"

"His wife Hallgerda got him into so many scrapes, that he was warned that his life was not safe if he remained in Iceland, but he could not tear himself away. One day his enemies surrounded his house; when he had shot eight, his bowstring broke, and he requested Hallgerda to give him one of her long curls to fit the bow."

"And she gave it like a lady of Carthage?" said Lodbrog.

> "She asked if his life absolutely depended on it. 'Absolutely,' said he. 'Then you will please to remember that you gave me a box on the ear three years ago,' retorted his spouse. And Gunnar was killed before her face."[25]

Darwin sees the saga episode as a clear demonstration of the wicked mindset of a sex with whom he cannot communicate. His companions see it as a lesson against domestic violence.[26] The flaws of accepted perceptions of the noble Norsemen (and indeed of noble Victorians) are inconveniently brought to light.

Where his reimaginings of northern chivalry were subject to questioning, Darwin drew the line at criticism of the sagas themselves, displaying a fierce devotion to the medieval texts.[27] Throughout the narrative Darwin is depicted as having little but Old Norse on his mind. He tells Umbra the plot of *Laxdæla saga* whilst they sit at the site of Kjartan's dwelling; he recites the tale of "Halfred, the Dangerous Bard"; he rails at the group's ignorance of Eddaic lore; he visits the sites of *Eyrbyggja saga*.[28] Yet despite all of this, at the end of their tour his companions seem to be more ignorant of Old Norse literature than when they arrived. On the ride back to Reykjavík, things get heated:

> "Ignorant, soulless being! Are these things not written about in the Saga?"
> "The Saga, Mr. Darwin?" said I. "I believe the Saga to be a humbug!"
> Scarcely had I let this imprudent word escape, than the Herculean frame of my friend was convulsed with passion. His eye glared with fury. Grasping the hammer of Mr. Digwell, which he chanced to have borrowed, he with one blow felled me from my horse. "Die, blasphemer, die!" shouted he, frantic with rage; and I have no doubt he was about to finish my existence, when the earth shook beneath us. A mightier power than – was abroad. A long-extinct volcano, resuming activity, suddenly woke to life. With horrid roar, with hideous belch, a column of mingled fire and smoke arose, and an enormous rocky mass, ninety tons in weight, upheaved three kilometres in air, descending, crushed Mr. Darwin and his horse flat as a pancake.[29]

Darwin's berserk saga-enthusiasm proves his undoing.

Saga Scholars in the Popular Eye

Clifford was by no means alone in his humorous characterization of northern scholars. Old Norse specialists from home and abroad were given equally bizarre descriptions. Bickford Dickinson, writing on the translator Sabine Baring-Gould, remarked that "beneath the surface of his genuinely spiritual nature, and often in conflict with it, lay strange depths that drew him to these dark byways that underlie all folklore."[30] Stefán Einarsson, writing on Eiríkur Magnússon, described him as "a man, a man of the North, a man in character as well as by descent [a] true son of the strong Vikings of old."[31] Elsewhere he further explained that Eiríkur "loved his friends and hated his foes. He had much of the temper of Egill Skallagrímsson who thanks Odin for being able to provoke his lurking foes to open fight ... Thus in a way he was a living illustration of the literature he spent his life in propagating."[32] And those were the complimentary descriptions. Less fortunate scholars might get something akin to Edmund Gosse's description of N. F. S. Grundtvig: "He looked like a troll from some cave in Norway; he might have been centuries old."[33] As if the point had not been stressed enough, Gosse proceeded to compare Grundtvig to a troll (again), an "old Pagan," and a "forgotten Druid."[34] Schizophrenia, extreme violence, and a monstrous aesthetic: in the field of Old Norse scholarship, you are what you read. The comparisons are (unwitting) examples of comedy of opposition. Saga-age imagery is humorous because it is out of place.

That these notions of the Old Norse scholar came together in the late nineteenth century is not surprising. Northern stereotypes were a common literary feature of the Victorian period. Take Mr. Josiah Bounderby of Charles Dickens's *Hard Times* (1854). A resident of northern industrial "Coketown," Bounderby is described, in terms common to both stereotypical northerners and to Icelandic settlers, as a figure who "could never sufficiently vaunt himself a self-made man."[35] The notion of the northerner's humble beginnings and self-sufficiency is ludicrously exaggerated:

> "I hadn't a shoe to my foot. As to a stocking, I didn't know such a thing by name. I passed the day in a ditch, and the night in a pigsty. That's the way I spent my tenth birthday. Not that a ditch was new to me, for I was born in a ditch."
>
> Mrs Gradgrind hoped it was a dry ditch.
>
> "No! As wet as a sop. A foot of water in it," said Mr Bounderby.
>
> "Enough to give a baby a cold," Mrs Gradgrind considered.
>
> "Cold? I was born with inflammation of the lungs, and of everything else, I believe, that was capable of inflammation."[36]

Dasent himself nurtured these stereotypes. He was not merely a victim of Clifford's wit. In his own collection of essays *Jest and Earnest*, Dasent similarly presented himself as a man torn between the respectable world and the wild one, between Victorian Britain and the saga-age North.[37] Saga-scholars became established figures of jest and eccentricity for the general public.[38] As comic characters, they commented on both variability and consistency of stereotypes within northern scholarship.[39]

The Sagasteads: Snarks and Argonauts

If saga scholars were prime targets for satire then the landscape of the sagas was too. Comedy frequently uses the return to a pastoral existence as the premise for humor, and the Victorians began to see the saga-age North as a utopian scene, an Edenic paradise in which a "Golden Age" of freedom and bravery had flourished. Dasent's translation marked a turning point in the focus of Anglo-Scandinavian travel accounts. Most travelers up to 1860 concentrated on Iceland as a site of geological or sociological interest. After 1860 the focus shifted to the literature of Iceland.[40] The number of informed references to the sagas, and to *Njáls saga* in particular, rose notably. With this came a blossoming reverence for the lands of the sagas. Yet the role of comedy is often to allow societies to question and disparage such idealism, and the Victorians were no exception.

William Mitchell Banks traveled to Iceland in 1880, hoping to emulate the tours of writers of the previous decades.[41] His work demonstrates the influence of Dasent's translation, in that it parodies an established popular knowledge of the saga and of Iceland.[42] Banks left for Iceland on June 19 in a party of fifteen travelers – including a designated "Sagaman" – aboard the "Argo." He molded his narrative between Lord Dufferin's earlier writings of the not-so-fearsome North and the open nonsense of Lewis Carroll's *The Hunting of the Snark*.[43] This style of comedy, initiated by Dufferin and described by comic travel writer Tim Moore as a mixture of "aristocratic understatement with Hunter S. Thompson hyperbole," is evident in much of the travel writing on Iceland of the period.[44] It is frequently unintentionally humorous and highly theatrical, as apparent in Frederick Metcalfe's *The Oxonian in Iceland*, where the Icelanders are described as a people living in "dark caverns."[45] Metcalfe warned his readers that the traveler's way was blocked, "not only by dangerous rivers, appalling lava streams, hidden pits of fire, and chasms of ice," but also by fiends of the imagination such as "chimeras dire" and "phantom gorillas."[46] This then was the territory of the renowned saga heroes of old – more Skull Island than Middle Earth.

On the voyage over, Banks was all enthusiasm, providing a *Snark*-esque poem introducing his companions and named "The Cata-log of the Argo: A Saga in Seventeen Snorts" by "Snorro Sknab" ("Banks" backwards).[47] Yet on arriving at the scenes described by numerous saga translations his disappointment was evident. The heroic landscape envisioned by British readers was simply not so: "some were astonished, but there is no use denying that some were not, and the latter were probably in the majority. Insurmountable rocks, arduous passes, gigantic waterfalls, and bottomless crevasses; where were they?"[48] In response to this deflation of expectations, Banks's fourth chapter was a parody of previous accounts of the terrible North.[49] The chapter was accompanied by the same "map" included with the *Snark*, namely a blank sheet with no features, and began with a quote from the fictional *Sniggurer's Saga*: "Thern everw asn osuch Thing [sic]."[50] Banks rewound the clock, and had the expedition start anew in Reykjavík, where group members left behind their gold and wrote a will.[51]

On their way to Geysir, Banks's party entered the terrible region of Burnt Njal – the saga now referred to as a geographical district rather than a tale: "we mounted our horses and rode rapidly forward through the arid and blasted district of Burnt Njal."[52] In this geographical realization of a saga, the earlier writings of masculine adventure and hyperbolic peril were made reality. "Words cannot do justice to the appalling spectacle which burst upon our view. The black and ghastly lava soil, begotten of cycles of ceaseless belching and vomiting from the now extinct crater of Spuemupp, was here riven and gashed as by the spade of a Titan. Before us lay a rent, its depths never fathomed by the plummet of man."[53] They overcome this terrifying obstacle only with the intuition of one of the party ("Mrs. Patchit"), who makes a rope from an unraveled Icelandic woolen sock.[54] Later they become lost in the mysterious "Black Forest of Iceland," where "gigantic trees, fully two feet high, with trunks of half-an-inch in circumference, reared their tall heads all around us."[55] Finally escaping from the perils of Burnt Njal, the group came across a pleasant green pasture. "To rest our eyes upon this, after the weary waste of the Burnt Njal, was an inexpressible relief."[56] Banks ended the chapter with a spoof newspaper article tearing apart his own parody.

Banks's account was not solely meant in jest. He had a deep appreciation for saga literature, and stressed this throughout the narrative.[57] On the return journey Banks remarked that the entire group had been influenced by the literature of the locations visited: "Our minds at that moment were somewhat tinged with Icelandic and Norse romance, and we were full of the reivings and blood-feuds of Njal and Skarphedin, of Kari and Flosi."[58] The disappointment on location was genuine, born jointly out of flourishing overseas interest and decades of unreliable travel accounts. Early travelers to Iceland described fantastical sights to match the tales from the sagas, demonstrating "Iceland on the brain," as Richard Burton put it.[59] Burton accused these writers of constructing a tired narrative "handed down from traveller to traveller" with little adherence to fact.[60] Such accusations went unheeded. The false narrative continued. Burton and Banks may have shared deflated expectations regarding the land of sagas, but their protestations merely denoted the sagas' notoriety. A lampoon implies importance, even canonization. No one writes a parody of an unknown genre.

Something Completely Different?

Evidently, the scholars and scenes of Old Norse literature did not match up to the Victorians' saga-fed imagination. The transformation from heroic saga imagery to everyday reality was the part-comic, part-tragic drama of Victorian saga scholarship. One might expect that an increase in public awareness of the "realities" of the Old North might diminish such sources of potential comedy. Conversely, the comedy of the twentieth century further stressed the contrast between the sagas and modernity.

In terms of the actual narrative, "Njorl's Saga" is a little disappointing for an Old Norse scholar. The sketch has little if any resemblance to the real-life *Njáls saga*. The Njorl of the title is in fact the non-patronymic surname of the priest Erik N-Jorl. The action is over a century later than the original saga's. On the positive side, the sketch does draw on the typical style of saga narratives, in particular with its emphasis on genealogies.[61] This is not unique to *Íslendingasögur*, but the formula is certainly recognizable to saga readers, and is particularly applicable to *Njáls saga*, the first two chapters of which start with extended character introductions, and which has an immensely complicated cast of interrelated characters.[62] Other aspects of the sketch which might be said to derive directly from the sagas include the mention of anonymous authorship, the relatively niche position the tale is said to have in popular culture, and the Scandinavian landscape.[63]

For the most part the humor relies on typical Norse stereotypes such as reveling in violence, the mixed-period medievalism of the costume design, and the dreaded horned helmets. By the end of the episode "Njorl's Saga" resembles a classic scene of swords and sorcery, rather than a family saga. Moreover, as the sketch progresses the comedy does not target recognizable features of the literary genre, but rather constructs a critique of BBC program planners: the unending genealogy is akin to a looped soundtrack or scripting error. Casual use of medieval aesthetic continues throughout the show. Critiquing television advertising culture, the Pythons derive humor from efforts of small contemporary businessmen cumbersomely juxtaposed with epic narrative. The relocation of Erik to the streets of 1970s North Malden is the surreal extreme of this process: a ridiculous combination of modern petty business concerns with medieval grandeur and hardship. Icelandic literature, with its frequent emphasis on the importance of self-reliance, provides a happy comedic antithesis to this atmosphere of friendly assistance and investment opportunities. The steady increase from one extreme towards the other in this sketch (much to the concern of the protagonist Erik) is typical of Monty Python's brand of humor.

As with Banks's preposterous saga-made-terrain and "Darwin" Dasent struggling to work out which century he is in, this episode attempts to deconstruct the notion of the hardy, masculine North, either by taking the notion to its ridiculous extreme or by inserting everyday mundanities. The early model for this humor can be seen in Michael Palin's and Terry Jones's project "The Complete and Utter History of Britain," which ran from January 12 to February 16, 1969.[64] As Palin explained, this was: "a fusion of the academic side of our upbringing and the comedy side: how you look at the world and make sense of it by turning it on its head."[65] Meanwhile, the origins of the Pythons' brief interaction with the sagas lie in the early education of medievalist historian Terry Jones, who was introduced to Old Norse under Bruce Mitchell while at Oxford. Through readings of medieval history, Jones became concerned at the misleading picture people held of the past, and endeavored to rewrite fundamental misinterpretations by exposing the ridiculous nature of modern medievalism.[66] Referring to the late Middle Ages in particular, Jones argues that an "unholy alliance of nineteenth-century novelists and painters with twentieth-century movie-makers" were to blame for erroneous notions of the past.[67] There is arguably a certain aspect of having one's cake and eating it here. The Pythons' image of the sagas is little more than that of the (admittedly self-aware) stereotypical Norsemen, complete with unattractive violence, squalor, and over-the-top costumes. "Njorl's Saga" has an initial element of intellectualism, of academic context, but it is quickly apparent that it requires no subject-specific knowledge to be humorous.[68] Does the terrible Njorl really make viewers question Norse stereotypes, or merely reinforce them?

Stereotypes abound in Jones's 1989 film *Erik the Viking*, which strays from the realm of *Íslendingasögur* and toward *Fornaldarsögur*.[69] Erik, the film's protagonist, lives in the age of Ragnarök. Fenrir has swallowed the sun and humanity is stuck in a seemingly endless (and pointless) cycle of violence.[70] Promised an end to the cycle, Erik sets out to find a magic horn, three blasts on which will deliver him to Asgard, awaken the gods, and bring him safely home again. He is hotly pursued by the casually violent Halfdan the Black (whose real-life namesake was Haraldr Hárfagri's father) and a pair of plotting blacksmiths, worried that the end of Ragnarök will take the bottom out of their market. Along the way the crew must overcome the politics of who sits where on a long ship, father–son antagonism on prematurely going berserk, and the terrifying prospect of an entire civilization of singing pacifists. Erik and his companions inhabit a world in which (to mis-quote Groucho Marx) humor is derived from reason gone berserk.

The comic manipulation of the Norse stereotype in *Erik the Viking* – particularly with its problematic jokes on the perceived culture of rape and violence – is made apparent by its absence in Jones's similarly-titled children's book *The Saga of Erik the Viking* (1983).[71] Here, Erik sets out on a long quest to find the land where the sun goes at night, in a tale clearly modeled on the adventures and travels of his namesake Eiríkr Rauði and his son Leifr Eiríksson in *Eiríks saga rauða* and *Grænlendinga saga*. Accompanied by a trusty band of fellow Vikings including Ragnar Forkbeard (who mirrors his namesake Ragnar Loðbrók by defeating a dragon, albeit using feathered pillows), Sven the Strong, and the wise Thorkhild, Erik successfully overcomes numerous Old Norse-derived obstacles, including surviving trials of fire against an impetuous Thangbrand and relieving a beautiful Freya from three demonic cats.[72] The accompanying players demonstrate Jones's wide knowledge of Norse sagas.[73] There are many literary elements here, but precious few jokes. It appears the comic incarnation of Erik(s) goes hand-in-hand with the formula of extreme violence.

The Last Laugh

This association makes comic interaction with the sagas problematic at best. Numerous works that appear to be humorous reimaginings of the sagas prove to have problems with their source texts, often because of certain inherent negative aspects in our current depiction of saga society and its related medievalism. The 1937 travel compilation *Letters from Iceland*, by W. H. Auden and Louis MacNeice, is one such example. Here, the sagas are treated with grave reverence and attempts by the authors to get enthusiastically entwined with their "gangster virtues" are tempered by their suspicion of fascist influence.[74] MacNeice's "Eclogue from Iceland" appears a fitting subject for the current theme, employing the ghost of Grettir Ásmundarsson as a comically distant comparative figure contemplating life's problems. Yet one could equally argue that Grettir fills the role of philosophical muse, and that the tone of the poem is grandly severe.[75]

In her book *English Poetry and Old Norse Myth*, Heather O'Donoghue demonstrates that the comic and yet often uncomfortable conflict created in comparing a romanticized Norse past and a present concerned with "realism" is a key feature of the work of several Norse-inspired writers, including the contemporary poet Ian Duhig. O'Donoghue remarks, "Duhig's attitude towards the past splits between bloke-ish jokiness and a serious exploration of the place of poetry" while simultaneously constructing a new relationship between the archaic and the contemporary.[76] Using this approach, Duhig's ideas are frequently "expressed through a satirical mode, a debunking of the past" which allows a simultaneous revelry in and criticism of accepted norms of reception.[77] Thus in Duhig's take on the character of Njáll in the poem "Wise, Brave Old Njal" the authorial voice can appear more violent and more cynical than the medieval blood feud it is depicting. Njáll here is an incessant bore, "His chosen weapon was the pointed saying: / 'The arm's joy in the blow is brief'; / 'Seines may miss where purse nets catch'; / 'Birds land on ears of wheat not spears.' / If I was with them I'd have lent a match."[78] The last laugh is a provocatively dark shade of humor. As O'Donoghue notes, there are two sides to this engagement. While Duhig's poetry has an aspect of relief, it would be wrong to classify it as wholly comic. Much like the saga-inspired work of George Mackay Brown, there may be elements of black humor to be gleaned, but the reader is not encouraged to laugh comfortably. The violence and sexuality intrinsic to the northern stereotype must be addressed one way or another.

Children's literature has proven a fertile field for comic reimaginings of potentially inappropriate saga themes. From the peaceful reign of Noggin the Nog to the highly successful franchise *How to Train Your Dragon*, the über-masculinity of the Norsemen has been transformed into thoughtful works which champion morality and intellect.[79] In 2015 the author of the latter, Cressida Cowell, became the first children's author to win *Philosophy Now*'s award for "Contributions in the Fight Against Stupidity": a prize for writers "combating poor reasoning, unexamined assumptions and entrenched habits of thought."[80] Such an approach suggests a promising mode for the comic rewriting of sagas for a variety of progressive ends, rather than adding to the already giddy quantity of "rape and pillage" jokes. British comedian Bridget Christie thus utilizes Norse stereotypes as an example of chauvinist historiography. Her jokes initially appear to follow the set routine of clichés: physicality, pillage, violence. ("What do you call a deaf Viking with one leg? You'd better not call him anything. He can lip-read and will slaughter you. You know what Vikings are like.")[81] Yet the humor derives from Christie's distinctive tone, combined with the recognizable, overused framework of the joke. Her argument demonstrates that feminism (the understood subject of this passage, and indeed of the book) is both pressingly relevant and funny, through demonstrating that Norsemen, at least in the tired format presented here, are neither. The formulaic northerners provide a comically humorless antithesis to comedy of progressive values.

Elsewhere, actual sagas have found their way into modern comedy in equally inventive ways, as shown by a 2013 episode of *The Simpsons* entitled "The Saga of Carl." In this episode, Homer and his colleagues win the lottery, but are alarmed to find that their friend Carl has run off with the winnings to his homeland of Iceland. Following hot on his heels (complete with a copy of travel guide *Lets Go Get Revenge … Iceland*) they discover his terrible reputation amongst Icelanders. It transpires that the notoriously cowardly Carlsons have their own Icelandic saga which paints them as treacherous and spineless: "This saga tells how Carl Carlson's family were the watchmen of our coast, always keeping an eye out for invading hordes," the group are informed at a

Reykjavík museum, "Iceland's safety depended on their vigilance. But the Carlsons failed in their duty. The enemy invaded, laying waste to our lava fields, burning our sweaters, and feasting upon our tiny horses."[82] Carl intends to use the lottery winnings to buy a missing page to the saga (here written entirely in runes), which he hopes will clear his ancestors' name. Although the episode portrays a situation in which the sagas are fit for comedy in their own right, and are not merely considered overly violent or dull, Carl's attempts backfire, as after his friends translate the saga into English, the missing page shows his ancestors to be even more cowardly and treacherous than previously thought. It seems even when a saga is not depicted as an object of tedious antiquarianism, it is not always what one wants it to be. Carl's attempts to find a more honorable version of history remind one of the recurring reimagining of the Saga Age. The result reflects the difficulty in consolidating what one finds in saga narratives with modern values.

Perhaps this too is a laughable exercise though, overestimating the extent to which our fundamental values have changed, assuming that the Nordic past really was the morally dubious sphere shown in numerous works of medievalism. Our modern entertainment often fits the sagas perfectly. Jackson Crawford's humorous take on the *Íslendingarsögur* genre, *Tattúínárdǿla saga*, is one such example, rewriting the *Star Wars* film franchise as an Old Norse text:

> A man was named Grídó, a retainer of King Jabbi; he did not like Hani and he coveted his ship. And when he learned that Hani had had his plunder stolen from him and had gone to Iceland, he asked the king: "Do you like the plunder which Hólmgöngu-Hani brings you, king?"
>
> "I like it well," said King Jabbi.
>
> "Then you would really like it," said Grídó, "If you had all of that which you own, but as it stands you have far from it. It is the much greater part, which Hani keeps to himself. He sends you as a gift three bearskins, but I know for certain that he keeps thirty of them to himself, which you own, and I think that the same must be true of other things. But now I have learned that he has gone to Iceland with a great deal of property which he intends to sell there, and you own all of that. Truly, king, if you gave me his good ship, I would bring you more plunder."
>
> And everything that Grídó said about Hani, his companions bore witness to. It came to the point that King Jabbi was at his angriest.
>
> "Bring me," said King Jabbi, "the ship, and everything that is on it, and kill Hólmgöngu-Hani Sólósson and Tsiubakka the Frisian, if they refuse to come before me."[83]

Crawford's rewriting combines an in-depth knowledge of saga scholarship (he provides extensive notes explaining possible theories for variant redactions, manuscript errors, and intercultural literary influences) with a playful use of the sagas themselves. The above passage humorously details the events leading to the bounty placed on Han Solo's head in *Star Wars: Episode IV – A New Hope* (1977) in the style of an Icelandic saga, but it also clearly mimics the vilifying of Egill Skallagrímsson's uncle Þorólfur from *Egils saga*. In doing so, Crawford not only shares a joke with readers of the original Old Norse saga, but also draws attention to the ease with which these two narratives coalesce.

Perhaps the popular sagas of the modern day are not as far removed from their Norse counterparts as we often like to think. Far from highlighting our own superiority, a more detailed comedic reimagining of the sagas might have the potential to demonstrate the absurdities of our own time, as well as an appreciation of the past.

Bibliography

Primary Sources

Adams, Douglas. *The Long Dark Teatime of the Soul*. London: Heinemann, 1988.

Auden, W. H. and Louis MacNeice. *Letters from Iceland*. London: Faber and Faber, 1985.

Banks, William Mitchell. *A Narrative Voyage of the Argonauts in 1880; Compiled by the Bard from the Most Authentic Records*. Edinburgh: unknown, 1881.

Baring-Gould, Sabine. *Iceland: Its Scenes and Sagas*. London: Smith, Elder, & Co, 1863.

Burton, Richard F. *Ultima Thule; or, A Summer in Iceland*. 2 vols. Edinburgh: William P. Nimmo, 1875.

Carroll, Lewis [Charles L. Dodgson]. *The Annotated Hunting of the Snark*. Edited by Martin Gardner. New York: W. W. Norton & Company, 2006.

Christie, Bridget. *A Book for Her*. London: Penguin, 2016.

[Clifford, Charles Cavendish.] *A Tour Twenty Years Ago*. Southampton: Hampshire Independent Office, 1863.

[Clifford, Charles Cavendish.] *Travels by "Umbra."* Edinburgh: Edmonston and Douglas, 1865.

The Complete Sagas of Icelanders. Edited by Viðar Hreinsson et al. 5 vols. Reykjavík: Leifur Eiríksson, 1997.

Crawford, Jackson. *Tattúínárdøla Saga: If Star Wars Were an Icelandic Saga*. https://tattuinar doelasaga.wordpress.com/2010/03/01/tattuinardoela-saga-if-star-wars-were-an-icelandic-saga/.

Dasent, George Webbe, trans. *The Story of Burnt Njal or Life in Iceland at the End of the Tenth Century*. 2 vols. Edinburgh: Edmonston and Douglas, 1861.

Dasent, George Webbe. "A Fortnight in Faroe." In *Jest and Earnest: A Collection of Essays and Reviews*, vol. 1, pp. 1–104. London: Chapman and Hall, 1873. [originally published in the *North British Review*. May 1864].

Dasent, George Webbe. *Popular Tales from the Norse. New Edition with a Memoir by Arthur Irwin Dasent*. Edinburgh: David Douglas, 1903.

Dasent, George Webbe, trans. *The Story of Burnt Njal*. With an introduction by E. O. G. Turville-Petre. London: J. M. Dent & Sons, 1971.

Dickens, Charles. *Hard Times*. Edited by Kate Flint. London: Penguin Books, 2003.

Dufferin, The Marquess of [Frederick William Hamilton Temple Blackwood]. *Letters from High Latitudes: Being Some Account of a Voyage in 1856 in the Schooner* Yacht *"Foam" to Iceland, Jan Meyen, and Spitzbergen*. London: John Murray, 1856. 11th ed. 1903.

Duhig, Ian. *The Lammas Hireling*. London: Picador, 2003.

Erik the Viking. Dir. Terry Jones. London: UIP, 1989. Film.

Halldór Kiljan Laxness. *Sjálfstætt folk*. Reykjavik: E. P. Briem, 1934–1935.

Halldór Kiljan Laxness,. *Gerpla*. Reykjavik: Helgafell, 1952.

Hooker, William Jackson. *Journal of a Tour in Iceland, in the Summer of 1809*. 2nd ed. London: Longman, Hurst, Rees, Orme, and Brown; and John Murray, 1813.

Jones, Terry. *The Saga of Erik the Viking*. London: Pavilion Books, 1983.

Metcalfe, Rev. Frederick. *The Oxonian in Iceland; or, Notes of Travel in that Island in the Summer of 1860, with Glances at Icelandic Folklore and Sagas*. London: Longman, Green, Longman, and Roberts, 1861.

Milo, Erika. "Norse of Course." http://www.odins-gift.com/poth/N/norseofcourse.htm.

Moore, Tim. *Frost on My Moustache: The Arctic Exploits of a Lord and a Loafer*. London: Abacus, 2000.

"The Saga of Carl." *The Simpsons*. Season 24, episode 21. Los Angeles: Fox, 2013. Television.

Waller, Samuel Edward. *Six Weeks in the Saddle: A Painter's Journal in Iceland* [with Illustrations]. London: Macmillan & Co, 1874.

"Whicker's World." *Monty Python's Flying Circus*. Series 3, episode 1. 27: 00.London: BBC, 1972. Television.

Þorðar saga Hreðu. In *Kjalnesinga saga*. Íslenzk fornrit 14, ed. Jóhannes Halldórsson, pp. 161–226. Reykjavík: Hið íslenzka fornritafélag, 1959.

Secondary Sources

Aronstein, Susan. "When Civilization Was Less Civilized: *Erik the Viking*." In *The Vikings on Film: Essays on Depictions of the Nordic Middle Ages*, edited by Kevin J. Harty, pp. 72–82. Jefferson, NC: McFarland, 2011.

Bergson, Henri. "Laughter." In *Comedy*, edited by W. Sypher, pp. 59–190. Baltimore: Johns Hopkins University Press, 1980.

Cederlund, Carl Olof. "The Modern Myth of the Viking." *Journal of Maritime Archaeology* 6, no. 1 (2011): 5–35.

Chapman, Graham, John Cleese, Terry Gilliam, Eric Idle, Terry Jones and Michael Palin. *The Pythons Autobiography by The Pythons*. London: Orion Books, 2005.

Cowan, Edward J. "Icelandic Studies in Eighteenth and Nineteenth Century Scotland." *Studia Islandica* 31 (1972): 107–51.

Dickinson, Bickford H. C. *Sabine Baring-Gould: Squarson, Writer and Folklorist, 1834–1924*. Newton Abbot: David & Charles, 1970.

Gosse, Sir Edmund William. *Northern Studies*. London: Walter Scott, 1890.

Gosse, Sir Edmund William. *Sir Edmund Gosse's Correspondence with Scandinavian Writers*. Edited by Elias Bredsdorff. London, Melbourne and Toronto: William Heinemann, 1960.

Hughes, Rebecca. "10 Unusual Degree Courses." *Which? University*. March 31, 2015. http://university.which.co.uk/advice/choosing-a-course/10-unusual-university-degrees.

Hume, Kathryn. "Beginnings and Endings in the Icelandic Family Sagas." *The Modern Language Review* 68, no. 3 (1973): 593–606.

Jón Karl Helgason. *Echoes of Valhalla: The Afterlife of the Eddas and Sagas*. Translated by Jane Victoria Appleton. London, Reaktion Books, 2017.

Jones, Terry and Alan Ereira. *Terry Jones' Medieval Lives*. London: BBC Books, 2005.

Nuttall, A. D. *Dead from the Waist Down: Scholars and Scholarship in Literature and the Popular Imagination*. New Haven, CT: Yale University Press, 2003.

O'Donoghue, Heather. *English Poetry and Old Norse Myth: A History*. Oxford: Oxford University Press, 2014.

"Saga, n.1." *OED Online*. Oxford University Press, June 2017. http://www.oed.com/.

Sigurdson, Erika Ruth. "Violence and Historical Authenticity: Rape (and Pillage) in Popular Viking Fiction." *Scandinavian Studies* 86, no. 3 (2014): 249–67.

Spray, Thomas. "Of Schooners and Sagamen: Anglo-Icelandic Tourism in the Nineteenth Century." In *Sea Lines of Communication: Construction*, edited by Joel Found, Maria Newbery and Ayan Salaad, pp. 161–74. Southampton: Southampton Marine and Maritime Postgraduate Group, University of Southampton, 2015.

Stefán Einarsson. "Eiríkr Magnússon and His Saga-Translations." *Scandinavian Studies and Notes* 13, no. 2 (1931): 17–32.

Stefán Einarsson. "Eiríkur Magnússon: The Forgotten Pioneer." In *Studia Centenalia. In honorem memoriae Benedikt S. Þórarinsson*, edited by B. S. Benedikz, pp. 33–50. Reykjavík: Typis Ísafoldianis, 1961.

Steinbauer, Anja. "News: December 2015 / January 2016." *Philosophy Now*. https://philoso phynow.org/issues/111/News_December_2015_January_2016#1.

Virno, Paolo. *Multitude: Between Innovation and Negation*. Los Angeles: Semiotext(e), 2008.

Wawn, Andrew. *The Vikings and the Victorians: Inventing the Old Norse in Nineteenth-Century Britain*. Cambridge: D. S. Brewer, 2000.

Weitz, Eric. *The Cambridge Introduction to Comedy*. Cambridge: Cambridge University Press, 2009.

Wilmut, Roger. *From Fringe to Flying Circus: Celebrating a Unique Generation of Comedy 1960–1980*. London: Eyre Methuen, 1980.

Notes

1. Douglas Adams, *The Long Dark Teatime of the Soul* (London: Heinemann, 1988); *Erik the Viking*, dir. Terry Jones (London: UIP, 1989), Film.
2. "Whicker's World," *Monty Python's Flying Circus*, series 3, episode 1, 27:00 (London: BBC, 1972), Television.
3. Ibid.
4. This essay deals exclusively with reception in the English language. For a masterful comedic reimagining of the *Íslendingasögur* in modern Icelandic see Halldór Kiljan Laxness's *Gerpla* (Reykjavik: Helgafell, 1952).
5. The *Oxford English Dictionary* notes that the modern definition encompasses "a long and complicated (account of a) series of more or less loosely connected events," "saga, n.1," *OED Online*, Oxford University Press, June 2017, http://www.oed.com/.
6. Adam Gopnik, in Lewis Carroll, *The Annotated Hunting of the Snark*, ed. Martin Gardner (London: W. W. Norton & Company, 2006), p. xvii.

7. Paolo Virno writes that a joke "puts into focus, in its own way, the variety of alternatives that come forth in applying a norm." Paolo Virno, *Multitude: Between Innovation and Negation* (Los Angeles: Semiotext(e), 2008), p. 103.

8. Or to give it its full title, *The Story of Burnt Njal or Life in Iceland at the End of the Tenth Century*, trans. George Webbe Dasent, 2 vols. (Edinburgh: Edmonston and Douglas, 1861).

9. Waller, Samuel Edward, *Six Weeks in the Saddle: A Painter's Journal in Iceland* [with Illustrations] (London: Macmillan & Co., 1874), p. 1. On Waller's relationship with Dasent's work see Jón Karl Helgason, *Echoes of Valhalla: The Afterlife of the Eddas and Sagas*, trans. Jane Victoria Appleton (London: Reaktion Books, 2017), pp. 105–7 and 113–15.

10. E. O. G. Turville-Petre (1957), in *The Story of Burnt Njal*, trans. George Webbe Dasent (London: J. M. Dent & Sons, 1971), p. xi.

11. Charles Cavendish Clifford, *A Tour Twenty Years Ago* (Southampton: Hampshire Independent Office, 1863); *Travels by "Umbra"* (Edinburgh: Edmonston & Douglas, 1865), pp. 1–164.

12. "I remember that Darwin once said, that to tell a saga wrong was a great offence against public morality! Therefore, O Reader, place implicit faith in my narrative." Clifford, *Travels by "Umbra,"* pp. 9–10.

13. He is not the only northern scholar. The "Mr. Jonson of Copenhagen" mentioned in chapter seven is Grímur Thompsen, Dasent's collaborator and guide in matters of Old Norse, see A. I. Dasent in George Webbe Dasent, *Popular Tales from the Norse, New Edition with a Memoir by Arthur Irwin Dasent* (Edinburgh: David Douglas, 1903), pp. xxix–xxxiii and Edward J. Cowan, "Icelandic Studies in Eighteenth and Nineteenth Century Scotland," *Studia Islandica* 31 (1972): 107–51 at 140.

14. Clifford, *Travels by "Umbra,"* p. 3.

15. Ibid., pp. 3–4. Andrew Wawn introduces the same passage on Dasent, although as a truth-bearing description rather than a comic rewriting, see *The Vikings and the Victorians: Inventing the Old Norse in Nineteenth-Century Britain* (Cambridge: D. S. Brewer, 2000). There is certainly much truth in the reimagined Dasent; his real-life counterpart was an outspoken supporter of slavery, anti-Semitism, Aryan science, and sexism.

16. Clifford, *Travels by "Umbra,"* p. 4.

17. Ibid., p. 8.

18. "I was not astonished – not at all – though perhaps the most remarkable spot in the world was beneath my feet; but I had been so sedulously instructed that I was to be surprised, that the foretold sensation could not take effect; a surprise expected cannot be a surprise." Ibid., p. 11.

19. Ibid., p. 14.

20. Ibid., p. 57.

21. Ibid., pp. 58–59.

22. An inability to socialize with women is a common feature of Victorian portraits of scholars, see A. D. Nuttall, *Dead from the Waist Down: Scholars and Scholarship in Literature and the Popular Imagination* (New Haven, CT: Yale University Press, 2003).

23. Clifford, *Travels by "Umbra,"* p. 15.

24. The passage mirrors Þangbrandr's unsuccessful exchange of skaldic verses with Steinunn in *Njáls saga*, chapter 102.

25. Clifford, *Travels by "Umbra,"* p. 121.

26. This is not so much out of respect as fear on the part of the young Lodbrog, who has promised six different ladies back home in Britain that he will bring them the feathers of

a Great Auk, only to discover to his alarm that the bird has been extinct since 1844 (Ibid., pp. 122–28).

27. This fierce devotion extends to his own translation. He gives Mr. X a copy to read. "'My dear X.,' said Darwin, 'you shall read my translation of the Saga. In it you will find, for the first time adequately rendered into English, the song of the Valkyries, that is, the Cor[p] se Choosers, or, as some term them, the Fatal Sisters'," Ibid., p. 23. Infuriatingly, after they go for a walk around the hot-springs at Geysir, the party return to find that Mr. X. has fallen asleep over the work. "'The brute! The insensate brute!' cried the enraged author. 'He has fallen asleep over the most interesting chapter in the whole Saga! … He should die for this; for a lesser offence Ella shut up Ragner in a dungeon with snakes; he should die'," Ibid., p. 25. Fortunately, Darwin decides that killing a sleeping man would be particularly unjust, pointing to Sigurðr's death in *Völsunga saga* as an example of the terrible consequences when people are assaulted in their bed. Mr. X. later wakes up, not realizing the close run with death he has just had. Ibid., p. 25.

28. Ibid., pp. 60–62; 64–70; 75; 77.

29. Ibid., p. 156.

30. Bickford H. C. Dickinson, *Sabine Baring-Gould: Squarson, Writer and Folklorist, 1834–1924* (Newton Abbot: David & Charles, 1970), p. 40.

31. Stefán Einarsson, "Eiríkur Magnússon: The Forgotten Pioneer," in *Studia Centenalia. In honorem memoriae Benedikt S. Þórarinsson*, ed. B. S. Benedikz (Reykjavík: Typis Ísafoldianis, 1961), pp. 33–50 at p. 49.

32. Stefán Einarsson, "Eiríkr Magnússon and His Saga-Translations," in *Scandinavian Studies and Notes* 13, no. 2 (1931): 17–32 at 31.

33. Sir Edmund William Gosse, *Northern Studies* (London: Walter Scott, 1890), p. 200.

34. Ibid., pp. 200–201 and p. 206. This was in fact the first and only time Gosse met Grundtvig, as it was the latter's last public sermon; he died a mere six weeks later, see Sir Edmund William Gosse, *Sir Edmund Gosse's Correspondence with Scandinavian Writers*, ed. Elias Bredsdorff (London, Melbourne and Toronto: William Heinemann, 1960), p. 4.

35. Charles Dickens, *Hard Times*, ed. Kate Flint (London: Penguin Books, 2003), p. 20. Bounderby's claims to a humble origin mirror those of Monty Python's "Yorkshiremen" sketch over a hundred years later. As a further comparison, consider Halldór Kiljan Laxness's destructively stubborn Guðbjartur Jónsson, of *Sjálfstætt folk* (Reykjavik: E. P. Briem, 1934–1935).

36. Dickens, *Hard Times*, p. 21. The sagas themselves ridicule over-valued self-sufficiency. In *Þórðar saga Hreðu* Skeggi advises Ásbjörn Þorsteinsson not to court Sigrid Þórdsdóttir, as her brothers are considered particularly violent men: "Ásbjörn svarar: 'Þat hafða ek ætlat at vera sjálfráði fyrir hverjum manni hér í landi.' Skeggi segir: 'Þat ferr sem reynist, hvárt þú ert þar einhlítr, áðr þér skilið, ef þú leitar nökkut á þá framar en þeim líkar'" ["I thought I would be my own master in this country," Asbjorn answered. [Skeggi said:] "We'll see just how 'independent' you are by the time they've finished with you"] *Þórðar saga Hreðu*, in *Kjalnesinga saga*, ed. Jóhannes Halldórsson, Íslenzk fornrit 14 (Reykjavík: Hið íslenzka fornritafélag, 1959), pp. 161–226 at p. 177, trans. Katrina C. Attwood, in *The Complete Sagas of Icelanders*, ed. Viðar Hreinsson et al. (Reykjavík: Leifur Eiríksson, 1997), vol. 3, chap. 3, p. 368. Clearly independence is only useful alongside common sense.

37. George Webbe Dasent, "A Fortnight in Faroe," in *Jest and Earnest: A Collection of Essays and Reviews*, vol. 1 (London: Chapman and Hall, 1873), pp. 1–104 at p. 104.

38. A 2015 article offering advice on choosing university degrees listed the study of Old Norse in the top ten "unusual degree courses" alongside such subjects as puppetry, spa management, equestrian psychology, and the educational context of Harry Potter, see Rebecca Hughes, "10 Unusual Degree Courses," *Which? University*, March 31, 2015. http://university.which.co.uk/advice/choosing-a-course/10-unusual-university-degrees.

39. See Henri Bergson, "Laughter," in *Comedy*, ed. W. Sypher (Baltimore: Johns Hopkins University Press, 1980), pp. 59–190.

40. See Thomas Spray, "Of Schooners and Sagamen: Anglo-Icelandic Tourism in the Nineteenth Century," in *Sea Lines of Communication: Construction*, ed. Joel Found, Maria Newbery and Ayan Salaad (Southampton: Southampton Marine and Maritime Postgraduate Group, University of Southampton, 2015), pp. 161–74.

41. See in particular Rev. Frederick Metcalfe, *The Oxonian in Iceland; or, Notes of Travel in that Island in the Summer of 1860, with Glances at Icelandic Folklore and Sagas* (London: Longman, Green, Longman, and Roberts, 1861); Sabine Baring-Gould, *Iceland: Its Scenes and Sagas* (London: Smith, Elder, & Co, 1863); Waller, *Six Weeks in the Saddle*; and Richard F. Burton, *Ultima Thule; or, A Summer in Iceland*, 2 vols. (London and Edinburgh: William P. Nimmo, 1875).

42. Banks himself recommended Dasent's book, urging any reader who wanted to get to grips with Iceland's history to "read the *Saga of Burnt Njal*, which, if he has any soul in him, will make his very toes tingle and his pulse beat higher at every fresh battle and duel." William Mitchell Banks, *A Narrative Voyage of the Argonauts in 1880; Compiled by the Bard from the Most Authentic Records* (Edinburgh: unknown, 1881), p. 13.

43. Banks, *Narrative Voyage*, p. 34. The Marquess of Dufferin (alias Frederick William Hamilton Temple Blackwood), *Letters from High Latitudes: Being Some Account of a Voyage in 1856 in the Schooner Yacht "Foam" to Iceland, Jan Meyen, and Spitzbergen* (London: John Murray, 1856) was one of Victorian Britain's most successful travel accounts. By the early 1900s it had gone through over ten editions. Banks, *Narrative Voyage*, p. 3.

44. Tim Moore, *Frost on My Moustache: The Arctic Exploits of a Lord and a Loafer* (London: Abacus, 2000), p. 6. Ostensibly a modern rewriting of Lord Dufferin's book, Moore's volume lacks the background reading and enthusiasm to provide any real commentary on the sagas. When he does discuss the genre (pp. 59 and 135–36), it is with thinly veiled disdain. Dufferin, by comparison, made well-informed references to both of the two sagas translated into English at the time of his voyage (George Stephens's translation of *Friðþjófs saga* and Walter Scott's *Eyrbyggja saga* extracts) and displayed significant knowledge of the sagas of Norwegian kings. The fact that Moore misses the first of these sagas, when his boat to Norway is the *Fridtjofen*, is particularly inexcusable, ibid., p. 152.

45. Metcalfe, *Oxonian in Iceland*, p. vi; Metcalfe's narrative was strongly influenced by Dasent's translation, and Dasent's introduction relied equally heavily on Metcalfe's field notes for geographical details.

46. Ibid.

47. Ibid., p. 12.

48. Ibid., pp. 32–33; Banks's comments were not an exaggeration of previous accounts: compare with Metcalfe, "To get drowned, to break your neck or your limbs, to be maimed, to be boiled alive, or, at the least, to be prostrated with rheumatism, are quite on the cards," ibid., p. 382.

49. Banks notably adapted the title from Dufferin's work: "Flecks from the Foam of an Icelandic Fritterer," by "Lord W. M. B.," Banks, *Narrative Voyage*, p. 38.

50. Ibid., p. 38. "He had brought a large map representing the sea, / Without the least vestige of land: / And the crew were much pleased when they found it to be / A map they could all understand." Carroll, *Hunting of the Snark*, p. 27.

51. Banks, *Narrative Voyage*, p. 41.

52. Ibid., p. 42.

53. Ibid., p. 41. Compare with a sobering description of Almannagjá from 1809: "a monstrous chasm, extending as far as we could see ... A more rugged pass can hardly be conceived," William Jackson Hooker, *Journal of a Tour in Iceland, in the Summer of 1809*, 2nd ed. (London: Longman, Hurst, Rees, Orme, and Brown; and John Murray, 1813), pp. 102–3.

54. Banks, *Narrative Voyage*, pp. 41–42.

55. Ibid., p. 46.

56. Ibid., p. 44.

57. See, for example, ibid., p. 75.

58. Ibid., p. 109.

59. Burton, *Ultima Thule*, vol. 1, p. x.

60. Ibid., p. 78.

61. This notion of taking a characteristic element of something and expanding it was a common feature of *Monty Python's Flying Circus*, the sketches of which frequently functioned on the basis of taking "ideas to their logical conclusion and then beyond that for a considerable way." Roger Wilmut, *From Fringe to Flying Circus: Celebrating a Unique Generation of Comedy 1960–1980* (London: Eyre Methuen, 1980), p. 198.

62. Kathryn Hume notes that even amongst scholars of Old Norse "disparagement of the sagas' extremities remains the standard attitude" and that the "intervening centuries have made the family history boring or even repellent," "Beginnings and Endings in the Icelandic Family Sagas," *The Modern Language Review* 68, no. 3 (1973): 593–606 at 593 and 597.

63. Although in fact this is filmed in Glen Coe in Scotland. It has also been suggested that the fact that the later sketches of the episode are set in a courtroom reflects the fact that Njáll was a lawyer, but this seems tenuous at best, particularly when one considers that the courtroom was a stock set for many of the Pythons' scenes and that the court depicted in those scenes in the "Njorl's Saga" episode is not particularly Nordic in nature.

64. Wilmut, *Fringe to Flying Circus*, p. 189.

65. Graham Chapman et al., *The Pythons Autobiography by The Pythons* (London: Orion Books, 2005), p. 181.

66. Ibid., p. 70. The term "medieval" was used in Jones's childhood home, as it frequently is in the media, as a "term of abuse," see Terry Jones and Alan Ereira, *Terry Jones' Medieval Lives* (London: BBC Books, 2005), p. 6.

67. Jones and Ereira, *Medieval Lives*, p. 13.

68. See Wilmut, *Fringe to Flying Circus*, pp. 216–17.

69. See Jón Karl Helgason, *Echoes of Valhalla*, pp. 182–83. Incidentally, "Erik Viking" was the name of the guitarist and vocalist in 1990s Swedish rock band "Odins Änglar," see Carl Olof Cederlund, "The Modern Myth of the Viking," *Journal of Maritime Archaeology* 6, no. 1 (2011): 5–35 at 25.

70. The comically pointless violence in *Erik the Viking* reflects a common delight taken in masculine aggression which characterizes depictions of Norsemen; this other side to the

comic appreciation of the sagas often resembles what Eric Weitz terms the "Grotesque" – comic narrative which "involves a conscious effort on the part of the producer to unsettle the reader or spectator," Eric Weitz, *The Cambridge Introduction to Comedy* (Cambridge: Cambridge University Press, 2009), p. 148.

71. On the attempted rape scene in *Erik the Viking* see Erika Ruth Sigurdson, "Violence and Historical Authenticity: Rape (and Pillage) in Popular Viking Fiction," *Scandinavian Studies* 86, no. 3 (2014), 249–67 at 249–51, and Susan Aronstein, "When Civilization Was Less Civilized: *Erik the Viking*," in *The Vikings on Film: Essays on Depictions of the Nordic Middle Ages*, ed. Kevin J. Harty (Jefferson, NC: McFarland, 2011), pp. 72–82 at pp. 72–75.

72. In the film it is Erik who defeats the dragon of the North Sea using his father's ancestral pillow. Erik's trial against Thangbrand in chapter 12 somewhat mirrors Þangbrandr's trial by fire in *Njáls saga*, chap. 103.

73. In names such as Olaf Hamundson and Gunnar Longshanks, Jones manages to combine elements of Iceland's most-beloved *Íslendingasaga* hero.

74. W. H. Auden and Louis MacNeice, *Letters from Iceland* (London: Faber and Faber, 1985), p. 117.

75. Ibid., pp. 122–33.

76. Heather O'Donoghue, *English Poetry and Old Norse Myth: A History* (Oxford: Oxford University Press, 2014), p. 208.

77. Ibid., p. 209.

78. Ian Duhig, *The Lammas Hireling* (London: Picador, 2003), p. 36. For other examples of Duhig's engagement with Norse literature see "Shanty," "A Line From Snorri Sturluson," and "Saga" in *Nominies* (Newcastle upon Tyne: Bloodaxe Books, 1998); and (via Wagnerian imagery) "The Badly Loved," in *The Bradford Count* (Newcastle upon Tyne: Bloodaxe Books, 1991).

79. Erika Milo's poem "Norse of Course: Egil's Seussian Saga" takes the notion one step further, using the context of the style of Theodor (Dr.) Suess Geiselson to highlight the simplistic elements of the Old Norse saga of Egill Skallagrímsson. See http://www.odins-gift.com/poth/N/norseofcourse.htm.

80. Anja Steinbauer, "News: December 2015 / January 2016," *Philosophy Now*, https://philosophynow.org/issues/111/News_December_2015_January_2016#1. (The previous year's winner was Noam Chomsky.)

81. Bridget Christie, *A Book for Her* (London: Penguin, 2016), p. 57.

82. "The Saga of Carl," *The Simpsons*, season 24, episode 21 (Los Angeles: Fox, 2013), Television. The show either intentionally or unwittingly misuses the patronymic system throughout the episode.

83. Jackson Crawford, "Tattúínárdǿla Saga: If Star Wars Were an Icelandic Saga," *Tattúínárdǿla saga* (blog), March 1, 2010, https://tattuinardoelasaga.wordpress.com/2010/03/01/tattuinardoela-saga-if-star-wars-were-an-icelandic-saga/.

Heather O'Donoghue

7 The One that Got Away in Old Norse Myth, *Moby-Dick*, and the Work of Hugh MacDiarmid

The World Serpent in Old Norse Myth

The story of Thor's encounter with the World Serpent out at sea is one of the best known episodes in Old Norse myth. The thirteenth-century Icelandic scholar and poet Snorri Sturluson tells it in his *Prose Edda* as a thrilling, half-comic, cartoonish adventure.[1] Thor, having been humiliated by a giant into thinking he was picking up a cat with its back arched and extended, when he was actually pulling, fruitlessly, on one of the mighty loops of the World Serpent itself, determines to get his revenge by hooking the World Serpent on a fishing line. He recruits another giant, the cowardly Hymir, to row him way out to sea, and baits his line with an ox head. The World Serpent takes the bait, and the god struggles mightily to land his enormous prize. The World Serpent's head finally breaks the surface of the waves, and for a few brief moments of heart-stopping tension, Thor and the Miðgarðsormr glare ferociously at each other, until the giant Hymir cuts the line, and ends the stand-off. In fury, Thor lashes out at Hymir, and he topples overboard. This is a story of the One that Got Away.

Snorri's entertaining narrative is not the only version of this confrontation in Old Norse tradition. There are references to it in two much older, pre-Christian, poems;[2] in one of the poems of the Poetic Edda;[3] and there are a number of Viking age stone carvings of the encounter, from Sweden, Denmark, and the British Isles.[4] Clearly it powerfully engaged the imaginations of artists who knew it. Unsurprisingly, the most successful representation is the one in which the World Serpent itself is not pictured: on the Danish Hørdum stone, Thor's boat is held at a terrifying angle against an unseen weight at the end of a long slender line which runs right off the edge of the stone.[5]

The many poetic names for the Miðgarðsormr are indicative of the creature's cosmic significance. The element *garðr* itself denotes an enclosed space, here the *miðgarðr* or middle-earth itself, of which the serpent is the encloser. Other poetic terms for the World Serpent are variations on this: "the edge-fish of all lands," for instance, or "the stiff boundary rope of the world."[6] The World

Heather O'Donoghue, University of Oxford

https://doi.org/10.1515/9781501513886-008

Serpent is the living manifestation of the circular horizon itself; like a vast belt, it holds the earth together. And with this one appalling exception which so mesmerized poets and artists, it is always just out of reach, just out of view. When Thor hooked it on his line, and dragged it up from the deep, the whole created world hung by a thread. And the serpent will not resurface until *ragnarök*, the Old Norse apocalypse, when it will meet again its old adversary, the god Thor, in the great battle at the end of the world.[7]

The broad-brush similarities between this story and Herman Melville's novel *Moby-Dick* are at once evident. But of course all man (or god) versus monster stories are liable to resemble one another in very general terms, and such encounters exist in most cultures, from the biblical references to God and Leviathan to struggles with serpent creatures in ancient mythologies all over the world. However, the parallels between Moby Dick and the Miðgarðsormr are not by any means limited to the outlines of their two stories. I will divide what follows into three sections: an introductory presentation of a set of often quite playful incidental allusions to Old Norse, showing Melville's perhaps unexpected familiarity with Old Norse; a detailed analysis of how Melville figures Captain Ahab as Thor, and the White Whale as a type of Miðgarðsormr; and finally, a discussion of close parallels in the two accounts of the climactic encounter, the not-landing of the monster, the One that Got Away.[8] As an epilogue, I will briefly consider the image of the sea-monster in the poetry of the Scots writer Hugh MacDiarmid, who read both *Moby-Dick* and the Old Norse mythological texts, and develops the hunt for the monster as an allegory of literary creativity – precisely what Melville himself claims to reject as a reading of *Moby-Dick*.

Incidental Allusions

With its encyclopedic and self-consciously didactic scope, there are lots of references to Icelandic (and Greenlandic) whaling and whalers in *Moby-Dick*, with whaling described as a "wild Scandinavian vocation,"[9] and the Spouter Inn, where Ishmael's story begins, said to be "cold as Iceland," perhaps a natural enough comparison in the context of a whalers' hostel.[10] By the same token, an incidental reference to Greenlandic whaling ships is attributed to a memoir perfectly plausibly entitled "A Voyage among the Icebergs, in quest of the Greenland Whale, and incidentally for the rediscovery of the Lost Icelandic Colonies of Old Greenland" although it has been suggested that this title is a playful fabrication.[11] Finally, in his negotiations with the landlord of the

Spouter Inn, Ishmael describes himself as being "as cool as Mt Hekla in a snow storm" – this clever reference to the Icelandic volcano once supposed to be the earthly mouth of Hell indicating that he is "hot within...but outwardly cool."[12]

Other allusions to Scandinavian history and Old Norse literature are equally playful. For example, in the very first chapter, amongst the "old established" families of North America listed by Melville – the Van Rensselaers, the Randolphs – we find the Hardicanutes.[13] Hardicanute was a historical figure, the last Danish king of England, the son of Canute the Great; he died without issue having reigned for only two years. As far as I can determine, his name was never perpetuated, in New England or anywhere else. This looks like a learned joke on Melville's part.

Given the prominence of actual Scandinavian whaling, incidental allusions in *Moby-Dick* are only to be expected, and I'm not going to go through them all. It is worth noting, though, that while it may be appropriate, given their trade, that Quaker whalers with their biblical names, like Bildad, are said to have "a thousand bold dashes of character, not unworthy a Scandinavian sea-king"[14] blended in with their Christian heritage, Melville seems particularly to stress the pre-Christian, pagan nature of whaling: the *Pequod*'s harpooners, for example, are a more "heathenish" crew than Ishmael has ever come across, and this is somehow connected with the "wild Scandinavian vocation" in which they are engaged.[15]

In chapter 16, there is an intriguingly arcane reference to Old Norse literature. Melville relates that Ahab's ship the *Pequod* has been ornamented in a manner "pertaining to the wild business that for more than half a century she had followed" – whaling. The boat has been inlaid as intricately as "Thorkill-Hake's carved buckler or bedstead."[16] This is ultimately a reference to chapter 119 of *Njáls saga*, in which Thorkell haki ("Thorkel Bully") appears as a very minor character. The editors of annotated editions and online resources have sometimes muddled this Thorkell with Thorkell inn Hávi, the Tall, who was part of the pre-Conquest Scandinavian invasion of England.[17] The saga author introduces him when the sons of the eponymous Njáll try to enlist the support of powerful men when they need to put up an intimidating defense against a murder charge. According to the saga, "Thorkel Bully had travelled abroad and earned fame in other lands." In Finland, "he met with a creature half-man, half-beast, and fought it off for a long time, and the fight ended with Thorkel killing the creature. Then he went south to Estonia; there he killed a flying dragon...he had these mighty feats of his carved above his bed closet and on a stool in front of his high seat."[18] Thorkell's exploits thus constitute a very carefully appropriate comparison for the heroic whale-hunting themes of the *Pequod*'s ornamentations. But ironically, in the saga itself Thorkell refuses to help the sons of Njáll, and when insulted and challenged by the most threatening of them, at once backs down and is out of the story. Thorkell haki and his mighty exploits turn out to be a damp squib, a bathetic non-event in a saga otherwise packed with dramatic confrontations and violent denouements.

Melville could scarcely have known the saga well enough to pluck out this bizarre little episode, for George Webbe Dasent's celebrated and popular translation of the saga was not published until a decade after the writing of *Moby-Dick*. Erik Yngvar Thurin is understandably puzzled, noting that Melville's reference does not precisely echo the Old Norse (which does not mention the buckler, or shield) and he suggests that Melville "knew the passage in question only from hearsay."[19] However, the reference can be traced to the eighteenth-century Swedish bishop Uno von Troil's *Letters on Iceland*; Melville's uncertainty as to where exactly the carvings were clearly derives from von Troil's (rather confused) account of Icelandic customs, which Melville evidently half-remembered, and not from the saga itself.[20]

Other references are equally arcane, but more obviously mock-learned: we are informed, for example, that "In old Norse times, the thrones of the sea-loving Danish kings were fabricated, saith tradition, of the tusks of the narwhale."[21] I have yet to find the source of this information,[22] but Melville's knowing archaism betrays his lack of total seriousness. Similarly, in chapter 24, Ishmael's narrative voice stoutly defends the "aesthetically noble associations" of whaling against the supposed (and slyly self-reflexive) taunt that no-one famous has written about whaling by citing "no less a prince than Alfred the Great, who, with his own royal pen, took down the words from Other, the Norwegian whale-hunter of those times."[23] This is a reference to the Old English translation of Orosius's *Historia adversum paganos*, long believed to be by Alfred himself, which contains a passage additional to the original in which (supposedly) King Alfred describes a visit to his Anglo-Saxon court by a Norwegian merchant and hunter, Ohthere (in Old Norse, Óttarr).[24] The opening chapters of *Moby-Dick* provide clear evidence that Melville was no mean medievalist; in addition, he seems to be setting up a distinctively medieval Scandinavian dimension to the context of Ishmael's voyage. This is a voyage both intellectual and physical: Ishmael says that "a whale-ship was my Yale College and my Harvard,"[25] and that he "swam through libraries" to tell his story[26] – this must be Melville's voice as much as Ishmael's.

Melville's debt to Old Norse becomes even more pronounced as we turn to the links Melville establishes between Captain Ahab and the Old Norse god Thor, on the one hand, and between the Great White Whale and the World Serpent, on the other.

Ahab as Thor

What primarily motivates Captain Ahab in his pursuit of the Great White Whale is revenge – for Moby Dick bit off Ahab's leg. Ahab is driven to a kind of madness by a passionate and overwhelming desire to be revenged on the monster: he had "purposely sailed upon the present voyage with the one only all-engrossing object of hunting the White Whale."[27] Further, "ever since that almost fatal encounter, Ahab had cherished a wild vindictiveness against the whale."[28] Similarly, Thor sets out on the fishing expedition in order to be avenged on the Miðgarðsormr. He is humiliated at the court of the giant Útgarða-Loki, who arranges for him to be tested in a series of unachievable tasks, including lifting up what appears to be the arched back of a cat, but is actually one of the great loops of the unseen Miðgarðsormr. We are struck not so much by the impossibility of the task, as by Thor's frustration about it, and his mortification at being fooled. The episode ends as follows: "But the fact is that he had then made up his mind to seek an opportunity for a meeting to take place between him and the Midgard serpent, as later occurred."[29] Snorri moves at once to the story of their encounter at sea.

Melville also plays with Thor's associations with a hammer, and with thunder – most obviously in chapter 119, during a great storm. Much is made of the thunder and lightning, and a gale "hammers" at the ship. Finally, to clinch the sequence, Starbuck asks of the darkness "Who's there?" and Ahab answers "Old Thunder!"[30] This is the most dramatic articulation of this particular link between Thor and Ahab, but in fact Ahab's very introduction into the narrative establishes the association. Ishmael and his friend Queequeg meet a mysterious stranger who speaks obliquely but clearly ominously about the captain of the *Pequod*, the ship they have just signed up for: " – ye hav'n't seen Old Thunder yet, have ye?" Ishmael responds, "Who's Old Thunder?" and the stranger replies "Captain Ahab."[31] The identification could hardly be more emphatically stated.

The Great White Whale and the World Serpent

Melville's sustained references to the ancient history of sea-monsters and their depiction in art and sculpture (for example in chapters 55, 57, and 82)[32] strongly suggest that the ageless Great White Whale is a contemporary manifestation of what was known to the Viking world as the World Serpent. Although Melville does not mention the Miðgarðsormr by name, the way he mythologizes – even deifies – the White Whale, and repeatedly alludes to its immense size, makes the identification inevitable. In chapter 41, for instance, we are told that "Moby Dick was ubiquitous...he had actually been encountered in opposite latitudes at one and the same instant of time,"[33] and further, that he was "not only ubiquitous, but immortal (for immortality is but ubiquity in time)."[34] This is a monster of mythic proportions, and that Melville had clearly envisaged the Miðgarðsormr as it is presented in Old Norse myth is evident from a reference in an earlier novel *Mardi*: "How undulated the horizon; like a vast serpent with ten thousand folds coiled all around the globe."[35]

The Climactic Encounter

Thor had three encounters with the World Serpent. The first – in the hall of the giant Útgarða-Loki – though abortive, is used by Snorri to motivate the second, the famous fishing expedition, which is in fact the only ocean-going encounter of the three. The third is at *ragnarök*, when the Miðgarðsormr flails its way up on to the land, and it results in the death of both parties. This final encounter of course depends on the World Serpent surviving the fishing expedition, and being accorded the role of the One that Got Away (which incidentally is not the case in all of the Old Norse texts). But the mutual survival version of the story does give rise to the dramatic, and at the same time anti-climactic, moment of the line being cut, and of course this is a major difference between the Old Norse story and the narrative of Melville's novel. In *Moby-Dick* there is no anti-climactic line cutting – the key element in the whole episode – and indeed, there could not be, for had there been, then Ahab and the *Pequod* would have survived the encounter, and the whole novel would have been completely different.

But Melville did not abandon the idea and the drama of the line cutting altogether, for there are no fewer than *three* accounts in *Moby-Dick* of how a line was cut so that a ship might be saved and the whale escape.

The first of these, in chapter 54, is quite perfunctory: in a story within the Story, told at the Golden Inn, the "Town-Ho's Story," a whale is harpooned, and threatens to drag down the boat,

> but a sudden terrific downward jerking of the boat quickly brought [the mariner's] knife to the line. He cut it; and the whale was free.[36]

Far more dramatic, and very like Snorri's account, is the version in chapter 81:

> With a grating rush, the three lines flew around the loggerheads with such a force as to gouge deep grooves in them...[the crew] caught repeated smoking turns with the rope to

hold on; till at last...the gunwales of the bows were almost even with the water; while the three sterns titled high in the air...Seems it credible that by three such thin threads the great Leviathan was suspended?[37]

The whale is caught, but its dead weight threatens to capsize the boat. Again, the improbably steep angle at which the boat is held – so vividly captured by the artist of the Danish Hørdum stone – is emphasized by Melville:

To cross to the other side of the deck was like walking up the steep gabled roof of a house. The ship groaned and gasped.[38]

Stubb the second mate shouts:

"Hold on, hold on, won't ye?...By thunder, men, we must do something...run one of ye for a prayer book and a pen-knife, and cut the big chains."

"Knife? Aye, aye," cried Queequeg, and seizing the carpenter's heavy hatchet, he leaned out of a porthole, and steel to iron, began slashing at the largest fluke-chains. But a few strokes, full of sparks, were given...With a terrific snap, every fastening went adrift: the ship righted, the carcase sank.[39]

It is worth noting Stubb's mention of thunder here.

The third version of cutting the line is different again; it is another mutual survival story. Pip has become entangled in the line, and

Tashtego stood in the bows...Snatching the boat-knife from its sheath, he suspended its sharp edge over the line, and turning towards Stubb, exclaimed interrogatively, "Cut?" Meantime Pip's blue, choked face plainly looked, Do, for God's sake! All passed in a flash. In less than half a minute, this entire thing happened.

"Damn him, cut!" roared Stubb; and so the whale was lost and Pip was saved.[40]

So if Melville denied himself the anti-climactic line-cutting in the final scene of the whale hunt, he nonetheless created three other versions of how a line was controversially cut to prevent a catastrophe. Further, throughout the novel, Ahab's crew – especially Starbuck and Stubb – are depicted as being unwillingly but helplessly caught up in Ahab's obsessive and vengeful hunt for the Great White Whale, just as Thor's companion, the giant Hymir, is shown to be unhappy about the hunt for the World Serpent. In fact, listening to his captain raving about his inability to resist the call of revenge, Starbuck is "blanched to a corpse's hue with despair,"[41] a clear echo of the way the giant Hymir "changed colour, went pale."[42] Much earlier in the novel, Starbuck laments both Ahab's obsession and his own inability to resist it: "I think I see his impious end; but feel that I must help him to it."[43] Only with hindsight can we see the full import of his next metaphor: "Will I, nill I, the ineffable thing has tied me to him; tows me with *a cable I have no knife to cut.*"[44] I will discuss the importance of the concept of ineffability shortly.

Interestingly, Melville also allowed himself three versions of the celebrated stand-off stare between Thor and the World Serpent in the closing moments of the Old Norse narrative, as Moby Dick rises up from the ocean to face his tormentor. As Snorri tells it, "And one can claim that a person does not know what a horrible sight is who did not get to see how Thor fixed his eyes on the serpent, and the serpent stared back up at him, spitting poison."[45] As Melville tells it, when Ahab closes in on the whale,

> Moby Dick moved on, still withholding from sight the full terrors of his submerged trunk, entirely hiding the wrenched hideousness of his jaw. But soon the fore part of him slowly rose from the water...the grand god revealed himself.[46]

Very shortly after this, as Ahab

> peered down and down into [the] depths, he profoundly saw a white living spot no bigger than a white weasel, with wonderful celerity uprising...and then there were plainly revealed two long crooked rows of white, glistening teeth...It was Moby Dick's open mouth...The glittering mouth yawned beneath the boat like an open-doored marble tomb.[47]

And finally,

> The bluish pearl-white of the inside of the jaw was within six inches of Ahab's head...With unastonished eyes Fedallah [Ahab's mysterious sidekick, and perhaps alter ego] gazed.[48]

These two sets of parallels, both enforced by triple repetition, are in my view impossible to dismiss. But at this point it may be worth mentioning one example of how the major generic differences between myth and novel may have made Melville's construction of these parallels a difficult task. In the myth, the whole cosmos seems to comprise Thor, the giant, the Miðgarðsormr, and the ocean. There is no other physical context, and no other living being. Thor rows out into the ocean, and thus, with the implicit inevitability of myth, it seems inconceivable that he and the giant will not find the monster. But the real – that is, novelistic – world is different, and Melville must go to considerable lengths to render at all plausible the possibility that given the run of all the oceans of the world, Ahab and Moby Dick will encounter one another. He addresses the problem directly: "it might seem an absurdly hopeless task thus to seek out one solitary creature in the unhooped oceans of this planet."[49] Most of chapter 44 is given over to rationalizing this difficulty.

One of the most intriguing aspects of *Moby-Dick* is the contrast between the bloody, almost documentary realism of the whale hunt, and the ineffability of Ahab's own quarry, Moby Dick himself. Even when he is detailing depictions of sea-monsters through the ages, Melville explains their great variety as follows:

you must needs conclude that the great Leviathan is that one creature in the world which must remain unpainted to the last. True, one portrait may hit the mark much nearer than another, but none can hit it with any very considerable degree of exactness.[50]

Moby Dick is elusive in more than just the physical sense. Elsewhere, Ishmael warns against the hubris of supposing that one might fully imagine such a beast from its physical remains: "How vain and foolish, then, thought I...to try to comprehend aright this wondrous whale, by merely poring over his dead, attenuated skeleton."[51] And I have already noted the physical impossibility of Moby Dick's cosmic ubiquity: that "he had actually been encountered in opposite latitudes at one and the same instant of time."[52]

But Melville insisted – although almost certainly disingenuously – that his novel was not "a monstrous fable, or still worse and more detestable, a hideous and intolerable allegory."[53] So I will not – at least, not here – pursue the claim that the hunt for Moby Dick is an allegory of literary creativity, and that the perfect literary artifact can never be "landed." However, as we shall see, when the Scottish poet Hugh MacDiarmid picked up the story of the Miðgarðsormr from his extensive reading of Old Norse literature and mythology and evidently linked it to his knowledge of Melville's novel – MacDiarmid knew Melville's work and in fact mentions him by name in "A Drunk Man Looks at the Thistle"[54] – the ungraspability or impalpability of the monster is the aspect of the material he engages with: the One that Got Away.[55]

Hugh MacDiarmid's Great Serpent

A World Serpent crops up a number of times in the poetry of Hugh MacDiarmid. In an early poem, "Sea-Serpent," MacDiarmid's monster has a strange status as half-abstraction, the unifying principle of God's first creation, and half-living thing – it "walloped in rings." Mysteriously, the serpent is simply too immense to be seen – "tint as the mid-day sun is tint / In the glory o' its rays."[56] In a very striking echo of *Moby-Dick*, MacDiarmid describes how the presence of a big fish may be evident only from what MacDiarmid terms "keethins" – a disturbance on the surface of the water – while Melville notes that while no "landsman" would suspect the presence of a whale, the experienced whaler would recognize "a troubled bit of greenish white water" and some "atmospheric waving and curling" above the submerged monster.[57]

What MacDiarmid makes of this mysterious serpent in his poem "To Circumjack Cencrastus, or, the Curly Snake" – note the name, from the Latin *circum jacere* (to lie encircling) – is even more abstract: it evokes what is in-effable – a principle like the creative life force of "Sea-Serpent," or even the poetic imagination itself.[58] Like the Miðgarðsormr, Cencrastus, always out of reach and barely apprehended at best, is also the One that Gets Away. Throughout the poem MacDiarmid imagines the poet as fisherman who – to quote Julian Meldon D'Arcy – "may struggle desperately with the monster, but must never actually land it, for to do so would signify the poet's doom as well as the serpent's."[59] At *ragnarök*, Thor will finally kill the Miðgarðsormr, but will die himself in the attempt.

Already in "A Drunk Man Looks at the Thistle" – drunk on the mead of poetry? – MacDiarmid acknowledges the hubris inherent in trying to capture this great thought-serpent. Early on in the poem, he cannily observes that "Content to glimpse its loops I dinna ettle / To land the sea serpent's sel' wi' ony gaff"[60] – a clear contrast with Thor's rash and almost catastrophic revenge attack on the Miðgarðsormr, and with Captain Ahab's maddened determination to capture the monster.

MacDiarmid tells a little anecdote in his autobiography *Lucky Poet* (1943) about his childhood in Langholm, when

> my brother and I were angling. He had hooked a trout and was greatly excited. My father nipped over to advise him in playing it, but by the time he reached my brother's side the trout had got off the hook. Instantly there was a tremendous splash; my brother had plunged into the pool after it.[61]

But MacDiarmid had made much more of this incident in a short story – "Andy," published in the Glasgow Herald in 1927.[62] Andy – MacDiarmid's brother – hooks the trout – "By jings, it's a whopper" – and the concentration on his face as he tries to land the fish is

> like a thunderclood – as if there was naethin' in the warld but him and this wallopin' troot and the need to land it.[63]

The scale has suddenly turned cosmic. Andy

> rung in till his rod was like a hauf-hoop and his line as ticht as the gut o' a fiddle – and there was its heid! It was a whopper and nae mistak'!...Snap! the line broke...Andy dived into the pool heid first.[64]

And with that one vivid interjection – "snap!" – we are back with the crew of the *Pequod*.

So we have seen the story of Thor and the World Serpent not only used by MacDiarmid as a symbol in modernist metaphysical poetry but also appropriated as ostensible autobiography. This in itself is a striking similarity with Herman Melville's curious – unique, in fact – blend of poetry and autobiography in *Moby-Dick*.

Further Parallels

I have drawn attention to some of the most striking parallels between *Moby-Dick* and the Old Norse story of the Miðgarðsormr. But I have only scratched the surface of Melville's debt to Old Norse, and haven't even begun to work out how Melville incurred it. As Erik Yngvar Thurin notes, Merton M. Sealts Jr., in *Melville's Reading: A Check-List of Books Owned and Borrowed*, with some additions and changes in *Pursuing Melville*, provides few clues, let alone answers.[65] However, I end with a few intriguing further parallels.

Melville several times describes how Ahab has customized the *Pequod* so as to accommodate his ivory leg the more securely to prop himself up firmly on deck (see chapter 50, for instance).[66] This is reminiscent of Önundr *tréfótr* (that is, wooden leg) in the Old Norse *Grettis saga*, a redoubtable Viking who similarly wedges his wooden leg on the deck of his boat when he is at sea.[67] When his grandson Grettir, the hero of the saga, undertakes a sea voyage, as Ishmael does, he too describes a mutinous crew, given to the satirical mocking of the captain.[68]

To turn back to Old Norse mythology, the dramatic scene in which Ahab consults the whale's head as an oracle – "Speak, thou vast and venerable head...and tell us the secret thing that is in thee...O head! thou hast seen enough to split the planets"[69] – recalls the god Odin who consults the head of the mysterious figure Mimir, in whose well wisdom and knowledge are contained.[70] And perhaps more strangely still, Melville describes in detail how Queequeg, close to death with a fever, orders the construction of his own coffin on board the *Pequod*. Queequeg recovers, but in the novel's epilogue, Ishmael tells us that when the *Pequod* sinks, Queequeg's coffin remains afloat, and Ishmael is saved from the wreck by clinging to this strange lifebuoy.[71] How odd, then, that in the Old Norse Eddic poem *Vafþrúðnismál*, we hear that "Countless years before the earth was created" a giant called Bergelmir was born, and placed in a box.[72] According to Snorri's retelling of the myth, when the cosmic giant Ymir was murdered by the sons of Bor, the blood from his wounds caused an almighty flood, and all the frost giants were washed away – except for one, Bergelmir, who with his wife, like Noah, was saved by climbing into a wooden box.[73] The sense of the Old Norse word for this box is uncertain, but the meaning "coffin" is possible.[74]

Finally, we might consider the bizarre episode of the hawk and the flag at the novel's denouement. It is such a strange passage that it is nearly impossible to paraphrase, so I shall quote it in full. The *Pequod* is sinking fast, when suddenly

> a red arm and a hammer hovered backwardly uplifted in the open air, in the act of nailing the flag faster and yet faster to the subsiding spar. A sky-hawk that tauntingly had followed the main-truck downwards from its natural home among the stars, pecking at the flag, and incommoding Tashtego there; this bird now chanced to intercept its broad fluttering wing between the hammer and the wood; and simultaneously feeling that ethereal thrill, the submerged savage beneath, in his death-grasp, kept his hammer frozen there; and so the bird of heaven, with archangelic shrieks, and his imperial beak thrust upwards, and his whole captive form folded in the flag of Ahab, went down with his ship.[75]

Obviously we cannot attribute every collocation of hawks and hammers to Old Norse influence.[76] Moreover, the dragging down of the "bird of heaven" with its "imperial" beak plainly has a number of allegorical possibilities. And yet, this whole episode is strongly evocative of the Old Norse tradition of the raven banner, which appears in a number of forms throughout medieval English and Old Norse literature. It is first mentioned in the Anglo-Saxon Chronicle for 878, and later accounts describe how the raven seems to flap its wings as if alive if the impending battle was to be a victory.[77]

This miscellaneous collection of Old Norse allusions – to saga, myth, and legend, sources widely separated in the literary and historical record – may be tenuous when regarded individually, but have a clear cumulative force. However, the sustained, close, and various parallels between *Moby-Dick* and the Old Norse myth of Thor and the World Serpent demonstrate beyond question Melville's knowledge and use of Old Norse sources in the writing of his novel.

In conclusion, I would like to add that this piece is no more than a cursory account of one strand in a literary relationship. No doubt there are more parallels in *Moby-Dick* itself than I have documented here. I have alluded to one reference to the World Serpent in another of Melville's novels, *Mardi*; I do not know how many Norse-derived allusions there may be elsewhere in his work.[78] I concluded this piece with some gestures towards possible evidence in *Moby-Dick* of Melville's Old Norse reading outside the story of Thor and the World Serpent, and doubtless this could be extended. And finally, as we have seen with the writing of Hugh MacDiarmid, Melville's own work had an influential afterlife. All this remains for others to explore.

Bibliography

D'Arcy, Julian Meldon. *Scottish Skalds and Sagamen: Old Norse Influence on Modern Scottish Literature*. East Linton, UK: Tuckwell Press, 1996.

FunTrivia. http://www.funtrivia.com/askft/Question124212.html.

Grettis saga. Translated by George Johnston as *The Saga of Grettir*. In *Three Icelandic Outlaw Sagas*, edited by Anthony Faulkes, pp. 69–263. London: Viking Society for Northern Research, 2014.

Húsdrápa. In *Poetry from Treatises on Poetics*, edited by Kari Ellen Gade and Edith Marold, vol. 1, pp. 402–24. Skaldic Poetry of the Scandinavian Middle Ages 3. Turnhout: Brepols, 2017.

Hymiskviða. In *The Poetic Edda*, edited by Ursula Dronke, vol. 3, pp. 67–108. Oxford: Clarendon Press, 1969–2011.

Lukman, Niels. "The Raven Banner and the Changing Ravens: A Viking Miracle from Carolingian Court Poetry to Saga and Arthurian Romance." *Classica et Medievalia* 19 (1958): 133–51.

MacDiarmid, Hugh. *Lucky Poet: A Self-Study in Literature and Political Ideas*. London: Methuen, 1943.

MacDiarmid, Hugh. *Complete Poems*. Edited by Michael Grieve and W. R. Aitken. Harmondsworth, UK: Penguin, 1985.

MacDiarmid, Hugh. *Annals of the Five Senses and Other Stories, Sketches and Plays*. Edited by Roderick Watson and Alan Riach. Manchester: Carcanet, 1999.

Melville, Herman. *Mardi and A Voyage Thither*. Edited by Harrison Hayford, Hershel Parker and G. Thomas Tanselle. The Writings of Herman Melville. The Northwestern-Newberry Edition, vol. 3. Evanston, IL: Northwestern University Press, 1970.

Melville, Herman. *Moby-Dick, or The Whale*. Edited by Harrison Hayford, Hershel Parker and G. Thomas Tanselle. The Writings of Herman Melville. The Northwestern-Newberry Edition, vol. 6. Evanston, IL: Northwestern University Press, 1988.

Melville, Herman. *Moby-Dick or The Whale*. Edited by David Herd. Ware, UK: Wordsworth Classics, 2002.

Njal's Saga. Translated by Robert Cook. London: Penguin, 2001.

O'Donoghue, Heather. "Miðgarðsormr." *Archipelago* 3 (2009): 20–33.

O'Donoghue, Heather. *English Poetry and Old Norse Myth: A History*. Oxford: Oxford University Press, 2014.

The Old English History of the World: An Anglo-Saxon Rewriting of Orosius. Edited by Malcolm R. Godden. Cambridge, MA: Harvard University Press, 2016.

Parker, Eleanor. *Dragon Lords: The History and Legends of Viking England*. London: IB Tauris, 2018.

The Poetic Edda. 2nd ed. Translated by Carolyne Larrington. Oxford: Oxford University Press, 2014.

Ragnarsdrápa. In *Poetry from Treatises on Poetics*. Edited by Kari Ellen Gade and Edith Marold, vol. 1, pp. 27–46. Skaldic Poetry of the Scandinavian Middle Ages 3. Turnhout: Brepols, 2017.

Snorri Sturluson. *Edda*. Translated by Anthony Faulkes. London: Dent, 1992.

Snorri Sturluson. *Edda: Skáldskaparmál*. Edited by Anthony Faulkes. London: Viking Society for Northern Research, 1998.

Snorri Sturluson. *Edda: Prologue and Gylfaginning*. Edited by Anthony Faulkes. London: Viking Society for Northern Research, 2005.

Sørensen, Preben Meulengracht. "Þorr's Fishing Expedition." In *The Poetic Edda: Essays on Old Norse Mythology*, edited by Paul Acker and Carolyne Larrington, pp. 119–38. London: Routledge, 2002.

Thurin, Erik Yngvar. *The American Discovery of the Norse: An Episode in Nineteenth-Century American Literature*. London: Associated University Presses, 1999.

Vafþrúðnismál. Edited by Tim William Machan. Durham, NC: Durham Medieval Texts, 1988.

Notes

1. Snorri Sturluson, *Edda: Prologue and Gylfaginning*, ed. Anthony Faulkes (London: Viking Society for Northern Research, 2005), pp. 43–45; for a translation see Snorri Sturluson, *Edda*, trans. Anthony Faulkes (London: Dent, 1992), pp. 46–47.
2. *Ragnarsdrápa* and *Húsdrápa*, in *Poetry from Treatises on Poetics*, ed. Kari Ellen Gade and Edith Marold, Skaldic Poetry of the Scandinavian Middle Ages 3 (Turnhout: Brepols, 2017), vol. 1, pp. 27–46 and 402–24.
3. *Hymiskviða*, in *The Poetic Edda*, ed. Ursula Dronke (Oxford: Clarendon Press, 1969–2011), vol. 3, pp. 67–108.
4. Preben Meulengracht Sørensen, "Þorr's Fishing Expedition," in *The Poetic Edda: Essays on Old Norse Mythology*, ed. Paul Acker and Carolyne Larrington (London: Routledge, 2002), pp. 119–38.
5. Ibid., p. 126.
6. See Dronke, *Poetic Edda*, vol. 3, pp. 94–100, and Snorri Sturluson, *Edda: Skáldskaparmál*, ed. Anthony Faulkes (London: Viking Society for Northern Research, 1998), vol. 1, pp. 14–17 (*Edda*, trans. Faulkes, pp. 72–74).
7. Snorri, *Edda: Prologue and Gylfaginning*, p. 50 (*Edda*, trans. Faulkes, p. 54).
8. For an invaluable exploration of some of Melville's Old Norse references, see Erik Yngvar Thurin, *The American Discovery of the Norse: An Episode in Nineteenth-Century American Literature* (London: Associated University Presses, 1999), chap. 4, pp. 61–76. Thurin is primarily concerned with Melville's references to Viking "sea-kings," and though he mentions the story of Thor and the World Serpent, he does not pursue the parallel in any detail.
9. Herman Melville, *Moby-Dick, or The Whale*, ed. Harrison Hayford, Hershel Parker and G. Thomas Tanselle, The Writings of Herman Melville: The Northwestern-Newberry Edition, vol. 6 (Evanston, IL: Northwestern University Press, 1988), p. 123. Page references are to this edition of the novel.
10. Melville, *Moby-Dick*, p. 14.
11. Ibid., p. 157; see for example Herman Melville, *Moby-Dick or The Whale*, ed. David Herd (Ware, UK: Wordsworth Classics, 2002), p. 477, n. 115.
12. Melville, *Moby-Dick*, p. 18, and n. 18.25, p. 833.
13. Ibid., p. 6.
14. Ibid., p. 73.
15. Ibid., pp. 122–23.
16. Ibid., p. 69.

17. See for instance the note in Melville, *Moby-Dick*, ed. Herd, p. 474, n. 62, or the website FunTrivia: http://www.funtrivia.com/askft/Question124212.html.
18. *Njal's Saga*, trans. Robert Cook (London: Penguin, 2001), pp. 202–3.
19. Thurin, *American Discovery of the Norse*, p. 156, n. 20. Thurin notes that many of the Old Norse references are "hidden," so it is not surprising that his piece is not a comprehensive account of Old Norse influence.
20. Melville, *Moby-Dick*, p. 839, n. 69.39.
21. Ibid., p. 129.
22. Thurin speculates on the possibility of "oral tradition" here, but recognizes that it was an "obscure" one (Thurin, *American Discovery of the Norse*, p. 156, n. 23).
23. Melville, *Moby-Dick*, p. 111.
24. Malcolm R. Godden, ed., *The Old English History of the World: An Anglo-Saxon Rewriting of Orosius* (Cambridge, MA: Harvard University Press, 2016), pp. 36–49.
25. Melville, *Moby-Dick*, p. 112.
26. Ibid., p. 136.
27. Ibid., p. 186.
28. Ibid., p. 184.
29. Snorri, *Edda: Prologue and Gylfaginning*, p. 43 (*Edda*, trans. Faulkes, p. 46).
30. Melville, *Moby-Dick*, p. 505.
31. Ibid., p. 92.
32. Ibid., pp. 260–71 and 361–63.
33. Ibid., p. 182.
34. Ibid., p. 183.
35. Herman Melville, *Mardi and A Voyage Thither*, ed. Harrison Hayford, Hershel Parker and G. Thomas Tanselle, The Writings of Herman Melville, The Northwestern-Newberry Edition, vol. 3 (Evanston, IL: Northwestern University Press, 1970), pp. 37–38. For a survey of Viking references in *Mardi* see Thurin, *American Discovery of the Norse*, pp. 63–64.
36. Melville, *Moby-Dick*, p. 257.
37. Ibid., pp. 355–56.
38. Ibid., p. 359.
39. Ibid., p. 359.
40. Ibid., p. 413.
41. Ibid., p. 545.
42. Snorri, *Edda: Prologue and Gylfaginning*, p. 45 (*Edda*, trans. Faulkes, p. 47).
43. Melville, *Moby-Dick*, p. 169.
44. Ibid., p. 169 (my italics).
45. Snorri, *Edda: Prologue and Gylfaginning*, p. 45 (*Edda*, trans. Faulkes, p. 47).
46. Melville, *Moby-Dick*, pp. 548–49.
47. Ibid., p. 549.
48. Ibid., p. 550.
49. Ibid., p. 199.
50. Ibid., p. 264.
51. Ibid., p. 453.
52. Ibid., p. 182.
53. Ibid., p. 205.

54. Hugh MacDiarmid, *Complete Poems*, ed. Michael Grieve and W. R. Aitken (Harmondsworth, UK: Penguin, 1985), vol. 1, pp. 81–167 at p. 135.
55. See Heather O'Donoghue, "Miðgarðsormr," *Archipelago* 3 (2009): 20–31, and *English Poetry and Old Norse Myth: A History* (Oxford: Oxford University Press, 2014), pp. 175–81.
56. MacDiarmid, *Complete Poems*, vol. 1, pp. 48–51 at p. 49.
57. Melville, *Moby-Dick*, p. 222.
58. MacDiarmid, *Complete Poems*, vol. 1, pp. 181–292.
59. Julian Meldon D'Arcy, *Scottish Skalds and Sagamen: Old Norse Influence on Modern Scottish Literature* (East Linton, UK: Tuckwell Press, 1996), p. 96.
60. MacDiarmid, *Complete Poems*, vol. 1, p. 87.
61. Hugh MacDiarmid, *Lucky Poet: A Self-Study in Literature and Political Ideas* (London: Methuen, 1943), p. 225.
62. Hugh MacDiarmid, *Annals of the Five Senses and Other Stories, Sketches and Plays*, ed. Roderick Watson and Alan Riach (Manchester: Carcanet, 1999), pp. 170–74.
63. Ibid., p. 173.
64. Ibid., p. 173.
65. Thurin, *American Discovery of the Norse*, p. 156, n. 20. But see the reference to Uno von Troil above, n. 20.
66. Melville, *Moby-Dick*, pp. 229–31.
67. *Grettis saga*, chaps. 2–4; see Anthony Faulkes, *Three Icelandic Outlaw Sagas* (London: Viking Society for Northern Research, 2014), pp. 69–263 at pp. 72–77.
68. *Grettis saga*, chap. 17, in Faulkes, *Three Icelandic Outlaw Sagas*, pp. 98–103.
69. Melville, *Moby-Dick*, pp. 311–12.
70. Snorri, *Edda: Prologue and Gylfaginning*, p. 17 (*Edda*, trans. Faulkes, p. 17).
71. Melville, *Moby-Dick*, p. 573.
72. *Vafþrúðnismál*, ed. Tim William Machan (Durham, NC: Durham Medieval Texts, 1988), p. 65, st. 35 (my translation).
73. Snorri, *Edda: Prologue and Gylfaginning*, p. 11 (*Edda*, trans. Faulkes, p. 11).
74. For discussion see Carolyne Larrington, trans., *The Poetic Edda* (Oxford: Oxford University Press, 2014), p. 288.
75. Melville, *Moby-Dick*, p. 572.
76. Thurin notes that red is "Thor's colour" but makes nothing of the hawk (*American Discovery of the Norse*, pp 70–71).
77. Niels Lukman, "The Raven Banner and the Changing Ravens: A Viking Miracle from Carolingian Court Poetry to Saga and Arthurian Romance," *Classica et Medievalia* 19 (1958): 133–51. For an authoritative and impressively scholarly account of the whole phenomenon, see Eleanor Parker, *Dragon Lords: The History and Legends of Viking England* (London: IB Tauris, 2018).
78. Thurin's chapter on Melville would be a good place to begin such an investigation: *American Discovery of the Norse*, pp. 60–76.

Richard North

8 Death ere the Afternoon: *Jómsvíkinga saga* and a Scene in Hemingway's *For Whom the Bell Tolls*

It is sometimes thought that the Icelandic sagas inspired the hard-boiled prose of Ernest Hemingway (1899–1961). Although there is nothing to show that he read translations of these, I shall argue that a motif in the tale told by Pilar about her husband's role in a series of executions in *For Whom the Bell Tolls*, chapter 10, is ultimately derived from the climax of *Jómsvíkinga saga*.[1] Let us see the comparison, then the suggested link.

Pilar's Tale and *Jómsvíkinga saga:* A Comparison

The motif in question is a heroic topos in which each warrior of an elite facing serial execution must put his courage to the ultimate test. The motif appears as a relatively small part of the action in *For Whom the Bell Tolls*, a novel which is set in May 1937 in the middle of the Spanish Civil War (1936–1939).[2] Hemingway's hero, Robert Jordan, is at once an American Hispanist professor, Republican sympathizer, and expert in explosives. The last skill puts him into a mission behind Nationalist lines to blow up a bridge in a pass in the Guadarrama mountains between Segovia and the north of Madrid. Having scouted the site and made his rendezvous with a band of guerrillas, Jordan settles down to wait, knowing that the bridge may not be blown until his commander, General Golz of the International Brigades, has launched a long-planned offensive. During this interval the resolve of the group's leader, Pablo, begins to waver and in chapter 10, while Jordan waits in the guerrillas' cave, he hears a tale about Pablo from the man's wife, the formidable Gypsy Pilar. As aware as others are of Pablo's unsuitability for the mission, Pilar aims to tell Jordan what a fine leader her husband was when he liberated a town at the beginning of the war. The night before the attack, according to Pilar, Pablo's men arrested all the fascists in the town. At dawn, having imprisoned them in the town hall, Pablo deals with the local Civil Guard. Having surrounded the barracks and killed all policemen inside and outside, Pablo

Richard North, University College London

https://doi.org/10.1515/9781501513886-009

organizes two lines from the courthouse door to the edge of a cliff, between which the town's mayor, landowners, and finally priest are made to pass under the blows of flails, each till he stumbles or is carried to the edge to be thrown to his death in the gorge. Motive for these murders is shown to be mostly drink, financial envy, or personal dislike; what starts as an orderly ritual descends into anarchy.

It is in the Civil Guard prelude that our parallel lies. Pilar says that the *guardias civiles* (Civil Guard) surrender soon after Pablo blows a hole in their building. There is a shout from the defenders to cease fire and four of them emerge with their hands in the air. Pablo tells his men to guard them: "The four *civiles* stood against the wall, dirty, dusty, smoke-grimed, with the four who were guarding them pointing their guns at them and Pablo and the others went in to finish the wounded."[3] Pablo shoots the wounded and reappears with a Mauser pistol with which he says the officer has shot himself. He asks one of the four *civiles*, all tall men who have been standing sweating and saying nothing during this shooting, to tell him how the Mauser works. The man instructs him twice in a voice which "was grayer than a morning without sunrise." For the *civiles* the next conversation is their last:

> "What are you going to do with us?" one asked him.
> "Shoot thee," Pablo said.
> "When?" the man asked in the same gray voice.
> "Now," said Pablo.
> "Where?" asked the man.
> "Here," said Pablo. "Here. Now. Here and now. Have you anything to say?"
> "*Nada*," said the *civil*. "Nothing. But it is an ugly thing."
> "And you are an ugly thing," Pablo said. "You murderer of peasants. You who would shoot your own mother."
> "I have never killed any one," the *civil* said. "And do not speak of my mother."
> "Show us how to die. You, who have always done the killing."
> "There is no necessity to insult us," another *civil* said. "And we know how to die."

Pablo orders them to kneel. One asks the other, the *civil* who helped Pablo with the pistol, what he thinks of this, and this man, a corporal, says that "It is as well to kneel," for "It is of no importance." There is an attempt at irony: "'It is closer to the earth,' the first one who had spoken said, trying to make a joke, but they were all too grave for a joke and no one smiled."

Then the corporal instructs the others to kneel facing the wall, they all do so and Pablo shoots each one in the back of the head. Although each bears up differently, all die with dignity, "and the four bodies were slumped against the wall when Pablo turned away from them and came towards us with the pistol still in his hand." This cold-blooded execution is the prelude to the more notorious scene in which Pablo orchestrates the murder of the town's fascists at the hands of farm laborers who have hated them all their lives. In comparison, the *civiles* are strangers. In their deaths too they appear to be different, an elite attempting a joke before dying.

In these elements the scene may be compared with the narrative climax of *Jómsvíkinga saga*, which is a story of tenth-century Vikings first written in Iceland in the early thirteenth century. The saga survives separately in five versions, as well as in distilled form within two Histories of Norwegian kings: in *Fagrskinna*, of the early thirteenth century; and in Snorri Sturluson's *Heimskringla* of ca. 1235.[4] As for the separate extant versions of *Jómsvíkinga saga*, the oldest consists of a partly incomplete and interpolated text in AM 291 4to, a manuscript from the first half of the thirteenth century. An Icelandic edition mostly of this text in *Fornmanna Sögur* (XI) served for an English novelization in 1875, on which more below.[5] The next oldest text, also the shortest, was copied into Codex Holmianus 7 4to, of the Royal Library of Stockholm, in the first third of the fourteenth century; this serves as the text for Norman Blake's edition and translation of 1962. The third version is the longest, in AM 510 4to, inscribed before the end of the fifteenth century. Fourth is a text which, though interpolated in two parts within the *Óláfs saga Tryggvasonar in mesta* (the greatest Saga of Óláfr Tryggvason), in five manuscripts, including Flateyjarbók in ca. 1390 (chaps. 70–87 and 123–63), is held to represent yet another version of *Jómsvíkinga saga*. The fifth and last version survives in a Latin adaptation which was made in the Copenhagen Royal Library by the Icelandic antiquarian Arngrímur Jónsson in 1592–1593.

However complex the transmission of their legend, historically the titular "Vikings of Jumne" seem to have been a nest of pirates with a fortress by Wolin at the mouth of the Oder on what is now the western Polish border.[6] In a stirring mixture of fact and fantasy, the saga portrays them as an elite cadre facing death with indifference. It says that Prince, soon to be King, Sveinn Haraldsson of Denmark, in revenge for their kidnapping him earlier and forcing him into a marriage, invites the Jómsborg leader Sigvaldi and his captains to a feast in which he tricks them all into swearing to attack his father's rebel vassal, Earl Hákon of Trøndelag. The next morning the Jómsvikings wake up to the knowledge that they must honor their oath. Despite misgivings they ready sixty ships for what will probably be their last expedition.

Sailing north, the Jómsvikings meet their fate in Hjǫrungavágr, a bay in north-western Norway, in a sea-battle which took place roughly in 985. For a while things seem to go their way, but when the hard-pressed Hákon takes a moment to sacrifice his young son to his tutelary goddess, Þorgerðr, the tide turns against the Danes and Jómsvikings, and Sigvaldi and his brother Þorkell the Tall sail off after the Danes, leaving their fellow Jómsvikings to be killed or captured. The episode of interest here comes after the battle and climactically on the morning of the following day, when the captives are bound to a log.

What follows tests the elite's ideology of courage in a sequence. Earl Hákon tours the scene with his sons Eiríkr and Sveinn, who have also fought in the battle. With them is Þorkell Leira, their headsman who is incidentally looking for Vagn Ákason, author of a vow which has preceded him to Norway. Seeing the seventy Jómsvikings tied up in a line on the log, Earl Hákon orders Þorkell to behead them all. First come the wounded:

> Three gravely wounded men were freed from the rope, and thralls were appointed to guard them and twist sticks in their hair. Þorkell leira now proceeded to cut off their heads.
>
> (chap. 36)[7]

As he warms to his task, Þorkell asks each man what he thinks about dying. According to the version in AM 291, it seems to be Hákon's idea to test the Jómsvikings' courage:

> And now Jarl Hákon and Þorkell intend to ask each of them before they are beheaded what they thought about death, and so to test the company, whether it was as tough as was said, and think it will be proved if none of them speaks a word of fear when they see death waiting for them.   (chap. 37)[8]

Some Jómsvikings memorialize the scene with jokes which include mockery of Þorkell their executioner. When, according to the text in Holmianus 7, a fourth wounded man is wrenched forward with sticks twisted in his hair:

> Þorkell said: "What do you think about dying?"
> "I am well content to die: I shall suffer the same fate as my father," Þorkell asked what that was.
> He said: "Strike; he died."
> Then Þorkell cut off his head.   (chap. 36)

The jokes come thick and fast, one in the name of scientific experiment, others again at Þorkell's expense:

> Then the seventh one was led forward and Þorkell asked him as usual. "I'm very content to die. But deal me out a speedy blow. I have here a dagger. We Vikings have often discussed whether a man knew anything after he had lost his head if it was cut off speedily. Let us make the following arrangement that I shall hold the dagger up if I know anything, otherwise it will fall down." Þorkell struck him and his head flew off, but the dagger fell down.
>
> Then the eighth man was brought up and Þorkell put the usual question to him. He said he was content to die. When he thought the blow was almost on him he said "Ram." Þorkell checked his hand and asked him why he said that.   (chap. 36)

The next joke depends on a barely translatable pun on Old Norse *á* "ewe" but also "ah!," as in the need for a *hrútr* "ram": *Þó mun eigi ofskipat til á-nna þeira er þér nefnduð í gær jarlsmenn, þá er þér fenguð á-verka* "They can't be too well provided for, those *ewes* [/*ah*'s] whose name you earl's men were calling out yesterday whenever you took a hit."[9] "Wretched fellow," says Þorkell, letting the blow crash down on him.

Hereupon the scene in the saga ends differently to that in Hemingway's *For Whom the Bell Tolls*. One of the Vikings, having asked for his locks to be held so that they are not bloodied, pulls forwards so that the sword cuts off the hands of the Norwegian holding his hair. Against his father Hákon's wishes, Earl Eiríkr pardons the insolent perpetrator, one Sveinn, son of Búi the Stout who was a leader of Jómsborg. The executions are set to continue, but for Vagn, the next victim. When Þorkell asks him what he thinks about dying, Vagn says that death will be fine as long as he has time to complete his vow, to sleep with Þorkell's daughter after killing her father. Þorkell makes for Vagn and then Bjǫrn *inn brezki* "the Welshman," Vagn's foster-father, trips up Vagn so that the blow goes over him and Þorkell, who falls over Vagn, accidentally cuts the rope. Vagn steps free, picks up the sword and lops off Þorkell's head. Despite another entreaty from his father, Eiríkr pardons Vagn and invites him to join his company. Vagn's condition, that the remaining Jómsvikings go free, is accepted and the executions stop. Despite this happy ending, Hemingway's scene and this one have three things in common: one is the morning setting, another a show of indifference, and the third, the illustration of an ideology with a joke before dying.

Hemingway and the Adaptations of *Jómsvikinga saga*

We now turn to the question of literary influence and how, if there was any, Hemingway might have made this startling vindication of Viking values into a model for the courage of *guardias civiles*. First, as noted, there is no evidence that he read the sagas of Iceland. It is true that Hemingway's library in Key West, Florida, before his initial move to Havana, Cuba, in 1939, contained a copy of *Kristin Lavransdatter*, a novel about medieval Norway by Sigrid Undset (1922), translated by Charles Archer and J. S. Scott (1930).[10] But Hemingway seems to have acquired most of his books relating to Iceland years after *For Whom the Bell Tolls* was published (on October 20, 1940).[11] First there is *Independent People*, J. A. Thompson's translation in 1945 of the novel *Sjálfstætt fólk* (published in two volumes in 1934 and 1935), partly for which Halldór Laxness won the Nobel Prize in 1955.[12] Thompson's translation sold 450,000 copies in the USA through *The Book of the Month Club,* the subscription service which, starting with *The Sun Also Rises* in 1926, had also launched Hemingway. Laxness, like Hemingway an admirer of Stalin's Soviet Union, had already translated *A Farewell to Arms* in 1941 (*Vopnin kvödd*). Then there is *The Viking Ships: Their Ancestry and Evolution* by A. W. Brøgger and Haakon Shetelig, which was published in 1951, as well as a book on Vineland the Good by Frederick Julius Pohl, *The Lost Discovery: Uncovering the Track of the Vikings in America,* which was published in 1952.[13] In the 1950s, along with hundreds of other books, these three were sent to La Finca Vigía near Havana, Hemingway's main home from 1940 to 1959.[14]

A fourth item, which Hemingway brought or had sent to Key West in or after 1954, is of greater interest. This is *The Long Ships: A Saga of the Viking Age,* Michael Meyer's translation of *Röde Orm,* a Swedish novel by Frans G. Bengtsson about a Viking from Skåne published in two parts, in 1941 and 1945.[15] As every fan of *The Long Ships* will know, Bengtsson puts the striking climax of *Jómsvíkinga saga* into the words of a survivor, one Sigurd Buesson – i.e., son of Búi the Stout – who tells his story in a yuletide feast at the court of King Harald Bluetooth in Denmark. Sigurd says that the morning after their defeat in the battle of "Jörundfjord," he and the other Jómsvikings were tied to a log along with Vagn Åkesson. News of the capture is sent to Jarl Haakon who orders them all beheaded at once. According to Sigurd:

> Jarl Erik, his son, and many of his followers, came to watch our end; for the Norwegians were curious to see how the Jomsvikings would conduct themselves in the face of death.
>
> (Part I, chap. 9)

Thorkell Leira swings with a will, working down the log towards our narrator, and never needing to strike twice. Bengtsson preserves the saga's humor in Sigurd's understated account:

> I think that those who were watching the scene had to admit that Vagn's and Bue's men knew how to conduct themselves in the face of death. Two who were seated not far from me began a discussion as to what it would feel like once one's head was off, and they agreed that it was one of those things that are difficult to foretell.
>
> One of them said, 'I have a brooch here in my hand. If my brain is still working after I have lost my head, I shall stick it into the ground.' Thorkell arrived at him, but as soon as the blow fell on his neck, the brooch dropped from his hand.   (Part I, chap. 9)

For his own part Sigurd asks Thorkell's brother-in-law to hold his silky hair to keep it clean. As the axe falls he pulls forward so that it cuts off the man's hands, allowing Thorkell to be tripped and beheaded by Vagn with the same axe. Erik Haakon's son, admiring the courage of Sigurd and the others, pardons them all on the spot, whereupon *The Long Ships* continues with more stories of adventure.

Meyer's translation probably arrived in Key West in or just after 1954, when Hemingway limped back from his second safari in Kenya,[16] so we know that he did read the Jómsviking story at least after he wrote *For Whom the Bell Tolls*. But there had been an English version of this story long before Hemingway started on his novel (in Havana in February 1939). Before and during his childhood, the Jómsvikings were widely known in the English-speaking world through *The Vikings of the Baltic: A Tale of the North in the Tenth Century*, by George Webbe Dasent, which appeared in three volumes in 1875.[17] Dasent had made popular translations of *Njáls saga* and *Gísla saga* respectively in *The Story of Burnt Njal* in 1861 and *Gisli the Outlaw* in 1866. By writing an English version of *Jómsvíkinga saga*, Dasent hoped to save a more exemplary saga for literature. "Jomsburg," he says in the preface, "was an asylum for all the bold spirits and dashing blades of the time"; he hopes "that something may be found of the strength and spirit with which the wonderful adventures of that famous company are narrated in the original."[18] His novel is a loose translation of AM 291 4to, packed with many additions of his own. When the battle of "the Voe" or the "Grange of Hjoring" in this episode is at last over, Earl Hacon has the Vikings bound to a log.[19] When Beorn the Welshman mocks the Norwegians, Hacon asks:

> "Is it not said, Sigmund, that these Jomsvikings are men of such hardihood, that no fear even makes them flinch?"[20]

Sigmund, a Faroese henchman whom Dasent has added in from elsewhere, in Flateyjarbók, assents and Earl Hacon turns his wit on the Jomsburg prisoners, reminding them of their rules:

> "No doubt such mighty champions as ye all are, the very flower of the Vikings of Jomsburg, will set the North an everlasting example how to die with hardihood."

Thorkel works his way through four captives, asking each one of them, on Hacon's instruction, whether he is afraid to die. One gives the scientific answer:

> "I think it very good to die," said the man, "and mind you behead me clean off at once. And now look here at this little knife, which I hold in my hand. We Jomsvikings have often wondered in our talk whether a man knows aught, or feels aught, when his head flies off, if he is beheaded in a trice, at one clean stroke. And now this shall be a sign to you – that I will make a point with this knife if I know anything. If I do not, it will fall down at once."

When the knife drops, another Jómsviking, when his name is called, calls out "Ram!" He is asked why:

> "Oh," said the Viking, "I thought a ram would not be out of place among the *Ohs* and *Ewes* and *Baas*, which ye warriors of the Earl uttered in your pain all yesterday whenever ye got a wound."

The man loses his head while his friends laugh at the joke, before the story of reprieve takes over, first with Sweyn son of Bui the Stout of Bornholm, then with Vagn (whose name is not rendered "Wayne"). After Thorkel's mishap with Vagn and the axe, Earl Eric recruits Vagn and the other survivors in defiance of his father Hacon. Dasent's story ends not too long after.

While there is no record of Hemingway reading it, there is no doubt that this novel – an edification for Victorians of empire, whether British or American – is the kind of book that he read as a teen. As Mrs Nina Grace, a retired teacher from the period after Hemingway in Oak Park High School, described the curriculum, "For years before I came, there had been in the senior year much organized collateral reading in eighteenth- and nineteenth-century English novels."[21]

Even so, it is more likely that Hemingway read a pastiche of the climax of *The Vikings of the Baltic* two decades after his childhood, within a novel which he appears to have bought in 1933 from Sylvia Beach's *Shakespeare & Company* bookshop in Paris.[22]

Hemingway and *The Men of Ness*

The Men of Ness: The Saga of Thorlief Coal-Biter's Sons is a novel which was written by Eric Linklater and published in London within a year of Hemingway's personal guide to bull-fights, *Death in the Afternoon* (1932).[23] Linklater was, like Hemingway, a successful novelist and travel writer with a distinguished record in the Great War. In recognition of his family's origins in Orkney, he set his novel in the early Viking Age, when Ivar the Boneless, son of Ragnar Hairy-Breeks, having killed two kings of England, leads his brothers up to Orkney to make a new base in the islands. Ivar murders a crofter there named Bui of Ness, rapes his widow Signy, and makes her his wife (chap. 2). Not long after, Ivar sails back to Northumbria with his brothers Halfdan and Ubbi, leaving behind Thorlief Coal-Biter, a fourth brother and pacifist whom Signy takes as her third husband.

One generation later, Signy eggs on the warlike Skallagrim and Kol, her sons by Thorlief, to avenge Bui and herself on their bad uncle Ivar in England (chap. 28). Skallagrim and Kol steer south while they watch their second ship go down with all hands in a storm in the Pentland Firth (chap. 29). Here Linklater's vivid detail doubtless caught the imagination of the sailor Hemingway, whom Beach, in the early 1930s, saw reading a book by Captain Marryat.[24] Having drifted under cloud for a while, Skallagrim's ship runs into a sandbar off Yorkshire. Making land, he and his crew learn of Ivar's whereabouts in a hall twenty miles away (chap. 39), where Skallagrim finds Ivar's son Ragnar at the head of thirty men. In the fight that follows the sons of Signy kill all but their cousin Ragnar (chap. 40), whom they spare with instructions to bring back Ivar. Ragnar, however, having lied about Ivar's distance from them, brings back his father plus Asbiorn, a local earl, later the same night, sooner than expected (chap. 43). Skallagrim's men are surprised in their house and all of them made prisoner but for his brother Kol, his dog, and an Orcadian joker by the name of Gauk, who have gone to see some women in another house (chap. 44). The next morning, Kol and Gauk witness Ivar and Asbiorn lead their friends and kinsmen to execution on the far side of a wood:

> The Orkneymen had been tied both at wrists and ankles till morning came, but then their ankles were loosed. Ivar made them sit together on the trunk of a tree that had been felled.
>
> (chap. 45)

Ivar mentions Signy to Skallagrim, his nephew and her son, saying that he thinks it was by her bidding that he came here; "Women's counsel is ever cruel," adds Asbiorn. With thuggish good humor, Ivar invites his prisoners to drink a toast before they die, which all but Skallagrim do. Then Ivar kills the man at the end of the log, after giving him the chance to run. The man had refused, saying he was too stiff to move, and the game continues:

> Then it came to Fridlief. Ivar said, "You are young and strong. Will you not run?"
> But Fridlief said, "I am at home out on Birsay, and that is too far for me to run to-day."
> So he also died without moving from where he sat. (chap. 45)[25]

Some rather more labored jokes follow. Ivar asks Thorgrim, who is sitting next to Skallagrim, if he will run:

> But Thorgrim said, "I never go from my bench while there is still ale in my cup." And he held the ale-horn in his hands.
> "Then you will lose your head," said Ivar. Skallagrim said, "strike off his hands rather than his head, for they will be the greater loss to him."
> Thorgrim said, "I do not think you are right in that, Skallagrim. For though there is much wisdom in my hands there is more in my head. And now I will prove it. For if my hands are as wise as my head they will still hold this horn when my head falls off. But if they are not so wise they will let it drop."
> Then Thorgrim's head was struck off, and the ale-horn fell out of his hands. (chap. 45)

Finally Kol shows himself, spears Asbiorn through and is captured and made to sit on the log next to Skallagrim, who grumbles that he might have come sooner. When Kol gives his uncle Ivar some invective concerning the killing of Bui of Ness, Ivar says that he speaks like Signy, "and now I am willing to believe that you are her son." Considering the nature of Thorlief, his father, Ivar tells Kol "it seems more likely that Signy got you on him." Here we might think of the way Pablo insults one *civil* victim by alluding to his mother, albeit he does so differently.

Kol asks Ivar to hold his hair. Ivar thinks this funny enough to grant the request, and so he holds Kol's hair:

> Then Kol said he was ready. The man with the axe stood in front of him. He swung his axe and hewed strongly at Kol's neck. But Kol lowered his head and thrust himself forward with a great jerk, and pulled Ivar after him. For Ivar's hand was caught in his hair. And the axe went higher than Kol's head, and fell on Ivar's forearm, and cut off his hand.
>
> (chap. 45)

Kol and Skallagrim throttle Ivar to death while his men cut both of them down. We see Gauk lying flat and watching this scene until the killing is over and Ragnar and his men ride away. Although he feels bad for not dying with his friends, Gauk survives to be witness, sailing back to Orkney and informing Signy and the other widows.

In all, these scenes by Linklater and Hemingway have more things in common than Hemingway's episode and the saga itself. There are five correspondences: the morning setting, an attack on a house, a joke in the face of death, the killer's reference to a prisoner's mother, and the lack of reprieve. Did Hemingway use a memory of Linklater's scene? It seems that each author read the other from 1929, when the new Penguin Books series in England published both Hemingway's *A Farewell to Arms* as its second book and an earlier novel by Linklater, *Poet's Pub*, as its third.[26] Hereafter Hemingway's library contained at least five of Linklater's novels: *The Men of Ness* (1933), *Magnus Merriman* (1934), *Juan in China* (1937), *Private Angelo* (1946), and *The Dark of Summer* (1956). Of the three that were in Key West before Hemingway moved from there to Cuba in 1939, only *The Men of Ness* was packed in 1940 for removal to La Finca Vigía after him.[27] The crates were carpentered by Toby Bruce, Hemingway's devoted driver, who typed the inventory. Bruce, under angry instruction from Hemingway's imminent ex-wife Pauline Pfeiffer, packed twenty-four crates with Papa's best books, twenty more with other effects, and a further two crates half-full with more books. These forty-six crates he kept locally (at Sloppy Joe's, a bar) until he was able to ship them to Cuba in 1941. *Kristin Lavransdatter* went in crate no. 7; *The Men of Ness*, Linklater's novel on the Vikings of Orkney, in no. 22, *inter alia* with books on fishing and medicine, a Spanish bullfighting annual, *The Voyage Out* by Virginia Woolf and Jane Austen's *Pride and Prejudice*.[28]

Conversely, Linklater reviewed in 1953 the first reprint of *The Old Man and the Sea* (1952). Perhaps it was by his recommendation that Hemingway, probably in 1954, bought Meyer's translation of Bengtsson, who had put some of Linklater's novels into Swedish, including *The Men of Ness* (*Männen från Ness*, 1933). In his review, Linklater claims to have read all of Hemingway's novels: "nowhere, I think, has his vision of the heroic scars of life been so surely realized."[29] Such "heroic scars" as are writ large here and in *For Whom the Bell Tolls* have figured less prominently in discussion of the latter, however, than the author's interest in medieval chivalry. That young Hemingway read books about chivalry is evident in the Oak Park High School curriculum and in later records in and after the first decade of the twentieth century.[30] At this time his reading included: *A Source Book of Mediæval History* by Francis Austin Ogg (1908, with a dense chapter on King Alfred and the Danes);[31] Sir Walter Scott's *Ivanhoe* (1820), given to Ernest by his uncle Leicester Hemingway over Christmas 1909;[32] Chaucer's *General Prologue* and *The Knight's Tale*, Edmund Spenser's *Faerie Queene* (vols. 1 and 2, of 1590), and Tennyson's *Idylls of the King* (1859–1873). Also, according to a contemporary biographer, Hemingway read translations of *Beowulf* and "*Deor's Lament*,"[33] Hemingway's letters show that he continued to read about medieval warfare as an adult, books which included translations of *La Chanson de Roland*, the *Chronicles of the Crusades* by Jean de Joinville and Geoffroy de Villehardouin, and Jean Froissart's *Chronicles*.[34] A letter by F. Scott Fitzgerald even refers to a plan by Hemingway for a story about crusaders.[35] Thus it appears likely that Hemingway, in writing *For Whom the Bell Tolls*, drew upon an ideal of knighthood with which to motivate the crusade of "Robert [i.e., King Robert of the river] Jordan" and his love for Maria. Confirming the professor's chivalry is a medievalized diction, almost ubiquitous to Hemingway's long passages of direct speech, which results from his literal rendering of Spanish:[36] "thou hast" for *tú has* and so on, or even the *civil*'s "There is no necessity to insult us" for *No hay necesidad de insultarnos*. However, the heroic note is stronger where the Civil Guard are concerned. Pilar's grim tale of execution owes nothing to chivalry, any more than Linklater's in *The Men of Ness*. It is the latter which Pilar's story resembles, chiefly in its morning setting, observation of a victim's humor, and lack of reprieve. For Linklater there, as perhaps for Hemingway, a man's courage before dying, however compromised, is truer to modern realism because it emulates not chivalry but the bleaker Jómsborg code.

Hemingway and the Massacre in Ronda

In the light of this comparison let us consider what real incidents might have given Hemingway the basis for Pilar's tale. Because Hemingway appears to have written it as a commentary on the failure of Socialist revolution at the start of the Spanish Civil War, Pilar's story is not only grim but controversial too.[37] Hemingway himself, in a letter to a friend in 1954, claimed to have made it up:

> We are old enough to try to talk truly and I tell you this only as a curiosity. A few other things which I invented completely such as the story in "For Whom the Bell Tolls" of Pablo and Pilar and their doing away with the Fascists in the village, I read, when by chance I have to do it, with complete astonishment that I could have invented as I did.[38]

Since Pilar and her husband are given as Castilians, it has been supposed that the town is located in their northern province, or even Cuenca, which overlooks its own drop far to the east of Madrid. Also after the Second World War, however, when one of Hemingway's admirers asked him "how much of the novel had come from actual events," he named a place, saying that "When Pilar remembers back to what happened in their village when the fascists came, that's Ronda, and the details of the town are exact."[39]

Ronda, dear to Hemingway for its bullfighting tradition, overlooks the most famous gorge in Spain, although the town lies far to the south of Castile in the province of Málaga. It has been noted that Hemingway's report on the disposal of dead horses there, in his *Death in the Afternoon* (1932), seems to pre-empt the way all the fascists are murdered in Pilar's story:[40]

> The bull ring at Ronda was built at the end of the eighteenth century and is of wood. It stands at the edge of the cliff and after the bullfight when the bulls have been skinned and dressed and their meat sent out for sale on carts they drag the dead horses over the edge of the cliff and the buzzards that have circled over the edge of the town and high in the air over the ring all day, drop to feed on the rocks below the town. (chap. 4)[41]

The handling of Pablo's Civil Guard victims is separate, like that of the bulls. Perhaps it is worth noting Hemingway's remark that Pablo was "really Rafael el Gallo," a self-preserving matador of the late 1920s, whom he also celebrates in *Death in the Afternoon* (chs. 2, 13, 15, 17–19).[42]

Records show that when the Nationalist uprising began in Morocco, on July 19, 1936, the commander of Ronda's garrison took a platoon to the town hall and ordered the mayor, a member of the ruling Popular Front, to declare martial law. The mayor disarmed the soldiers with the help of peasants outside who had gathered in greater numbers. These were anarchists, members of the *Confederación Nacional de Trabajo* (CNT) whose committees were busy taking over Andalusia. The CNT held Ronda nominally for the Republican government until September 18. In practice, however, they declared a revolution which had been long in the making. This started to get out of hand on July 24, when 200 peasants removed Ronda's college of priests to the prison whence they took them out of town to be shot. Out of the total number of victims of this terror, which is put at between 200 and 600, one person is thought to have killed himself by jumping into the gorge. Other Andalusian towns have terror stories closer to Hemingway's, but in Ronda it seems that most victims were shot.[43]

Less than a month later, however, the Nationalists put out an even more dramatic story. On August 18, General Queipo de Llano, who had taken Seville for the rebels, gave a radio broadcast in which he claimed that 400 *personas de orden* ("people of standing") of Ronda had been massacred by order of the local committee:

> Those they haven't thrown into the gorge, they have dragged through the streets, tied to the tail of a horse to the edge of town, where a pile of some three hundred unburied corpses lies openly decomposing.[44]

In the last analysis, it seems likely that a version of the Radio General's fiction lies somewhere behind the story in *For Whom the Bell Tolls*,[45] in which Pilar, recalling an anarchist massacre of landowners from the beginning of the war, lets us infer that the town is in Castile and under Nationalist rule and that Pablo's guerrillas are taking, not retaking, this town for the Republic. By the same token Pablo's men appear not to be Republican loyalists, but anarchist insurgents; his Civil Guard victims not Nationalist rebels, but policemen doing their job.

Hemingway and the Vikings: A Reflection on Their Refraction

To sum up, the well-known tale told by Pilar, of the anarchist liberation of a town in Castile in chapter 10 of *For Whom the Bell Tolls*, may seem shocking to us not only in its brutality but also in its apparent admiration for the courage of *civiles* who are fighting for General Franco. Yet more surprising is the possibility argued here that Hemingway modeled this courage on that of Viking avengers from Orkney who are themselves modeled on an elite in *Jómsvíkinga saga*. In this way it seems that Hemingway has used the Vikings, or rather Linklater's pastiche of Dasent's eclectic novelization of Jómsvíkings in the saga tradition of thirteenth-century Iceland, as the heroic template for an enemy he admired.

How could the Vikings have served him here but as the model of a manly indifference to death? Henceforth perhaps we may need to credit them with influence of a wider kind. The force of their refraction in this novel, if this particular influence is accepted, is a matter not of style but of stylization, for in Hemingway's case it seems that the Vikings, appearing as his prelude to a bitter recrimination against anarchists in a war only lately lost, have been used to stylize modern history.

Bibliography

Bengtsson, Frans G. *The Long Ships: A Saga of the Viking Age*. Translated by Michael Meyer. London: Collins, 1954.

Blake, Norman F., ed. and trans. *Jómsvíkinga saga: The Saga of the Jomsvikings*. London: Thomas Nelson and Sons, 1962.

Brasch, James D. and Joseph Sigman. *Hemingway's Library: A Composite Record*. Garland Reference Library of the Humanities 29. Boston: John F. Kennedy Library e-publications, 1981.

Buckley, Ramon. "Revolution in Ronda: The Facts in Hemingway's *For Whom the Bell Tolls*." *The Hemingway Review* 17 (1997): 49–57.

Dasent, George Webbe. *The Vikings of the Baltic*. 3 vols. London: Chapman and Hall, 1875.

Davies, Richard. "The Birth of Penguin Books." https://www.google.co.uk/search?tbm=bks&hl=en&q=ichard+davies+the+birth+of+penguin+books&=#q=ichard+davies+the+birth+of+penguin+books&hl=en&spf=1500205193604.

Finlay, Alison. "*Jómsvíkinga Saga* and Genre." *Scripta Islandica: Isländska sällskapets årsbok* 65 (2014): 63–79.

Gibson, Ian. *Queipo de Llano: Sevilla, verano de 1936 (con las charlas radiofónicas completas)*. Barcelona: Ediciones Grijalba, 1986.

Hallberg, Peter. *The Icelandic Saga*. Translated with notes and introduction by Paul Schach. Lincoln: University of Nebraska Press, 1962.

Hemingway, Ernest. *Death in the Afternoon*. London: Grafton Books, 1977. [New York: Charles Scribner's Sons, 1932].

Hemingway, Ernest. *For Whom the Bell Tolls*. London: Arrow Books, 1994. [New York: Charles Scribner's Sons, 1940].

Hemingway, Ernest. *Ernest Hemingway: Selected Letters 1917–1961*. Edited by Carlos Baker. St Albans and London: Granada Publishing, 1981.

Hotchner, A. E. *Papa Hemingway: A Personal Memoir*. London: Weidenfeld and Nicholson, 1966. [First published 1955].

Hutchisson, James M. *Ernest Hemingway: A New Life*. University Park: The Pennsylvania State University Press, 2016.

Linklater, Eric. *The Men of Ness: The Saga of Thorlief Coal-Biter's Sons*. London: Jonathan Cape, 1933.

Linklater, Eric. "'My Marks and Scars I Carry with Me': Announcing as Our October 'Extra' – a Special Illustrated World Books Edition of *The Old Man and the Sea* by Ernest

Hemingway." *World Books Broadsheet: Bulletin of World Books: The Reprint Society, Ltd.* August 1953.

Moreland, Kim. *The Medievalist Impulse in American Literature: Twain, Adams, Fitzgerald, and Hemingway.* Charlottesville and London: University Press of Virginia, 1996.

Ogg, Francis A. *A Source Book of Mediæval History: Documents Illustrative of European Life and Institutions from the German Invasions to the Renaissance.* New York, Cincinnati and Chicago: American Book Company, 1908.

Ólafur Halldórsson, ed. *Jómsvíkinga saga.* Reykjavík: Prentsmiðja Jóns Helgasonar, 1969.

Preston, Paul. *The Spanish Holocaust: Inquisition and Extermination in Twentieth-Century Spain.* London: Harper Press, 2012.

Reynolds, Michael S. *Hemingway's Reading, 1910–1940: An Inventory.* Princeton, NJ: Princeton University Press, 1981.

Wawn, Andrew. *The Vikings and the Victorians: Inventing the North in Nineteenth-Century Britain.* Cambridge: D. S. Brewer, 2002.

Zernack, Julia. "Artistic Reception," trans. Matthias Ammon. In *The Routledge Research Companion to the Medieval Icelandic Sagas*, edited by Ármann Jakobsson and Sverrir Jakobsson, pp. 327–41. Abingdon and New York: Routledge, 2017.

Notes

1. Peter Hallberg, *The Icelandic Saga*, trans. with notes and introduction by Paul Schach (Lincoln: University of Nebraska Press, 1962), p. 78. For skepticism, Julia Zernack, "Artistic Reception," trans. Matthias Ammon, in *The Routledge Research Companion to the Medieval Icelandic Sagas*, ed. Ármann Jakobsson and Sverrir Jakobsson (Abingdon and New York: Routledge, 2017), pp. 327–21, esp. p. 336.
2. Ernest Hemingway, *For Whom the Bell Tolls* (London: Arrow Books, 1994).
3. Ibid., pp. 107 ff.
4. *Jómsvíkinga saga: The Saga of the Jomsvikings*, ed. and trans. N. F. Blake (London: Thomas Nelson and Sons, 1962), pp. xv–xix. Blake's translation will be used in this essay.
5. The modern edition is *Jómsvíkinga saga*, ed. Ólafur Halldórsson (Reykjavík: Prentsmiðja Jóns Helgasonar, 1969).
6. *Jómsvíkinga saga*, ed. and trans. Blake, pp. vii–ix. For discussion of attempts by archaeologists to find evidence linking Wolin with the Jómsvikings, see Gardeła's chapter in this volume, and particularly pp. 65–66, 70, and 75.
7. *Jómsvíkinga saga*, ed. and trans. Blake, pp. 40 ff.
8. Translated in Alison Finlay, "*Jómsvíkinga Saga* and Genre," *Scripta Islandica: Isländska sällskapets årsbok* 65 (2014): 63–79, esp. 75.
9. *Jómsvíkinga saga*, ed. and trans. Blake, p. 41. My translation, based on Blake.
10. James D. Brasch and Joseph Sigman, *Hemingway's Library: A Composite Record*, Garland Reference Library of the Humanities 29 (Boston: John F. Kennedy Library e-publications, 1981), pp. 44 (key to abbreviations) and 355, n. 6681.
11. On the dates of writing, see James M. Hutchisson, *Ernest Hemingway: A New Life* (University Park: The Pennsylvania State University Press, 2016), pp. 161–65.
12. Brasch and Sigman, *Hemingway's Library*, p. 221, n. 3763.
13. Ibid., pp. 83, n. 834 and 287, n. 5251.

14. Michael S. Reynolds, *Hemingway's Reading, 1910–1940: An Inventory* (Princeton, NJ: Princeton University Press, 1981), pp. 28–29.
15. Frans G. Bengtsson, *The Long Ships: A Saga of the Viking Age*, trans. Michael Meyer (London: Collins, 1954), pp. 136–37.
16. Brasch and Sigman, *Hemingway's Library*, pp. 24 and 69, n. 526.
17. George W. Dasent, *The Vikings of the Baltic*, 3 vols. (London, 1875). Andrew Wawn, *The Vikings and the Victorians: Inventing the North in Nineteenth-Century Britain* (Cambridge: D. S. Brewer, 2002), pp. 175–82.
18. Dasent, *Vikings of the Baltic*, vol. 1, pp. v–vi.
19. Ibid., vol. 3, p. 23, chap. 2.
20. Ibid., vol. 3, pp. 205 ff.
21. Reynolds, *Hemingway's Reading*, p. 13.
22. Ibid., p. 150, n. 1330.
23. Eric Linklater, *The Men of Ness: The Saga of Thorlief Coal-Biter's Sons* (London: Jonathan Cape, 1933).
24. Brasch and Sigman, *Hemingway's Library*, p. 21; cf. p. 243, ns. 4275–79.
25. Linklater, *The Men of Ness*, pp. 239 ff.
26. Richard Davies, "The Birth of Penguin Books," https://www.google.co.uk/search?tbm=bks&hl=en&q=ichard+davies+the+birth+of+penguin+books&=#q=ichard+davies+the+birth+of+penguin+books&hl=en&spf=1500205193604.
27. Brasch and Sigman, *Hemingway's Library*, p. 227, respectively ns. 3915, 3914, 3913, 3916, 3912.
28. Ibid., pp. 22–25. Reynolds, *Hemingway's Reading*, pp. 50 and 67.
29. Eric Linklater, "'My Marks and Scars I Carry with Me:' Announcing as Our October 'Extra' – a Special Illustrated World Books Edition of *The Old Man and the Sea* by Ernest Hemingway," *World Books Broadsheet: Bulletin of World Books*, August 1953.
30. Reynolds, *Hemingway's Reading*, pp. 12, 26–27 and 41–42.
31. Francis A. Ogg, *A Source Book of Mediæval History: Documents Illustrative of European Life and Institutions from the German Invasions to the Renaissance* (New York, Cincinnati and Chicago: American Book Company, 1908), pp. 181–95.
32. Kim Moreland, *The Medievalist Impulse in American Literature: Twain, Adams, Fitzgerald, and Hemingway* (Charlottesville and London: University Press of Virginia, 1996), pp. 161–200.
33. Reynolds, *Hemingway's Reading*, p. 75, ns. 287 and 288; citing Charles A. Fenton.
34. Moreland, *The Medievalist Impulse*, p. 176.
35. Ibid., p. 172.
36. Ibid., pp. 163–71; Hutchisson, *Hemingway: A New Life*, pp. 168–69.
37. Ramon Buckley, "Revolution in Ronda: The Facts in Hemingway's *For Whom the Bell Tolls*," *The Hemingway Review* 17 (1997): 49–57.
38. *Ernest Hemingway: Selected Letters 1917–1961*, ed. Carlos Baker (St. Albans and London: Granada Publishing, 1981), pp. 837–38, esp. p. 837 (September 24, 1954, to Bernard Berenson).
39. A. E. Hotchner, *Papa Hemingway: A Personal Memoir* (London: Weidenfeld and Nicholson, 1966), p. 129 (at Cervecería Alemana, Pla. St. Ana, Madrid).
40. Note from Edward Stanton, in Buckley, "Revolution in Ronda," p. 54.
41. Ernest Hemingway, *Death in the Afternoon* (London: Grafton Books, 1977), p. 44.

42. *Hemingway: Selected Letters*, ed. Baker, pp. 507–10, esp. 508 (August 15, 1940, to Charles Scribner).
43. Buckley, "Revolution in Ronda," 49–54.
44. Ian Gibson, *Queipo de Llano: Sevilla, verano de 1936 (con las charlas radiofónicas completas)* (Barcelona: Ediciones Grijalba, 1986), p. 370: "A los que no despeñaron por el tajo, los arrastraron por las calles, atados a la cola de un caballo, hasta la salida del pueblo, donde se hacinan unos trescientos cadáveres insepultos, en plena putrefacción." My translation.
45. Paul Preston, *The Spanish Holocaust: Inquisition and Extermination in Twentieth-Century Spain* (London: Harper Press, 2012), p. 171.

Carolyne Larrington

9 "(No More) Reaving, Roving, Raiding, or Raping": The Ironborn in George R. R. Martin's *A Song of Ice and Fire* and HBO's *Game of Thrones*

An Ironborn Ethnography

The Ironborn, the fierce sea-raiders in George R. R. Martin's *A Song of Ice and Fire* and HBO's *Game of Thrones*, are a reimagining of the Vikings within the series' fantasy universe.[1] Their ruling dynasty, the Greyjoys, are the principal Ironborn characters; it is largely through their eyes that the customs, distinctive religion, ethos, and ambitions of this combative and independent community are mediated. The series lies squarely within the cultural domain of medievalism, understood as "a discourse of contingent representations derived from the historical Middle Ages, composed of marked alterities to and continuities with the present," in Nickolas Haydock's definition.[2] Yet, since *A Song of Ice and Fire* and *Game of Thrones* draw primarily on popular knowledge and second-order reimaginings about the Vikings, they should also be regarded as neomedievalist instantiations, "a post-postmodernist medievalism: fragmentary, fluid, attempting to encompass all truths, yet also brazenly fictionalizing these apparent truths," as Carol. L. Robinson and Pamela Clements define it in a now-classic article.[3] For, "[n]eomedievalist works reflect, or pass through, earlier medievalist works, rather than looking directly to the Middle Ages … [t]he reader or viewer is assumed to know, and appreciate, how many levels of literary artifice are being employed."[4] Thus Martin's fictional universe is in continuing dialogue with that of J. R. R. Tolkien, and with worlds created by other writers of medieval fantasy; he is also inspired by the French author Maurice Druon (as discussed below). Yet Martin's imagination is not simply a second-order phenomenon; it is clear that he has read widely in medieval history and literature, including that of northern Europe: in particular, Norse mythology, Viking history, and Icelandic sagas.[5] In the course of the novel sequence – – at least in the volumes published so far – – Martin charts the history of the Ironborn as a culture in the grip of far-reaching (and, to modern eyes, progressive) social change.[6] The TV show adopts some of these themes, but here the drama of the Ironborn's struggle

Carolyne Larrington, St. John's College, University of Oxford

https://doi.org/10.1515/9781501513886-010

for self-determination, the battle for gender equality, and their responses to the shifting politics of the continent of Westeros are secondary – though not unrelated – to the show's larger themes.

The Ironborn inhabit a group of thirty-one rocky islands (the Iron Islands) in the Sunset Sea, about two-thirds of the way up the western coast of Westeros.[7] There are seven principal islands; Pyke is the home of the ruling family, the Greyjoys. Castle Greyjoy was once situated on the Pyke mainland, but is now distributed across several rock-stacks, separated by perilous swaying bridges; it is from one of these that Balon Greyjoy, the Ironborn king, falls to his death.[8] Other islands have names which are either descriptive (Saltcliffe, Blacktyde), or Norse- or Scottish-sounding: Great and Old Wyk, Orkmont, and Harlaw. The two Wyks nod to the Viking connection; *vík* is a Norse place-name element meaning "bay" or "inlet," and the etymology of "Viking" seems likely to be connected to it.[9] The terrain is rocky and largely barren; sheep are grazed on some islands, but the economy of the Ironborn depends on raiding ("reaving" in the books' parlance), fishing, farming, and mining. The seas around the Iron Islands are notoriously stormy and the islands themselves offer few safe harbors. Consequently the Ironborn are famed for their seamanship and their skill in building fast, maneuverable longships. The islands are most likely named for iron deposits found there in ancient times, though the Ironborn themselves claim that the designation "Iron" is metonymic for their own toughness.

Except for Balon's daughter, Asha, whose name seems to echo ON *askr* (ash, longship) or Old English *æsc* with similar meanings, the Greyjoys have names which sound Greek: Balon may echo Balor One-Eye, an Irish deity (though he has two eyes); his brother Euron may be named for the East wind (Eurus) while the other brother, Victarion, has a hybrid Latin-Greek name.[10] The name of Theon, Balon's only surviving son, may allude, perhaps ironically, to Greek *theos* (god) or a contracted form of OE *þeoden* (prince), a name Martin would have found in Tolkien. Other Ironborn have more authentically Norse-sounding names such as Thormor, often with appended nicknames that follow Norse byname patterns. They make reference to physical characteristics or occupations: Dagmer Cleftjaw, or Erik Ironmaker. Scottish-type names, such as Andrik the Unsmiling are also to be found. Leaders of Houses are sometimes referred to, Scots-style, as "The Harlaw" or "The Merlyn."

The Ironborn are descendants of the First Men, the aboriginal inhabitants of Westeros; their origin-myth claims that they emerged from the sea, while another, more learned, tradition speculates that they migrated from an unknown western territory across the Sunset Sea.[11] Their traditional way of life, known as the "Old Way," was predicated on warfare and raiding along the coasts of Westeros, where they are still widely feared. "The ironborn are a race of pirates and thieves," notes a member of a neighboring House.[12] However, after the Seven Kingdoms were conquered by Aegon Targaryen, around three hundred years ago in the series-internal history, they were forced to abandon their attacks on their neighbors and thus redeployed their raiding fleets eastwards to the seas off the continent of Essos. Balon Greyjoy, the king occupying the Salt Throne at the beginning of the series, rebelled against the Iron Throne some ten years previously; the rebellion was quashed and two of his three sons were killed. Theon, the surviving youngest son, was sent to live as a hostage at the northern castle of Winterfell with the Stark family, while Balon came to regard his daughter Asha (Yara in the show) as his true heir.

The social and economic organization of the Ironborn is not entirely clear. The rank system, a clear division between the high-born and the "smallfolk," pertains here as in the rest of the Seven Kingdoms. Ironborn women are largely invisible, apart from Asha (see below), whose exceptionalism is marked in every possible way. Ironborn are permitted by custom to take concubines when they are at sea; these are known as "salt wives." Back at home, only one legal wife, the "rock wife," is allowed. The upper social rank lives by raiding and its spoils. The House Word, or motto, of the Greyjoys is "We Do Not Sow," boasting that they do not work the land. The "smallfolk" crew the longships, or scrabble for a living as farmers, fishermen, and miners. Thralls provide labor for individual lords; these are usually captives of war. They may not be sold and their children are free, provided that they accept the religion of the Drowned God (see below).[13] An artisan class works in metal, smithing tools and weapons; there is no real equivalent to the Scandinavian or Icelandic rank of *bændr* (farmers / freeholders). Life on the islands is hard and unromantic; it harbors no Gunnarr of Hliðarendi looking longingly at his south Icelandic farm and seeing beauty in the landscape.[14] Rather, as Theon notes, returning to his homeland:

> The islands are stern and stony places, scant of comfort and bleak of prospect. Death is never far here, and life is mean and meagre. Men spend their nights drinking ale and arguing over whose lot is worse, the fisherfolk who fight the sea or the farmers who try and scratch a crop from the poor thin soil. If truth be told, the miners have it worse than either, breaking their backs down in the dark, and for what? Iron, lead, tin, those are our treasures. Small wonder the ironmen of old turned to raiding.[15]

The Ironborn follow a distinctive religion. It is broadly dualist, predicated on two opposing forces: the Drowned God and the Storm God who are locked in constant conflict, reflected in storms and tempests. This particular model seems likely to derive from Martin's reading of Maurice Druon, whose seven-volume sequence of historical novels based on fourteenth-century French history he cites as an inspiration.[16] Druon's novels begin with the burning of the Grand Master of the Templars in Paris in 1314. Much later, in the sixth novel, Béatrice Hirson, a Templar adherent, expounds the tenets of her version of the Templar faith to her lover: "There is not one God; there are two, the god of light and the god of darkness, the prince of Good and the prince of Evil. Before the creation of the world, the inhabitants of darkness rebelled the inhabitants of light, and the vassals of Evil, in order to exist – for Evil is death and annihilation, devoured part of the principles of Good."[17] Although this is scarcely an accurate account of Templar belief – Béatrice's auditor dismisses it (rightly) as "ill-digested scraps of Manichaeism and corrupt elements, ill-transmitted and ill-understood, of the doctrines of the Cathars" – Béatrice's credo offers a basis not only for Martin's conceptualization of the Faith of the Red God, R'hllor – one of the series' major religions – but also of the Ironborn creed. Entry to the religion is by a ceremony in which the devotee is "drowned," held down underwater until he (or she?) loses consciousness.[18] Thereafter the adherent is deemed to be already "dead"; the paradoxical Ironborn proverb "What is Dead Can Never Die" rehearses the belief that the ritual confers immunity from drowning.

Once Balon Greyjoy is dead, more information about Ironborn post-mortem beliefs is imparted. Balon's brother, Aeron Damphair, a priest in the religion of the Drowned God, has seen the next world for himself and speaks with authority: "My brother Balon made us great again, which earned the Storm God's wrath. He feasts now in the Drowned God's watery halls, with mermaids to attend his every want. It shall be for us who remain behind in this dry and dismal vale to finish his great work."[19] The Ironborn's model of the afterlife suggests a version of Valhöll, an eternity of feasting, with mermaids substituting for Valkyries. What the dead feast on is not entirely clear – it is unlikely to be a self-reconstituting boar like the Old Norse Sæhrímnir who feeds the Einherjar in Óðinn's hall. Possibly it is octopus, for the House sigil (or crest) is a kraken, though consumption of the flesh of the House symbol is more likely taboo. The Drowned God's hall also has a touch of Davy Jones' locker: the submarine destination of drowned sailors, presided over by the fiend-like Davy.[20] Folklore, myth and popular medievalism combine in Martin's conceptualization of the Ironborn religion, though its liturgical details are not clearly fleshed out beyond the drowning ritual.

The "Old Way," closely connected with the Ironborn faith, is, in its strongest form, a romanticized and popular version of what might be loosely described as a "Viking mindset." "War was an ironman's proper trade. The Drowned God had made them to reave and rape, to carve out kingdoms and write their names in fire and blood and song," Theon muses.[21] Nostalgic for the good old days, and, given the chaos engulfing the Westeros mainland in consequence of the War of the Five Kings and the Targaryen invasion, its practitioners are eager to resume their old ways. They begin to harry their neighbors once more, in raids usually reported in the capital, rather than narrated at close quarters. The "Old Way" decrees that seaborne raiding and the taking of booty, including slaves, is the only honorable way to live; trading, except in human lives, is despised.[22] Thus when Theon Greyjoy returns home wearing velvet and silk and a gold chain, the costume that is fashionable in the north where he has been living, his father snarls at him: "That bauble around your neck – was it bought with gold or with iron?" In the Old Way, Theon recalls too late, "women might decorate themselves with ornaments bought with coin, but a warrior wore only the jewelry he took off the corpses of enemies slain by his own hands." "You blush red as a maid, Theon . . . Is it the gold price you paid or the iron?"[23] Balon already knows the answer; he yanks the chain from his son's neck and casts it in the brazier.

Archaeology shows of course that real-life Vikings exhibited no such nicety about masculine adornments, brightly-colored clothing, nor indeed about trading rather than relying on pillage to supply their needs. The 2014 "Vikings" exhibition at the British Museum bore ample witness to the wide range of neck- and arm-rings, and other jewelry that followed Viking Age owners to their graves or that was incorporated into hoards of hack-silver and gold.[24] Moreover, even the Great Army which invaded England in the 860s and 870s was actively involved in trade in its winter-quarters: sets of weights and scales have been excavated from Torksey where the Army overwintered in 871.[25] Likewise Viking settlers are credited with having introduced the manufacture and sale of cheese to Seville and Cordoba.[26] Trade was crucial to Viking Age economies, fueling the growth of towns as commercial centers; saga evidence suggests that Icelanders were only too pleased to return from Norway or further afield with brightly dyed clothing and handsome weapons, sometimes given as gifts but often purchased with ready coin.[27] Life in the Iron Islands without the luxuries produced elsewhere in the Seven Kingdoms, or further afield in the Free Cities of Essos would be bleak indeed.

The Ironborn have some distinctive skills. Balon Greyjoy is remembered by his brother as embodying all that makes a true Ironborn / Viking leader. "At thirteen he could run a longship's oars and dance the finger dance as well as any man in the isles. At fifteen he had sailed with Dagmer Cleftjaw to the Stepstones and spent a summer reaving. He slew his first man there and took his first two salt wives. At seventeen Balon captained his own ship."[28] Running along the oars of a moving longship is a feat credited to Óláfr Tryggvason by Snorri Sturluson: "Óláfr konungr gekk eptir árum útbyrðis, er menn hans røru á Orminum, ok hann lék at þrimr handsöxum, svá at jafnan var eitt á lopti, ok hendi æ meðalkaflann." (King Óláfr used to walk along the oars over the side while his men were rowing on Ormrinn [the "Long Serpent"], and he would juggle with three knives, so that there was always one in the air, and he caught them always by the handle.)[29] Martin's casual inclusion of the oar-running feat may seem to suggest detailed research into the kings' sagas, but it is more likely that he draws upon the famous scene in the film *The Vikings* (1958) in which Kirk Douglas as Einar performs the feat, "jump[ing] from one oar held horizontally to the next all around the ship."[30] Moreover, Douglas insisted on doing the stunt himself. "'Nobody had seen the running of the oars in the past thousand years,' says [Richard] Fleischer [the director], marveling at the power of the camera to capture the past."[31] Here, as in Martin's discussion of his debt to Tolkien in the 2014 interview, we see a fusion of medievalism and neomedievalism, the tropes of Viking heroism relayed through popular culture into the epic fantasy genre.[32] The finger dance was a competition in which the Ironborn threw weapons at one another's outstretched hands – and could be extremely dangerous: "A flying axe took off half of Urri's hand when he was ten-and-four, playing at the finger dance whilst his father and his elder brothers were away at war," recalls Aeron Damphair of his beloved older brother – and it was Aeron who threw it.[33] Urri's hand was treated not by traditional Ironborn remedies but rather with poultices and potions from the "green lands" as the non-Iron Island territories are derisively known; he contracted sepsis and died. The finger dance sounds both macho and ridiculous; real-life fighters seem unlikely to court maiming in such a gratuitous way.[34] The show, wisely, eschews both these unique Ironborn identity markers.

Other well-known Viking tropes are employed to construct the Ironborn heroic identity. "It was said that the ironmen of old had oft been blood-drunk in battle, so berserk that they felt no pain and feared no foe," recalls Theon.[35] In the series' present, two of Balon's brothers, Victarion and Euron best incarnate the Viking / Ironborn ideal. Victarion is a largely sympathetic character, clinging to the heroic paradigms of the "Old Way." Euron, like Victarion, a contender for the Salt Throne after Balon's death, fulfils an impressive number of stereotypes. Known as Crows-Eye, he sports an eye-patch beneath which a terrifying black eye is rumored to roll. He is mad, even in the estimation of other Ironborn, "Balon was mad, Aeron is madder and Euron is the maddest of them all," observes one of the more sensible Ironborn to Victarion, tactfully omitting his interlocutor from his assessment of the Greyjoy brothers' sanity.[36] Fearless and godless, Euron scorns Aeron's devotion to the Drowned God, sneering: "Horse gods and fire gods, gods made of gold with gemstone eyes, gods carved of cedar wood, gods chiseled into mountains, gods of empty air ... I know them all."[37] Euron's skepticism meshes with the tendency of some Viking Age figures in the sagas, often berserks or other social undesirables, to believe only in their own *mátt ok megin* (might and main), rather than worshiping either Þórr or the Christian God, the "White Christ." Euron's characterization and sadistic behavior exaggerates and surpasses even such legendary Viking cruelty as the cutting of the blood-eagle or forcing the unhappy Bróðir after the Battle of Clontarf to walk around a stake, unwinding his own guts.[38] The most villainous of villains, he fails to keep faith with his own family; he is implicated in Balon's murder, seduces and impregnates his brother's wife, mutilates his crew, and sports his piratical eye-patch, primarily, or so it is rumored, in order to increase his mystique, rather than to disguise a disability.

A New King (or Queen) on the Salt Throne

Leadership of the Ironborn after Balon's death is contested between Euron and the more reasonable Victarion. Asha, Balon's daughter, also puts herself forward as a candidate. Aeron Damphair has called a "kingsmoot," a kind of *Alþingi* at which the new ruler makes a pitch, offers chests full of booty, and waits for acclamation. Victarion's promise is essentially of "business as usual." Asha understands that the expansionist acquisitions that the Ironborn have made in the North are untenable; while the Great Army that harried much of England in the mid-ninth century had the capacity to pursue military objectives on land as well as sea, to seize horses and fight, even at some distance from their ships, the Ironborn – as Theon's history bears out – flounder when they can no longer exploit their superiority on the water. Asha believes that she could negotiate real territorial inroads for the Ironborn, extending their domain from their rocky islands onto the mainland, if they were prepared to conclude an alliance with the men of the North. "Peace . . . land. Victory. I'll give you Sea Dragon Point and the Stony Shore, black earth and tall trees and stones enough for every younger son to build a hall."[39] Her chances of success were slim from the outset and her vision for the Ironborn's future does not chime with the lords' idea of themselves. Euron, who carries the day, promises glory, listing all the regions of the Seven Kingdoms and bombastically declaiming: "I say we take it *all*! I say we take Westeros!"[40]

The show refracts the choices that the Ironborn face at the kingsmoot rather differently. Yara (as she is called here) and Theon flee with fifty ships after she fails to win assent at the kingsmoot. They sail east for Meereen where they find Daenerys Targaryen. Daenerys's claim to the Iron Throne derives from her father, Aerys, the Mad King, who had ruled the Seven Kingdoms before his deposition by Robert Baratheon, the reigning monarch when the series begins. In exchange for naval support in her quest to seize the Iron Throne, Daenerys agrees to support Yara's bid for the Salt Throne – but on one condition:

"No more reaving, roving, raiding or raping." And, with only a momentary hesitation, Yara looks her in the eye and consents.[41]

The Ironborn then are at a crossroads at this particular point in their history. The "Old Way" could be abandoned for ever, peace concluded with neighboring territories. In the books, the Stony Shore and Sea Dragon Point would open up new lands (rather like the colonization of Iceland and Greenland), offering opportunities for younger sons to acquire land, clear forests to build halls and, it is intimated, turn to a more peaceful life of farming and trading – very likely woolen products, walrus ivory and dried fish, the staples of the medieval Icelandic export trade – with the people of the "green lands." So too, at the end of the Viking Age (considered as the failure of Haraldr harðráði's invasion of England in 1066), Scandinavians had already begun to adapt to alternative modes of living. Icelanders were farmers or traders; only a few young men could not adapt to the new realities. Among them was Grettir Ásmundarson, the troubled hero of *Grettis saga*, who in an earlier century might have carved out a profitable career for himself as a Viking (like his great-grandfather Önundr *tréfótr*, memorably described as the "most famous and nimblest one-legged man in Iceland").[42] In mainland Scandinavia, farming, trading, and mercantile activities fueled the economy; Bergen's medieval prosperity was built on its membership of the Hanseatic League. "Scandinavians instead opted to join Europe, embracing Christianity and other ideologies, and adopting European artistic ideals, military tactics, and trading patterns. When Scandinavians became the subjects of kings and the servants of the universal Church, they were no longer Vikings," notes Anders Winroth.[43]

The Ironborn are not great readers, and they set little store by Maesters (the independent order of learned men who act as teachers, healers, secretaries, and communicators in the rest of the Seven Kingdoms). Theon can offer to show the Ironborn occupying a captured mainland fortress a letter he bears, supposedly guaranteeing safe-conduct; he is confident that no-one will be able to read it. Yet, even in the Iron Islands, cultural change is underway. Literacy may be a key to the future. Asha's maternal uncle, Rodrik Harlaw, who has spent some time in the "green lands," keeps a magnificent collection of books at his castle and is known as "The Reader," a nickname that reflects a qualified respect, even if "his love of written words" was something "so many ironborn found unmanly and perverse."[44] Although Rodrik is also a redoubtable fighter, he has little time for Ironborn heroics: "I prefer my history dead. Dead history is written in ink, the living sort in blood." When Asha taunts him: "Do you want to die old and craven in your bed?" he responds, "How else? Though not till I'm done reading."[45] Rodrik's connections with the mainland allow him to add to his library, and, until the Faith of the Seven (the series' equivalent of the Catholic Church) was forbidden on the Iron Islands, he had also employed septons (priests of the Seven) to care for his books. Rodrik and Asha thus represent one future course – one akin to that of medieval Scandinavia – that the Ironborn might choose. Profound cultural change is associated with new gender patterns, and possibly with religious skepticism too, for Asha is not a particularly strong adherent of the Drowned God. In a moment of peril in *A Dance with Dragons*, she prays: "'God of my fathers, if you can hear me in your watery halls beneath the waves, grant me just one small throwing axe.' The Drowned God did not answer. He seldom did. That was the trouble with gods."[46] Although raised Catholic, Martin himself is not religious and does not endorse as transcendent any faith within his invented world.[47]

Asha is also a ship's captain, a formidable commander and fighter in her own right. Martin has noted how important unconventional women are to his series. "The books reflect a patriarchal society based on the Middle Ages … my heroes and viewpoint characters are all misfits. They're outliers … They're 'cripples, bastards, and broken things' – a dwarf, a fat guy who can't fight, a bastard, and women who don't fit comfortably into the roles society has for them."[48] To be a successful epic fantasy author in the twenty-first century demands, as Martin recognizes, a move beyond the simplistic, monolithic model of the male hero taking on the forces of evil – the basic pattern of the superhero movie. He is explicit about the importance of creating characters who are not straightforwardly good or evil; even some of the initially most dislikeable characters have a chance of redemption.[49] Women too – from Arya Stark who learns to become an effective assassin, Brienne of Tarth, the idealistic female knight, and Asha / Yara herself, reflect a modern gender politics: women who are the equal of or better than men. Asha confounds her culture's gender expectations, encouraged by her father who regards her as his *de facto* son once Theon has gone to live with the Starks. In some ways Asha recalls such medieval fantasy figures as Alvild in Saxo Grammaticus's *Gesta Danorum* (History of the Danes). Alvild's chamber had been enclosed in the coils of a pair of poisonous serpents; these were slain by a Danish hero named Alf, who expected to marry Alvild as his reward. Nettled by her mother's comment that her daughter appears to be ready to marry the first dragon-slayer to come along, Alvild and a band of like-minded girls commandeer a ship and set sail in the Baltic where they embark on successful careers as pirates. Alf and his men set out in pursuit and eventually find themselves in combat with Alvild's ship. The Danes board the vessel and are astonished by the "graceful, shapely limbed opponents"; Alvild's helmet, in a classic Amazon trope, is pulled from her head, and her sex revealed: "They ought not to be fighting with weapons, but kisses."[50] Alvild is made to resume female clothing, is wed to Alf, and once she becomes a mother her Viking days are definitively over.

Medieval Icelandic writers were interested – as interested as modern fantasy authors – in thought-experiments about reversing gender roles. The so-called "maiden-king sagas" feature women like Asha, who are their royal fathers' heirs, who don male costume, lead armies, rule their kingdoms, and refuse to marry. Eventually, they are brought to heel; sometimes through appalling sexual mistreatment as in *Sigurðar saga þögla* and *Clári saga*, sometimes through teaching their suitors that hyper-masculine force is not the way to a woman's heart, as in *Nitiða saga*.[51] This saga "suggests that wooers should not proceed with force and the intention to dominate, but win a noble maiden's trust and love through courtly and restrained behavior. The woman should not be bullied or forced into marriage, or humiliated for having the audacity to exercise agency and autonomy."[52] Questions about the value of virginity and female honor are at stake in these tales, signaling changing views about sexual mores for well-born Icelandic women in the years after the submission to the Norwegian Crown.

I doubt whether George R. R. Martin has read any maiden-king sagas, but he is certainly aware of continuing speculation about whether Viking women did in fact wield weapons.[53] The series draws heavily upon neomedievalist stereotypes of the fighting Viking woman, framing Asha / Yara as sexually adventurous. Determined not to marry, Asha shocks her childhood friend, now a romantically inclined suitor, Tristifer Botley, with her sexual frankness.[54] Yara visits brothels alongside her men and is on the verge of an erotic encounter with her new ally Ellaria Sand when her ship is attacked by her uncle Euron.[55]

In those books published so far in Martin's series, Euron's star is in the ascendant. He has successfully raided the Shield Islands at the mouth of the Mander river, and now styles himself king of the Isles and the North. He has ordered his brother Victarion to set sail for the distant east, to Meereen, to bring him Daenerys Targaryen as his bride. Victarion has indeed reached Meereen in one of the published chapters of *The Winds of Winter*.[56] Asha has been taken captive by Stannis Baratheon, and, although she has been reunited with her brother Theon, their prospects are uncertain. Stannis is trapped in a snowstorm in the north and his followers suggest sacrificing Asha or Theon to R'hllor, the Red God, in the hope that the snows will melt.[57] In the show, Yara was last seen as Euron's captive, paraded through the streets of the capital of the Seven Kingdoms, King's Landing. There has been some fan speculation as to whether Yara's tongue has been cut out – in the books Euron's ship, the *Silence*, is entirely crewed by mutes. Show and books appear to promise political change, epitomized by Daenerys's famous speech in which she vows that she will not just stop the wheel (of history, or in a medieval context, of fortune), but rather that she will break the wheel.[58] Yara's promise to reform the Ironborn way of life was part of that project; whether she will survive to fulfil it remains to be seen.

Theon has mobilized a crew of Ironborn to set out to rescue her. The crew's captain refuses the mission, claiming that he and his men would rather "sail east, find a nice quiet island, kill all the men and take their wives for ourselves": a classic iteration of the "Old Way."[59] In response, Theon invokes Yara's new vision: "We're done with that … Yara … made a pledge," and his readiness to reassert the Ironborn version of masculinity – by beating the captain to death – wins the crew's acclaim. With cries of "For Yara!," they have set off for King's Landing.

In the books, Asha's dream of the Ironborn's future is endorsed through the prophetic vision of her uncle Aeron Damphair, priest of the Drowned God. Aeron has repeatedly declared that a "godless man," such as Euron is, shall never sit in the Seastone Chair.[60] Rather, or so Aeron foretells: "The ironborn shall be waves … not the great and lordly, but the simple folk, tillers of the soil and fishers of the sea. The captains and the kings raised Euron up, but the common folk shall tear him down."[61] Prophets are not always without equivocation in the *Song of Ice and Fire* world, but it may be that Aeron can indeed correctly foresee the Ironborn's future – perhaps as a medieval Icelandic-type commonwealth.

The Ironborn and Neomedievalism

While Yara's fortunes took a turn for the worse in Season Seven, Euron, played by the Danish actor Pilou Asbæk, seized the center stage. Allying himself with Queen Cersei who tenaciously clings to power in King's Landing – in exchange, he hopes, for her hand in marriage – Euron swaggers about the court. Clad in rock-star leathers and wearing eyeliner, he cuts a disturbing, yet glamorous, figure. His styling meshes with that of the Vikings in the *Vikings* TV show and in *The Last Kingdom*, though here facial tattoos, hipster beards, and man-buns complement the furs, leather, and open shirts, making literal the popular idea of the berserk. "These are grimy Vikings – disheveled with greasy crow's nest hair, smudged faces, and dull and tattered clothes augmented with animal furs – and the run-down, snow-swept village they live in seems to have used Jorvik as a model; you can almost whiff the smell-o-vision," Susan Aronstein notes of Terry Jones's *Erik the Viking* (1989), the film that established the current Viking visual aesthetic.[62] Such is the popularity of the cool hipster Viking, preferably played by well-built Scandinavian actors, that, in a classic neomedievalist move, quite ignoring traditional chronology, a crew of them, led by noted Swedish heart-throb actor Mikael Persbrandt, turn up as allies of villainous King

Vortigern in Guy Ritchie's 2017 movie *King Arthur*.[63] By the end of the film however, even they willingly acknowledge Arthur's sovereignty.

Game of Thrones departs from the neomedievalist tendency to emphasize Vikings as strongly homosocial and group-oriented, competing with one another in courage and risk-taking; in contrast the show focuses on individual Ironborn characters – Balon, Theon, Euron, Yara, and Aeron – anonymizing their crewmen and supporters. The books call on a much larger cast of Ironborn, and the account of the Battle of the Shield Islands gives an authentic sense of Viking-style sea-battles of the type recounted in the sagas.[64] There is a stronger emphasis on bravery and solidarity – "manly men doing manly things in a manly way," as Elizabeth Sklar characterizes the ethos of the Viking-Rus' film *The Thirteenth Warrior* (1999).[65] Although the Ironborn's future is treated as relatively unimportant across both the series media in comparison with the battle for the Iron Throne, nevertheless the Iron Islands' fate echoes in miniature the series' larger themes. A new cadre of young rulers is poised to come to power, and its members are determined to eschew the conservatism, adherence to tradition, madness, and tyranny of their parents' generation. Daenerys Targaryen promises social reform, rule which benefits the interests of the smallfolk rather than the Great Houses; Asha / Yara imagines a future in which the "Old Way" is definitively consigned to the past, where a transition to a post-Viking existence and modernization of economic and cultural priorities becomes a real possibility. That this new, optimistically inflected future should be incarnated by young women who have set aside the imperatives of the patriarchy – importantly including religious faith – is significant. Daenerys and Asha / Yara are not exactly maiden-kings of the type found in Old Norse saga, but they are equally determined to rule well, to avoid subjection to a husband and to resist being deprived of agency and autonomy.

Will Asha / Yara succeed in her quest to ascend the Seastone Chair and bring peace to the Iron Islands? "You may dress an ironman in silks and velvets, teach him to read and write and give him books, instruct him in chivalry and courtesy and the mysteries of the Faith, but when you look into his eyes, the sea will still be there, cold and grey and cruel," write Elio Garcia and Linda Antonsson in their encyclopedic guide to the World of Ice and Fire.[66] In this comment I hear echoes of Rudyard Kipling's "Harp Song of the Dane Women," a poem that gives voice to Viking women's powerlessness in the face of their husbands' longing for the "Old Way" and the sea, "the old grey widowmaker."[67] Yet it is the function of medievalist fantasy not only to recreate the medieval past, but also to reconfigure it – and thereby to signal ways in which our present may also be reconfigured.

Bibliography

Primary Sources

Brennu-Njáls saga. Edited by Einar Ólafur Sveinsson. Íslenzk fornrit 12. Reykjavík: Hið
Íslenzka fornritafélagið, 1954.
Druon, Maurice. *Les Rois maudits* (édition integrale). Paris: Plon, 2014.
Druon, Maurice. *The Accursed Kings*. Translated by Humphrey Hare. London: HarperCollins,
2013–2015; *The Iron King* (1956/ repr. 2013); *The Strangled Queen* (1956/ repr. 2013); *The
Poisoned Crown* (1957/ repr. 2013); *The Royal Succession* (1958/ repr. 2014); *The She-
Wolf* (1960/ repr. 2014); *The Lily and the Lion* (1961/ repr. 2014); *The King without a
Kingdom*. Translated by Alan Simpkin (1977/2015).
Grettis saga. Edited by Guðni Jónsson. Íslenzk fornrit 7. Reykjavík: Hið Íslenzka
fornritafélagið, 1936.
HBO TV. *Game of Thrones*. Produced by David Benioff and Daniel Weiss. 2011–.
Kipling, Rudyard. *Puck of Pook Hill*. London: Macmillan, 1906.
Martin, George R. R. *A Clash of Kings*. London: Harper Voyager, 1998.
Martin, George R. R. *A Storm of Swords*. London: Harper Voyager, 2000.
Martin, George R. R. *A Feast for Crows*. London: Harper Voyager, 2005.
Martin, George R. R. *A Dance with Dragons*. London: Harper Voyager, 2011.
Saxo Grammaticus. *Gesta Danorum: The History of the Danes*. Edited by Karsten Friis-Jensen,
translated by Peter Fisher. 2 vols. Oxford: Oxford University Press, 2015.
Snorri Sturluson. *Óláfs saga Tryggvasonar*. In *Heimskringla*, edited by Bjarni Aðalbjarnarson.
3 vols. Íslenzk fornrit 26–28. Reykjavík: Hið íslenzka fornritafélag, 1941–1951.

Secondary Works

Aronstein, Susan. "When Civilization Was Less Civilized: Erik the Viking (1989)." In *The
Vikings on Film: Essays on Depictions of the Nordic Middle Ages*, edited by Kevin J. Harty,
pp. 72–82. Jefferson, NC: McFarland, 2011.
Bjarni Einarsson. "The Blood-Eagle Once More: Two Notes." *Saga-Book* 23 (1990): 80–81.
Brink, Stefan, with Neil Price. *The Viking World*. London: Routledge, 2008.
Frank, Roberta. "Viking Atrocity and Skaldic Verse: The Rite of the Blood Eagle." *English
Historical Review* 99, no. 391 (1984): 332–43.
Frank, Roberta. "The Blood-Eagle Again." *Saga-Book* 22 (1988): 287–89.
Frank, Roberta. "Ornithology and Interpretation of Skaldic Verse." *Saga-Book* 23 (1990): 81–83.
Garcia, Elio and Linda Antonsson, in association with George R. R. Martin. *The World of Ice
and Fire*. London: Harper Voyager, 2014.
Germani, Erik. "The Redemption of Jaime Lannister." http://atseajournal.com/asoiaf/essays/
jaimes_redemption.html.
Gilmore, Mikal. "George R.R. Martin: The Rolling Stone Interview." *Rolling Stone*, May 8, 2014.
https://web.archive.org/web/20180220172219/https://www.rollingstone.com/tv/news/
george-r-r-martin-the-rolling-stone-interview-20140423.
Hadley, Dawn M. and Julian D. Richards et al. "The Winter Camp of the Viking Great Army AD
872–3, Torksey." *The Antiquaries Journal* 96 (2016): 23–67.

Haydock, Nickolas. "Medievalism and Excluded Middles." In *Defining Medievalism(s)*, vol. 2, Studies in Medievalism 18, edited by Karl Fugelso, pp. 17–30. Cambridge: D. S. Brewer, 2010.

Hedenstierna-Jonson, Charlotte et al. "A Female Viking Warrior Confirmed by Genomics." *American Journal of Physical Anthropology* 164, no. 4 (2017): 853–60.

Hibberd, James. "George R.R. Martin Explains Why There's Violence against Women on *Game of Thrones*." http://ew.com/article/2015/06/03/george-rr-martin-thrones-violence-women/?xid=IFT-Trending.

IMDb. "Erik the Viking (1989)." http://www.imdb.com/title/tt0097289/.

IMDb. "The 13th Warrior (1999)." http://www.imdb.com/title/tt0120657/.

IMDb. "King Arthur: Legend of the Sword (2017)." http://www.imdb.com/title/tt1972591/.

Jóhanna Katrín Friðriksdóttir. "'From Heroic Legend to Medieval Screwball Comedy?' The Development and Interpretation of the *meykongr* Motif." In *The Legendary Sagas: Origins and Development*, edited by Annette Lassen, Agneta Ney and Ármann Jakobsson, pp. 229–49. Reykjavík: Háskólaútgáfan, 2012.

Jóhanna Katrín Friðriksdóttir. *Women in Old Norse Literature: Bodies, Word, and Power*. New York: Palgrave Macmillan, 2013.

Kelly, Kathleen Coyne. "'The Trope of the Scopic in *The Vikings* (1958)." In *The Vikings on Film: Essays on Depictions of the Nordic Middle Ages*, edited by Kevin J. Harty, pp. 9–23. Jefferson, NC and London: McFarland, 2011.

Kennedy, Hugh. *Muslim Spain and Portugal: A Political History of Al-Andalus*. London: Routledge, 2014.

Larrington, Carolyne. *Winter Is Coming: The Medieval World of Game of Thrones*. London: I. B. Tauris, 2015.

Martin, George R. R. Blog. March 30, 2013. http://www.georgerrmartin.com/maurice-druons-the-iron-king/.

Martin, George R R.. "My Hero: Maurice Druon." *The Guardian*, April 5, 2013. https://www.theguardian.com/books/2013/apr/05/maurice-druon-george-rr-martin.

Moss, Emma-Lee. "Game of Thrones Announces New Season Five Cast Members." *The Guardian*, July 26, 2014. https://www.theguardian.com/culture/tvandradioblog/2014/jul/26/game-of-thrones-announces-new-season-five-cast-members.

OED Online. Oxford University Press, June 2017. http://www.oed.com/.

Robinson, Carol. L. and Pamela Clements. "Living with Neomedievalism." In *Defining Medievalism(s)*, vol. 2, Studies in Medievalism 18, ed. Karl Fugelso, pp. 55–77. Cambridge: D. S. Brewer, 2010.

Sif Rikhardsdóttir. *Emotion in Old Norse Literature*. Woodbridge: Boydell & Brewer, 2017.

Sindbæk, Søren M. "Networks and Nodal Points: The Emergence of Towns in Early Viking Age Scandinavia." *Antiquity* 81, no. 311 (2007): 119–32.

Sklar, Elizabeth S. "Call of the Wild: Culture Shock and Viking Masculinities in *The Thirteenth Warrior* (1999)." In *The Vikings on Film: Essays on Depictions of the Nordic Middle Ages*, edited by Kevin J. Harty, pp. 121–34. Jefferson, NC and London: McFarland, 2011.

Williams, Gareth, Peter Pentz and Matthias Wemhoff. *Vikings: Life and Legend*. London: British Museum, 2014.

Winroth, Anders. *The Age of the Vikings*. Princeton, NJ: Princeton University Press, 2014.

Notes

1. The terms "books" and "show" are self-explanatory; where my comments apply to the narrative across both media I use the term "series." The books are cited by chapter; the show is cited by season and episode number.
2. Nickolas Haydock, "Medievalism and Excluded Middles," in *Defining Medievalism(s)*, vol. 2, Studies in Medievalism 18, ed. Karl Fugelso (Cambridge: D. S. Brewer, 2010), pp. 17–30 at p. 19.
3. Carol. L. Robinson and Pamela Clements, "Living with Neomedievalism," in *Defining Medievalism(s)*, vol. 2, ed. Fugelso, pp. 55–77 at p. 61.
4. Ibid., p. 63.
5. Martin claims not to be a historian though he frequently invokes medieval history in discussion of his inspirations, notably in the important interview by Mikal Gilmore in *Rolling Stone*, May 8, 2014, https://web.archive.org/web/20180220172219/https://www.rollingstone.com/tv/news/george-r-r-martin-the-rolling-stone-interview-20140423. For analysis of the Old Norse-Icelandic historical and literary parallels to the series' evocation of the Ironborn, the North and the Three-Eyed Raven, see Carolyne Larrington, *Winter Is Coming: The Medieval World of Game of Thrones* (London: I. B. Tauris, 2015), pp. 58–74.
6. At the time of writing, five novels had been published in the "A Song of Ice and Fire" sequence; volume six, *The Winds of Winter* was eagerly awaited.
7. The continent of Westeros maps roughly onto Western Europe plus Iceland and Greenland. It is bisected by a seven-hundred-mile long and three-hundred-foot high wall of ice. North of the Wall live prehistoric tribal peoples of various kinds; south of the Wall are the Seven Kingdoms. The right to sit on the Iron Throne and rule over the Seven Kingdoms is at stake in the wars that have rent Westeros since the end of the first book, *A Game of Thrones* and show season 1. For more on the geography of Westeros, see Larrington, *Winter Is Coming*.
8. George R. R. Martin, *A Storm of Swords* (London: Harper Voyager, 2000), chap. 45, "Catelyn V"; *Game of Thrones*, 6.2, "Home."
9. The OED entry for "viking" has not been revised since 1917, and casts some doubt over *viking* as Scandinavian in origin. "Viking, n.," *OED Online*, Oxford University Press, June 2017, http://www.oed.com/. For an extensive discussion of the etymology and usage of the term, see the chapter by Driscoll in this collection, esp. pp. 26–30.
10. Thanks to Professor Ayelet Lushkov for this suggestion.
11. A reverse version of the Old Norse legends of *Hvítramannaland* (White Men's Land) across the western ocean, where, according to *Eyrbyggja saga* chap. 64, Björn Breiðvíkingakappi is thought to have ended his days.
12. Martin, *Storm of Swords*, chap. 78, "Samwell V"; in the most recent season of the show, Jaime Lannister sneers: "They're not good at anything. I know the Ironborn, they're bitter, angry little people. All they do is steal things they can't build or grow themselves." *Game of Thrones*, 7.1, "Dragonstone." Martin consistently uses a lower-case spelling "ironborn," but most critical writing, and the show and book wikis, capitalize the first initial.
13. George R. R. Martin, *A Feast for Crows* (London: Harper Voyager, 2005), chap. 29, "The Reaver."
14. *Brennu-Njáls saga*, ed. Einar Ólafur Sveinsson, Íslenzk fornrit 12 (Reykjavík: Hið Íslenzka fornritafélagið, 1954), p. 182.

15. George R. R. Martin, *A Clash of Kings* (London: Harper Voyager, 1998), chap. 11, "Theon I."
16. Maurice Druon, *Les Rois maudits* (édition integrale) (Paris: Plon, 2014); translations: *The Accursed Kings*, trans. Humphrey Hare. Reprint (London: Harper Collins, 2013–2015); *The Iron King* (1956/2013); *The Strangled Queen* (1956/2013); *The Poisoned Crown* (1957/ 2013); *The Royal Succession* (1958/2014); *The She-Wolf* (1960/2014); *The Lily and the Lion* (1961/2014); *The King without a Kingdom*, trans. Alan Simpkin (1977/2015). See Martin's Foreword(s) to the 2013–2015 republished editions and George R. R Martin, "My Hero: Maurice Druon," *The Guardian*, April 5, 2013, https://web.archive.org/web/ 20180221111732/https://www.theguardian.com/books/2013/apr/05/maurice-druon-george-rr-martin; compare Martin's blog, March 30, 2013, https://web.archive.org/web/ */http://www.georgerrmartin.com/maurice-druons-the-iron-king/.
17. Druon, *The Lily and the Lion*, pp. 132–33.
18. Whether women also undergo this ceremony remains uncertain.
19. Martin, *Feast for Crows*, chap. 1, "The Prophet."
20. See "Davy Jones, n.," *OED Online*, Oxford University Press, June 2017, http://www.oed. com/. The first citation here is Tobias Smollett from 1751, though there is an earlier usage in Daniel Defoe, *Four Years Voyages of Capt George Roberts*, from 1726.
21. Martin, *Clash of Kings*, chap. 11, "Theon I."
22. Victarion Greyjoy, in Martin, *Feast for Crows*, chap. 29, "The Reaver."
23. Martin, *Clash of Kings*, chap. 11, "Theon I."
24. See Gareth Williams, Peter Pentz and Matthias Wemhoff, *Vikings: Life and Legend* (London: British Museum, 2014) and Stefan Brink with Neil Price, ed., *The Viking World* (London: Routledge, 2008).
25. See Dawn M. Hadley and Julian D. Richards et al., "The Winter Camp of the Viking Great Army AD 872–3, Torksey," *The Antiquaries Journal* 96 (2016): 23–67; https://www.cam bridge.org/core/journals/antiquaries-journal/article/winter-camp-of-the-viking-great-army-ad-8723-torksey-lincolnshire/C54BB610EA9E0E567DC2C0622BA753EB, and the findings of Gareth Williams at the so-called "Riverine Site near York."
26. Hugh Kennedy, *Muslim Spain and Portugal: A Political History of Al-Andalus* (London: Routledge, 2014), p. 47.
27. See Søren M. Sindbæk, "Networks and Nodal Points: The Emergence of Towns in Early Viking Age Scandinavia," *Antiquity* 81, no. 311 (2007): 119–32.
28. Martin, *Feast for Crows*, chap. 1, "The Prophet."
29. Snorri Sturluson, *Óláfs saga Tryggvasonar*, in *Heimskringla*, ed. Bjarni Aðalbjarnarson. 3 vols. Íslenzk fornrit 26–28 (Reykjavík: Hið íslenzka fornritafélag, 1941–1951), vol. 1, p. 333.
30. Kathleen Coyne Kelly, "The Trope of the Scopic in *The Vikings* (1958)," in *The Vikings on Film: Essays on Depictions of the Nordic Middle Ages*, ed. Kevin J. Harty (Jefferson, NC and London: McFarland, 2011), pp. 9–23 at p. 12.
31. Ibid., p. 12.
32. See footnote 5.
33. Martin, *Feast for Crows*, chap. 1, "The Prophet."
34. The finger-dance may be another neomedievalist trope, possibly originating in the axe-throwing scene that begins the 1989 British comedy-fantasy movie, *Eric the Viking*, directed by Terry Jones. See Susan Aronstein, "When Civilization was Less Civilized: Erik the Viking (1989)," in *The Vikings on Film*, ed. Harty, pp. 72–82.
35. Martin, *Clash of Kings*, chap. 37, "Theon III."
36. Martin, *Feast for Crows*, chap. 29, "The Reaver."

37. Ibid., chap. 19, "The Drowned Man."
38. On the "blood-eagle," see Roberta Frank, "Viking Atrocity and Skaldic Verse: The Rite of the Blood Eagle," *English Historical Review* 99, no. 391 (1984): 332–43; Roberta Frank, "The Blood-Eagle Again," *Saga-Book of the Viking Society* 22 (1988): 287–89; Roberta Frank, "Ornithology and Interpretation of Skaldic Verse," *Saga-Book* 23 (1990): 81–83 and Bjarni Einarsson, "The Blood-Eagle Once More: Two Notes," *Saga-Book* 23 (1990): 80–81; *Njáls saga*, ed. Einar Ólafur Sveinsson, p. 453.
39. Martin, *Feast for Crows*, chap. 19, "The Drowned Man."
40. Ibid., chap. 19, "The Drowned Man."
41. *Game of Thrones*, 6.9, "Battle of the Bastards." Sovereignty over the Ironborn is symbolized by the "Salt Throne," also called the "Seastone Chair."
42. *Grettis saga*, ed. Guðni Jónsson, Íslenzk fornrit 7 (Reykjavík: Hið Íslenzka fornritafélagið, 1936), pp. 25–26.
43. Anders Winroth, *The Age of the Vikings* (Princeton, NJ: Princeton University Press, 2014), p. 247.
44. Martin, *Feast for Crows*, chap. 11, "The Kraken's Daughter."
45. Ibid., chap. 11, "The Kraken's Daughter."
46. George R. R. Martin, *A Dance with Dragons* (London: Harper Voyager, 2011), chap. 62, "The Sacrifice."
47. In April 2014. Martin remarked: "Religion is an important part of the world and should be depicted, but I won't endorse one over the other. I wouldn't choose one particular god." Emma-Lee Moss, "Game of Thrones Announces New Season Five Cast Members," *The Guardian*, July 26, 2014, https://www.theguardian.com/culture/tvandradioblog/2014/jul/26/game-of-thrones-announces-new-season-five-cast-members.
48. James Hibberd, "George R.R. Martin Explains Why There's Violence against Women on *Game of Thrones*," https://web.archive.org/web/20180226183218/http://ew.com/article/2015/06/03/george-rr-martin-thrones-violence-women/?xid=IFT-Trending.
49. See Erik Germani, "The Redemption of Jaime Lannister," http://atseajournal.com/asoiaf/essays/jaimes_redemption.html for a good account of Martin's treatment of Jaime Lannister.
50. Saxo Grammaticus, *Gesta Danorum: The History of the Danes*, ed. Karsten Friis-Jensen, trans. Peter Fisher, 2 vols. (Oxford: Oxford University Press, 2015), vol. 1, pp. 470–77.
51. See Jóhanna Katrín Friðriksdóttir, *Women in Old Norse Literature: Bodies, Word, and Power* (New York: Palgrave Macmillan, 2013), pp. 107–34 and Jóhanna Katrín Friðriksdóttir, "'From Heroic Legend to Medieval Screwball Comedy?' The Development and Interpretation of the *meykongr* Motif," in *The Legendary Sagas: Origins and Development*, ed. Annette Lassen, Agneta Ney and Ármann Jakobsson (Reykjavík: Háskólaútgáfan, 2012), pp. 229–49; see also Sif Rikhardsdóttir, *Emotion in Old Norse Literature* (Woodbridge: Boydell & Brewer, 2017), pp. 146–74.
52. Jóhanna Katrín Friðriksdóttir, *Women in Old Norse Literature*, p. 129.
53. See Charlotte Hedenstierna-Jonson, Anna Kjellström, Torun Zachrisson et al., "A Female Viking Warrior Confirmed by Genomics," *American Journal of Physical Anthropology* 164, no. 4 (2017): 853–60. Compare the figures of Lathgertha in the History channel's *Vikings* show, and Brida in the BBC's *The Last Kingdom*.
54. Martin, *Feast for Crows*, chap. 11, "The Kraken's Daughter."
55. *Game of Thrones*, 7.2, "Stormborn."

56. Martin's sixth volume, *The Winds of Winter*, is in preparation at the time of writing; parts of it have been published online. There is no guarantee that they will not be revised before final publication. The plots of the TV show and the novels have now diverged considerably, once the show's chronology overtook that of the books at the beginning of Season Five.

57. Asha endeavors to save Theon from the pyre in a published *Winds of Winter* chapter.

58. *Game of Thrones*, 5.8, "Hardhome."

59. Ibid., 7.7, "The Dragon and the Wolf."

60. An alternative term for the Salt Throne.

61. Martin, *Feast for Crows*, chap. 29, "The Reaver."

62. Aronstein, "When Civilization Was Less Civilized," p. 77.

63. "King Arthur: Legend of the Sword," IMDb, http://www.imdb.com/title/tt1972591/ Viking / Arthurian crossover originates in the Prince Valiant comics, first published in 1937.

64. Martin, *Feast for Crows*, chap. 29, "The Reaver."

65. Elizabeth S. Sklar, "Call of the Wild: Culture Shock and Viking Masculinities in *The Thirteenth Warrior* (1999)," in *The Vikings on Film*, ed. Harty, pp. 121–34 at p. 128; "The 13th Warrior," IMDb, http://www.imdb.com/title/tt0120657/.

66. Elio Garcia and Linda Antonsson, in association with George R. R. Martin, *The World of Ice and Fire* (London: Harper Voyager, 2014), "The Old Way and the New."

67. Rudyard Kipling, "Harp Song of the Dane Women," https://www.poetryfoundation.org/poems/47691/harp-song-of-the-dane-women, first published in *Puck of Pook Hill* (London: Macmillan, 1906).

Kendra Willson
10 A Saga King in a Finnish Beijing Opera

Introduction

Sigurd Ring is a Beijing opera-style theatrical performance produced in Finland in Swedish in 2016, based on a legendary Danish-Swedish king of the eighth century, whose story is mediated through various medieval sources in Old Norse and Latin, a seventeenth-century Latin paraphrase of a lost saga, and a nineteenth-century Swedish Romantic play. The visual, kinetic, and musical language of the opera contains some striking analogues to commonplaces of saga style. The modern fusion of traditions highlights affinities in the ethos of the worlds represented in the very different genres.

Many of the Old Norse texts written in Iceland in the thirteenth and fourteenth centuries lend themselves naturally to dramatic performance. Some may have their origins in ritual drama.[1] Sagas and Eddic poems have been adapted for the stage in modern times in many different ways, from the *Gesamtkunstwerk* of Richard Wagner's *Der Ring der Nibelungen* to *Mr. Skallagrímsson*, Benedikt Erlingsson's one-man comic take on *Egils saga Skallagrímssonar*.

Adaptations of stories across media, centuries, and traditions show the versatility of the narratives. Different tellings, interpretations, and adaptations bring out different aspects of a story. This applies both to narratives that are retold in oral tradition and in the fluid authorship of medieval literature, as well as to dramatic texts as performed. As Reba Gostand writes, "Drama, as an art form, is a constant process of translation."[2] Each new production involves an interpretation of a text from a written medium to a live performance, tied to a specific place and time. This holds especially for productions that move the text into a different cultural idiom and tradition. Shaping the story of Sigurd Ring into a form from a non-Western culture makes it less of a period piece and shifts it away from Nordic nationalistic traditions. It highlights archetypes and universals that can be clothed in very different trappings.

Sigurd Ring in Sagas and Saxo

The eighth-century king Sigurd Ring (Sigurðr hringr Randversson) is mentioned briefly in numerous Old Norse sources, mainly of the types classified as kings'

Kendra Willson, University of Turku

https://doi.org/10.1515/9781501513886-011

sagas (*konungasögur*) and legendary sagas (*fornaldarsögur*), as well as in the twelfth-century Latin history *Gesta Danorum* by Saxo Grammaticus.[3] Sigurðr belongs to the time treated in the thirteenth- and fourteenth-century sagas as the ancient past, before the settlement of Iceland in the ninth and tenth centuries. Nonetheless, in many ways the social structures and values depicted in the legendary sagas and the modes of narration invoked are similar to those seen in sagas of Icelanders (*Íslendingasögur*).[4]

Sigurðr himself is a minor character in these sources. He is described as having been the ruler of Svealand and Västergötland. He is noted primarily for having defeated his uncle King Haraldr hilditönn (Wartooth) at the battle of Brávellir, thereby becoming ruler of Sweden and Denmark. The longest preserved narrative about Sigurðr, in book 8 of *Gesta Danorum* by Saxo Grammaticus, focuses on this battle.[5] The fragmentary saga (*Sögubrot*) breaks off in the middle of the account of Sigurðr and the battle,[6] but the first parts of the story more or less align with Saxo. Another legendary saga, *Bósa saga ok Herrauðs*, mentions a lost saga of Sigurd Ring,[7] so it is likely that a longer tradition attached to him.

Sigurd Ring's main significance is as part of a succession. He belongs to one of the most famous families in Old Norse literature: Sigurðr is the father of Ragnarr loðbrók (Hairy-breeches), whose legendary saga (*Ragnars saga loðbrókar*) continues the lineage from *Völsunga saga*. This genealogical link connects the story of Sigurd Ring to the "other" Ring opera, Richard Wagner's cycle *Der Ring der Nibelungen*. Ragnarr's mother Áslaug is the daughter of the dragon-slayer Sigurðr Fáfnisbani and the Valkyrie Brynhildr. However, there are some discrepancies in the genealogies. According to *Sögubrot af nokkrum fornkonungum* and *Skjöldunga saga*, Ragnarr's mother was named Álfhildr. The genealogical connection between Ragnarr and Sigurðr Fáfnisbani is perhaps contrived in order to give a divine/mythic pedigree for the royal lineage.[8] It has been suggested that the traditions about Ragnarr and his sons conflate several (semi-)historical figures.[9]

The saga fragment known as *Sögubrot af nokkrum fornkonungum* (Fragmentary saga of some ancient kings) contains a chapter on Sigurd Ring that ends in a lacuna. It praises the lineage of Sigurðr's first wife Álfhildr, Ragnarr's mother, and begins to describe a battle that takes place in Sigurðr's old age.[10] The account of Sigurd Ring in *Hervarar saga ok Heiðreks* comprises just a few sentences, focusing on his battle prowess and genealogical position.[11] The image of Sigurd Ring that emerges from the different sources is of a powerful warrior king, who retained authority into his older age and was ambitious in marriage.

The proximate source for the play by Stagnelius comes from *Skjöldunga saga*. The lost saga concerns the Scylding dynasty known from *Beowulf* and is one of the eventual sources for Shakespeare's *Hamlet*. Bjarni Guðnason believes that *Skjöldunga saga* dated from around or before 1200.[12] Although the saga has not survived as a whole, parts of it are preserved or reworked in other texts.

The Icelander Arngrímur lærði (the learned) Jónsson (1568–1648), who had access to a version of *Skjöldunga saga* that is now lost, gives a Latin retelling of the story, with some of his own interpolations and speculation.[13] Jakob Benediktsson argues that the structure of *Skjöldunga saga* can be inferred by comparing Arngrímur's account to preserved analogues for various parts of the text.[14] Bjarni Guðnason argues that Arngrímur Jónsson's seventeenth-century translation followed its source fairly closely,[15] and shows that, for the parts of Arngrímur's account for which other versions are known, Arngrímur's narrative is at least as full as the comparanda. Arngrímur's model most likely had a lacuna that extended to part of the story of Sigurd Ring.[16]

Arngrímur's text contains a narrative in which Sigurðr, following the death of his first wife, Ragnarr's mother Álfhildr, decides to take a second wife. During a sacrificial celebration (*blót*) at Skíringssalr in Vík in Norway he notices Álfsól, daughter of Álfr, a Vendel king. He asks for her hand, but her two brothers Álfr and Yngvi refuse, which enrages Sigurðr. Once the sacrificial sanctuary has ended, they fight with armies. Both brothers are slain, but they have contrived first to poison their sister so that she will not fall into the victor's hands.[17] When the victorious but wounded Sigurðr hears of Álfsól's death, he prepares and burns a funerary boat piled with corpses and boards it to sacrifice himself alive.[18]

Saxo's account of Sigurd Ring does not include this late-life wooing story, although some of the same motifs occur in different configurations: Omund appears as an unwelcome suitor to Sigurd's own daughter,[19] and Sigurd prepares an elaborate funeral pyre for his defeated uncle Harald rather than for himself.[20] *Sögubrot* breaks off early in the story of Sigurd Ring.

Arngrímur Jónsson's text was not published until 1894, almost eighty years after Stagnelius wrote his play *Sigurd Ring: Sorgspel*. Stagnelius may have known the Sigurd story from P. F. Suhm's *Historie af Danmark*;[21] the story was also popularized through *Swerges historia för ungdom* by Magnus Bruzelius[22] (see Henrikson[23]). Whatever the source Stagnelius used, he treated the subject freely as the basis for a Romantic tragedy. It is possible that Sigurd Ring appealed as a subject in part because he is mentioned in enough texts to be considered historical, but his story is sufficiently fragmentary and little-known to allow the poet space to shape the narrative for his own purposes.[24] The story as transmitted involves a number of conventional tropes, perhaps filling gaps in historical memory, that have potential as dramatic elements: valiant resistance in the face of overwhelming odds, the tragic death of a reluctant would-be bride, and the pageantry of pagan rituals such as the elaborate funeral. *Sigurd Ring* is a stylized story with a simple, classical structure and widespread analogues. At the same time, the psychological depth and ambivalent view of the heroic ethos also make it modern.

Stagnelius: *Sigurd Ring: Sorgspel*

Erik Johan Stagnelius (1793–1823) was a Swedish Romantic poet and playwright, who has been compared with the English poet Percy Bysshe Shelley.[25] Stagnelius worked extensively with Old Norse themes as well as with classical ones. *Sigurd Ring: Sorgspel* (tragedy) was the first of his "nordiska dramer" (Nordic dramas), followed by *Wisbur* and the fragment *Svegder*,[26] both of which are based on subjects from *Völsunga saga*. *Sigurd Ring* was most likely written around 1817 (when the story of Sigurd Ring became available through Bruzelius) or a couple of years later, but was published only posthumously.[27]

Here is a brief plot summary: the powerful king Sigurd demands to marry Hilma, who was supposed to marry Ragnar that day. When he encounters resistance, Sigurd challenges Ragnar and Hilma's brother Alf to combat, defeats them and triumphantly approaches Hilma – only to find her a corpse. She had preferred death and poisoned herself. In his despair Sigurd boards his ship beside Hilma's corpse and abandons himself to the flames.

The tone of the play is tragic throughout. Even when Hilma first appears on what is supposed to be her wedding day, before Sigurd has arrived, she is already in despair, having had a premonition of doom. The focus is less on action than on mood. Stagnelius introduces a love triangle by making Ragnar Hilma's betrothed, and presents both Hilma's and Sigurd's deaths as suicides.

Henrikson notes that "*Sigurd Ring* präglas av en överflödande rikedom på bilder som på ett framträdande sätt förmedlar vanitassymbolik"[28] (*Sigurd Ring* is characterized by an overwhelming richness of images which in a prominent way convey symbolism of vanity). This is stripped out of the Beijing opera adaptation, which replaces verbal imagery with the rich multimodal language of stagecraft.

Beijing Opera

Beijing or Peking opera (*jingju*, or "capital city theater") is a codified theater form with strict rules. It is the best-known genre of Chinese theater abroad. The genre emerged near the end of the eighteenth century. Despite its name, it did not originate in Beijing, but in provincial areas. It developed from "rustic" folk dramas known collectively as *huabu*, particularly those of the middle and lower Yangtze valley in the eighteenth century,[29] but *jingju* also absorbed influences from and eventually supplanted the previously dominant *kunqu* tradition when it was imported to the capital in the early nineteenth century.[30]

Traditional Chinese theater in general is anti-realistic, stylized, and based on types. All traditional Chinese theater forms are music-based.[31] Beijing opera does not classify stories as tragedy or comedy, but as military drama (*wuxi*) and civil drama (*wenxi*).[32] Wusheng Company's productions, including *Sigurd Ring*, are military dramas (the name *Wusheng* means "male warrior"). Characters in Beijing opera are divided into well-defined types. The main character types are *sheng* (male characters), *dan* (female characters), *jing* (painted-face characters like Sigurd Ring), and *chou* ("ugly," clown characters).[33] Types are further divided by age, military skills, and social class. One criterion in Edström's selection of *Sigurd Ring* as a subject was that the characters in the play could be fit into the types of Beijing opera.

Chinese Theater in Finland

Chinese drama has been performed in Finland since the first visit by a Chinese company in 1955.[34] From 1997 to 2016, the annual festival Aasia Helsingissä (Asia in Helsinki) brought visiting companies from different Asian countries to perform in Helsinki.[35] This festival indirectly inspired the foundation of Wusheng Company: seeing a performance of Beijing opera at the festival led Antti Silvennoinen to study the art in Beijing.[36] Silvennoinen has since spread this interest to others, including Elias Edström.

Silvennoinen and Edström founded Wusheng Company in 2011 in order to create opportunities to perform Beijing opera in Finland, the only company of its kind in the world producing professional Beijing opera abroad.[37] Over the period 2011–2016 the company produced a dozen plays, ranging from classical Beijing operas to fusion productions such as *Sigurd Ring*. Edström left Wusheng Company in 2016 and in 2017 founded Matchbox Company, which produced additional performances of *Sigurd Ring* in Kajaani in 2017.[38]

Sigurd Ring is Elias Edström's (b. 1988) debut as director and playwright. Edström (Figure 10.1) studied physical theater at Svenska yrkeshögskolan in Vaasa (now part of Novia University of Applied Sciences). Part of the program involved becoming acquainted with a different theatrical tradition, so in the

Figure 10.1: Elias Edström as Sigurd Ring (image used in production poster). Photo by Mitro Härkkönen.

third year of the four-year program, Edström spent four months on exchange in China. Beijing opera appealed to him as a way of combining his interests in martial arts and physical theater.[39] After completing the program at Vaasa he went to China to continue his studies. In 2015, Edström was the first European to complete a Master's degree at The National Academy for Chinese Theater Arts, where he was one of only five Europeans among 2000 students.[40]

The other actors, Satu Mäkelä, Niko Arola, and Talvikki Eerola, were recruited for the production via an advertisement. The performers are Finns with professional education in different performing arts. All were around thirty at the time of the production. They trained intensely for two months in the techniques of Beijing opera.

From Saga to Romantic Play to Beijing Opera

Elias Edström created this production in seeking a way to connect the Chinese theatrical tradition he had studied to his own Nordic heritage. Edström's text is freely adapted from *Sigurd Ring*. The text is distilled from approximately eight thousand to around one thousand words: the opening monologues in which the characters introduce themselves and briefly present their situation at the start of the play, three short scenes of dialogue, and a final scene consisting of two songs. However, most of the hour-long show consists of wordless movement and music, including courtship dances by Alf and Hilma and especially fight scenes. While Stagnelius puts all the battles offstage, in Edström's version they are the center of the action. The number of characters is reduced to four, eliminating Hilma's mother Gerda, "en kämpe" (a warrior), and two choruses, one of serving girls and one of warriors. While Stagnelius wrote in rhymed couplets, Edström's script is pared down to its essence as an operatic libretto, with the dignity and distance of a slightly archaic style.

The plot is fairly simple. Hilma has ruled the kingdom of Jutland after her father's death and in her brother Alf's absence. She has refused all suitors because her heart has gone to Ragnar, her brother's ally. Alf is now home; today Ragnar will return and ask for Hilma's hand in marriage. Alf has sacrificed his dignity and made peace with their father's killer, King Sigurd of Sweden. King Sigurd has decided he needs a wife to bring him comfort and an heir in his old age, and comes to Jutland to demand Hilma's hand. Alf refuses, saying that Sigurd has gone too far. Alf has suffered enough humiliation from Sigurd, and Hilma is engaged to Ragnar. Sigurd says that Ragnar and Alf must die if he does not get Hilma's hand. Alf and Ragnar fight Sigurd, first separately and then together. In a pause, Hilma asks if the battle is over. She urges them to flee – why fight a battle that is already lost? Sigurd will return with all his army. The others say that this is why they must defeat Sigurd now while he is alone and vulnerable: "Det finns mycket här att vinna" (There is much here to gain), while Hilma warns them, "Och än mer att förlora" (and even more to lose). The fighting resumes. Sigurd slays first Alf, then Ragnar. The bereaved Hilma takes up a sword against Sigurd, but he wrests it from her and slays her with it. In the final scene Sigurd holds the dying Hilma and says that "sköna Hilma all min kärlek har" (beautiful Hilma has all my love).[41]

Edström has commented that while Stagnelius gives the text a tragic tone throughout, the adaptation combines elements of love and humor for a more varied emotional palette.[42] In contrast to the dramatic funeral pageant of the Romantic and Early Modern versions, this play has a haunting, ambiguous ending – Sigurd's words present macabre irony. The villain has lost everything and becomes almost pitiable.[43]

Scenery and Lighting

The stage was bare apart from a rectangular green mat, a station for musicians with instruments stage left (audience right), and black curtains framing the scene. Two simple chairs were used in the scene in which Alf receives Sigurd. The bare stage is in accordance with the Chinese tradition, in which the actor is supposed to evoke the environment (setting, season, mood) through use of body, costume, and sound.[44]

The lighting was designed by Milka Timosaari. The lighting filled the backdrop with solid (or gradually shading) color in ways that would change by character and mood – blue at the start, blood red after Sigurd kills Ragnar and Alf, purple when Hilma comes to avenge. Each character was associated with a color. Sigurd is associated with the color red and Alf with blue. The hues correspond to colors in their costumes. When two characters or moods meet, the light colors blend. Finnish translations of the Swedish text were also projected onto the back wall.

This use of lighting departs from traditional Beijing opera, in which, as Rosenberg put it, there are two settings: "Valot pois ja valot päällä" (lights off and lights on).[45] However, the spirit of simplicity is retained, while allowing the use of varied lighting as a dimension of the performance.

Music

Pekka Saarikorpi, best known as a jazz musician, has worked with Wusheng Company since 2011. In this production, Saarikorpi played four Chinese percussion instruments. Senni Eskelinen played the electric kantele (a modern variation on an iconic Finnish folk instrument), which was used for more melodic and lyrical moments, especially accompanying Hilma. The music for the play was based on the basic rhythms of traditional Beijing opera, with a rhythmical score written out by Edström. The music was not traditional, but the ways of combining music and movement were based on tradition. In the rehearsal process, the musicians and actors worked together to develop the music and movements.

In addition to the rhythmical music performed by the instrumentalists, the opera includes two songs sung by actors: a Finnish folk melody, "Läksin minä kesäyönä käymään" (I went out on a summer night), sung by Hilma in Western style with lyrics loosely based on text from the play by Stagnelius, and a traditional Beijing opera melody performed by Sigurd in Chinese style. These comprise the libretto for the final scene. Both are brief, just a few lines, but provide variety in the texture and emotional palette of the play.

Costumes

The costumes were authentic Beijing opera costumes ordered from China; they had originally been designed for a different production and were reused for *Sigurd Ring*. In Beijing opera tradition each element of the costume has significance. The audience can instantly see the character's age, social status and whether he is good or bad. Much of this symbolism may be lost or understood differently by a foreign audience. In the Finnish production, however, the costumes are used "incorrectly" according to tradition. Nonetheless, they have evocative connotations even to a naïve audience, as well as contributing to the spectacle.

The costumes function as an extension of the body, and shape and amplify its movement. Some central costume elements are used from the beginning of the rehearsal process as central to character development.

Edström as Sigurd (Figures. 10.1 and 10.2) wore a white silk robe with elaborate brocade, red trousers, and knee-high boots with platform soles. His face

Figure 10.2: Sigurd Ring (Elias Edström) holds the dying Hilma (Talvikki Eerola). Photo by Kari Rosenberg.

was painted white with black details as a mask, whereas the other characters had pink faces with emphasized rising diagonals at the temples but more "naturalistic" makeup. The painted-face type (*jing*) is the role-type that Edström had studied in China. *Jing* characters are typically powerful and high-ranking. A white face in a *jing* character "indicates cunning and treachery."[46] The symbolism of white in Chinese tradition is the opposite of the canonical association of white with "good" and black with "evil" in Western tradition, but gives him in Western eyes perhaps the appearance of a ghost or otherworldly figure. High platform shoes with wedged angles at toe and heel emphasized his height over the other characters and shaped his movements.[47]

Also in contrast to the Western convention of black costumes for "bad guys" and white for good, the "good guy" warriors had costumes that were predominantly black. Ragnar wore a black martial arts uniform with orange and red trim, drawing attention to an orange and red sash. This was a *bingyi* or *kuaiyi* costume associated with the *wusheng* "male warrior" character type.[48] Ragnar's sash and Hilma's sleeves become important foci for movement and expression. They hit each other with these costume extensions but also reach for each other longingly. Hilma drags Ragnar offstage by the sash, with erotic overtones.

Hilma's costume (Figure 10.2) combined elements of *wudan* "warrior woman" and *qingyi* "noble woman" types but departed substantially from Beijing opera tradition.[49] Hilma's expressive, overly long white sleeves (*shuixiu* "water sleeves") serve as an extension of her body. The water sleeves are an important accoutrement and support technique in Beijing opera.[50] In *Sigurd Ring*, Hilma's sleeves sometimes appear as weapons. Sometimes they are extensions of her arms reaching longingly toward her lover. They tremble to reveal emotion while the rest of her body remains restrained. In her last scene Hilma trades the pink bridal robe for a purple one that leaves her sword arm free. The rippling sleeve waves as she dies, like a white flag of surrender and a suggestion of flowing blood.

A significant departure from Beijing opera tradition was that Hilma was barefoot. In traditional Beijing opera, characters are never barefoot on stage.[51] The bare feet highlight Hilma's vulnerability and humanity, as well as the contrast with Sigurd's height and platform shoes.[52] Both Hilma and Ragnar were also bare-headed, another departure from tradition. In Beijing opera the full coverage of the costumes assists in concealing the individual features of the actors and emphasizes the types.[53] However, Western audiences may seek connection with the "human" side of the characters.

Alf's costume included a close-fitting coat over a suit, in dark blue and black. This was a *jianyi* or "archer's robe"[54] with some added decoration to suggest rank. Edström said in an interview that he would have liked to have a more elaborate costume for Alf.[55] Sigurd and Alf had long false beards, attached to wires, which they manipulated during their speeches. Alf's was black and Sigurd's dark grey. In the symbolism of Beijing opera, a black beard means that a character is at least forty years old, a grey beard that he is at least fifty. They wore headdresses with dangling balls, which evoke royal crowns and which draw attention to the actor's face.

Saga Narration and Beijing Opera

The points of contact between Beijing opera and saga narrative are partly coincidences, partly reflections of honor-based societies which idealize a kind of warrior elite and storytelling styles refined from oral tradition, not to mention universal archetypes.

A number of points in the structure and narrative form of the *Sigurd Ring* production echo characteristic features of saga narrative, what has been termed the "folklig stil" (folk style) for its deceptive simplicity and apparent similarity to oral narrative. This style is most associated with sagas of Icelanders from the thirteenth century, but also applies to varying extents to other genres.

Character Introductions

In Beijing opera, when each character appears on the stage for the first time, he or she performs a two- to three-minute movement sequence that expresses or represents character. The character's first speech, following this "dance," states explicitly who he is, the situation, and his goal. The pattern of self-presentations can be compared to formulaic character introductions in sagas, a striking feature of saga style. The degree to which a saga personage's genealogy, appearance, and character are described indicates the importance of the character.[56] Genealogies are important for explaining loyalties, as well as being of interest to the medieval Icelandic audiences who traced their ancestry to persons mentioned in sagas.[57]

Varied Pacing

The pace of *Sigurd Ring* varies between very slow build-up and rapid fight scenes. Battle scenes are elaborately choreographed. The delay – punctuated by percussion – before a reaction evokes "the mask's time," a deliberateness and slowness common to stylized dramatic traditions. It contributes to the sense of deliberateness and otherworldliness. It also evokes the self-discipline and emotional control valued in the saga world, where characters in the midst of battle or immediately before a violent death still take the time to make a laconic *bon mot*, and where vengeance may be plotted for years.

Dual Focus on Action and Psychology

In Beijing opera the focus is on acrobatic virtuosity, whereas Western theater is about interpersonal relationships and character development. This production had perhaps a dual focus, with the tragic story and relationships (expressed in constrained ways) coming across clearly as the frame, but a dramatic high point and substantial fraction of stage time devoted to the choreographed battles. This is reminiscent of saga narrative, where intense conflicts – with words and weapons – alternate with periods of waiting and political regrouping.

Tight, Laconic Dialogue; Songs Used to Highlight Emotions

One characteristic of saga style is its conciseness. Dialogue in particular is pithy, brief, and laconic. The characters are people of few words. Gestures all have significance. Emotions may be expressed through gesture. Characters have a restrained mode of expression. The formalized style and minimal text of the Beijing opera production resonates with this aesthetic.

The two songs in *Sigurd Ring* highlight moments of particular emotion and provide a change of rhythm from the acrobatic movement and battle scenes. Their function can be compared to some of the uses of skaldic verse in saga narration: a personal voice for a character, with somewhat more emotional openness than is seen in the highly constrained dialogue and narration.

Ambivalent Portrayal of Honor Society

Both *Sigurd Ring* and sagas represent an honor society. Like many sagas, Wusheng Company's *Sigurd Ring* can be read either as endorsing or as critical of or ambivalent toward the honor society and its ethical code.[58] Alf has compromised his and his family's honor by seeking conciliation with his father's killer in the interest of peace. However, Sigurd is uncompromising and Alf's diplomacy ill rewarded – which can be read as a warning: "Give 'em an inch and they'll take a mile." Hilma advises flight after the first round: why fight a battle that is already lost? Alf and Ragnar assure her they will win, but they are mistaken and their bravado may be misguided. This contrasts with their pessimism in the version by Stagnelius. Sagas regularly portray characters going into battles or traps despite warnings that they are unlikely to come out alive, sometimes to avoid the appearance of cowardice, sometimes citing the inevitability of fate.[59]

One manifestation of the honor society is that trivial actions are imbued with significance for the power dynamics among the characters. A scene in which Alf and Sigurd make an elaborate show of each asking the other to sit down first, with politeness thinly veiling hostility, recalls scenes in sagas (notably *Brennu-Njáls saga*) in which characters quarrel over seating arrangements at feasts with their attendant symbolism of status.[60]

Warrior Women

In *Sigurd Ring*, the one female character Hilma includes elements of the type of character known in Chinese as *wudan* (female with martial skills).[61] She dies fighting Sigurd, rather than from poison as in the versions of the story by Arngrímur and Stagnelius. In her introduction, Hilma states that she has ruled Jutland justly in the absence of her male relatives. Hilma's role as a warrior gives her a stronger position than the Romantic feminine ideal represented in the nineteenth-century play. Nonetheless Hilma's character is represented as "softer" than the male characters, associated with more melodic kantele music and blue and pink colors.

The character of the woman who takes up arms after her male allies have fallen resonates with the women warriors, maiden kings, and Valkyries of Norse legendary history. The historical basis for the trope has been much debated.[62] Although in Arngrímur's version Sigurðr's desired match Álfsól is not presented as a warrior woman, there are numerous women warriors and maiden kings in book 8 of Saxo, in and around the story of Sigurd Ring,[63] and *Sögubrot* mentions shield maidens Vebjörg and Visina as leaders in the battle of Brávellir.[64]

As Grimstad discusses, express suicide is rare in Old Norse literature.[65] In *Völsunga saga* it is a solution used by women in response to conflicting loyalties and dilemmas – in fulfilling the obligation for revenge on blood kinsmen, they have transgressed against their husbands and/or children whom they are also required to avenge, and so have no other way out. This has been interpreted as reflecting Continental influence; it can also be seen as a way for women to participate in bloodfeud. In shifting the ending from suicide and self-sacrifice to loss in a valiant but hopeless (perhaps foolhardy) battle and an ambiguous continuation, the Beijing opera moves away from Romantic melodrama and closer to modern sensibilities, as well as to general saga ethos.

"Opera"

The term "opera" evokes a grand scale of stylized musical drama and spectacle. As mentioned above, the Mandarin name for what is called Peking or Beijing opera in English is actually *jingju* "capital city theater." *Sigurd Ring* by Stagnelius has, however, been characterized as having operatic overtones. Malmström notes that while Stagnelius intended the choruses in the play to evoke Greek tragedy, in many ways their function is more reminiscent of that of choruses in Western opera,[66] as Henrikson summarizes:

> Malmströms stilistiska studier har visat hur körerna i Stagnelius' nordiska sorgspel rent formellt befinner sig i en mellanfas: de är samtidigt präglade av såväl operan och kantaten som en tydlig antikiserande ambition.[67] (Malmström's stylistic studies have shown how the choruses in the Nordic tragedies of Stagnelius are situated in an intermediate stage on a purely formal level: they simultaneously show features of opera and cantata and of a clear classisizing ambition.)

The title *Sigurd Ring* (particularly paired with the word "opera") also evokes Richard Wagner's *Der Ring des Nibelungen*. The name *Sigurd* (or *Siegfried*) is of course also that of the dragon-slayer in the Nibelung material, and as mentioned above, Sigurd Ring is genealogically connected to the Volsungs. This may prime viewers to expect a visual and musical spectacle, at a grand scale and a slow pace, based on mythical materials from the Germanic past.

Renewal through Synthesis

The fusion between ancient traditions seen in *Sigurd Ring* brings a fresh view to both Beijing opera and the saga tradition. Rosenberg has speculated that if the production were to tour in China, it might help revitalize interest in Beijing Opera among a younger Chinese audience by showing its potential for renewal.[68] When excerpts from Wusheng Company's productions have been performed at festivals in China, they have received positive responses and media attention. In 2017, Wusheng Company was awarded second prize in a Global Beijing Opera Fans Contest in the Garden Expo Park in Beijing.[69]

The synthesis also revives a long-dead Viking king and a rarely performed Romantic play. The ethos of the Viking world and of the traditional Chinese opera have some features in common that are not shared with the Romantic era. Connecting different traditions produces something new. In this case, the Beijing opera form takes the story of Sigurd Ring out of the Nordic historical context and into a formalized, archetypal space, with a slowed pace and condensed script that bring focus to fundamentals. The Viking spirit is not represented by blond beards and horned helmets, but by warrior codes of conduct, problematic honor societies, pride and betrayal, valiance in the face of overwhelming odds, fatal strategic blunders, and attempts at heroic death.

The Wusheng Company artists respect Chinese expertise and seek it out, for instance taking the cast of *Viimeinen taistelija* (The Last Warrior), including the well-known ballet dancer and choreographer Tero Saarinen, to Beijing for a crash course in Beijing opera technique.[70] However, Edström has said that his goal is less to perform traditional Beijing opera than to draw on the possibilities offered by its many-sided training and techniques in conjunction with other techniques and styles.[71] Fusion productions such as *Sigurd Ring* celebrate eclectic hybridity in a way that is part of modern national and other identities in a globalized world. They belong to an inclusive artistic discourse that brings Asia to Helsinki, Finns to China, and a saga king to a Finnish Beijing opera.

Bibliography

Arngrímur Jónsson. "Svíakonungatal Arngríms lærða." In *Danakonunga sǫgur. Skjǫldunga saga. Knýtlinga saga. Ágrip af sǫgu Danakonunga*, edited by Bjarni Guðnason, pp. 72–77. Íslenzk fornrit 35. Reykjavík: Hið Íslenzka fornritafélag, 1987.

Bjarni Guðnason. *Um Skjöldungasögu*. Reykjavík: Bókaútgáfa Menningarsjóðs, 1963.

Bjarni Guðnason. "Skjǫldunga saga." In *Kulturhistoriskt lexikon för nordisk medeltid. Från vikingatid till reformationstid 15: Samisk språk – Skude*, edited by Helge Pohjolan-Pirhonen, pp. 596–98. Helsinki: Akademiska bokhandeln, 1970.

Bonds, Alexandra B. *Beijing Opera Costumes: The Visual Communication of Character and Culture*. Honolulu: University of Hawai'i Press, 2008.

"Bósa saga ok Herrauðs." In *Fornaldarsögur Norðrlanda*, edited by Valdimar Ásmundarson, vol. 3, pp. 243–72. Reykjavík: Sigurður Kristjánsson, 1889.

Brennu-Njáls saga. Edited by Einar Ól. Sveinsson. Íslenzk fornrit 12. Reykjavík: Hið Íslenzka fornritafélag, 1954.

Bruzelius, Magnus. *Swerges historia för ungdom*. Lund: s.n., 1817.

Böök, Fredrik. *Erik Johan Stagnelius*. Stockholm: Albert Bonniers förlag, 1919.

Callow, Christopher. "Reconstructing the Past in Medieval Iceland." *Early Medieval Europe* 14, no. 3 (2006): 297–304.

Clark, George. *Gender, Violence, and the Past in Edda and Saga*. Oxford: Oxford University Press, 2012.

Eddison, E.R. *Styrbiorn the Strong*. London: Jonathan Cape, 1926.

Edström, Elias. "Sigurd Ring." Manuscript, 2016.

Edström, Elias. Interview taken by the author, October 9, 2016.

Edström, Elias. "Taiteilijahaastatteluja: Elias Edström." In *Ikkunat auki itään!" 100 vuotta Aasiaa Suomen näyttämöillä*, edited by Anna Thuring, Jukka O. Miettinen and Veli Rosenberg, pp. 208–11. Teatterikorkeakoulun julkaisuja 65. Helsinki: Taideyliopiston teatterikorkeakoulu, 2018.

Einar Ólafur Sveinsson. "Íslendingasögur." In *Kulturhistoriskt leksikon for nordisk middelalder: fra vikingetid til reformationstid 7: Hovedstad – Judar*, edited by Georg Rona, pp. 496–513. Copenhagen: Rosenkilde and Bagger, 1962.

Gardeła, Leszek. "Amazons of the Viking World: Between Myth and Reality." *Medieval Warfare* 7, no. 1 (2017): 8–15.

Gostand, Reba. "Verbal and Non-Verbal Communication: Drama as Translation." In *The Languages of Theatre: Problems in the Translation and Transposition of Drama*, edited by Ortrun Zuber, pp. 1–9. Oxford: Pergamon Press, 1980.

Granroth, Ann-Catrin and My Tengström. "Han vägrar bli kändis i Kina." X3M, February 11, 2015. https://svenska.yle.fi/artikel/2015/02/11/han-vagrar-bli-kandis-i-kina.

Grimstad, Kaaren. "Introduction." In *Völsunga saga. The Saga of the Volsungs: The Icelandic Text according to MS Nks 1824 b, 4o with an English Translation, Introduction and Notes*, edited and translated by Kaaren Grimstad, pp. 13–72. Bibliotheca Germanica, Ser. Nova 3. Saarbrücken: AQ-Verlag, 2000.

Gropper, Stephanie. "Fate." In *The Routledge Research Companion to the Medieval Icelandic Sagas*, edited by Ármann Jakobsson and Sverrir Jakobsson, pp. 198–209. New York and London: Routledge, 2017.

Gunnell, Terry. *The Origins of Drama in Scandinavia*. Cambridge: D. S. Brewer, 1995.

Hedenstierna-Jonson, Charlotte et al. "A Female Viking Warrior Confirmed by Genomics." *American Journal of Physical Anthropology* 164, no. 4 (2017): 853–60.

Henrikson, Paula. *Dramatikern Stagnelius*. Eslöv: Brutus Östlings bokförlag Symposion, 2004.

Hervarar saga ok Heiðreks. Edited by Gabriel Turville-Petre, introduction by Christopher Tolkien. London: Viking Society for Northern Research, 1956.

Holmqvist-Larsen, H. N. *Møer, skjoldmøer og krigere: En studie i og omkring 7. bog af Saxo's Gesta Danorum*. Studier fra Sprog- og Oldtidsforskning 304. Copenhagen: Museum Tusculanum, 1983.

Hsü Tao-Ching. *The Chinese Conception of the Theatre*. Seattle: University of Washington Press, 1985.

Jakob Benediktsson. *Arngrímur Jónsson and His Works*. Copenhagen: Ejnar Munksgaard, 1957.

Jesch, Judith. *The Viking Diaspora*. London: Routledge, 2015.

Malmström, Sten. *Studier över stilen i Stagnelius lyrik*. Stockholm: Svenska bokförlaget / Bonniers, 1961.

McTurk, Rory. *Studies in Ragnars saga loðbrókar and Its Major Scandinavian Analogues*. Oxford: Society for the Study of Mediaeval Languages and Literature, 1991.

Miettinen, Jukka O. and Veli Rosenberg. "Aasia Helsingissä 20 vuotta." Lecture at Stoa Helsinki, October 8, 2016.

Miettinen, Jukka O. and Veli Rosenberg. "Aasia Helsingissä -festivaali 1997–2016." In *Ikkunat auki itään!" 100 vuotta Aasiaa Suomen näyttämöillä*, edited by Anna Thuring, Jukka O. Miettinen and Veli Rosenberg, pp. 129–70. Teatterikorkeakoulun julkaisusarja 65. Helsinki: Taideyliopiston Teatterikorkeakoulu, 2018.

Ney, Agneta. *Bland ormar och drakar. Hjältemyt och manligt ideal i berättartraditioner om Sigurd Fafnesbane*. Lund: Nordic Academic Press, 2017.

Rosenberg, Veli. "Enemmän irti esityksestä: Sigurd Ring." Lecture at Kanneltalo, Helsinki, March 11, 2016.

Rosenberg, Veli. "Kuinka Kiina astui Suomen näyttämöille." In *"Ikkunat auki itään!" 100 vuotta Aasiaa Suomen näyttämöillä*, edited by Anna Thuring, Jukka O. Miettinen and Veli Rosenberg, pp. 63–96. Teatterikorkeakoulun julkaisusarja 65. Helsinki: Taideyliopiston teatterikorkeakoulu, 2018.

Rothberg, Isabella. "För långa ben, konstigt ansikte." *Hufvudstadsbladet*, March 5, 2016. https://www.hbl.fi/artikel/for-langa-ben-konstigt-ansikte/.

Saxo Grammaticus. *The History of the Danes. Books I–IX. Volume 1: English Text. Volume 2: Commentary*. Edited and translated by Hilda Ellis Davidson and Peter Fisher. Cambridge: D. S. Brewer, 1979–1980.

Saxo Grammaticus. *Gesta Danorum: The History of the Danes*. Edited by Karsten Friis-Jensen. Translated by Peter Fisher. 2 vols. Oxford: Clarendon Press, 2015.

Schulman, Jana K. "'A Guest Is in the Hall': Women, Feasts, and Violence in Icelandic Epic." In *Women and Medieval Epic: Gender, Genre, and the Limits of Epic Masculinity*, edited by Sara S. Poor and Jana K. Schulman, pp. 209–33. The New Middle Ages. London: Palgrave Macmillan, 2007.

Stagnelius, Erik Johan. "Sigurd Ring." In *Samlader skrifter. IV. Dramatiska dikter II. Prosa och brev*, edited by Fredrik Böök, pp. 1–57. Stockholm: Albert Bonniers förlag, 1915.

Strand, Birgit. "Kvinnor och män i Gesta Danorum." Ph.D. dissertation, University of Gothenburg, 1980.

Suhm, P. F. *Historie af Danmark*. 14 vols. Copenhagen: s.n., 1782–1828.

Sweet, Henry. *Shelley's Nature Poetry*. London: Printed for private circulation, 1891.

"Sǫgubrot af fornkonungum." In *Danakonunga sǫgur. Skjǫldunga saga. Knýtlinga saga. Ágrip af sǫgu Danakonunga*, edited by Bjarni Guðnason, pp. 46–71. Íslenzk fornrit 35. Reykjavík: Hið Íslenzka fornritafélag, 1982.

"Sǫgubrot af fornkonungum." In *Sǫgur Danakonunga. 1. Sǫgubrot af fornkonungum. 2. Knytlinga saga*, edited by Carl af Petersens and Emil Olson, pp. 1–25. Copenhagen: Samfund til udgivelse af gammel nordisk litteratur, 1919–1925.

"'Theatre of the Capital' or Peking Opera." In *Asian Traditional Theatre and Dance*, edited by Jukka O. Miettinen. Helsinki: Theatre Academy Helsinki, 2010. http://www.xip.fi/atd/china/theatre-of-the-capital-or-the-peking-opera.html.

Wawn, Andrew. "Foreword." In *Old Norse Made New: Essays on the Post-Medieval Reception of Old Norse Literature and Culture*, edited by David Clark and Carl Phelpstead, pp. v–vii. London: Viking Society for Northern Research, 2007.

Willson, Kendra. "Inside and Outside in *Gísla saga Súrssonar* and *Hrafnkels saga Freysgoða*." In *The Book of Nature and Humanity in the Middle Ages and the Renaissance*, edited by David Hawkes and Richard G. Newhauser, pp. 287–307. Turnhout: Brepols, 2013.

Xu Chengbei. *Peking Opera*. Cambridge: Cambridge University Press, 2012.

Zung, Cecilia S. L. *Secrets of the Chinese Drama: A Complete Explanatory Guide to Actions and Symbols as Seen in the Performance of Chinese Dramas. With Synopses of Fifty Popular Chinese Plays and 240 Illustrations*. New York: Benjamin Blom, 1937.

Notes

1. Terry Gunnell, *The Origins of Drama in Scandinavia* (Cambridge: D. S. Brewer, 1995).
2. Reba Gostand, "Verbal and Non-Verbal Communication: Drama as Translation," in *The Languages of Theatre: Problems in the Translation and Transposition of Drama*, ed. Ortrun Zuber (Oxford: Pergamon Press, 1980), pp. 1–9 at p. 1.
3. The main sources for Sigurd Ring – *Hervarar saga ok Heiðreks, Sögubrot af nokkrum fornkonungum*, and Arngrímur Jónsson's Latin retelling of parts of the lost **Skjöldunga saga*, as well as *Gesta Danorum* by Saxo Grammaticus – are discussed below. Sigurd is also mentioned in passing in some other texts, including *Hversu Noregr byggðisk, Haralds saga hárfagra* in Snorri Sturluson's *Heimskringla, Ragnars saga loðbrókar, Ragnarssona þáttr, Bósa saga ok Herrauðs, Gríms saga loðinkinna, Örvar-Odds saga*, and *Norna-gests þáttr*.
4. Kaaren Grimstad discusses this in the case of *Völsunga saga*. Kaaren Grimstad, "Introduction," in *Völsunga saga. The Saga of the Volsungs. The Icelandic Text according to MS Nks 1824 b, 4o with an English Translation, Introduction and Notes*, ed. and trans. Kaaren Grimstad. Bibliotheca Germanica, Ser. Nova 3 (Saarbrücken: AQ-Verlag, 2000), pp. 13–72 at p. 41.
5. Saxo Grammaticus, *History of the Danes. Volume 1: Text*, ed. Hilda Ellis Davidson, trans. Peter Fisher (Cambridge: D. S. Brewer, 1979), pp. 238–46.
6. "Sǫgubrot af fornkonungum," in *Danakonunga sǫgur. Skjǫldunga saga. Knýtlinga saga. Ágrip af sǫgu Danakonunga*, ed. Bjarni Guðnason, Íslenzk fornrit 35 (Reykjavík: Hið Íslenzka fornritafélag, 1982), pp. 46–71 at p. 71.
7. "þá skyldi vera bardagi á Brávöllum, er mestr hefir verit á Norðrlöndum, sem segir í sǫgu Sigurðar hrings, fǫður Ragnars loðbrókar" (then there would be a battle at Brávellir, the greatest that has taken place in the Nordic countries, as is told in the saga of Sigurðr hringr, the father of Ragnarr loðbrók). "Bósa saga ok Herrauðs," in *Fornaldarsögur Norðrlanda*, ed. Valdimar Ásmundarson, vol. 3 (Reykjavík: Sigurður Kristjánsson, 1889), pp. 243–72 at p. 259.
8. Agneta Ney, *Bland ormar och drakar. Hjältemyt och manligt ideal i berättartraditioner om Sigurd Fafnesbane* (Lund: Nordic Academic Press, 2017), p. 68.
9. Rory McTurk, *Studies in Ragnars saga loðbrókar and Its Major Scandinavian Analogues* (Oxford: Society for the Study of Mediaeval Languages and Literature, 1991); Saxo Grammaticus, *Gesta Danorum: The History of the Danes*, ed. Karsten Friis-Jensen, trans. Peter Fisher (Oxford: Clarendon Press, 2015), vol. 1, pp. 628–29, n. 4.
10. "Sǫgubrot af fornkonungum," in *Sǫgur Danakonunga. 1. Sǫgubrot af fornkonungum. 2. Knytlinga saga*, ed. Carl af Petersens and Emil Olson (Copenhagen: Samfund til udgivelse af gammel nordisk litteratur, 1919–1925), pp. 1–25 at p. 25.
11. *Hervarar saga ok Heiðreks*, ed. Gabriel Turville-Petre and Christopher Tolkien (London: Viking Society for Northern Research, 1956), p. 68.
12. Bjarni Guðnason, *Um Skjöldungasögu* (Reykjavík: Bókaútgáfa Menningarsjóðs, 1963), pp. 284–85.
13. Arngrímur Jónsson, "Svíakonungatal Arngríms lærða," in *Danakonunga sǫgur. Skjǫldunga saga. Knýtlinga saga. Ágrip af sǫgu Danakonunga*, ed. Bjarni Guðnason. Íslenzk fornrit 35 (Reykjavík: Hið íslenzka fornritafélag, 1987), pp. 72–77.

14. Jakob Benediktsson, *Arngrímur Jónsson and His Works* (Copenhagen: Ejnar Munksgaard, 1957), pp. 107–17.
15. Bjarni Guðnason, "Skjǫldunga saga," in *Kulturhistoriskt lexikon för nordisk medeltid. Från vikingatid till reformationstid 15: Samisk språk – Skude*, ed. Helge Pohjolan-Pirhonen (Helsinki: Akademiska bokhandeln, 1970), pp. 596–98 at p. 596.
16. Bjarni Guðnason, *Um Skjöldungasögu*, p. 307.
17. The phrasing is ambiguous as to whether she is aware that her brothers are poisoning her and whether she takes the poison willingly: "priusqvam ad bellum proficiscerentur, sorori venenum proprinant, ne victori præda foret" (before setting out to battle, they gave their sister poison to drink, so that she would not fall to the victor as booty), Arngrímur Jónsson, "Svíakonungatal Arngríms lærða," p. 74.
18. Ibid., p. 74.
19. Saxo Grammaticus, *The History of the Danes*, vol. 1, pp. 245–46.
20. Ibid., vol. 1, pp. 243–44.
21. P. F. Suhm, *Historie af Danmark*, 14 vols. (Copenhagen: s.n., 1782–1828).
22. Magnus Bruzelius, *Swerges historia för ungdom* (Lund: s.n., 1817).
23. Paula Henrikson, *Dramatikern Stagnelius* (Eslöv: Brutus Östlings bokförlag Symposion, 2004), p. 135.
24. The use of an obscure historical figure, allowing the modern author free rein, may also be seen in Ernest Rücker Eddison's choice of protagonist for his novel *Styrbiorn the Strong* (London: Jonathan Cape, 1926); see Andrew Wawn, "Foreword," in *Old Norse Made New: Essays on the Post-Medieval Reception of Old Norse Literature and Culture*, ed. David Clark and Carl Phelpstead (London: Viking Society for Northern Research, 2007), pp. v–vii at p. vi.
25. Henry Sweet, *Shelley's Nature Poetry* (London: Printed for private circulation, 1891), p. 298.
26. Fredrik Böök, *Erik Johan Stagnelius* (Stockholm: Albert Bonniers förlag, 1919), p. 290.
27. The play appears in Erik Johan Stagnelius, *Samlader skrifter. IV. Dramatiska dikter II. Prosa och brev*, ed. Fredrik Böök (Stockholm: Albert Bonniers förlag, 1915), pp. 1–57.
28. Henrikson, *Dramatikern Stagnelius*, p. 138.
29. Xu Chengbei, *Peking Opera* (Cambridge: Cambridge University Press, 2012), p. 15.
30. "'Theatre of the Capital' or Peking Opera," in *Asian Traditional Theatre and Dance*, ed. Jukka O. Miettinen (Helsinki: Theatre Academy Helsinki, 2010), http://www.xip.fi/atd/china/theatre-of-the-capital-or-the-peking-opera.html.
31. Veli Rosenberg, "Enemmän irti esityksestä: Sigurd Ring," lecture at Kanneltalo, Helsinki, March 11, 2016.
32. "'Theatre of the Capital' or Peking Opera."
33. Alexandra B. Bonds, *Beijing Opera Costumes: The Visual Communication of Character and Culture* (Honolulu: University of Hawai'i Press, 2008), p. 3.
34. Veli Rosenberg, "Kuinka Kiina astui Suomen näyttämöille," in *"Ikkunat auki itään!" 100 vuotta Aasiaa Suomen näyttämöillä*, ed. Anna Thuring, Jukka O. Miettinen and Veli Rosenberg (Helsinki: Taideyliopiston teatterikorkeakoulu, 2018), pp. 63–96 at pp. 78–80.
35. Jukka O. Miettinen and Veli Rosenberg, "Aasia Helsingissä -festivaali 1997–2016," in *"Ikkunat auki itään!" 100 vuotta Aasiaa Suomen näyttämöillä*, ed. Anna Thuring, Jukka O. Miettinen and Veli Rosenberg (Helsinki: Taideyliopiston Teatterikorkeakoulu, 2018), pp. 129–70.
36. Jukka O. Miettinen and Veli Rosenberg, "Aasia Helsingissä 20 vuotta," lecture at Stoa, Helsinki, October 8, 2016.

37. Rosenberg, "Enemmän irti esityksestä."
38. Elias Edström, email correspondence, January 14, 2018.
39. Ann-Catrin Granroth and My Tengström, "Han vägrar bli kändis i Kina," X3M, February 11, 2015, https://svenska.yle.fi/artikel/2015/02/11/han-vagrar-bli-kandis-i-kina.
40. Isabella Rothberg, "För långa ben, konstigt ansikte," *Hufvudstadsbladet*, March 5, 2016, https://www.hbl.fi/artikel/for-langa-ben-konstigt-ansikte/.
41. Elias Edström, "Sigurd Ring," manuscript, 2016.
42. Elias Edström, interview taken by the author October 9, 2016.
43. Edström, interview.
44. "'Theatre of the Capital' or Peking Opera."
45. Rosenberg, "Enemmän irti esityksestä."
46. "'Theatre of the Capital' or Peking Opera."
47. On the use of platform shoes in Beijing opera see Hsü Tao-Ching, *The Chinese Conception of the Theatre* (Seattle and London: University of Washington Press, 1985), p. 151.
48. Elias Edström, email correspondence, April 3, 2018.
49. Ibid.
50. Cecilia S. L. Zung, *Secrets of the Chinese Drama: A Complete Explanatory Guide to Actions and Symbols as Seen in the Performance of Chinese Dramas. With Synopses of Fifty Popular Chinese Plays and 240 Illustrations* (New York: Benjamin Blom, 1937), p. 79.
51. Post-performance discussion March 12, 2016; Edström, interview.
52. Edström, interview.
53. Rosenberg, "Enemmän irti esityksestä."
54. Bonds, *Beijing Opera Costumes*, p. 151.
55. Edström, interview.
56. Kendra Willson, "Inside and Outside in *Gísla saga Súrssonar* and *Hrafnkels saga Freysgoða*," in *The Book of Nature and Humanity in the Middle Ages and the Renaissance*, ed. David Hawkes and Richard G. Newhauser (Turnhout: Brepols, 2013), pp. 287–307 at p. 290; Chris Callow, "Reconstructing the Past in Medieval Iceland," *Early Medieval Europe* 14, no. 3 (2006): 297–324 at p. 300; Einar Ólafur Sveinsson, "Íslendingasögur," in *Kulturhistoriskt leksikon for nordisk middelalder: fra vikingetid til reformationstid 7: Hovedstad – Judar*, ed. Georg Rona (Copenhagen: Rosenkilde and Bagger, 1962), pp. 496–513 at p. 508.
57. Callow, "Reconstructing the Past," p. 300; Einar Ólafur Sveinsson, "Íslendingasögur," p. 508.
58. For a reading of Norse heroic materials as critical of vengeance, see George Clark, *Gender, Violence, and the Past in Edda and Saga* (Oxford: Oxford University Press, 2012).
59. Well-known examples include Eyvindr disregarding repeated warnings to flee Hrafnkell in chapter 8 of *Hrafnkels saga Freysgoða*, Vésteinn ignoring attempts to warn him in chapter 12 of *Gísla saga Súrssonar*, and Gunnarr deciding not to leave Iceland after he falls off his horse in chapter 75 of *Brennu-Njáls saga*. On fate and fatalism in Icelandic sagas, see Stephanie Gropper, "Fate," in *The Routledge Research Companion to the Medieval Icelandic Sagas*, ed. Ármann Jakobsson and Sverrir Jakobsson (New York and London: Routledge, 2017), pp. 198–209.
60. See, for instance, *Brennu-Njáls saga*, ed. Einar Ól. Sveinsson. Íslensk fornrit 12 (Reykjavík: Hið Íslenzka fornritafélag, 1954), chap. 35, pp. 90–92; c.f. Jana K. Schulman, "'A Guest Is in the Hall': Women, Feasts, and Violence in Icelandic Epic," in *Women and Medieval Epic: Gender, Genre, and the Limits of Epic Masculinity*, ed. Sara

S. Poor and Jana K. Schulman. The New Middle Ages (London: Palgrave Macmillan, 2007), pp. 209–33 at pp. 211 and 215.

61. Xu Chengbei, *Peking Opera*, pp. 53–54.

62. Very selected recent references include Leszek Gardeła, "Amazons of the Viking World: Between Myth and Reality," *Medieval Warfare 7*, no. 1 (2017): 8–15; Charlotte Hedenstierna-Jonson et al., "A Female Viking Warrior Confirmed by Genomics," *American Journal of Physical Anthropology 164*, no. 4 (2017): 853–60; Judith Jesch, *The Viking Diaspora* (London: Routledge, 2015), pp. 104–7.

63. On Saxo's women warriors and maiden kings see H. N. Holmqvist-Larsen, *Møer, skjoldmøer og krigere: En studie i og omkring 7. bog af Saxo's Gesta Danorum.* Studier fra Sprog- og Oldtidsforskning 304 (Copenhagen: Museum Tusculanum, 1983); Birgit Strand, "Kvinnor och män i Gesta Danorum" (Ph.D. dissertation, University of Gothenburg, 1980), pp. 110–17.

64. "Sǫgubrot af fornkonungum," ed. Bjarni Guðnason, pp. 67–68.

65. Grimstad, "Introduction," pp. 55–56.

66. Sten Malmström, *Studier över stilen i Stagnelius lyrik* (Stockholm: Svenska bokförlaget / Bonniers, 1961), p. 71.

67. Henrikson, *Dramatikern Stagnelius*, p. 132.

68. Rosenberg, "Enemmän irti esityksestä."

69. Elias Edström, e-mail correspondence, January 14, 2018.

70. Miettinen and Rosenberg, "Asia Helsingissä 20 vuotta"; Edström, interview.

71. Elias Edström, "Taiteilijahaastatteluja: Elias Edström," in *"Ikkunat auki itään!" 100 vuotta Aasiaa Suomen näyttämöillä*, ed. Anna Thuring, Jukka O. Miettinen and Veli Rosenberg. Teatterikorkeakoulun julkaisuja 65 (Helsinki: Taideyliopiston teatterikorkeakoulu, 2018), pp. 208–11 at pp. 209, 211.

Maja Bäckvall

11 "Pick up Rune": The Use of Runes in Digital Games

Introduction

Runes live a life of their own in popular culture. While closely associated in the public mind with Viking culture, they can also appear in contexts completely separate from such a culture. In fact, much of what is called "runes" in popular culture is not the historically attested writing system, but can refer to all kinds of mysterious symbols. Calling them "runes" is a conscious choice, meant to evoke a certain response in the audience. In digital games – that is, computer and video games – the use of runes appears to be widespread, but this use has not been studied closely. To runologists and Old Norse scholars, the use of runes in games can give an idea of how the general public understands the runic tradition. The context in which runes appear can also throw light on which characteristics of rune-using cultures – that is, Vikings – the developers wish to evoke. This essay will discuss the different uses of runes in a selection of games, considering them as semiotic resources (as explained below).

The games I draw my examples from range from small independent games to big, so-called "triple-A" games, the Hollywood blockbusters of gaming. They are generally either role-playing or strategy games, and most engage with a historical or mythologized past. The selection of games is admittedly eclectic and is not intended to represent all possible uses of runes in digital games. The individual games are presented briefly in the endnotes when they are mentioned.

There are different kinds of rune usage discussed in this essay. Runes can be represented visually, either in the form of historically attested runes or as rune-like symbols. They can also be exclusively mentioned in writing – that is, using the words "rune(s)" or "runestone(s)." For the sake of simplicity, I will occasionally use "runes" in this essay to cover use both of actual symbols and of the words "rune" and "runestone," unless otherwise specified. The essay is divided into sections following the three most common functions of runes found in the games discussed. They can be physical objects, a shorthand for arcane writing, and/or denote a Viking-like Norse culture. While these functions often overlap, they will be presented and discussed separately.

Maja Bäckvall, Uppsala University

https://doi.org/10.1515/9781501513886-012

Historical Runes

In this essay, when I mention "historical runes" or "the runic tradition," I am referring to the writing system used in the Germanic-speaking areas of Europe from, roughly, the third century to the thirteenth century CE.[1] Largely inspired by the Mediterranean alphabets (especially the Latin alphabet, but possibly also the Greek), it appears on a wide range of objects. Early finds from Central Europe are mainly small, personal objects bearing a personal name or a word for the inscribed object (one of the earliest extant inscriptions is a bone comb carrying the inscription "kaba" for *kamba*, "comb"). Later, during the Iron and Viking Ages in Scandinavia (ca. 500–1100 CE), longer, epigraphic inscriptions on public runestones come into vogue.

A runic alphabet is called a "futhark" or "futhorc," and inscriptions can be dated and placed geographically based on which futhark is used. The Older Futhark has twenty-four runes and was in use in central and northern Europe from the third century CE until about 800 CE. The thirty-four-character Anglo-Saxon or Anglo-Frisian Futhorc was used during the same time period in what is now England and the Netherlands. Finally, the Younger Futhark was used from about 800 CE to the thirteenth century, predominantly in Scandinavia, and has eighteen runes. Runes continued to be used into the Middle Ages in Scandinavia, but lost their role as the primary vernacular writing system.

One of the biggest differences between how runic writing was used historically and its usage in popular culture is the use of individual runes. The futharks in their own time were primarily alphabets, and runic inscriptions are typically words or phrases. There are few one-rune inscriptions in the corpus. As examples in this essay will show, in video games, as in popular culture in general, single runes are common.

Semiotic Resources

My analysis will be based on the notion of semiotic resources, a term taken from multimodal analysis. The "modes" in "multimodal" are the forms of communication that can be used to make meaning. Language is only one mode among many, potentially equally important, modes.[2] As an example, the layout of a piece of writing may be the only difference between reading it as a poem or a diary entry. In speech, altering the way a word is said (in pitch, volume, etc.) can completely change the meaning of the word. What can be counted as a mode in a given situation varies with the social and cultural setting; in order to function as a semiotic mode, a form of communication must be conventionalized within a culture.[3] Line breaks only indicate verse if there is a shared assumption between writer and reader about layout and its relation to poetry.

Slightly simplified, any factor that contributes to the intended meaning of a text (in this case, a game) is a semiotic resource. A combination of semiotic resources, conventionalized as described above, is what makes up a semiotic mode. As Carey Jewitt puts it, "people express meanings *through their selection* from the semiotic resources that are available to them in a particular moment: meaning is a choice from the system."[4] There is rarely just one way of conveying a meaning, and the ways in which you choose to get your specific meaning across are in themselves meaningful. An example of this may be signaling "danger" with the intention of instilling fear in the audience of a horror film. This could be done in several, equally effective ways: a monster jumping out from behind a door is very different from a doll slowly opening its eyes, but both convey similar meanings.

Because they have culturally encoded connotations, runes are one semiotic resource among many that game developers can choose from. The aim of this essay is not only to discuss what meanings runes carry in the games mentioned, but also why runes specifically were chosen as opposed to other resources that may carry similar connotations. Viewed as a semiotic resource, what is the cultural encoding of runes for the intended audience of the game? What connotations are the developers making use of, and in what situations?

Runes as Physical Objects

The title of this essay, "Pick up Rune," is taken from the *Dishonored* game series,[5] where that phrase is a command prompt shown on the screen whenever the player finds a rune. In these games, the object called a "rune" is a slightly glowing piece of bone, carved with a symbol and with metal clamps attached to it. Runes in *Dishonored* are hidden in different places throughout the game. Alongside other secrets, runes are found through using a magical object called the Heart, which beats faster as the player approaches an object of interest. Finding them is voluntary, although encouraged both in the gameplay and via in-game benefits such as increased health or damage. The runes are equipped to inventory slots, presumably on the player character's gear, and improve the main character's abilities. These abilities take the form of different kinds of magic, which in turn is connected to a slightly disturbing trickster god, The Outsider.[6]

A similar use of portable, magic runes can be seen in the *Dragon Age* series.[7] Here, runes are connected to dwarves, who are also associated with smithing. The crafting of runes in *Dragon Age* is referred to as "enchanting" and is the only kind of magic dwarves can perform in this world. Where runes in *Dishonored* upgrade the main character's abilities, *Dragon Age* runes are used to enhance weapons and armor. Like in *Dishonored*, the process of finding runes in *Dragon Age* is not part of the main storyline, but an optional task the player can pursue. New runes are discovered by the player by illuminating hidden wall inscriptions with magical fire. Within the game's world, the assumption is that once you find the design of a rune, the enchanter can inscribe it on your gear to improve it.

Objects called "runestones" are used in a similar way in *The Witcher 3*.[8] Runestones in this game can be found, bought or made by a smith, and the recipes are likewise found or bought. In keeping with the eastern European inspirations for *The Witcher 3*, the runestones are named after gods in the Slavic pantheon, such as *Dazhbog* or *Chernbog*.

Practically speaking, there is no difference between what is called a "rune" in one game and a "runestone" in another. They are all visualized as a small, physical object meant to be attached to the player's gear. Perhaps confusingly, a "rune" in *Dragon Age: Inquisition* is made (by the player in a crafting system) by combining an item called a "blank runestone" with various other items. For instance, to make a Cleansing Rune, which enhances a weapon's attack power against undead enemies, the player combines a blank runestone and six corpse hearts. Schematics for upgrading your weapons and armor in all the games mentioned here show slots for placing the runes. In *Dishonored*, the design of the runic objects themselves shows their use as something you equip.

Visually, none of the three game series I discuss here uses runes from any of the extant futharks (runic alphabets) to represent the physical runes. *The Witcher 3* comes closest, with simple, angular symbols, some of which are close to futhark runes. *Dishonored*'s runes are all the same symbol, which is also used as a symbol for the game itself on websites and promotional materials. The design of runes in the *Dragon Age* series changes from game to game, from relatively complex designs in *Dragon Age: Origins* to simple elemental symbols in *Dragon Age 2*, to not being shown at all in *Dragon Age: Inquisition*.

The option to upgrade abilities and gear is a commonplace in role-playing games. In a game set in modern times, or in the future, you would still upgrade your weapons, but then the upgrades are usually part of the gear – a new muzzle for your gun, a visor for your helmet, etc. These are upgrades that are probably easier for the player to imagine than how they might improve a sword or other pre-modern weapon. Upgrades tend to function as an intermediary step to make your gear better before you replace it altogether. They may also pose a minor dilemma for the player, who has to choose between keeping an upgraded weapon or switching to a new one and starting over on the upgrades, which are usually not replaceable. The main difference between "modern" and "fantasy" upgrades is that while the modern ones will be things like better accuracy or more ammunition, the fantasy ones will add some kind of magical effect. In both the *Dragon Age* games and *The Witcher 3*, these are effects like freezing or setting the enemy on fire. Physical runes, then, fill functions that most games have – leveling up, upgrading gear – and do so through a filter of magic.

Runes as Arcane Writing

In a pivotal scene in the early hours of *Dragon Age: Inquisition*, one of the main characters declares that the Inquisition for which the game is named is being reinstated. She does this by hefting a huge, leather-bound book which opens to show briefly a page fully written in runes. The book is clearly meant to be an ancient tome of religious texts or laws, and its age and importance is reinforced by the use of runes alongside mysterious diagrams. This is also one of the few uses of actual runes to represent runic writing,[9] although they are J. R. R. Tolkien's revised futhark from *The Hobbit*, where it is the writing system of the dwarves.[10]

Elsewhere in the same game, a quest has the player reveal runes with the same magic fire that they use for the crafting runes mentioned above. Here, however, the runes are not standalone magical symbols used for crafting, but something approaching writing, although still magical. One prompt during this quest tells the player "Staring at this set of unreadable runes conjures up strong feelings of bitterness and arrogance in equal measure. They fade, slowly."[11]

An example from a very different game is from the space exploration game *No Man's Sky*.[12] Here, the player can discover monoliths and ruins belonging to various cultures. The information given at these sites is opaque, often written in an unknown language with only a few words decipherable. The results of interacting with the monuments depend on the player's choices. In one instance, the text the player encounters is as follows:

> There are three vast columns of words on the ancient structure, each written in a different alphabet. The first column's words are like savage runes scratched in sand, the second shows precise sequences of dots. The final column has wide and welcoming letters, almost appearing hand-written in hard stone.
> The dirt and blood of ancient hand prints cover the base of each column.[13]

The player is then prompted to either press their hand against the "letters," the "dots," or the "runes." Depending on which writing system they choose, they will learn a word from one of the three non-human factions in the game. The runes are associated with the militaristic Vy'keen, characterized as aggressive warriors and designed with big, square jaws and glaring eyes. In the passage quoted, the runes are described in a way – "savage runes scratched in sand" – that hints at this association, not least through being called "runes" in the first place. To the player who has met members of the three factions, the way each writing system is described makes it relatively clear which faction it belongs to.[14] Because of the way the game is structured, a player may also come across this text before encountering all factions, in which case it functions as a hint at their respective characteristics.

The word "runes" is used one other time in *No Man's Sky* about writing on a monolith, but there in a more generalized fashion: "I'm running my fingers over the ancient, glowing runes."[15] In this case, the use is similar to the "unreadable runes" in *Dragon Age: Inquisition* mentioned above: to indicate arcane and impenetrable writing.

Runes as Norse Culture

Runes and runic inscriptions may, of course, also be used in games more obviously inspired by the Viking Age. While there are no historically attested runes in the Norse mythology-inspired *The Banner Saga*,[16] the game employs a rune-like font (for the Latin alphabet) on its world map, as well as a design taken from a Swedish runestone. The same font is used on the so-called "godstones," enormous inscribed monoliths the player comes across, whose design is clearly inspired by Swedish eleventh-century runestones. Each stone belongs to a god in the game world's pantheon, all of whom are dead in the time period when the game takes place. Accompanied by a short text about each god, the godstones' function in the narrative is to provide the player with background information about the world. The death of the gods and the end of the world are overarching themes in *The Banner Saga*.

Almost all godstones have writing on them, at least the name of the god if nothing else. By far the most writing can be found on that of the god of knowledge, Ingrid, and the accompanying text reinforces the importance of writing on this particular monument:

> Ingrid's godstone is carved with ancient runes which don't make much sense to you, though Eyvind tells you some of the menders have deciphered them. It's how the menders

learned the language of the gods. Past the largest stone a long series of slabs contain more writing all the way down the hill. The odd thing, he tells you, is that the writing occasionally changes depending on who is reading it. Usually it describes the history of the gods but it can be about nearly any topic.[17]

As opposed to the writing on the other godstones, which are relatively easy to read for the player, the text on Ingrid's godstone is both reversed and upside down, a way to indicate that the "ancient runes" on these stones are different from the others. It is possible to make out shorter sentences in transliterated English, such as in one case "We know these things to be true, that all men are responsible for their own actions." Other, minor stones around the godstones bear lists of modern-sounding names, which may be of people who have helped fund or otherwise make the game, although this is not explained anywhere. However, the text is very small on the screen; the primary function of the writing is clearly not for it to be deciphered. Instead, the runes are there to reinforce the Viking-themed setting while being another example of the "runes as arcane writing" theme described above. The general sense conveyed from these encounters with rune-inscribed monuments is one of awe and wonder.

In a similar fashion, the runestones in *Year Walk* add to the sense of mystery in this atmospheric game.[18] Perhaps unsurprisingly for a game made by Swedish developers, the runestones in this game are among the ones that look the most like actual runestones out of the games discussed in this essay. They appear to be carved monuments slightly smaller than a person, and the runes are written in a band around the outer edge of the stone face. The design also uses the red color used to paint the lines on runestones in modern Sweden. However, the runes are not immediately decipherable, nor are all of them attested runes. The player comes across them, like all other things in the game, in a snow-filled forest. Their function in the gameplay is as puzzle pieces; each stone shows a combination of lines that the player needs to replicate in another part of the game.

Year Walk's runestones are not there as part of the culture the game is set in. The story is centered on creatures from Swedish folklore and is set in the nineteenth century, the time when many of these tales were collected for the first time. The addition of runestones to this environment ties back to the mysterious folklore elements of the game, as well as to the part runestones play in the landscape of central and southern Sweden.

Neither *The Banner Saga* nor *Year Walk* (nor any of the games discussed so far) claim to be historically accurate, nor is historical accuracy a selling point for them. However, the case is slightly different for historical strategy games such as *Civilization VI*[19] and *Crusader Kings II*.[20] While the latter is set on a map of the world, in a specific time in history (with all expansions, 769–1453 CE),[21] the former builds its gameplay around civilizations and nations that exist or have existed, but sets it on a randomly generated map. Both games employ what Adam Chapman calls "conceptual simulations" of history: they focus on historical processes and concepts – for example, hierarchical structures, the pros and cons of various technological advances, strategic placement of cities – rather than visual representation.[22] When both of these games use runestones, then, it is not for the visual impact like, in part, *The Banner Saga* and *Year Walk*.

In *Civilization VI*, runes are only ever mentioned in a line of dialogue uttered by the leader of Norway, Harald Hardrada: "I have sent you traders with gifts of rune stones. They are powerful – the stones, not the traders."[23] This indicates an image of runestones more akin to the small, magical objects as seen above in *Dragon Age* and *The Witcher* than to the historical reality of inscribed memorials. It is not surprising, however, because the framing of Viking civilizations in these games is based on a public conception of Vikings rather than on historical research. This is especially obvious in the case of religion: Harald Hardrada's lines often mention Valhalla and Odin, despite the historical king being Christian. The same goes for his equally Christian predecessor Harald Bluetooth[24] in *Civilization V*. The idea of Odin-worshipping Vikings clearly overrides the need for historical accuracy in the *Civilization* games.

Runestones in *Crusader Kings II*, on the other hand, are a good example of a historical process being used as a gameplay element. The game is almost exclusively played through an interface that is a zoomable world map with pop-up windows describing events. Playing as a leader belonging to either the North Germanic Culture or the Norse Pagan Religion gives you the opportunity to decide to raise a runestone, as long as the year has not passed 1150.[25] This costs 100 Gold, a relatively high amount, and rewards the player with Prestige, another important metric in the game. The player can choose whether the runestone is raised in memory of a dead parent or after themselves. In the former case, Prestige is awarded based on how the parent died, while in the latter, it is calculated from which in-game traits the player character has cultivated. As a simulation of the historical process of commissioning a runestone, it is fairly accurate. That it involves exchanging Gold for Prestige makes sense, as does the choice of whom to commemorate and the time span in which it is possible. It does, however, maintain the same image of pagan Vikings as discussed above in *Civilization*, when in fact, the majority of Swedish runestones were raised as a show of Christianity.[26]

The resulting runestone texts are often entertaining, for example when combining the formulaic phrasing of Viking Age runestones ([N.N.] had this stone made in memory of [N.N.], their [relation]) with absurd formulations based on the traits of the player character. An example from the *Crusader Kings II* forums is a runestone raised by a character with the trait Mad:

The runestone you commissioned has been finished and raised on the spot you chose for it. You examine the runes:

Hrafn, proud son of a holy union between Odin, a wild mare, and three forest gnomes paid Óleifr handsomely to carve these runes. With his flying longship and its crew of twelve singing rabbits, Hrafn earned his fame by sailing across the Norse lands solving crime. May the Shining Tentacle preserve us all.

You leave the stone, content in the knowledge that many centuries from now, when its paint has long since faded, scholars will be studying these rune carvings in an effort to glean the wisdom of their words.[27]

The developers have clearly done their research and then decided to have fun with it: the basic formula can be sensed, and the accompanying illustration shows a runestone painted in red, white, and black, in accordance with what we know about the coloring of runestones.[28]

Why Runes in Games?

The semiotic resource "runes" in digital games is relatively far removed from runic inscriptions in reality. In the games discussed here, runes are predominantly used as individual magic symbols and artifacts, and are not something ordinary people understand. They convey a sense of magic power, arcane and hidden knowledge. Probably through association with the popular idea of Viking culture, the games' runes can also be used as a shorthand for a harsh and perhaps primitive warrior culture. While there is some basis in the source material for individual runes having their own magic significance, this was in all likelihood a peripheral notion compared to their more straightforward use as a writing system.[29]

Of course, the purpose of this essay is not to bemoan the lack of historical accuracy in games' use of runes, but to describe and discuss what cultural notions of runes can be gleaned from how they are used. Shiloh Carroll, citing Helen Young,[30] describes a "feedback loop" of medievalism in fantasy literature where

readers are exposed to a medievalist version of the Middle Ages through fantasy. They then come to believe that this medievalist version is an "accurate" portrayal of the Middle Ages. Having done that, people then insist on this version of the Middle Ages in future literature because it is "accurate."[31]

Runes seem to have gone through a similar feedback loop in regard to their magical properties, to a point where magic runes are the norm. Their portrayal as ancient and mysterious is of course not just limited to games; runes play a similar role in TV series and films. A simple internet search for "runes" will result in a large number of websites about the healing and divinatory properties of runes. For example, this description, taken from a knitting pattern for a *Rune Shawl*, seems to sum up popular conceptions of runes quite well:

> Found carved into ancient artefacts, monuments and standing stones scattered across the north, runes carry stories across thousands of years. Every rune was much more than a simple letter in an alphabet. Each one was also a symbol of power, revered as magical, used in divination and charms. To inscribe or invoke a rune was to invoke the force for which it stood.[32]

The runes' role as a writing system is downplayed in favor of their use in magic, much as they are in the examples from the games discussed here. The feedback loop of ideas about runes moves between fiction and factoid. It is likely that the origin of "runestone" in the sense of a small object with a rune on it has its origin in the modern divination form using small stones painted with individual runes. As a result, as we have seen, a "runestone" in a fantasy game like *The Witcher 3* is such an object, and even *Civilization VI*, a game with more historical heft, portrays runestones as magic and portable rather than inscribed memorials.

There are probably other uses of runes in digital games, and definitely in many more games than I have discussed here. However, the association between runes and magic seems to be clear. It would be interesting to see how runes function together with other semiotic resources to build a fictional world; not least how the connotation of belonging to a harsh warrior culture comes into play. From the examples I have discussed in this essay, runes are clearly associated with something rugged and dark; there is nothing ethereal about their magic. Instead, they are primitive, roughly hewn symbols. In this, there seems to be a certain masculinity encoded in them, similar to the masculinity arguably associated with the Vikings. Runes belong to the bearded, axe-wielding dwarves, not the mild, slender elves. This is less a connotation inherent in the runes themselves (although certain qualities of runes, such as their angular shape, probably help) than it is one they have picked up from being associated with Vikings. In turn, that association is used to tell the players of these games what to think of rune-using cultures.

Bibliography

The Banner Saga. Developed by Stoic. Austin: Versus Evil, 2014. Various Formats.
The Banner Saga 2. Developed by Stoic. Austin: Versus Evil, 2016. Various Formats.
"The Banner Saga Godstones." The Banner Saga wiki. https://bannersaga.gamepedia.com/The_Banner_Saga_godstones.
Barnes, Michael. *Runes: A Handbook*. Woodbridge: Boydell & Brewer, 2012.

"Beneath the Mire." Dragon Age wiki. http://dragonage.wikia.com/wiki/Beneath_the_Mire.
Carroll, Shiloh. "Race in A Song of Ice and Fire: Medievalism Posing as Authenticity." *The Public Medievalist* (blog). November 28, 2017. https://www.publicmedievalist.com/race-in-asoif/.
Chapman, Adam. *Digital Games as History: How Videogames Represent the Past and Offer Access to Historical Practice.* New York and London: Routledge, 2016.
Crusader Kings II. Developed by Paradox Development Studio. Stockholm: Paradox Interactive, 2012. PC.
"Decisions." Crusader Kings II wiki. https://ck2.paradoxwikis.com/Decisions.
Dishonored. Developed by Arkane Studios. Rockville, MD: Bethesda Softworks, 2012. Various Formats.
Dishonored 2. Developed by Arkane Studios. Rockville, MD: Bethesda Softworks, 2016. Various Formats.
Dragon Age: Inquisition. Developed by BioWare. Redwood City, CA: Electronic Arts, 2014. Various Formats.
Dragon Age: Origins. Developed by BioWare. Redwood City, CA: Electronic Arts, 2009. Various Formats.
Dragon Age 2. Developed by BioWare. Redwood City, CA: Electronic Arts, 2011. Various Formats.
"Favorite Runestone So Far." Crusader Kings II forum. June 27, 2015. https://forum.paradox plaza.com/forum/index.php?threads/favorite-runestone-so-far.866366/.
Findell, Martin. *Runes.* London: The British Museum Press, 2014.
"Harald Hardrada." Civilization VI wiki. http://civilization.wikia.com/wiki/Harald_Hardrada_ (Civ6).
Jewitt, Carey. "An Introduction to Multimodality." In *The Routledge Handbook of Multimodal Analysis*, edited by Carey Jewitt, pp. 14–27. New York and London: Routledge, 2009.
Kress, Gunther. "What Is Mode?" In *The Routledge Handbook of Multimodal Analysis*, edited by Carey Jewitt, pp. 54–67. New York and London: Routledge, 2009.
MacLeod, Mindy and Bernard Mees. *Runic Amulets and Magic Objects.* Woodbridge: Boydell Press, 2006.
McKinnell, John and Rudolph Simek, with Klaus Düwel. *Runes, Magic and Religion: A Sourcebook.* Studia Medievalia Septentrionalia 10. Vienna: Fassbaender, 2004.
Monforton, Hazel. "Uncovering the Meaning of The Outsider, Dishonored's Misunderstood God." *PC Gamer.* December 20, 2016. https://www.pcgamer.com/uncovering-the-meaning-of-the-outsider-dishonoreds-misunderstood-god/.
"Monolith Puzzle Solutions, No Man's Sky." GosuNoob. August 29, 2016. http://www.gosu noob.com/no-mans-sky/monolith-puzzle-solutions/.
No Man's Sky. Developed by Hello Games. Guildford: Hello Games, 2016. Various Formats.
Sid Meier's Civilization V. Developed by Firaxis Games. Novato, CA: 2K Games, 2010. PC.
Sid Meier's Civilization VI. Developed by Firaxis Games. Novato, CA: 2K Games, 2016. PC.
"Start Date." Crusader Kings II wiki. https://ck2.paradoxwikis.com/Start_date.
Stewart, Helen. "Rune Shawl Knitting Pattern." https://www.ravelry.com/patterns/library/rune-shawl.
Þorhallur Þráinsson. "Traces of Colour." In *Runestones: A Colourful Memory*, edited by Eija Lietoff, pp. 21–30. Uppsala: Museum Gustavianum, 1999.
Williams, Henrik. "Runstexternas teologi." In *Kristnandet i Sverige. Gamla källor och nya perspektiv*, edited by Bertil Nilsson, pp 292–312. Projektet Sveriges kristnande Publikationer 5. Uppsala: Lunne Böcker, 1996.

The Witcher 3: Wild Hunt. Developed by CD Projekt Red. Warsaw: CD Projekt, 2015. Various Formats.

Year Walk. Developed by Simogo. Malmö: Simogo, 2013. Various Formats.

Young, Helen. "'It's the Middle Ages, Yo!': Race, Neo/ medievalisms,and the World of Dragon Age." *The Year's Work in Medievalism* 27 (2012). https://sites.google.com/site/theyears workinmedievalism/all-issues/27-2012.

Notes

1. For general introductions to runes, see Michael Barnes, *Runes: A Handbook* (Woodbridge: Boydell & Brewer, 2012); and Martin Findell, *Runes* (London: The British Museum Press, 2014).
2. Carey Jewitt, "An Introduction to Multimodality," in *The Routledge Handbook of Multimodal Analysis*, ed. Carey Jewitt (New York and London: Routledge, 2009), pp. 14–27 at p. 14.
3. Gunther Kress, "What Is Mode?," in *The Routledge Handbook of Multimodal Analysis*, ed. Carey Jewitt (New York and London: Routledge, 2009), pp. 54–67 at p. 59.
4. Jewitt, "An Introduction," p. 23 (emphasis mine).
5. *Dishonored*, developed by Arkane Studios (Rockville, MD: Bethesda Softworks, 2012), Various Formats; and *Dishonored 2*, developed by Arkane Studios (Rockville, MD: Bethesda Softworks, 2016), Various Formats; both are stealth-based games set in a steampunk world centered on whaling and sea travel.
6. See Hazel Monforton, "Uncovering the Meaning of The Outsider, Dishonored's Misunderstood God," *PC Gamer*, December 20, 2016, https://www.pcgamer.com/uncover ing-the-meaning-of-the-outsider-dishonoreds-misunderstood-god/.
7. *Dragon Age: Origins*, developed by BioWare (Redwood City, CA: Electronic Arts, 2009), Various Formats; *Dragon Age 2*, developed by BioWare (Redwood City, CA: Electronic Arts, 2011), Various Formats; and *Dragon Age: Inquisition*, developed by BioWare (Redwood City, CA: Electronic Arts, 2014), Various Formats. These are fantasy games set in a world mainly inspired by medieval Europe.
8. *The Witcher 3: Wild Hunt*, developed by CD Projekt Red (Warsaw: CD Projekt, 2015), Various Formats. This is the third in a series of games based on the fantasy novels of Andrzej Sapkowski, set in a world inspired by medieval Europe, especially eastern Europe.
9. Another example is from the *Ultima* series of games, where a runic writing system can be found. It is almost identical to the Anglo-Saxon Futhorc, but with a couple of runes switched for unclear reasons. I am unfortunately not familiar enough with the series to be able to discuss it further at this point.
10. Upon closer inspection, the text written in runes turns out to be information about the font, including that it is free to use as long as it is accompanied by this text.
11. "Beneath the Mire," Dragon Age wiki, http://dragonage.wikia.com/wiki/Beneath_the_ Mire.
12. *No Man's Sky*, developed by Hello Games (Guildford: Hello Games, 2016), Various Formats. At the time of writing, *No Man's Sky* has little narrative. Its world is randomly generated by algorithms rather than being fixed beforehand by the developers.

13. "Monolith Puzzle Solutions, No Man's Sky," GosuNoob, August 29, 2016, http://www.go sunoob.com/no-mans-sky/monolith-puzzle-solutions.
14. The other two being the Korvax, a species of sentient robots, focused on science and technology, and the Gek, a species of kind, froglike people who operate as merchants.
15. "Monolith puzzle solutions."
16. *The Banner Saga*, developed by Stoic (Austin: Versus Evil, 2014), Various Formats; and *The Banner Saga 2*, developed by Stoic (Austin: Versus Evil, 2016), Various Formats. Two adventure games in a planned trilogy inspired by Norse mythology but not set in our world.
17. "The Banner Saga Godstones," The Banner Saga wiki, https://bannersaga.gamepedia. com/The_Banner_Saga_godstones.
18. *Year Walk*, developed by Simogo (Malmö: Simogo, 2013), Various Formats. A puzzle game based on Swedish folklore and set in and around a fictional nineteenth-century Swedish village.
19. *Sid Meyer's Civilization VI*, developed by Firaxis Games (Novato, CA: 2K Games, 2016), PC. Part of a long-running series of strategy games where the player leads a culture from its first settlement to, at the latest, the year 2050 CE.
20. *Crusader Kings II*, developed by Paradox Development Studio (Stockholm: Paradox Interactive, 2012), PC. A strategy game based on historical leaders and places.
21. "Start Date," Crusader Kings II wiki, https://ck2.paradoxwikis.com/Start_date.
22. Adam Chapman, *Digital Games as History: How Videogames Represent the Past and Offer Access to Historical Practice* (New York and London: Routledge, 2016), pp 69–79.
23. "Harald Hardrada," Civilization VI wiki, http://civilization.wikia.com/wiki/Harald_ Hardrada_(Civ6).
24. In his own words, from the younger Jelling stone (DR 42), "that Harald who won for himself all of Denmark and Norway and made the Danes Christian."
25. "Decisions," Crusader Kings II wiki, https://ck2.paradoxwikis.com/Decisions.
26. Henrik Williams, "Runstenstexternas teologi," in *Kristnandet i Sverige. Gamla källor och nya perspektiv*, ed. Bertil Nilsson, Projektet Sveriges kristnande Publikationer 5 (Uppsala: Lunne Böcker, 1996), pp. 292–312 at p. 310.
27. "Favorite Runestone So Far," Crusader Kings II forum, https://forum.paradoxplaza.com/ forum/index.php?threads/favorite-runestone-so-far.866366/.
28. Þorhallur Þráinsson, "Traces of Colour," in *Runestones: A Colourful Memory*, ed. Eija Lietoff (Uppsala: Museum Gustavianum, 2009), pp. 21–30.
29. See Mindy MacLeod and Bernard Mees, *Runic Amulets and Magic Objects* (Woodbridge: Boydell Press, 2006), p. 9; John McKinnell and Rudolph Simek with Klaus Düwel, *Runes, Magic and Religion: A Sourcebook*, Studia Medievalia Septentrionalia 10 (Vienna: Fassbaender, 2004), p. 7.
30. Helen Young, "'It's the Middle Ages, Yo!': Race, Neo/medievalisms, and the World of Dragon Age," *The Year's Work in Medievalism* 27 (2012): https://sites.google.com/site/ theyearsworkinmedievalism/all-issues/27-2012.
31. Shiloh Carroll, "Race in A Song of Ice and Fire: Medievalism Posing as Authenticity," *The Public Medievalist* (blog), November 28, 2017, https://www.publicmedievalist.com/ race-in-asoif/.
32. Helen Stewart, "Rune Shawl Knitting pattern," https://www.ravelry.com/patterns/li brary/rune-shawl.

Roderick Dale
12 From Barbarian to Brand: The Vikings as a Marketing Tool

Introduction

The Viking brand is ubiquitous throughout Europe and North America: a quick search on the internet reveals many companies using the Vikings, defined in the broadest possible meaning of the word, to promote their products, and many websites devoted to the topic. Its popularity is reflected in television programs like *Vikings* and *The Last Kingdom* which use that popularity for their own promotion, but which also enhance it in a self-sustaining, uroboric feeding frenzy. It should come as no surprise, then, that the World-Tree Project was able to source, through community collection, more than four thousand items related to the Vikings for its digital archive, many of them reflecting modern interpretations of the Viking past.

The World-Tree Project was the first large-scale community collection initiative in the field of Viking and Old Norse Studies, and was funded by a 15-month Irish Research Council "New Horizons" grant. Its goal was to create an interactive digital archive for the teaching and study of Old Norse literature and Viking culture that would benefit both the scholarly community and the non-specialist audience. By putting the onus for contribution on both specialists and non-specialists, the project was able to plot responses to Norse and Viking heritage within the wider community, showing how and where Viking influence was felt, and to show what people perceived as "Viking".

The use of Vikings to market products was especially highlighted by user contributions to the World-Tree Project and featured in one of the online exhibits which showed just how wide an array of items might be marketed using "Viking" imagery.[1] A search on the World-Tree website for the tag "branding" produced nearly three hundred items submitted by users at the time of writing, and over one hundred items where a Viking-themed logo was tagged.[2] Similarly, horned helmets were tagged nearly one hundred times in the collection.[3] These items provide evidence for the popularity of Vikings as a product and in advertising. Drawing on the World-Tree Project data, this essay examines how Vikings are used and repurposed to suit modern commercial needs. It discusses which attributes of the Vikings are emphasized in their use as a brand, and how this shapes the narrative around products, showing that a

Roderick Dale, University of Nottingham

https://doi.org/10.1515/9781501513886-013

diverse range of attributes are ascribed to the Vikings, not least strength, adventurousness, and endurance, while other attributes are diminished or ignored in the quest to co-opt the powerful semiotics of the Vikings. The use of figures from Norse mythology to shape brands through identification with the attributes of the gods, such as Thor Motocross gear which must be robust like Thor, or the seductiveness of Freya Lingerie, is also discussed.[4] In creating and engaging with this narrative, advertisers and producers have given the Viking brand a life separate from, but based on aspects of, historical Vikings. They have taken the historical Vikings, and adapted and repurposed them to suit modern needs. As a corollary to this colonization of the past from the present, the essay considers how this apparently separate existence affects the basic assumptions about, and the need for, "mythbusting." It considers whether such "mythbusting" is necessary, productive or useful given how modern people engage daily with "Viking" brands without necessarily connecting those brands to the historical Vikings, and shows how marketing builds on a collective perception of the Vikings rooted in popular culture without directly engaging with the history.

It is not surprising that the Vikings should be so ubiquitous. Popular interest in them has existed in western Europe since at least the early nineteenth century when they were used as part of the campaigns to establish and promote national identities.[5] They still do sterling service in support of modern Scandinavian national identities with all of the Nordic countries deploying horned-helmeted images as part of their approach to engaging with tourist expectations.[6] In Norway, the Viking is often combined with troll images to establish a distinctly Norwegian "Vikingness" that harks back to the national romanticism of Ibsen's *Peer Gynt*.[7] As a result, the Vikings have a legendary history over and above their historical reality, and many calls are made upon that legendary history to reinforce brand identity, as well as for political purposes.

Misuse of the Vikings by fascist groups in early twentieth-century Germany, and by neo-Nazi and white supremacist groups in the later twentieth and early twenty-first centuries also speaks to their power as a symbol of identity. Trafford and Pluskowski considered their appeal as icons of hard rock and heavy metal, and showed how the Vikings were adapted and adopted as symbols of these musical genres and yet with radically different political views.[8] Bands like Type O Negative adopted a Norse identity through their Vinland iconography that was later adopted as the Vinland flag by US neo-Nazis.[9] This use of the Vikings as a strong, independent, but, more importantly, malleable identity is mirrored in the material submitted to the World-Tree Project.

The classic Viking is readily identifiable. More often than not the male Viking has a horned helmet where Valkyries are depicted with winged helmets. Both depictions appear to derive from Doepler's costumes for the 1876 staging of Wagner's Ring cycle, a point when Vikings generally switched from having winged helmets to horned helmets.[10] It is notable that Valkyries retained the winged helmet where male Vikings followed the new fashion. If Wagner's opera had as great an effect on popular culture depictions as it appears to have had, then it led the way in changing public perceptions of how the Vikings looked and introduced the concept of the horned helmet to the world. This was an enduring change that has survived to the present day in Viking branding, as the many examples of horned helmets on the World-Tree Project show.

In advertising, the construction of meaning must happen in the audience's mind. Rarely is an explicit statement of value and meaning made, but rather value is implied by association and an emotional appeal is made to the audience.[11] The value of the Viking brand lies in approximately two hundred years of popular history and representation of the Vikings in popular culture. It is reinvented or redirected at regular intervals so that it can be appropriated in new ways. Thus, the Capital One advertising campaign with its increasingly comical, marauding Vikings presented them as pillagers of your wallet who only attacked the unwary.[12] The fiscally savvy were safe from their depredations. In similar ways, the Vikings became proto-capitalists as the doctrine and ideology of the free market became more popular: these different meanings are all present in the World-Tree Project collection.

The Data

Where other studies have focused on the output from a single country or based on a single theme, this essay adopts a transnational approach in line with the broader remit of the World-Tree Project,[13] and considers a wide range of material themed around the Vikings or given a Viking brand. While the World-Tree Project focused primarily on Denmark, Ireland, Norway, and the United Kingdom, contributors from many other countries submitted items relating to branding to the project, some of which are considered here.

Examples of Viking branding were documented using online community collection. Public calls were put out on social media (specifically Twitter and Facebook) asking for the submission of any and all Viking-related items that contributors might encounter, and a small number of contributors became sufficiently enthused by the project to contribute a majority of the items, as expected based on current research.[14] The call for submissions resulted in a wide variety of items ranging from pedagogical materials to pop culture references. Some of these items were text files to download while others were photographs or links to blog posts. No attempt was made to control or direct the type of material submitted. The project relied solely on its contributors deciding what was suitable, because the intent was to review and engage with what the contributors considered to be "Viking." This resulted in an eclectic mix of items ranging from the Asgard Bestattungen in Berlin (Asgard funeral home) to Thor and Balder bread rolls from the 7-Eleven in Denmark.[15]

The material collected on the World-Tree Project was sent in by a wide range of contributors, from members of the public to academics from whom submissions were solicited directly. No controls were placed on who could contribute or what they could contribute. It was anticipated that some contributions might need to be edited or not approved for public upload due to the types of content that could potentially have been submitted. This type of content could have included explicitly white supremacist material, or material that could not be added to the website for copyright reasons. However, in the end the vast majority of material submitted was uploaded.

No analysis has been undertaken of the contributors themselves, and data collected was only used to communicate with the contributor about their contribution. Nevertheless, they all have some key factors in common. They had to be interested enough in the Vikings to take time to submit material to the World-Tree Project. They needed access to the internet to be able to submit material. Most needed to be able to communicate in English, although the project accepted submissions in Norwegian and Danish specifically, and was open to submissions in other languages. Attempts were made to access communities that did not fit these criteria, but with limited success. The project team wrote to local libraries in the target countries asking them to post notices about the project with the intention of engaging with library users who might not be habitual users of the internet, and who might not have a sufficiently good command of English to be willing to submit. However, the results of this exercise were poor, while direct contact with potential users yielded better results, as, for example, in the cases where individuals or online groups were approached and asked for specific submissions. Although this did limit the scope of the submissions, the range was still substantial, and several clear trends in the branding of the Vikings can be identified.

Strength and Endurance

Popular images of Vikings see them as strong and capable of enduring a lot without complaint. As sailors, they sailed to Newfoundland across seas that others dared not cross. They lived in the snowy northlands and survived all that the elements could throw at them. For these reasons, they are often seen as symbols of hardihood.

This endurance is co-opted by Viking Tyres which uses a logo of a Viking in a horned helmet standing strong with his sword by his side and his shield in his hand.[16] This Viking looks like he is on guard, and his sword is pointing to the floor in a defensive, non-aggressive posture. Upon closer inspection, his shield is actually a tire, indicating that the tires will protect the purchaser. This theme is further expanded upon in the section of the website about the company where the website explains that the company began its life in Norway and that by 1970 "nearly every Norwegian knows the brand and trusts its tyres."[17] Given the nature of the product, it is unsurprising that the website repeatedly references the quality, reliability and endurance of these tires. Nevertheless, to drive the point home, the slogan "Strong as a Viking" is adopted as a heading for the page about the brand.

Viking Life-Saving Equipment is another product that draws on this sense of endurance, and, in this case, is more closely related to the sea.[18] The company was set up in Esbjerg, Denmark where fishing was a major industry as the company website notes: "The story of VIKING begins in a town where people know that the sea gives and the sea takes away. For decades, anxious women have waited through storms for signs of life from their men at sea. Some in vain, others relieved when their loved ones managed to defy nature's power and rescue themselves."[19] The website immediately sets the scene for a conflict between humans and the sea. The language is dramatic and timeless. It is as easy to imagine Viking women waiting for their men to return, as it is to imagine the fishing families of more modern times anxiously awaiting news of the sailors' return. The website then continues: "The fishermen have almost disappeared from Esbjerg, Denmark's most western town. But VIKING remains – now as a global corporation that has long since conquered the world's oceans and whose name is synonymous with safety at sea. For fishermen, merchant seafarers, ship passengers, offshore workers, sports and leisure sailors, and everyone who sails the seas."[20] The company appropriates the strength and endurance of the Vikings to show how it has survived against nature. However, it goes further. It states that it has conquered the sea, a truly Viking-like achievement, because the Vikings were the sailors *par excellence* of all time, and warriors who could conquer anything, even nature. From its origins in Denmark to its logo, and its statements about its heritage, Viking Life-Saving Equipment draws on the common tropes of the hardiness of the Vikings without ever overtly claiming a Viking connection beyond the company's name.

The Norwegian outdoor clothing and sportswear brand Norrøna also exploits this traditional image of Vikings as hardy, outdoor folk. Its logo in 1929 featured a Viking-like figure on skis with a shield in his hand and a pair of skis emblazoned on the shield.[21] The skis the figure is wearing and on the shield have been stylized to represent the company's founder's name Jørgen Jørgensen: "The initials JJ from the original company name is symbolized in the skis and the shield of the Viking."[22] The identification of this figure as a Viking is made in passing on the company website, as if it were so obvious that it need not be mentioned. The same webpage references the figure as a *Birkebeiner* when discussing the 1977 logo, again as if the connection were obvious and requires no explanation: "We missed the *Birkebeiner* in the logo, so Kjell Witberg made a new styled edition."[23] The modern logo has been cropped and updated to show a head in a Viking-style helmet with long hair flowing behind it as if the figure's body is skiing downhill.[24] In all cases, there is a strong resemblance to Bergslien's 1869 painting "Birkebeinerne på Ski over Fjeldet med Kongsbarnet" and it seems likely that the original logo referenced the painting to provide an image of strength, endurance, and a willingness to push oneself as hard as possible.[25] While the logo is referred to both as a Viking and as a *Birkebeiner* by the company website, the connection to Bergslien's painting is never made explicit in the company's history of itself. The imagery of the Viking and the *Birkebeiner*, and the conflation of two related but not historically contemporary concepts, speaks to a desire to connect the company's products to the outdoors, toughness, and endurance. It also references a common body of knowledge, suggesting that in the popular consciousness in Norway the *Birkebeinere* are seen as Vikings. The fact that Norrøna makes sailing gear as well as other types of outdoors wear makes it logical to link the product to the Vikings as great sailors and to the *Birkebeinere* whose frantic dash across the mountains on skis is the epitome of legendary endurance and sportiness. It shows that the products are rugged and able to cope in all weathers and environments.

THOR MX takes its name from a serendipitous acronym combining the founder's name and product: Torsten Hallman Original Racewear.[26] In doing so, it references Hallman's Swedish birth through the reference to Norse mythology, and it draws on the legendary strength of the god of thunder, linking the brand to a god known primarily for his strength and willingness to fight to protect his people.[27] By combining Thor's strength and warlike nature with the competitive nature of motocross, and by linking the brand to Vikings through a logo that combines the name Thor and a half-profile Viking in a horned helmet, THOR MX draws on stereotypes of the strength and aggression of the Vikings. The sense of danger and aggression is enhanced by the horns on the helmet being jagged, making them more threatening. Furthermore, the use of THOR as the acronym is likely to set up associations with Marvel's superhero version of Thor in the modern mind, especially given his recent cinematic exposure.[28] Together, these elements create a sense of excitement in the viewer as if they are traveling on one of Thor's journeys, ready to go into battle against the giants, or perhaps to battle Loki's latest machinations in the Marvel cineverse. Thus, THOR MX incorporates not just strength and endurance, but also offers a gateway to the adventurousness of the Vikings.

Adventurousness and Exploration

The adventurousness of the Vikings is epitomized in the ways that Vikings have been linked to transport and travel. As mentioned above, linking moto-cross gear to the Vikings makes it more exciting and adventurous, but other elements of transport and travel incorporate the Vikings for more passive thrill-seekers, as is the case with Viking Cruises which offers tourists the opportunity to "plunder" the culture of their destinations. As with many similar companies, Viking Cruises was founded by a Scandinavian, the Norwegian billionaire Torstein Hagen, so the name references his cultural heritage, although most passengers will not realize this. Instead, they will see the exciting red background of the logo and the Viking ship in full sail that suggests the thrill and adventure of voyages into the unknown.[29] Viking Cruises is just one way that the tourist industry uses the Vikings as a symbol of adventure and exploration.

The Vikings have been used to entice visitors to come to Scandinavia. "See the Lands of the Vikings" declares one 1930s poster under a brightly colored image of a Viking ship in full sail with two Vikings visible on board, resplendent in their winged helmets.[30] The bright colors promise an exciting adventure, as the ship crests a wave towards the Scandinavian coastline. Norwegian American Line offers a calmer adventure with less dramatic colors on its poster that entreats the reader to "Enjoy your trip – go by ship."[31] In this case the ship, a drawing of the Oseberg ship, appears almost to be beached on the grass beside a peaceful fjord with dramatic mountains rising in the background and the full sun top center of the poster, hinting at the long days of the midnight sun. This adventure promises more exploration than danger, but still it relies on Viking imagery to sell it.

On a more local level, the excitement of joining a Viking voyage of exploration is offered to tourists in Dublin, where one may see the sights of the city on an interactive Viking-themed tour (Figure 13.1).[32] Visitors board a DUKW amphibious vehicle and are encouraged to don a plastic helmet with huge horns, and to roar like Vikings before the tour sets off. They are then taken around

Dublin both by road and river. While the tour does cover Viking Dublin, the main appeal of the theme is the idea that the tourists become a band of Viking explorers. In doing this, the tour draws on people's expectations of the adventurous Vikings who traveled through all dangers to new places.

This sense of exploration and adventurousness is often felt in relation to travel and transport. Rover cars featured a Viking ship in full sail on a heading directly towards the viewer.[33] This logo appeared on their cars from 1929 onwards. Between the connotations of the company name and the Viking ship imagery, the brand sought to sell itself as latter-day rovers of the highways, emphasizing the opportunity to explore and have adventures as one traveled, alongside the implications of technological innovation that Viking ships represent. The logo and name also suggest that the drivers of these cars could rule the roads, much as the Vikings ruled the seaways in the early medieval period.

In the same way as Rover cars might rule the road, small boats named for Viking-related themes are common. Contributors submitted pictures of boats named "Viking," "Oden," "Thor," "Troll," "Ringhorne," and "Loke," among others. In some cases, as with the name "Viking," several examples of different boats with the same name were submitted.[34] Many of these names may have specific significance to their owners, and examples like "Ringhorne," which was spotted in Norway, may be an appeal to the owner's Scandinavian, and thus Viking, heritage.[35] However, they also reference the seafaring heritage of the Vikings, and thus are an appeal to an adventurous and daring spirit that led the Vikings to travel across the globe from Newfoundland to Baghdad. They impart a vicarious thrill of participation in these daring voyages, if only by proxy, as is also the case with the other examples cited in this section.

Jovial, Feasting Vikings

Unsurprisingly, given the usual feasting scenes in Viking movies and TV series, for which the feasting scene in *The Vikings* (1958) is archetypal, beer is closely associated with the Vikings and that connection is exploited mercilessly by producers of alcohol.[36] A search for "beer" on the World-Tree Project website yields thirty-four hits, but a little exploration around the subject reveals many more examples that were not submitted to the project.[37] Red Erik beer by Ceres Brewery (now owned by Unibrew)[38] in Århus, Denmark, is a typical example, and sports a Viking wearing the classic horned helmet to reinforce its connection to the Viking brand.[39] Horned helmets, as in many other areas, are a popular element in giving beer a Viking brand. Rudgate Brewery in York exploits

York's own Viking connection with its Viking ale and Battle Axe bitter, and the bottle of its Ruby Mild featured in the photograph submitted to the World-Tree Project makes the Viking connection by featuring a helmet, an axe, and a tankard of foaming ale.[40] Other beers, like the beers from Ægir Bryggeri, a Norwegian micro-brewery, link their products to Norse mythology.[41] Thus Ægir Bryggeri takes its name from the Norse ruler of the sea who is known for having to hold a feast for the gods and thus having to brew enough ale for them all. In addition to being named for a mythological personage, Ægir Bryggeri gives several of its beers names from Norse mythology: Nagelfare Nut Brown Ale from *naglfari*, one of Night's husbands; Ratatosk Double IPA from the squirrel *Ratatoskr*; and Tors Hammer Barleywine from Thor's Hammer *Mjöllnir*.[42] This branding sells beers by connecting to the stereotype of the jovial, ale-quaffing Viking and suggesting that the drinker can partake of the uninhibited pleasure of which the barbarian Vikings partook, unhindered and unfettered by the restraints placed on civilized people.

This image of the Vikings is further encouraged and reinforced by two Icelandic T-shirt images that were submitted to the project. One T-shirt encourages the reader to "Drink like a Viking" with an image of a Viking in a horned helmet to which are attached tins of "Viking brew" with straws to the Viking's mouth.[43] So, the Viking is being related to images of people in beer hats. The other is advertising for Egil's Brewery.[44] It features a slightly madly staring Viking with his tongue lolling out of his mouth as he presents a foaming horn of ale to the viewer while holding a bottle of Egils beer in the other hand. He is obviously ecstatic about his choice of brew, and this is reinforced by the slogan on the T-shirt: "Choice of Vikings." Vikings, who all know their beer, would choose Egils and it would drive them into a transcendent state of unbridled, perhaps even berserk, pleasure. Untrammeled by the crushing weight of civilization, these barbarian Vikings reflect ideas of the noble savage, whose approach to life is more honest and open than that of civilized people, and thus they can enjoy their beer without complication.

While these beers all play up the stereotype of Vikings who love their beer, they also draw on local connections. Viking branding is ubiquitous throughout the Nordic countries, Orkney, Shetland, and the Hebrides, as a means of harking back to the "good old days" in much the same way as, for example, the Hovis "Bike" advert drew on wholesome images of a baker's boy pushing his bicycle up a hill to create a sense of nostalgia for simpler, better times in the audience, and to relate that to their product.[45]

In the same way that Vikings are connected to alcohol, they are also connected to food and for much the same reason. Food is the other part of the stereotypical Viking feast, and not just any food: roast meat is top of the menu. While roast meat is not broadly represented in the World-Tree Project archive, other foodstuffs are present. Forty-two food-related items were submitted, and many are only tangentially related to the Vikings, despite being marketed as "Viking."[46]

Two of these, Wickie Chicken-Nuggets and Wickie Abenteuer Salami, build on the popularity of Wickie der Wikinger (Vicky the Viking) among both children and adults in Germany, a popularity that ensures good sales of almost anything branded with Wickie.[47] These products promise an adventurous and exciting meal by being associated with the popular children's character in particular and with the Vikings more generally. The images on the packaging show Wickie at sea, windsurfing on the chicken nuggets, and Wickie inviting the viewer to board the ship on the salami packaging. The color and motion of the depictions is such as to draw the viewer in.

Other foodstuffs have little or no obvious thematic connection to the Vikings, despite carrying Viking branding. Odin Potetbrød is a type of gluten-free flatbread whose only connection to the Vikings is in the reference to Odin.[48] Knorr Wikingertopf is a powdered sauce marketed as Viking but with no obvious connection to the Vikings.[49] Snowcream milk uses a Viking ship to promote it, but, again has no direct connection to the Vikings, although it is produced in Co. Waterford and may, therefore, be an appeal to nostalgia via the Viking heritage of the area.[50] These items show that, no matter how spurious, a connection to the Vikings has strong marketing value.

The Viking Brand

So, how does the Viking, this dangerous alterity, become a family-friendly symbol of aspiration, adventure, or strength? The answer, as with many perspectives on the Vikings, lies initially in the nineteenth-century use of the Vikings to promote ideals of nationalism. The Vikings, as distant historical figures with connections throughout Europe, were sufficiently malleable to have many different attributes mapped onto them based on their activities. It was easy to downplay the violence and terror that they caused, or even to transmute it, in favor of accentuating those attributes that were most desirable. For the English, Viking sea-power played up to nationalist perspectives that Britannia ruled the waves. Exploration was a strong part of the English colonial mentality, and it was easy to find similar activities among the Vikings. Thus, they were ready-made for use in the creation and bolstering of national identity.[51] Similar contortions surrounded the Vikings in other countries. The Vikings were used to bolster and to underpin nascent national identity in Scotland, as they were throughout Scandinavia and western Europe. Every nation state could find in the Vikings something to emphasize and support whatever identity suited them best. While the uses to which Vikings are put have changed, this adaptability has not. As the examples from the World-Tree Project show, Vikings and Viking-related themes have a strong and malleable enough marketing identity that they can be used for almost any product.

The use of Viking themes to sell products varies. Some products borrow from the success of other successful brands, as in the case of the Wickie Chicken Nuggets and Abenteuer Salami. Others use the popularly understood attributes of the Norse gods or the Vikings themselves, as in the case of Freya Lingerie. Others appeal to heritage. For example, a Viking sprinkler alarm made in Hastings, Michigan, plays up to local identities, and to the identity of the Viking Group's founder, Emil Tyden, a Swedish immigrant. Tyden became involved in the production of sprinkler systems in the 1920s when he bought The Viking Corporation which is now a subsidiary of Viking Group Inc.[52] The association of Hastings with Vikings is ahistorical but makes sense in the broader overview of the events of 1066 too. It roots the company's identity in its ostensible founder's nationality, a trait that is found throughout Minnesota where a large proportion of Scandinavians settled, as is evidenced by the choice of Minnesota Vikings as an identity for the area's NFL team. These identities were seen as particularly important in the late nineteenth and early twentieth centuries when Scandinavian immigrants felt they were losing touch with their heritage and needed a strong identity to cope with the discrimination against them. In the face of such difficulties, appeals to heritage are particularly strong and forge local identities that buffer people against the worst that is thrown against them. Given the malleability of the Vikings, it is unsurprising that they were and are used in this manner, and that they create strong associations with the specific attributes identified in this essay in the minds of those that engage with them.

This strong brand identity is evident in the range of material branded as "Viking." It works through a combination of nostalgia for a simpler past that never was and builds on the sense that modern, civilized life is constricting and leaves little room for the adventurous soul to express themselves. By identifying with the Viking brand, people are able to take ownership of some of that adventurousness and to claim a Viking identity of their own. This may be pure wish-fulfilment, as in the case of making salami adventurous by branding it as Wickie the Wiking, or it may be a national identity and a call to the homeland, as in the case of Viking fire sprinklers. These brands are central to the myth-building that goes into establishing a group identity.

The use of Viking imagery is a central element in modern Viking identities. It means different things in different places, and often has little connection to the realities of the past. Instead, the imagery builds on and co-opts more recent interpretations that have caught the public imagination. One case in point is the ubiquitous horned helmet. Academics and reenactors decry this aspect of the popular-culture Viking and it is usually one of the first elements mentioned in any attempt at mythbusting the Vikings, but it is such a strong symbol of Viking identity that it has gained a life of its own. Most people are already aware of the lack of evidence for horned helmets, but the brand value of the horned helmet is too strong for advertisers to ignore. As a result, many advertisers and brands play on it to ensure that their product has that essential and immediately recognizable relationship to the Viking past. In doing this, commercial uses of the Vikings as a brand demonstrate that the popular-culture Viking has a separate existence from the historical reality of the Vikings and that people can accommodate both meanings in their lives.

Branding may be seen as a type of play activity. The marketers play with and develop the Vikings, through their interaction and presentation of it. Use of the Viking brand is playing with the past, a game that is culturally specific, but for which most know the rules and boundaries. Sometimes this play leads to usage of Norse material that seems particularly apposite, as in the case of the M/S Sigyn, a nuclear waste carrier named for Loki's wife who caught the poison dripping into his eyes and carried it away, or an incinerator on the Isle of Man that was designed to evoke the image of a Viking longship so that anything burnt on it was being burnt on a Viking funeral pyre.[53] The marketers use these rules and boundaries to shape the relationship that people have with their products through the medium of the Vikings. This play offends some who consider it to be distasteful or irksome because it does not accord with their understanding of history. Certainly, the marketers' use of history does not adhere closely to the probable historical reality. However, this new Viking identity exists separately from the historical reality, having a life of its own that is unlikely to be crushed by historical arguments in the short or medium term. This play recreates the present in the past, permitting modern ideas to colonize the past for their own purposes. It gives it currency because it references modern attitudes and concerns. It is an emotional, affective engagement with the past, not engagement with any kind of Rankean past "wie es eigentlich gewesen" (as it really was) if such a thing ever even existed.[54] As such, it is a past of the imagination that has particular resonance with the individual and which can become a strong part of their identity, yet has never existed anywhere but in the popular mind. Challenging these ideas can be met with strong pushback precisely because they are so intertwined with identity, and thus people are resistant to change. This resistance necessarily dictates the types of approaches that must be taken in seeking to counter it and to educate people about the historical Vikings.

Mythbusting

In a post on his *Archaeodeath* blog, Professor Howard Williams took issue with mythbusting the horned helmet.[55] It is an easy thing to do, given that no horned helmets of Viking Age date have been found yet, but Williams argued that it was not a productive use of scholars' time. It creates a situation where those with actual or claimed authority speak down to others, and is not necessarily a good method of educating them. The study of the medieval period as depicted in movies shows that much academic analysis often seeks to position movies as an alterity distanced from reality; the "reel/real" distinction that Haydock discusses.[56] Just as analysis of movies purely in terms of their authenticity does not address the imaginary space in which those movies exist, mythbusting and debunking of pop-culture Vikings situate the mythbuster as an authority but fail to address the nature of the spaces in which pop-culture Vikings exist and how they came to be created.

The horned helmet of the pop-culture Viking has a separate identity from the non-horned historical Viking. These identities exist in almost completely separate continua, perhaps uneasily, but nevertheless separate and distinct from each other. Images of the Vikings found in advertising and as brands continue to perpetuate nineteenth-century stereotypes for the most part, while the historical Viking has moved on and has been incorporated into modern narratives, as new evidence has emerged. The gulf between the two images continues to widen, and it may well be futile to attempt to reconcile them now that the stereotype has its own separate existence.

As the reporter says in *The Man Who Shot Liberty Valance*, "When the legend becomes fact, print the legend."[57] One might well say the same of the popular-culture Viking. This Viking has a life of its own that has little to do with historical Vikings, and much to do with people's need to have a readily identifiable symbol of "Vikingness." As Service writes, the Vikings could have many attributes mapped onto them from uncouth barbarians whose appetites remained unfettered by civilization to adventurers, merchants, and poets.[58] Each of these attributes has had its use in the construction of modern identities, and still has its uses in the emergence of Vikings as a strongly marketable brand. In the face of this separate brand identity, it seems unnecessary to repeat the mantra that Vikings never had horns on their helmets or indulge in other mythbusting that privileges the mythbuster over the recipient of their knowledge. There are more important areas of popular usage and reinvention where that same energy might be better spent countering modern toxic narratives, such as the use of Norse myth and Viking masculinity to support white supremacist ideologies, as Steel notes.[59] These narratives were not encountered directly by the

World-Tree Project, which elicited more contributions focused on pop culture, marketing, and daily life, but they are clearly present in the wider arena and are a useful focus for our energy.

Bibliography

AMA Motorcycle Hall of Fame. http://www.motorcyclemuseum.org/halloffame.

Anti-Defamation League. "General Hate Symbols: Vinland Flag." https://www.adl.org/educa tion/references/hate-symbols/vinland-flag.

Flåmsbrygga. http://flamsbrygga.no.

Frank, Roberta. "The Invention of the Horned Helmet." In *International Scandinavian and Medieval Studies in Memory of Gerd Wolfgang Weber: Ein Runder Knauel, So Rollt' Es Uns Leicht Aus Den Handen*, edited by Michael Dallapiazza, Olaf Hansen, Preben Meulengracht Sørensen and Yvonne Bonnetain, pp. 199–208. Trieste: Parnaso, 2000.

Freya Lingerie and Swimwear. http://www.freyalingerie.fr/.

Harty, Kevin J. "Introduction: 'Save Us, O Lord, from the Fury of the Northmen'; or 'Do You Know What's in Your Wallet?'" In *The Vikings on Film: Essays on Depictions of the Nordic Middle Ages*, edited by Kevin J. Harty, pp. 3–7. Jefferson, NC and London: McFarland, 2011.

Haydock, Nickolas. *The Imaginary Middle Ages: Movie Medievalism*. Jefferson, NC and London: McFarland, 2008.

Hovis "Bike" Advert. Dir. Ridley Scott. London: Alan Parker Film Company, 1973. Television.

LeMans Corporation. http://www.thormx.com.

Lönnroth, Lars. "The Vikings in History and Legend." In *The Oxford Illustrated History of the Vikings*, edited by Peter Sawyer, pp. 225–49. Oxford: Oxford University Press, 1997.

The Man Who Shot Liberty Valance. Dir. John Ford. London: Paramount British Pictures, 1962. Film.

Merchant, Altaf, Kathryn Latour, John B. Ford and Michael S. Latour. "How Strong Is the Pull of the Past? Measuring Personal Nostalgia Evoked by Advertising." *Journal of Advertising Research* 53, no. 2 (2013): 150–65.

Muehling, Darrel D. and Vincent J. Pascal. "An Involvement Explanation for Nostalgia Advertising Effects." *Journal of Promotion Management* 18 (2012): 100–18.

Norrøna Sports AS. https://www.norrona.com.

O'Donoghue, Heather. *From Asgard to Valhalla: The Remarkable History of the Norse Myths*. New York: I. B. Tauris, 2007.

Oomen, Johan and Lora Aroyo. "Crowdsourcing in the Cultural Heritage Domain: Opportunities and Challenges." In *Proceedings of the 5th International Conference on Communities and Technologies*, edited by Marcus Foth, Jesper Kjeldskov and Jeni Paay, pp. 138–49. New York: ACM, 2011.

Royal Unibrew. http://www.royalunibrew.com.

Rudgate Brewery. http://www.rudgatebrewery.co.uk/.

Service, Alexandra. "Popular Vikings: Construction of Viking Identity in Twentieth Century Britain." Unpublished D.Phil. thesis, University of York, 1998.

Snowcream. http://snowcreamdiscoverwaterford.com.

Steel, Karl. "Bad Heritage: The American Viking Fantasy, from the Nineteenth Century to Now." In *DEcolonial Heritage: Natures, Cultures, and the Asymmetries of Memory*, edited by Aníbal Arregui, Gesa Mackenthun and Stephanie Wodianka, pp. 75–96. Münster: Waxmann, 2018.

Stormfront. "Classified ads." https://www.stormfront.org/forum/t916169/.

Thor. Dir. Kenneth Branagh. London: Channel 4 Television Corporation, 2011. Film.

Thor: The Dark World. Dir. Alan Taylor. Burbank, CA: Walt Disney, 2013. Film.

Thor: Ragnarok. Dir. Taika Waititi. Burbank, CA: Walt Disney, 2017. Film.

Trafford, Simon and Aleks Pluskowski. "Antichrist Superstars: The Vikings in Hard Rock and Heavy Metal." In *Mass Market Medieval: Essays on the Middle Ages in Popular Culture*, edited by David W. Marshall, pp. 57–73. Jefferson, NC: McFarland, 2007.

Viking Group Inc, "Homepage," http://www.vikinggroupinc.com.

Viking Life-Saving Equipment. https://www.viking-life.com.

Viking River Cruises. http://www.vikingrivercruises.com.

Viking Tyres. https://www.viking-tyres.com.

The Vikings. Dir. Richard Fleischer. London: United Artists, 1958. Film.

Wawn, Andrew. *The Vikings and the Victorians: Inventing the Old North in Nineteenth-Century Britain*. Cambridge: D. S. Brewer, 2000.

Williams, Howard. Archaeodeath Blog. https://howardwilliamsblog.wordpress.com.

Wilson, David. "The Viking Age in British Literature and History in the Eighteenth and Nineteenth Centuries." In *The Waking of Angantyr: The Scandinavian Past in European Culture*, edited by Else Roesdahl and Preben Meulengracht Sørensen, pp. 58–71. Aarhus: Aarhus University Press, 1996.

The World-Tree Project. http://www.worldtreeproject.org.

Notes

1. The World-Tree Project, "Exhibit: Viking Branding," http://www.worldtreeproject.org/exhibits/show/viking-branding.
2. The World-Tree Project, "Branding [search term]," http://www.worldtreeproject.org/items/browse?tags=Branding.
3. The World-Tree Project, "Horned Helmet [search term]," http://www.worldtreeproject.org/items/browse?tags=Horned+Helmets.
4. LeMans Corporation, "Thor: Homepage," http://www.thormx.com; The World-Tree Project, "Thor Motocross Gear in Dublin," http://www.worldtreeproject.org/document/2905; Freya Lingerie and Swimwear, "Homepage," http://www.freyalingerie.fr/; The World-Tree Project, "Freya Lingerie," http://www.worldtreeproject.org/document/2834.
5. See, for example, Andrew Wawn, *The Vikings and the Victorians: Inventing the Old North in Nineteenth-Century Britain* (Cambridge: D. S. Brewer, 2000); David Wilson, "The Viking Age in British Literature and History in the Eighteenth and Nineteenth Centuries," in *The Waking of Angantyr: The Scandinavian Past in European Culture*, ed. Else Roesdahl and Preben Meulengracht Sørensen (Aarhus: Aarhus University Press, 1996), pp. 58–71; and Lars Lönnroth, "The Vikings in History and Legend," in *The Oxford Illustrated History of the Vikings*, ed. Peter Sawyer (Oxford: Oxford University Press, 1997), pp. 225–49.

6. See for example: The World-Tree Project, "Denmark Snow-globe Souvenir with Horned Helmet," http://www.worldtreeproject.org/document/1101; "The Great Valkyrie Keyring by Ninna Thorarinsdottir," http://www.worldtreeproject.org/document/694; and "3 Fridge Magnets," http://www.worldtreeproject.org/document/2897.
7. See for example: The World-Tree Project, "Viking-themed Souvenirs in a Shop in Oslo," http://www.worldtreeproject.org/document/2261.
8. Simon Trafford and Aleks Pluskowski, "Antichrist Superstars: The Vikings in Hard Rock and Heavy Metal," in *Mass Market Medieval: Essays on the Middle Ages in Popular Culture*, ed. David W. Marshall (Jefferson, NC: McFarland, 2007), pp. 57–73.
9. Stormfront, "Classified Ads," https://www.stormfront.org/forum/t916169/; Anti-Defamation League, "General Hate Symbols: Vinland Flag," https://www.adl.org/educa tion/references/hate-symbols/vinland-flag.
10. Roberta Frank, "The Invention of the Horned Helmet," in *International Scandinavian and Medieval Studies in Memory of Gerd Wolfgang Weber: Ein Runder Knauel, So Rollt' Es Uns Leicht Aus Den Handen*, ed. Michael Dallapiazza et al. (Trieste: Parnaso, 2000), pp. 199–208.
11. Darrel D. Muehling and Vincent J. Pascal, "An Involvement Explanation for Nostalgia Advertising Effects," *Journal of Promotion Management* 18 (2012): 100–18.
12. K. J. Harty, "Introduction: 'Save Us, O Lord, from the Fury of the Northmen'; or 'Do You Know What's in Your Wallet?,'" in *The Vikings on Film: Essays on Depictions of the Nordic Middle Ages*, ed. Kevin J. Harty (Jefferson, NC and London: McFarland, 2011), pp. 3–7 at p. 3.
13. The World-Tree Project, "About," http://www.worldtreeproject.org/about.
14. Johan Oomen and Lora Aroyo, "Crowdsourcing in the Cultural Heritage Domain: Opportunities and Challenges," in *Proceedings of the 5th International Conference on Communities and Technologies*, ed. Marcus Foth, Jesper Kjeldskov and Jeni Paay (New York: ACM, 2011), pp. 138–49 at p. 146.
15. The World-Tree Project, "Item 2879: Asgard Bestattungen (Funeral Home) in Berlin," http://www.worldtreeproject.org/document/2879; The World-Tree Project, "Item 1034: Thor and Balder Bread Rolls," http://www.worldtreeproject.org/document/1034.
16. Viking Tyres, "Homepage," http://www.viking-tyres.com/; "Item 68: Viking Tyres," The World-Tree Project, http://www.worldtreeproject.org/document/68.
17. Viking Tyres, "The Brand," https://www.viking-tyres.com/car/the-brand.
18. Viking Life-Saving Equipment, "Homepage," https://www.viking-life.com; "Item 849: Viking Life-Saving Equipment," The World-Tree Project, http://www.worldtreeproject.org/document/849.
19. Viking Life-Saving Equipment, "Our Heritage," www.viking-life.com/en/about-us/our-heritage.
20. Ibid.
21. Norrøna, "The History of Norrøna," https://www.norrona.com/en-GB/about-norrona/the-history-of-norrona/; The World-Tree Project, "Item 2851: Norrøna Logo from 1929," http://www.worldtreeproject.org/document/2851.
22. Norrøna, "The History of Norrøna," https://www.norrona.com/en-GB/about-norrona/the-history-of-norrona/.
23. Ibid.
24. The World-Tree Project, "Item 2267: Norrøna Shop, Oslo," http://www.worldtreeproject.org/document/2267.

25. See The World-Tree Project, "Item 2843: Birkebeinerne på Ski over Fjeldet med Kongsbarnet," http://www.worldtreeproject.org/document/2843.
26. AMA Motorcycle Hall of Fame, "Torsten Hallman," http://www.motorcyclemuseum.org/halloffame/detail.aspx?RacerID=188&lpos=0px&letter=H&txtFname=&rblFname=S&txtLname=&rblLname=S&discipline=0.
27. The World-Tree Project, "Item 2905: Thor Motocross Gear in Dublin," http://www.world treeproject.org/document/2905.
28. *Thor*, dir. Kenneth Branagh (London: Channel 4 Television Corporation, 2011), Film; *Thor: The Dark World*, dir. Alan Taylor (Burbank, CA: Walt Disney, 2013), Film; and *Thor: Ragnarok*, dir. Taika Waititi (Burbank, CA: Walt Disney, 2017), Film.
29. Viking River Cruises, "Homepage," http://www.vikingrivercruises.com; The World-Tree Project, "Item 65: Viking Cruises," http://www.worldtreeproject.org/document/65.
30. The World-Tree Project, "Item 2831: 'See the Lands of the Vikings' Vintage Poster," http://www.worldtreeproject.org/document/2831.
31. The World-Tree Project, "Item 2839: Norway – Enjoy Your Trip Go By Ship," http://www.worldtreeproject.org/document/2839;
32. The World-Tree Project, "Item 1897: Photographs of Viking Splash Tours, Dublin," http://www.worldtreeproject.org/document/1897; see also p. 235 in this collection.
33. The World-Tree Project, "Item 2828: Logo of Rover Company," http://www.worldtreeproject.org/document/2828 sourced via https://en.wikipedia.org/wiki/Rover_Company.
34. The World-Tree Project, "Item 1258: Boat Named 'Viking,' Photographed on Aldeburgh Beach," http://www.worldtreeproject.org/document/1258; "Item 2902: Boat Named Viking Photographed in Amsterdam," http://www.worldtreeproject.org/document/2902; and "Item 1343: Canal Boat Named Viking," http://www.worldtreeproject.org/document/1343.
35. The World-Tree Project, "Item 2463: Ringhorne: Boat Name with Rune-like Script," http://www.worldtreeproject.org/document/2463.
36. *The Vikings*, dir. Richard Fleischer (London: United Artists, 1958), Film.
37. The World-Tree Project, "Beer [search term]" http://www.worldtreeproject.org/search?query=beer&query_type=keyword&record_types%5B%5D=Item&record_types%5B%5D=File&record_types%5B%5D=Collection&record_types%5B%5D=Exhibit&record_types%5B%5D=ExhibitPage&record_types%5B%5D=SimplePagesPage&submit_search=Search.
38. Royal Unibrew, "Homepage," http://www.royalunibrew.com.
39. The World-Tree Project, "Item 2881: Photograph of Red Erik Beer – Ceres, Århus, Denmark," http://www.worldtreeproject.org/document/2881.
40. Rudgate Brewery, "Rudgate: Brewed in the Vale of York," http://www.rudgatebrewery.co.uk/; The World-Tree Project, "Item 1423: Photograph of Viking & Battle Axe Bitter Ale by Rudgate Brewery," http://www.worldtreeproject.org/document/1423.
41. Flåmsbrygga, "Homepage," http://flamsbrygga.no; The World-Tree Project, "Item 2607: Ægir Bryggeri Littlebro," http://www.worldtreeproject.org/document/2607.
42. Flåmsbrygga, "Ølutval frå Ægir," http://flamsbrygga.no/aegir-bryggeripub/olutval/.
43. The World-Tree Project, "Item 564: Icelandic T-Shirt, 'Drink Like a Viking,'" http://www.worldtreeproject.org/document/564.
44. The World-Tree Project, "Item 559: Icelandic T-Shirt, Egils Beer," http://www.worldtreeproject.org/document/559.
45. *Hovis "Bike" Advert*, dir. Ridley Scott (London: Alan Parker Film Company, 1973), Television.

46. The World-Tree Project, "Food [search term]," http://www.worldtreeproject.org/items/browse?tags=Food.
47. The World-Tree Project, "Item 308: 'Viking' Chicken Nuggets and 'Viking' Salami," http://www.worldtreeproject.org/document/308.
48. The World-Tree Project, "Item 2072: Odin Potetbrød," http://www.worldtreeproject.org/document/2072.
49. The World-Tree Project, "Item 2554: Knorr Wikingertopf (Powdered Sauce)," http://www.worldtreeproject.org/document/2554.
50. Snowcream, "Homepage," http://snowcreamdiscoverwaterford.com; The World-Tree Project, "Item 2936: Snowcream Milk, with Viking Ship Branding," http://www.worldtreeproject.org/document/2936.
51. Heather O'Donoghue, *From Asgard to Valhalla: The Remarkable History of the Norse Myths* (New York: I. B. Tauris, 2007), p. 131.
52. Viking Group Inc, "Homepage," http://www.vikinggroupinc.com; The World-Tree Project, "Item 2856: Viking Sprinkler Alarm," http://www.worldtreeproject.org/document/2856.
53. The World-Tree Project, "Item 831: MS Sigyn," http://www.worldtreeproject.org/document/831; "Item 440: Incinerator on the Isle of Man, Designed to Evoke a Viking Ship," http://www.worldtreeproject.org/document/440.
54. Altaf Merchant, Kathryn Latour, John B. Ford and Michael S. Latour, "How Strong Is the Pull of the Past? Measuring Personal Nostalgia Evoked by Advertising," *Journal of Advertising Research* 53, no. 2 (2013): 150–65.
55. Howard Williams, "I Believe in Horned Helmets," *Archaeodeath* (blog), May 25, 2016, https://howardwilliamsblog.wordpress.com/2016/05/05/i-believe-in-horned-helmets.
56. Nickolas Haydock, *The Imaginary Middle Ages: Movie Medievalism* (Jefferson, NC and London: McFarland, 2008), p. 6.
57. *The Man Who Shot Liberty Valance*, dir. John Ford (London: Paramount British Pictures, 1962), Film.
58. Alexandra Service, "Popular Vikings: Constructions of Viking Identity in Twentieth Century Britain" (Unpublished D.Phil. thesis, University of York, 1998), pp. 38–43.
59. Karl Steel, "Bad Heritage: The American Viking Fantasy, from the Nineteenth Century to Now," in *DEcolonial Heritage: Natures, Cultures, and the Asymmetries of Memory*, ed. Aníbal Arregui, Gesa Mackenthun and Stephanie Wodianka (Münster: Waxmann, 2018), pp. 75–96 at pp. 88–90.

Rebecca Boyd
13 Raiding the Vikings: How Does Ireland Consume Its Viking Heritage?

Finding the Vikings

For most people growing up in Ireland, our first encounters with the Vikings take place in school history classes. The Vikings are introduced as part of the Early Peoples and Ancient Societies strand to children around eight years old. Within these classes, pupils learn about the Viking world, the types of archaeological and historical evidence we have, and fit the Vikings into the wider timeline of Irish history.[1] History textbooks from the 1990s show that pupils first met the Vikings as ferocious raiders, attacking Ireland's churches and monasteries.[2] More recent texts[3] and online teaching resources[4] discuss housing, runes, ships, and the Wood Quay controversy, introducing a more diverse idea of the Viking world. This means that until the 2000s, Irish schoolchildren were primarily exposed to the Vikings as raiders. These schoolchildren, now adults, are the people who are the targets of today's many Viking-themed promotions, festivals, and marketing campaigns.

There seems to be no limit to what we can attach a Viking label to – popcorn, fitness regimes, beer festivals, marathons – and whilst some of these do have a Viking connection, many do not. Dublin Port have made two Viking-themed advertisements – in 1988, to coincide with the Dublin millennial celebrations, and in 2008.[5] These ads correctly reference the role of the Viking in creating Dublin Port and celebrate its trade and economic importance thanks to their legacy. A more tenuous connection is that of TonedFit, a Dublin gym which advertises a Viking Fitness approach.[6] If you train with them, you will "go to war," fight through your pain levels, and reach an unspecified but presumably terrifying "Viking Level" of fitness. Even snack foods can be turned into Vikings: a single kernel of popped popcorn, adorned with a penciled-on horned helmet and a beard marauds around the packaging of Pop Notch's Sweet and Salty flavored popcorn.[7] An American delicacy, popcorn was only introduced to Europeans after the discovery of that continent in 1493, quite some time after the Viking era. When I asked Pop Notch why they chose a Viking, they admitted that "in reality, we just liked the picture with the Viking hat."[8]

Rebecca Boyd, University College Cork

https://doi.org/10.1515/9781501513886-014

Vikings also appear with some regularity in our media, and not just as news articles. One of Ireland's major claims to fame is that blockbuster dramas such as *Vikings* and *Game of Thrones* are filmed on this island. These series popularize the Vikings and medieval Ireland and pique the public's interest in what life in the Viking Age was like. *Vikings* is filmed in Wicklow at Ashford Studios. This commercial television studio has just been granted planning permission for a €90 million expansion on the basis of its *Vikings* success.[9] This made news as a financial success story, but equally, it can read as a success story based on the popularity of the subject matter of the show – Vikings. The Vikings do not usually make it into the financial pages of the newspapers; more commonly, they appear in news items relating to excavation findings. Early in 2018, we saw a series of articles in the national media discussing new eleventh-century Viking finds excavated during the development of the Beamish and Crawford Brewery site in the medieval heart of Cork city. Journalists reported the recovery of a rare wooden weaver's sword, houses, and land reclamation programs dating to about the turn of the twelfth century.[10] However, they referred to these finds interchangeably as Viking and Hiberno-Norse, despite the fact that the Viking era proper in Ireland dates to the tenth century. These finds were even used to add to a long-running feud between Cork and Waterford as to which city is the oldest, inspiring yet more column inches about Vikings.[11] Of course, the truth is that neither of these cities is Ireland's oldest, that honor goes to Dublin whose earliest Viking find dates from the first half of the ninth century. After more than half a century of archaeological excavations in Dublin, there is still a palpable sense of excitement in the media when a new Viking site is uncovered. In March 2018, media reported the excavation of Viking houses and artifacts, including a key, leather shoes, bowls, and spoons, underneath a new hotel in the Coombe in Dublin.[12] The hotel developers stated that they would now incorporate that Viking heritage into the "hotel experience," again demonstrating the value of Vikings, in this case, as a tourist attraction and as something which would add extra value to the hotel.[13]

The Vikings were a powerful force in ninth- and tenth-century Ireland, and they remain so today, appearing in many different guises: as news reports, advertisements, entertainment, as part of the school curriculum, and of course at museums and heritage venues. The story of the Vikings is as complex today as it was 1200 years ago, but using a series of conceptual frames (of places, stories, and worlds), this essay will explore how Vikings appear in twenty-first-century Ireland.

Making Viking – Places

Dyflinn – Dublin

Dublin, Viking Dyflinn, was Ireland's first town. Founded by Vikings in the ninth century, it was a major international port and urban center within a few decades of its foundation.[14] It is the original Viking "place" in Ireland. Archaeologists and historians have spent more than a century studying Viking Dublin, but were still ignored by Dublin Corporation when it sought to build new headquarters right at the heart of the Viking settlement in the 1970s.[15] This battle became the Wood Quay saga and the derisory attitude of the Corporation towards its heritage was a national scandal. Twenty thousand protesters participated in the "Save Wood Quay" march in 1978 with no success. Layers of priceless archaeological remains were threatened by bulldozers, resulting in a twenty-day occupation of the site by a core of committed protesters. Ireland's Supreme Court upheld the Corporation's position but allowed the archaeologists a further two years to excavate and record the site prior to construction of the Civic Offices.[16] In 1986 the Corporation decided that a millennium celebration was needed to boost the city's morale, deep in economic recession. This marked a step forward for the city, and a step away from the Wood Quay debacle, and made Dublin the first town in Ireland to celebrate its Viking heritage. In a year-long celebration of the city,[17] the Corporation went to great lengths to encourage civic pride. They released special edition 1988 Dublin Milk Bottles, planted 1000 trees and 500,000 flowering plants, floated a statue of Gulliver (from Swift's *Gulliver's Travels*) down the Liffey, unveiled public sculptures, planned a new Viking Adventure Centre, and issued a 1988 Millennium fifty pence piece. Whilst historians criticized the accuracy of the chosen date,[18] the public thoroughly enjoyed these celebrations and even now children of the 1980s reminisce about the millennium milk bottles.

The 1990s marked a new era for Dublin: the recession was lifting, and new developments were springing up around the city. One of the biggest proposals was the redevelopment of Temple Bar. Its developers envisaged a "a bustling cultural, residential and small-business precinct that will attract visitors in significant numbers."[19] Given its location, just down the road from Wood Quay, archaeological interventions were expected and were planned into the redevelopment. Temple Bar Properties recognized the potential of this heritage and planned to incorporate heritage into its management of the area. A single archaeological consultancy was appointed to the project and together the archaeologists and Temple Bar Properties created a public engagement campaign. This included viewing platforms allowing people to watch the excavation of

Viking Dublin in progress, opportunities to "Meet the Archaeologist,"[20] and an extensive publication program for the results of the excavations.[21] These excavations revealed significant Viking and medieval remains which were used to inform the character of Temple Bar's redevelopment.[22] This archaeological information was then incorporated into an informational scheme across Temple Bar,[23] promoting the Viking heritage of the area.

At this time, two new Viking-inspired heritage centers opened their doors – the Viking Adventure Centre (announced in 1988) and Dublinia. The Viking Adventure opened in 1996 and employed live actors to animate scenes based around the Wood Quay findings. The Viking Adventure closed in 2002,[24] citing the decline in American tourists post 9/11 as one factor. Dublinia is the museum of Dublin's Viking and medieval history and in 2018, it celebrates its twenty-fifth anniversary. It has four permanent exhibitions and is one of Dublin's premier visitor attractions.[25] The end of the 1990s saw another Viking-themed tourist attraction begin operations – the Viking Splash Tour.

This is a light-hearted tour of Dublin aboard a World War Two DUKW – a motorized vehicle which drives on road and water. Tour guides (Figure 13.1, nick-named Ger the Hoarse Norse, Anto the Atrocious, and Vinny the Voracious)[26] take tourists on a jaunt around Dublin's history with special emphasis on its Viking

Figure 13.1: A tour guide at the Viking Splash Tour. Image © Viking Splash Tours.

roots and the ability to roar like Vikings at rival tour buses. These three commercial attractions date to the 1990s, emphasizing the popularity of Vikings to visitors and the critical role which Vikings played in developing Dublin as a tourist destination.

There are also a number of Viking-themed attractions which are free of charge to visitors. Chief amongst these is the National Museum of Ireland which has a large permanent Viking exhibition, as well as a temporary exhibition on the Battle of Clontarf. Its popularity clearly reflects the free entry policy of Ireland's national cultural institutions – more than 450,000 visitors entered its halls in 2015.[27] Another free-entrance site is the National Botanic Gardens which contains a replica Viking house and garden: its visitor numbers were 553,348 in the same year, many of whom will have seen this replica house.[28] There are also a number of pieces of public art located around Wood Quay (many installed in 1988), including a longship sculpture, bronze plaques depicting artifacts excavated at Wood Quay, and the outlines of one of the houses excavated. Visitors can view sections of the Viking city walls at Wood Quay and St. Audeon's Gate, while the foundations of Isolde's Tower can be seen in Temple Bar. Dublin City Council has also developed a number of walking tours which allow visitors to explore Viking and medieval Dublin at their own pace.

When considered as a whole, it becomes clear that Dublin has, for the past forty years, based a very significant portion of its civic identity on this Viking heritage. This identity was heavily drawn upon by users from multiple backgrounds including heritage institutions (for example, National Museum of Ireland, Dublinia, National Botanic Gardens), educational partners (Dublinia, School of Irish Archaeology), commercial enterprises (Dublin Port, Viking Splash, Temple Bar Properties), and traditional marketing teams (Fáilte Ireland). Indeed, up until 2017, the Ireland.com website (the main portal for tourists to Ireland) had these lines opening its Dublin webpage:

> Dublin's streets are a busy fusion of both past and present – a 1,000–year-old mix that has inspired writers, visitors and political firebrands alike. From the city's Viking roots by the banks of the river Liffey, to its atmospheric medieval churches along gracious Georgian streets, walk these streets and you'll be taking a journey through history.[29]

For both locals and visitors, Dublin's history and character were a major selling point and the Vikings were a headline act. This changed following the collapse of the Celtic Tiger. Dublin's tourist numbers fell significantly enough to prompt Fáilte Ireland (Ireland's National Tourism Development Authority) to rebrand the city, saying that the city's image had become stale.[30] This resulted in a new branding campaign entitled "Dublin – a breath of fresh air." It positions Dublin's landscape (from the mountains to the seas) as the backdrop to cultural urban experiences.[31] The accompanying website – www.visitdublin.com – emphasizes events (St. Patrick's Day or New Year's Eve festivals), themes (Dublin on a Budget, Hiking and Walking, or This City's Got Love), and food and drink attractions (a chocolate factory or, of course, the Guinness Storehouse). Heritage, from being one of Dublin's key attractions, no longer appears as a compelling factor to attract visitors to Dublin.

Veðrafjǫrðr – Waterford

Waterford is Ireland's second Viking city, but it has taken a very different approach to its Viking heritage. The quality of its archaeological and historical evidence is similar to Dublin's, but on a smaller scale. The first excavations of Viking Waterford took place in the late 1980s, following which Waterford County Council developed a medieval themed Museum of Treasures to display the related artifacts. This visitor attraction opened in 1998, but a decade later, the museum director Eamonn McEneaney proposed a new vision – the Waterford Viking Triangle. According to McEneaney, the Vikings are an easy concept for people to grasp and accept, while their international connections and mobility resonate with modern audiences.[32] There is a public awareness around the Vikings which make them a more acceptable concept than their Norman descendants. Leading up to the 1100th anniversary of the city in 2014, these Vikings were to become the key to the regeneration of the city. Using the slogan "It begins here," the Viking Triangle begins at Reginald's Tower with the Viking foundation of the town, before traveling through "1000 years of history in 1000 paces."[33]

Reginald's Tower is located on the quays at the apex of the original Viking settlement of Waterford. A small triangular network of streets and surviving medieval and post-medieval architecture radiates out from the tower. Three new museums (focusing on the Vikings at Reginald's Tower, medieval Waterford in the new Medieval Museum, and Georgian Waterford in the Bishop's Palace) are located in the Triangle. Street signs, banners, and promotional flyers adorned with the project logo loudly proclaim its existence. Waterford's Viking Triangle represents one of, if not the most, clearly defined uses of the Vikings for branding purposes. A comprehensive guidance document[34] details the appropriate use of the Viking Triangle brand: the use of the logo and slogan, their placement on documents, correct font, size and color, as well as the need to include customer relevant messages. The emphasis is on making the Viking Triangle stand out.[35]

The Waterford Experience Report details Waterford City Council's vision for the city: through the Viking Triangle project, it wanted to create "a truly unique and authentic visitor attraction."[36] Whilst its aim was to increase tourist revenues, it wanted to do so in a way which combined urban and economic regeneration with its riverside street layout, heritage aspects, and its association with the internationally renowned Waterford Crystal factory.[37] It was "devised to appeal to a broad cohort of the tourism market"[38] and to have a global reach. The campaign is driven by the need to generate revenue for the city through increasing tourist numbers, but it does so by placing at its core the historic environment and heritage potential of Waterford, spearheaded by the Vikings.

Unfortunately, the Vikings have proven to be too successful for their own good here in Waterford and, to an extent, the overall concept of the Triangle has been hijacked by the Vikings. The original vision was that Waterford began with the Vikings but that the story continues through another thousand years of history.[39] Visitors encounter the Viking Triangle brand and immediately assume that the city has a dominant Viking presence rather than a gradual story of urban development. To counter this and provide some of the Viking exposure that the public want, Waterford Viking Triangle have installed a 23-meter-long carved wooden sword outside a new virtual reality attraction – the King of the Vikings. These are located around the corner from Reginald's Tower, creating a permanent Viking presence within Waterford's Viking Triangle which the project hopes will go some way towards putting the Vikings on the ground in the Triangle.

At this point, it feels necessary to compare these two cities. Dublin and Waterford share a common point of (Viking) origin but they have very different marketing stories. Whilst Dublin was the original Viking city, its "Breath of Fresh Air" campaign has definitely moved away from promoting a Viking heritage towards emphasizing a very contemporary cultural experience. In contrast, Waterford's branding strategy embraces its history, placing particular emphasis on its Viking heritage. I wonder if these two approaches are simply evidence of the two cities being at different points in their branding journeys. Heritage attractions can provide a simple initial hook to entice visitors to a place. In the aftermath of the 1988 celebrations, 1990s Dublin was full of Vikings – from the Viking Adventure to the Museum, to the viewing platforms at archaeological excavations in Temple Bar. A decade later, when the Viking Adventure closed in 2002, Temple Bar Properties noted that "a Viking dimension isn't a requirement now."[40] With the benefit of hindsight, this comment is ominous, as if forewarning (like Hugin and Munin, Odin's ravens) of the overhaul of Dublin's image to the detriment of its Viking heritage. The Vikings became less relevant, perhaps even over-exposed in Ireland's capital. Waterford, on the other hand, is at a much earlier point in its branding journey. It is a much smaller city in terms of both population[41] and geography – it requires a more tightly defined brand to promote itself precisely because it has fewer tourist attractions to offer than Ireland's capital city.

Telling Viking Stories

At the recent Veðrafjǫrðr festival,[42] one of the most successful attractions was the Storyteller. He sat at the top of Reginald's Tower, overlooking the harbor, enthralling children and adults with his tales of Viking adventurers. His stories were evocative, particularly in that setting, and emphasized the power of the stories and the spoken word. Storytelling was a vital entertainment and educational tool in the Viking world and the power of storytellers is still potent. In fact, it is stories that are at the heart of Fáilte Ireland's newest advertising campaign – Ireland's Ancient East. Market research carried out for Fáilte Ireland indicated one crucial thing – that what visitors to Ireland want to hear are stories about people. Initial responses from their target audience (the "culturally curious": people traveling alone or in a couple, aged over forty, and willing to pay for "authentic" experiences)[43] revealed these travelers were primarily attracted by Ireland's "culture" – history, landscape, and getting "off the beaten track." Rather than dates and places, these consumers want to hear about people – the people living (upstairs and downstairs) in a Big House, about the people who made our archaeological treasures, or the people who used them.

Using these insights, Fáilte Ireland created their newest "destination brand": Ireland's Ancient East. This multi-million-euro campaign will increase tourist footfall and revenues in Ireland's south and east. Visitors to Ireland encounter this brand while planning their holiday and use the bespoke website to create their own journey around Ireland's Ancient East. The website presents nine themes told through a series of stories. One of the most popular is the Viking theme:

> A terrifying new power came racing across the seas from the north. At first they were raiders – then traders and settlers. You can still find traces of the Vikings in Ireland – but you'll need to know where to look.[44]

Clicking on the Viking theme opens a homepage[45] with images of longships, the reconstructed Viking settlement at Ireland's National Heritage Park, and artifacts from Wood Quay and Waterford. There is also a one-minute video clip which gives a potted (and accurate) history of the Vikings, discusses family names of Norse origin, and the genetic origins of Ireland's red hair. The text reveals a very simple story – the Vikings came to Ireland, they raided, then they settled down to trade, found cities, and integrate with the Irish. Visitors can follow Viking-themed touring itineraries, such as "Explore the legacy of the Vikings' arrival on Irish shores." This five-day trip begins in Tippperary at Lough Gur (the location of a Viking silver hoard) and Cashel (home of Brian Boru, a famous Irish hero), moving on to Waterford's Viking Triangle, and to Wexford's Irish National

Heritage Park. Visitors then head back west to Clonmacnoise and the Rock of Dunamase, before finishing in Carlingford where, they say, Vikings would once have run in their longships on the river Newry to pillage Ireland's heart.[46] This is an extensive itinerary covering 715 kilometers, nine counties, and several major tourist attractions. However, its Viking associations are, by and large, tangential: with the exception of Waterford, these are places that the Vikings visited, perhaps only once or twice, rather than settled.

This makes Fáilte Ireland's recently announced development very interesting indeed. Under the auspices of Ireland's Ancient East, they have commissioned the creation of a "motivating visitor experience" along a Viking Coast through counties Wicklow, Wexford, and Waterford. From a historical perspective, this part of Ireland certainly experienced Viking activity – we have historical evidence for raids, place names with Viking origins, and, of course, Waterford. In terms of Viking attractions, Waterford is the star attraction, followed by the Irish National Heritage Park at Ferrycarrig. But, outside of these, there is little else to see – this is an "intangible" heritage.[47] The tender documentation indicates that this Viking Coast experience should include Viking themed festivals and events, associations with fire and water and interactive activities to fill in the gaps to create a "best in class" and unique visitor experience.[48] A significant challenge to this proposal is the exclusion of Dublin and its major Viking attractions. At this point in time, the project is still in its early development stages and no further details are available.

The launch of this new and focused cultural trail emphasizes that Vikings really do provide an exciting and attractive selling point for Ireland. The Vikings are an international phenomenon and the public has an immediate image of what makes a Viking – they are a good motivating factor for visitors. However, the "culturally curious" visitors who are Fáilte Ireland's target audience are highly educated with a desire to "delve deeper into the history of a location."[49] Yet the stories provided on the website are very simplistic and prioritize entertainment rather than education and Gillian O'Brien wonders if there is enough depth to these stories to satisfy that target audience.[50] Additionally, a closer look at the Viking homepage on the Ireland's Ancient East website reveals a number of mistakes: one of the Ferrycarrig images is not from the Viking settlement, the Wood Quay artifacts are from Dublin, which is not included in Ireland's Ancient East, and the cloth of gold vestments are fifteenth century in date and so not from the Viking Age at all. Fáilte Ireland's business is to promote and market Ireland as a tourist destination, they are not custodians of Ireland's heritage. They do, however, have a duty of care towards that heritage to ensure accuracy and responsible storytelling.

Creating Viking Worlds

A third way to encounter the Vikings is to attend a Viking festival or event, for example the Battle of Clontarf Festival in 2014 or the Follow the Vikings Roadshow which visited both Dublinia and Waterford in 2018. At these events, entertainment and education are provided by historical reenactment groups. These groups are dedicated to teaching, through example, what life was like at a particular point in history. Displays by reenactment groups usually promote two ways of engaging with the past – through displays of living history and fighting. Groups such as Fingal Living History and Déise Medieval (Figure 13.2) meet on a weekly basis to train and discuss their research. When members join, they are assigned a role (cook, weaver, moneyer, warrior) which they maintain for two to three years before swapping roles. They will participate in two or three weekend events a month from April to September. When attending events, the group erects a tented Viking village for the duration of the event, sleeping in this village overnight. When in character, each member will carry out their assigned tasks (polishing weapons, sewing, preparing food) and must be able to do this whilst talking to visitors. It is through this dialogue that re-enactors find the best opportunities to connect with the public and, through a dialogue, teach them about the real Viking world.

Figure 13.2: Déise Medieval at Gallows Hill in Co. Waterford, 2017. Image © John Foley Images.

Denise Colbert, a reenactor with Déise Medieval, says that visitors generally have an image of a raiding Viking in their minds but they have no idea what followed the raids –settlement, inter-marriage, farming, and daily life.[51] The fighting displays are the most visually striking parts of reenactment events, but reenactors find that the living history displays are what really capture the imagination. This presentation of a Viking world is very different from a static museum display or a textual or digital display panel – it is a sensual world. Visitors can see, touch, smell, taste, and hear the reenactors as they work, play, fight, cook, and live as Vikings did. These displays present a totally different picture to the onlooker: one with families, children, parents, farmers, traders, and craftspeople, as well as raiders and warriors.

Through living history displays, the public meet a new and different type of Viking and have their preconceptions challenged. According to Colbert, audience reactions to the reenactors vary from amused to confused, with plenty of "are you crazy" questions thrown in. Children often provide the best questions and comments at these events, as they have learned a little about the Vikings and early medieval Ireland in school. They are particularly taken by the opportunity to touch and feel the objects, bringing the words to life and making the experience real and authentic. Another vocal part of the audience consists of viewers of *Game of Thrones* and *Vikings*. Whilst we can argue about their accuracy and authenticity, the fact remains that these shows are extremely popular and influential and they have impacted upon what the public expects of the Viking period.[52] The on-screen portrayals of characters stimulate viewers to learn more about the real world which these shows use as their foundations. These viewers often express surprise at how the reenactors' costumes do not resemble those of the shows – they are less "flashy," wear less make-up, and their gear is altogether more practical. In these situations, reenactors find themselves emphasizing their authentic evidence-based approach and educating the visitors as to authenticity versus the dramatics of television.[53]

Raiding the Vikings?

Running throughout this discussion has been the presence of Fáilte Ireland – Ireland's National Tourism Development Agency. Fáilte Ireland are one of the biggest promoters of Ireland's heritage both nationally and internationally and their market research confirms that Vikings, as noted earlier, are indeed "trending" right now. The idea of Vikings, of their mobility and international scope, and their glamor and drama appeal to audiences. Within their tender documents for the Viking Coast experience, Fáilte Ireland state that the public expect three things of Viking attractions: an interactive or immersive activity, an association with fire, and a big, hairy Viking.[54] The first of these is simple enough to provide at museums, events, or roadshows: my own children were delighted by striking Viking coins at the Viking Waterford festival, while I have already mentioned the popularity of the Storyteller there. The public's association with fire is inspired by references to fire within Ragnarok and well-known festivals such as Up Helly Aa. It is the third element which is most troubling to me, the evocation of "a big hairy Viking" as standard.

Figure 13.3 shows the prize medals and participation T-shirts for the 2018 Waterford Viking Marathon. We might compare this to the Viking Splash tour guide, to the Pop Notch popcorn Viking, to the stereotypical Viking raider as portrayed in those 1990s history textbooks, or even the photographs chosen to illustrate news reports of the Battle of Clontarf Festival.[55] If we take a closer look at this Viking, we see some basic similarities. Firstly, this Viking is male, usually bearded, and has long flowing hair. Secondly, he is always in an action pose – running, jumping, or smashing through the wall (in the case of the marathon medal). At all times, he carries his weapons (shield, sword, axe, and helmet) indicating that he has the potential to create violence and is ready to do battle. In sum, this Viking is a man of action, a force to be reckoned with, and a threat to any people he will encounter. This Viking represents a very traditional

Figure 13.3: The race medals and T-shirts for the 2018 Waterford Viking Marathon. Image © Waterford Viking Marathon.

stereotype which emerged as a romantic ideal in the Victorian era.[56] This is Fáilte Ireland's "big hairy Viking" – a highly recognizable product which has two centuries of stereotype reinforcement to support it. Using this Viking to advertise products (whether that is popcorn, a marathon, or a multi-million-euro tourist drive) is virtually guaranteed to boost public interest, increase visitor numbers, and drive revenues upwards.

However, Viking scholars now recognize that while these Vikings – the big, hairy raiders – played a very important role in the Viking world, they did not represent the majority of the population or their lifestyle. Scholars now accept a plurality of what we might broadly term "Vikings" – men, women, children, old, young, middle-aged, healthy, infirm, ageing, living, dying (see Price's contribution to this collection) – whose daily lives included a myriad of tasks – weaving, repairing ships, building houses, rearing children, farming, telling stories – not just fighting or sailing. The challenge is that this complex image of Norse culture has not translated from academia to the public who still expect to meet the big, hairy Viking. This is something which reenactors regularly encounter at events – audience surprise that Vikings come in different ages, genders, and characters (see again Figure 13.2). Interestingly, while visitors are initially attracted by the fighting displays, weapons, and battle reenactments, they spend much more time within the Viking Village exploring the Living History displays. Colbert puts this down to the interactive nature of Living History – the fighting displays are just that, displays which the audience watches but does not participate in. The power of reenactment lies in the tangible and sensory nature of their interactions with their audience. The key word which Colbert kept using was "authenticity," that reenactment must be authentic or genuine. When presenting Viking societies, it is not authentic to present a world that is only peopled by young male warriors. An authentic Viking world must encompass young and old, male and female, warriors and every other role.

One of the attractions of the Vikings is their mythic quality, the way that they can change and shift as new evidence comes to light. Wawn says that the Vikings' "capacity to undergo cultural transformation, reconstruction, and reassessment" is pivotal to their continuing attraction for us.[57] Yet, this transformative capacity is not evident in that Viking stereotype of "the big, hairy Viking." The challenge in changing public perceptions lies here – in providing authenticity while reeducating the public as to the realities of the Viking world. Fáilte Ireland have a great opportunity here with their Viking Coast to step away from this stereotype and to send the "big, hairy Viking" on his funeral ship to Valhalla while ushering in a more nuanced Viking to the general public.

Acknowledgements: I would like to thank the following for their contributions to this research: Eamonn McEneaney, Director Waterford's Viking Triangle; Jenny de Saulles, Head of Ireland's Ancient East; Ruth Johnson, Dublin City Archaeologist; Neil Jackman, Abarta Heritage; and Denise Colbert, Déise Medieval. I am grateful to the editors Tom Birkett and Roderick Dale for their invitation to contribute this paper and finally, my thanks to Simon, Jim, Ben, and Scott for their patience during its preparation.

Bibliography

Byrne, L. "'Graffiti' among Treasure Trove of Viking Artifacts Found on Dublin Building Site." *Irish Independent*, March 23, 2018. https://www.independent.ie/irish-news/news/graffiti-among-treasure-trove-of-viking-artifacts-found-on-dublin-building-site-36735495.html.

Central Statistics Office. *Census 2016 Summary Results. Part 1: Government of Ireland*. Dublin: Government Publications, 2017.

Cullinan, E. A. "Temple Bar Dig." *The Irish Times*, November 28, 1996. https://www.irishtimes.com/opinion/letters/temple-bar-dig-1.110884.

Deegan, G. "Vikings Film Studio Gets Go-ahead for Expansion." *The Times*, March 15, 2018. https://www.thetimes.co.uk/article/vikings-film-studio-gets-go-ahead-for-expansion-cxd26nctk.

Drohan, F. "Newly Found Viking Artifacts Suggest Cork Is Ireland's Oldest Urban Settlement." *IrishCentral*, January 10, 2018. https://www.irishcentral.com/roots/history/newly-found-viking-artefacts-suggest-cork-could-be-ireland-s-oldest-urban-settlement.

Fáilte Ireland. "A Breath of Fresh Air for Dublin as New Brand and Marketing Campaign Launched." http://www.Fáilteireland.ie/Utility/News-Library/A-Breath-of-Fresh-Air-for-Dublin-as-New-Brand-and.aspx.

Fáilte Ireland. "Culturally Curious." http://www.Fáilteireland.ie/International-sales/International-sales/Culturally-Curious.aspx.

Fáilte Ireland. "Invitation to Tender: Product Development Plan for the Development of a Viking Coast Visitor Experience." https://irl.eu-supply.com/app/rfq/publicpurchase_frameset.asp?PID=125679&B=ETENDERS_SIMPLE&PS=1&PP=ctm/Supplier/PublicTendersp/rfq/publicpurchase_frameset.asp?PID=125679&B=ETENDERS_SIMPLE&PS=1&PP=ctm/Supplier/PublicTenders.

Fáilte Ireland. "Top Visitor Attractions in 2015 Revealed." http://www.Fáilteireland.ie/Footer/Media-Centre/Top-Visitor-Attractions-in-2015-Revealed.aspx.

Government of Ireland. *Primary School Curriculum: History*. Dublin: Government Publications, 1999. https://www.curriculumonline.ie/getmedia/4b95f9d8-a307-4ef0-bbf0-b3b9047f31f0/PSEC03a_History_Curriculum.pdf.

Grow Dublin Taskforce. *Destination Dublin: A Collective Strategy for Tourism Growth to 2020*. http://www.failteireland.ie/FailteIreland/media/WebsiteStructure/Documents/4_Corporate_Documents/Strategy_Operations_Plans/Dublin-a-Collective-Strategy-for-Tourism-Growth.pdf.

Halloran, C. "A Thousand Years of Dublin, 1987." *RTE News* (Archives), November 17, 1987. http://www.rte.ie/archives/2017/1116/920531-dublin-millennium-launch/.

Hernon, L. *Ages Ago*. Dublin: Folens, 1996.

Ireland.com. "Dublin City: See, Do, Experience." Archived webpage available at: https://web. archive.org/web/20170606103811/http://www.ireland.com/en-us/what-is-available/ sightseeing/destinations/republic-of-ireland/dublin/dublin-city/.

Ireland's Ancient East. "Explore the Legacy of the Vikings' Arrival on Irish Shores." https:// www.irelandsancienteast.com/plan-a-trip/itineraries/limerick-to-louth-five-day-itinerary.

Ireland's Ancient East. "Vikings." https://www.irelandsancienteast.com/discover/stories/ themes/vikings.

The Irish Times. "Vikings Routed Again as Adventure Centre Closes." *The Irish Times*, April 24, 2002. https://www.irishtimes.com/life-and-style/homes-and-property/vikings-routed-again-as-adventure-centre-closes-1.1086323.

The Irish Times. "Battle of Clontarf Re-enactment Attracts 40,000 Spectators." *The Irish Times*, April 19, 2014. https://www.irishtimes.com/news/ireland/irish-news/battle-of-clontarf-re-enactment-attracts-40-000-spectators-1.1768143.

McDonald, F. "'Bogus' Selection of Date to Mark Dublin's Millennium." *The Irish Times*, January 8, 1986. https://www.irishtimes.com/opinion/8-january-1986-bogus-selection-of-date-to-mark-dublin-s-millennium-1.1266478.

McDonald, F. "Temple Bar, 25 Years On." *AI Extra* (blog), *Architecture Ireland*, July 3, 2016. http://architectureireland.ie/temple-bar-25-years-on.

Montgomery, B. *Past Times History Workbook Middle Standards Book 1*. Dublin: Folens, 1993.

Montgomery, B. *Past Times History Workbook Middle Standards Book 2*. Dublin: Folens, 1993.

O'Brien, G. "Ireland's Ancient East: When East Is Not Always East." *RTE Brainstorm* (blog), February 9, 2018. https://www.rte.ie/eile/brainstorm/2018/0208/939258-irelands-an cient-east-when-east-is-not-always-east/.

Ó Loingsigh, C., H. Goff and H. MacHale. *History All Around Me 3*. Dublin: Educational Company of Ireland, 2003.

Roche, B. "Viking Centre Discovered in Cork City Predates Waterford Settlement." *The Irish Times*, January 10, 2018. https://www.irishtimes.com/news/ireland/irish-news/viking-centre-discovered-in-cork-city-predates-waterford-settlement-1.3350654.

Royal Institute of the Architects of Ireland. "Residential Tower (Wooden Building), Temple Bar." http://www.irisharchitectureawards.ie/annual-awards/2001/residential-tower-wooden-building-temple-bar.

Simpson, L. *Directors First Findings: Temple Bar West*. Dublin: Temple Bar Properties, 1999.

Simpson, L. "Heritage Outrage: Wood Quay." *History Ireland*, 22, no. 2 (2014). https://www. historyireland.com/volume-22/heritage-outrage-wood-quay/.

Viking Splash. "Our Vikings." www.vikingsplash.com/about-viking-splash/viking-staff/.

Wallace, P. F. *Viking Dublin: The Wood Quay Excavations*. Dublin: Academic Press, 2016.

Waterford City Council. "The Waterford Experience: Two Centuries of Tradition and a Thousand Years of History." http://waterfordvikingtriangle.com/assets/The-Waterford-Experience-Report.pdf.

Waterford Viking Triangle Trust. "Introducing Waterford's New Cultural and Heritage Quarter." http://waterfordvikingtriangle.com/assets/WVT-Fact-Sheet.pdf.

Waterford Viking Triangle Trust. "Waterford Viking Triangle Brand Guidelines 2012." http:// waterfordvikingtriangle.com/assets/WVT_Brand-Guidelines_2012.pdf.

Wawn, A. "The Viking Revival." *BBC History*, February 2, 2011. http://www.bbc.co.uk/history/ ancient/vikings/revival_01.shtml.

Notes

1. Government of Ireland, *Primary School Curriculum: History* (Dublin: Government Publications, 1999).
2. Examples of these older school textbooks are: B. Montgomery, *Past Times History Workbook Middle Standards Book 1* (Dublin: Folens, 1993); B. Montgomery, *Past Times History Workbook Middle Standards Book 2* (Dublin: Folens, 1993); and L. Hernon, *Ages Ago* (Dublin: Folens, 1996).
3. C. Ó Loingsigh, H. Goff and H. MacHale, *History All Around Me 3* (Dublin: Educational Company of Ireland, 2003).
4. Many teachers now prefer to use digital hubs such as https://my.cjfallon.ie/ to create personal portfolios of teaching resources instead of relying on textbooks, Stephanie Pardy, Phone call to author, April 29, 2018. However, on viewing these resources, the content of these hubs is very similar to the textbooks published in the 2000s.
5. These ads can be viewed at http://www.lecraic.com/2008/12/11/relax-dublin-port-company-is-there/ and http://eastwallforall.ie/?p=1062.
6. Toned Fit, "Viking Level," http://www.tonedfit.com/vikingtraining.
7. You can see the Pop Notch Viking popcorn and his friends at the website of "Atto Partners," https://www.attopartners.com/case-studies/popnotch/.
8. Pop Notch, Facebook message to author, November 27, 2017.
9. G. Deegan, "Vikings Film Studio Gets Go-ahead for Expansion," *The Times*, March 15, 2018.
10. B. Roche, "Viking Centre Discovered in Cork City Predates Waterford Settlement," *The Irish Times*, January 10, 2018.
11. F. Drohan, "Newly Found Viking Artifacts Suggest Cork Is Ireland's Oldest Urban Settlement," *IrishCentral*, January 10, 2018.
12. L. Byrne, "'Graffiti' among Treasure Trove of Viking Artifacts Found on Dublin Building Site," *Irish Independent*, March 23, 2018.
13. Ibid.
14. P. F. Wallace, *Viking Dublin: The Wood Quay Excavations* (Dublin: Academic Press, 2016).
15. L. Simpson, "Heritage Outrage: Wood Quay," *History Ireland* 22, no. 2 (2014).
16. Wallace, *Viking Dublin*.
17. C. Halloran, "A Thousand Years of Dublin, 1987," *RTE News Archives*, November 17, 1987, http://www.rte.ie/archives/2017/1116/920531-dublin-millennium-launch/.
18. F. McDonald, "'Bogus' Selection of Date to Mark Dublin's Millennium," *The Irish Times*, January 8, 1986.
19. Quoted in F. McDonald, "Temple Bar, 25 Years On," *AI Extra* (blog) *Architecture Ireland*, July 3, 2016, http://architectureireland.ie/temple-bar-25-years-on.
20. E. A. Cullinan, "Temple Bar Dig," *The Irish Times*, November 28, 1996.
21. L. Simpson, *Director's First Findings: Temple Bar West* (Dublin: Temple Bar Properties, 1999).
22. An example is the award-winning Wooden Building whose design was inspired by the Viking post-and-wattle houses found on the site: Royal Institute of the Architects of Ireland, "Residential Tower (Wooden Building), Temple Bar," Irish Architecture Awards, http://www.irisharchitectureawards.ie/annual-awards/2001/residential-tower-wooden-building-temple-bar.
23. Simpson, *Director's First Findings*.

24. The Irish Times "Vikings Routed Again as Adventure Centre Closes," *The Irish Times*, April 24, 2002.
25. Visitor numbers rose to 161,054 admissions in 2015, Fáilte Ireland, "Top Visitor Attractions in 2015 Revealed," http://www.Fáilteireland.ie/Footer/Media-Centre/Top-Visitor-Attractions-in-2015-Revealed.aspx.
26. Viking Splash Tours, "Our Vikings," www.vikingsplash.com/about-viking-splash/vi king-staff/.
27. 457,057 visitors, Fáilte Ireland, "Top Visitor Attractions in 2015."
28. Ibid.
29. www.Ireland.com, "Dublin City: See, Do, Experience," Archived at https://web.archive. org/web/20170606103811/http://www.ireland.com/en-us/what-is-available/sightsee ing/destinations/republic-of-ireland/dublin/dublin-city/.
30. Grow Dublin Taskforce, *Destination Dublin: A Collective Strategy for Tourism Growth to 2020*, http://www.Fáilteireland.ie/FáilteIreland/media/WebsiteStructure/Documents/4_ Corporate_Documents/Strategy_Operations_Plans/Dublin-a-Collective-Strategy-for-Tourism-Growth.pdf.
31. Fáilte Ireland, "A Breath of Fresh Air for Dublin as New Brand and Marketing Campaign Launched," http://www.Fáilteireland.ie/Utility/News-Library/A-Breath-of-Fresh-Air-for-Dublin-as-New-Brand-and.aspx.
32. Eamonn McEneaney, Phone call to author, April 17, 2018.
33. Waterford Viking Triangle, "Introducing Waterford's New Cultural and Heritage Quarter," http://waterfordvikingtriangle.com/assets/WVT-Fact-Sheet.pdf.
34. Waterford Viking Triangle, "Waterford Viking Triangle Brand Guidelines 2012," http:// waterfordvikingtriangle.com/assets/WVT_Brand-Guidelines_2012.pdf.
35. Ibid., p. 47.
36. Waterford City Council, "The Waterford Experience: Two Centuries of Tradition and a Thousand Years of History," http://waterfordvikingtriangle.com/assets/The-Waterford-Experience-Report.pdf, p. 2.
37. Ibid., p. 7.
38. Ibid., p. 2.
39. McEneaney, Phone call to author, April 17, 2018.
40. *Irish Times*, "Vikings Routed."
41. Waterford's population is 53,504 compared to 1,173,179 in Dublin. Central Statistics Office, *Census 2016 Summary Results. Part 1: Government of Ireland* (Dublin: Government Publications, 2017).
42. Veðrafjǫrðr – Waterford's International Viking Festival and Roadshow – took place from April 1 to April 2, 2018.
43. Fáilte Ireland, "Culturally Curious," http://www.Fáilteireland.ie/International-sales/ International-sales/Culturally-Curious.aspx.
44. Ireland's Ancient East, "Vikings," https://www.irelandsancienteast.com/discover/sto ries/themes/vikings.
45. Ibid.
46. Ireland's Ancient East, "Explore the Legacy of the Vikings' Arrival on Irish Shores," https://www.irelandsancienteast.com/plan-a-trip/itineraries/limerick-to-louth-five-day-itinerary.
47. Jenny de Saulles, Phone call to author, April 4, 2018.

48. Fáilte Ireland, "Invitation to Tender: Product Development Plan for the Development of a Viking Coast Visitor Experience," https://irl.eu-supply.com/app/rfq/publicpurchase_fra meset.asp?PID=125679&B=ETENDERS_SIMPLE&PS=1&PP=ctm/Supplier/PublicTendersp/ rfq/publicpurchase_frameset.asp?PID=125679&B=ETENDERS_SIMPLE&PS=1&PP=ctm/ Supplier/PublicTenders.
49. Fáilte Ireland, "Culturally Curious."
50. G. O'Brien, "Ireland's Ancient East: When East Is Not Always East," *RTE Brainstorm* (blog), February 9, 2018, https://www.rte.ie/eile/brainstorm/2018/0208/939258-irelands-an cient-east-when-east-is-not-always-east/.
51. Denise Colbert, phone call to author, April 23, 2018.
52. Ibid.
53. Ibid.
54. De Saulles, phone call to author.
55. The Irish Times, "Battle of Clontarf Re-enactment Attracts 40,000 Spectators," *The Irish Times*, April 19, 2014, https://www.irishtimes.com/news/ireland/irish-news/battle-of-clontarf-re-enactment-attracts-40-000-spectators-1.1768143.
56. A. Wawn, "The Viking Revival," *BBC History*, February 2, 2011, http://www.bbc.co.uk/his tory/ancient/vikings/revival_01.shtml.
57. Ibid.

Eleanor Rosamund Barraclough

14 The Great Viking Fake-Off: The Cultural Legacy of Norse Voyages to North America

In recent years, the history of the Norse on the fringes of the North American continent has proved fertile ground for authors. In Neil Gaiman's modern classic *American Gods*, the Norse arrive in North America in 813 CE. This fictional episode is set significantly earlier than the known historical Norse expeditions that took place around 1000 CE (indeed, neither Iceland nor Greenland had been settled in 813 CE). Understandably, the men lament: "We are far, far from our homes and our hearths, far from the seas we know and the lands we love. Here on the edge of the world we will be forgotten by our gods."[1] Despite the fictional nature of this episode, there are similarities with the expeditions described in the Old Norse sagas. The new arrivals encounter natives whom they call "scraelings" (ON *skrælingar*, used in medieval Norse texts of both the non-Norse inhabitants of Greenland and North America). As in the sagas, cross-cultural relations deteriorate into violence, but in this reimagined version of history the Norse sacrifice a scraeling to Odin before being killed by a retaliating war party. Gaiman nevertheless concludes the episode by linking it to historical reality:

> It was more than a hundred years before Leif the Fortunate, son of Erik the Red, rediscovered that land, which he would call Vineland. His gods were already waiting for him when he arrived: Tyr, one-handed, and gray Odin gallows-god, and Thor of the thunders. They were there. They were waiting.[2]

More recently, Rick Riordan's fantasy trilogy stars Magnus Chase, a bolshie homeless orphan living on the streets of Boston. He also happens to be the son of the pagan god Freyr, and destined for an afterlife in Valhalla. The premise of the Young Adult novel is that Norse travelers made it as far south as Boston. Riordan references the historical debates of the nineteenth century in which individuals tried to prove this was the case: "many people over the centuries have known. They've *felt* it instinctively, even if they had no proof. This area wasn't just *visited* by the Vikings. It was *sacred* to them."[3] Readers don't have to know their Norse historiography or mythology to appreciate these novels, but those with a little more knowledge can sit back and enjoy Riordan's sharp reuse of debunked historical theories and the pagan myths. Picture the sea god

Eleanor Rosamund Barraclough, Durham University

https://doi.org/10.1515/9781501513886-015

Njord reimagined as a hipster obsessed with microbreweries, or a Thor obsessed with farting and streaming TV shows through his hammer, and you will understand his playful approach.

Despite such modern incarnations of Norse history, interest in the legacy of the expeditions to North America around 1000 CE is far from a recent phenomenon. Long before the excavations at L'Anse aux Meadows in the 1960s confirmed the historicity of these voyages, the topic had been a matter of considerable interest and speculation. In the absence of concrete proof, individuals sought, imagined, and even fabricated evidence in a way that was less about shaping the theory to fit the data, and more about shaping data to fit the theory. In what follows, I will examine the sort of "evidence" that surfaced in North America and consider the continued development of a Norse cultural legacy that very often had little to do with historical reality. This invites the broader question: how often does historical enquiry have less to do with establishing past facts, and more to do with the establishing of present identity?

Viking Voyages

On September 22, 1998, a reconstructed Norse ship called *Snorri* reached its final destination: L'Anse aux Meadows on the northern coastline of Newfoundland. It had been built by an American–Danish team who aimed to retrace the route taken by Erik the Red's son, Leif the Lucky, from Greenland to the edge of North America. After an abortive attempt the year before, when the ship's rudder had broken in the middle of the Davis Strait, they arrived at L'Anse aux Meadows after 87 days at sea.

For Hodding Carter, the American leader of the expedition, inspiration came less from historical knowledge of this chapter in Norse history, and more from the romance and challenge of following in the footsteps of adventurers of the past. As he wrote in his account of the voyage:

> Why not retrace the Viking voyages to the New World? I get ideas like this all the time. Some people sit in rush hour traffic fantasizing about bashing their fellow drivers with a sizable ham hock. When I find myself delayed, I decide it's high time to ride an elephant across Hannibal's route through the Alps, although I know nothing about elephants or war ... In the case of the Vikings, I initially did just enough research to find that Leif Eriksson had sailed to a place he called Vinland ... That was enough for me ... Mostly, though, I have an unyielding need to walk in much bigger shoes than my own. I crave to see just how brave, stoic, undaunted, or even insane our historical figures were. In following Hannibal or Leif Eriksson, I put myself in their situation, get in way over my head, and then attempt to survive.[4]

Even so, this voyage taps into a long-held, deep cultural interest in the Norse in America that can be traced back at least to the nineteenth century, long before there was any hard archaeological evidence for Norse activity in the New World. As Carter's comments indicate, historical accuracy has not always been the most pressing concern. In the cultural mentality of America's immigrant nation, the Norse who came to North America were very different in character to the Norse who arrived on the shores of the British Isles and Western Europe: not raiders and pillagers but far-traveling, independent-minded adventurers. These associations have undoubtedly colored the significance that has been attached to these early Nordic voyagers and to Leif the Lucky in particular.

Snorri was far from the first replica Norse ship to sail west to America. Over a century earlier in 1893, the "World's Fair: Columbian Exposition" was held in Chicago to celebrate the 400th anniversary of Columbus' arrival in America. The fair included three life-size replicas of Columbus' ships, constructed in Spain and sailed to America for the exhibition. But the vessels had competition. Another star of the show was the *Viking*, a reconstructed Norse ship based on the recently excavated Gokstad ship in Norway. The *Viking* had sailed all the way from Bergen in Norway to Chicago via Cape Cod, New York, the Erie Canal and the Great Lakes. This was a blatant challenge to received historical orthodoxy, described by Elisabeth Ward as a "brazen bit of ethnic one-upmanship" on the part of many Scandinavian-Americans. She continues:

> While the Viking longship in Europe still evokes the idea of the Viking raids, the image of a Viking ship in the United States is more apt to prompt an association with sea voyaging, heroic exploits, and long-distance contact. Scandinavian-Americans highlighted this heroic aspect of their Viking heritage as a defining characteristic of their identity.[5]

Two years earlier, the Leif Eriksson Memorial Association in Oslo (then Christiania) held a competition: artists were tasked with creating a painting of Leif Eriksson discovering America. The winning entry was to be displayed at the Chicago World Fair, to coincide with the arrival of the reconstructed *Viking*. The prize was awarded to Christian Krohg for his *Leiv Eriksson oppdager America* ("Leif Eriksson Discovers America"), now hanging in the stairwell of the National Gallery in Oslo.[6] A sturdy, strawberry-blond Leif stands on the deck wearing a bright mustard-colored tunic, one hand on the rudder, the other pointing to land on the horizon. He radiates strength and leadership, his purposefulness contrasted with the men huddled on the deck, apparently in the throes of seasickness.

Few visual representations of Leif Eriksson in North America correlate with historical reality. North of the border, a statue of Leif was unveiled at L'Anse aux Meadows only as recently as 2013. Yet further south in the United States are statues dating back to the nineteenth century, commissioned for locations entirely unconnected with the historical Norse voyages. Leif statues can be found in places such as Boston (Massachusetts), Chicago (Illinois), Newport (Virginia), St. Paul (Minnesota), Duluth (Minnesota), Minot (North Dakota), Cleveland (Ohio), and Seattle (Washington). Each has its own background story and significance; the origins of the Boston statue will be returned to later on. But to focus on one example, since the erection of the Leif statue in Seattle in 1962, the names of over two thousand Scandinavian immigrants have been carved into its base. There could be no clearer physical manifestation of Leif's value to Americans of Scandinavian heritage as a trailblazing immigrant from Nordic lands. This is despite the fact that Leif never visited any part of what is now the United States and could hardly be counted as an immigrant, having only overwintered at the edge of the continent.

Leif was far from the only medieval Norse visitor to North America. But equally important far-travelers such as Thorfinn Karlsefni and his wife Gudrid hardly get a look in. In the early twentieth century, the Icelandic sculptor Einar Jónsson was commissioned to create a statue of Karlsefni, installed in Fairmont Park in Philadelphia and unveiled in 1920. The commissioner was Joseph Bunford Samuel at the bequest of his wife Ellen, who left a fund for the creation of sculptures "emblematical of the settlement of our great country."[7] A cast of the statue stands in Reykjavik, Iceland. Also in Iceland is a modern statue of Gudrid, created by artist Ásmundur Sveinsson and located where she was born in Laugarbrekka, Snæfellsnes. Yet despite the prominence of her character in the Vínland sagas, she does not seem to have captured the North American imagination in the same way as Leif, more's the pity.

Over the course of the twentieth century, Leif Eriksson continued to grow as a popular figure in American communities of Scandinavian descent. In 1918 the Supreme Lodge of the Sons of Norway (a fraternal organization representing those of Norwegian heritage in North America) instigated the celebration of "Leif Erikson Day" on October 9. In 1929, Wisconsin became the first state to adopt "Leif Erikson Day" as a state holiday. The day is still observed – albeit with far less enthusiasm than Columbus Day – particularly in the Upper Midwest where Scandinavian communities settled during the course of the nineteenth and twentieth centuries. Yet it is significant that this region does not correlate with the geographical area that Leif likely visited. Moreover, the date has nothing to do with the events of Leif's life. Rather, this is the date when, in 1825, the ship *Restauration* arrived in New York from Stavanger in Norway, signaling the official start of Scandinavian immigration to America.

While the medieval Nordic world did not have the same concepts of nationality and ethnicity as we do today, the fact that the Norwegians claim Leif as their own is highly contentious. After all, Leif was born in Iceland, and raised in Iceland

and Greenland. A statue of Leif stands on the hill outside Hallgrímskirkja in Reykjavik, appropriately a gift from the United States to commemorate the millennial anniversary of the Alþingi (Iceland's parliament) in 1930. Carved into the stone at the back of the statue are the words: "LEIFR EIRICSSON SON OF ICELAND DISCOVERER OF VINLAND." Yet the misconception of his Norwegian identity continues. On October 9, 2015, Barack Obama issued a proclamation in which he described Leif's voyage to the west as marking "the beginning of a meaningful friendship between Norway and the United States."[8] In fact, the statement is meaningless, since Leif's voyage took him to what is now Canada. The following year, Obama's proclamation was rather vaguer, describing Leif as a "Scandinavian explorer" and with rather more use of the catchall word "Nordic."[9] It may have come as something of a relief that this was the final proclamation before his term of office ended, just in case the Greenlanders decided to get involved in the argument. After all, if any country could claim to have been the link between the Old and New Worlds, it is Greenland. It seems that Leif Eriksson's popularity has less to do with historical veracity and more to do with cultivating modern cultural identity rooted in a past so vague and inaccurate that it may be said to shade into legend rather than history.

Material Evidence

At present, L'Anse aux Meadows is the only Norse archaeological site on the North American continent about which there is certainty. During excavations in the 1960s, the remains of eight Norse-style, turf-walled buildings were discovered, which have been dated to around 1000 CE. Some were probably larger halls built for habitation, while others were workshops. As the archaeologist Birgitta Linderoth Wallace notes, "The traces indicate the presence of a male work force performing tasks such as carpentry, iron manufacture, boat repair, and exploration."[10] Given that the middens were relatively empty and no burials have been found, it seems the site was not occupied for long.

To L'Anse aux Meadows we can add a meager handful of material artifacts that testify to links (direct or indirect) between the Norse and the inhabitants of North America. For example, the Maine Penny is a silver coin of Norse origin, dating from ca. 1065–1080.[11] The fact that it was found at a major historical trading site on the Maine coastline, far to the south of areas known to have been visited by the Norse, is not evidence of a Norse presence in the region. More likely, the penny made its way south via the long-distance indigenous trading routes, although of course the possibility of Norse visitors cannot be ruled out. The penny's date – several decades after the known voyages – may suggest that the extent of Norse activities in North America were more substantial and chronologically extensive than the sagas suggest. After all, the Icelandic annals record that in 1347 a Greenlandic ship drifted to Iceland en route back from Markland (the Norse name for what is most likely a forested section of the Labrador coastline):

> Then a ship came from Greenland, smaller in size than little Icelandic boats … It was anchorless. There were seventeen men on board, and they had sailed to Markland but were later shipwrecked here.[12]

On the other hand, the penny may have passed from Norse to non-Norse hands in Greenland rather than North America, and then been traded on further west by the ancestors of modern-day Greenlanders (Inuit). This would be less remarkable given that we know rather more about the timeframe for Norse activities in this part of the world than in North America, and there is evidence of contact between the Norse and non-Norse inhabitants of Greenland at a far later date.[13]

In the past few years, there have been some additional developments with regard to material evidence for Norse activities on the fringes of North America. Several sites were discovered on Baffin Island (or Helluland, to give it its Norse name) with artifacts that appeared to have been manufactured using European technologies. These include yarn spun from local animal fur, whetstones, and wooden objects with notched sticks, all of types associated with Norse culture. At one site in the Cape Tanfield area, archaeologists discovered a structure with long walls made from boulders and turf (not typically associated with indigenous culture in the Canadian Arctic) and a stone vessel containing traces of bronze and glass.[14] Moreover, in 2016 newspaper reports started to appear concerning another possible Norse site at Point Rosee on the south-west tip of Newfoundland, although further investigations are necessary.[15] The announcement attracted considerable interest in the international media, with articles declaring that the new find could "rewrite history."[16] This claim is something of an exaggeration: after all, we already know the Norse reached Newfoundland, and the discovery of butternuts and butternut wood at the L'Anse aux Meadows site suggests that they traveled at least as far south as the New Brunswick / Nova Scotia area.[17] Even so, such dramatic media headlines indicate the continued significance that the Norse voyages hold in the popular imagination.

Before the discovery of the site at L'Anse aux Meadows, knowledge of the Norse expeditions to North America came primarily from *Eiríks saga rauða* (The Saga of Erik the Red) and *Grœnlendinga saga* (The Saga of the Greenlanders). Known collectively as the Vínland sagas, they had appeared in editions, translations, and summaries from the end of the seventeenth century onwards.[18]

The first modern edition of the sagas was published by the Danish scholar Carl Christian Rafn in 1837, under the title *Antiquitates Americanae*. As Geraldine Barnes has noted,

> Many reviewers . . . saw the work as a challenge to the image of America as a land unseen, unnamed, and otherwise without mortal creator before 1492. Uncontroversial in England, in America the Vínland sagas impinged upon questions of national history and identity.[19]

Taken in isolation, the historical value of the Vínland sagas is difficult to ascertain. The details provided are relatively sparse and sometimes conflicting (although given that the two sagas seem to draw on a collective pool of oral information, the many similarities are perhaps more remarkable). As is often the case in sagas, certain episodes appear fantastical by modern standards, not least tales of plague victims returning from the dead, a murderous uniped, and a sea full of flesh-eating worms. The sagas were also recorded several centuries after the events described (possibly the first decades of the thirteenth century), and preserved today only in manuscripts from the fourteenth and fifteenth centuries. Yet given the many geographical descriptions and navigational details included in both sagas, it is not surprising that attempts have been made to identify the regions visited by the Norse. Broadly speaking, the modern-day consensus is that Helluland (Stone-Slab Land) seems to be part of Baffin Island, Markland (Forest Land) the wooded coastline of Labrador, and Vínland (Vine Land) the area south of Newfoundland.[20]

Carl Christian Rafn had other ideas. In *Antiquitates Americanae*, he posited the theory that the area of New England was the Vínland described in the sagas. The volume included his correspondence with members of the historical societies of Rhode Island and Massachusetts, in which they discussed the possible Norse origins of unexplained edifices and constructions in New England. These included the mysterious inscriptions on the so-called Dighton Rock by the Taunton River at Berkley, MA. As Thomas Webb, secretary of the Rhode Island Historical Society, wrote to Rafn, "No one, who examines attentively the workmanship, will believe it to have been done by the Indians."[21] The scratches on the rock were painstakingly "translated" as runes by Rafn's assistant Finn Magnusen.[22] Likewise, Norse origins were ascribed to a ruined tower in Newport, Rhode Island, although it was actually a seventeenth-century windmill belonging to Governor Benedict Arnold.[23]

While scholarly opinion was divided on the veracity of Rafn's theories, they found a degree of support amongst non-specialists.[24] In the 1870s, a bronze statue of Leif was erected in Boston, Massachusetts, more Roman warrior than Norse explorer, with runes on the pedestal that identify him as "Leif the Lucky, Erik's Son." The project found support from individuals including prominent

Norwegian violinist Ole Bull, who had been influenced by Rafn's theories.[25] However as Geraldine Barnes has pointed out, the statue was never destined for Boston. It was meant to stand in front of the main building of the Madison campus of the University of Wisconsin, as part of a promotional venture to advance the University of Wisconsin as the premiere center for Scandinavian studies in the USA. The problem was that not enough subscriptions could be drummed up from the Scandinavian community in the Midwest, and so the project was transferred to Boston, where it met with a more enthusiastic reception.[26]

Incidentally, the statue also features in the opening chapters of Rick Riordan's *Magnus Chase* trilogy. As the protagonist says, "My mom and I used to joke about Leif. His armor was on the skimpy side: a short skirt and a breast-plate that looked like a Viking bra."[27] In fact, part of the old debate as to whether the Norse reached Boston or not is outlined in the opening pages of the first novel: "That statue of Leif Erikson . . . that was the pet project of a wishful thinker in the 1800s, a man named Eben Horsford. He was convinced that Boston was the lost Norse settlement of Norumbega, their furthest point of exploration. He had an instinct, a gut feeling, but no real proof. Most historians wrote him off as a crackpot."[28] Later on, when Magnus is standing on the Longfellow Bridge above the Hudson River, his uncle points out the longship designs carved onto the pier (the poet Longfellow also being inspired by the possibility of Norse visitors to New England). In this fantasy version of history, the wreck of a real longship lies in the water below the bridge, holding a mythological sword. Even better, it turns out that the entrance to "Hotel Valhalla" is located on nearby Beacon Street. Thus Riordan riffs off the old historiographical debates to create a fantasy world in which the truth is even more colorful than a "crackpot" such as Horsford could have conjured. It is significant that in the cases of both Riordan and Gaiman, what is distilled from the grains of historical truth are reworked versions of Norse mythology, not tales of Norse humans.

Fakes and Football

Where proof couldn't be read into preexisting features in the landscape, it might be fabricated. Unsurprisingly, what was "discovered" in this way tended to be sexier than the lumps and shadows on the ground, or clumps of animal fur woven into yarn.[29] One of the most famous of these fakes is the Kensington Stone, which came to light in 1898. It was apparently tangled in the roots of a tree on a Minnesota farm belonging to a Swedish immigrant called Olof Ohman. The runes translate as:

> Eight Goths and 22 Norwegians on an exploration journey from Vinland to the west. We had [a]? camp by 2 skerries one day's journey north from this stone. We were [out] to fish. One day after we came home [we] found 10 men red of blood and dead. AVM Save [us] from evil. [We] have 10 men by the sea to look after our ships 14 days' travel from this island [In the year] 1362.[30]

Swiftly, the experts brought in to examine the runes came to the opinion that they were a modern fake. However, proving the authenticity of the stone became the life's work of a Norwegian-born amateur archaeologist called Hjalmar Holand, who published five books and many articles on the subject. From 1948 to 1953 it was put on display in the Smithsonian Institution in Washington DC, with an accompanying press release that described it as "A stone carved with Norse runes, the authenticity of which now is widely accepted by archaeologists."[31] Birgitta Wallace has pointed out that runic script was still used in Sweden at this time, particularly in remote rural areas such as the one that Olof Ohman's family came from. He was also the owner of rather a large library, and would have had a lot of historical information at his disposal. As Wallace notes,

> History demonstrates that humans have a unique capacity for recreating and reshaping their past to suit social, political, or emotional needs. History suggests that new Norse "discoveries" will continue to be made by the ardent or the duplicitous.[32]

While this is undoubtedly true at times, sometimes fakes can just be clever pranks. In the 1970s during the making of a TV documentary "The Riddle of the Runestone," an interview was conducted with Frank Walter Gran, the son of one of Olof's neighbors. According to Gran, Ohman had chiseled the inscription with Frank's dad Jonas before the pair buried it under the roots of a tree to be found several years later. This was a joke: "the biggest haha . . . in their life," as Frank Gran put it.[33] Just as significant as the creation of these artifacts is how they are interpreted by others with agendas to push; in this case taken on as a personal crusade by Holand. Moreover, Henrik Williams has argued that the worth of the Kensington Runestone lies in its role as "an effective catalyst of scientific and scholarly debate," inviting a series of questions that scholars must ask themselves if they are to maintain relevance and credibility: "How do we tell what is true or false, and how do we convey our scientific results to non-academics? What role does an object of this kind play as a symbol of or an instrument in creating identity? And what do we learn about the uses and abuses of historical objects?"[34]

The Kensington Runestone may be widely recognized by scholars as a fake, but in its hometown of Alexandria, Minnesota, this fact seems to have been conveniently forgotten. The town is also home to Big Ole, a 25-foot Viking statue built in 1965 for the New York World Fair. The words on his shield read: "Alexandria: Birthplace of America." Also in Alexandria, the Runestone Museum has its own tableaux of sexy Viking waxworks, a replica longship, and a cardboard cut-out Viking for photo ops. Indeed, outside the academic community and in popular discourse, belief in the runestone's authenticity continues. On one website, Olof Ohman is presented as the passive victim of ruthless scholars intent on destroying his reputation:

> Scholars dismissed the Runestone as impossible, and Ohman as either a fraud or a fool. Disheartened, he used the slab as a doorstep, then sold it to a guy in Wisconsin for ten bucks. With the passage of time, experts have become more accepting of the Runestone (although it still has skeptical foes).[35]

Today, there is no need to create fakes in order to prove the Norse reached North America. But in some areas – particularly parts of the United States with a strong Scandinavian heritage – there is still a marked investment in Viking-American heritage that moves beyond historical reality. For example, Minnesota is home to the "Vikings" American football team, named in 1960 to reflect the state's importance in Scandinavian-American culture. Again, despite the fact that there is no evidence of any medieval Norse activity in the area, their official logo is a Viking with enormous inauthentic horns on his helmet and plaited blonde hair. Yet the creation of an (in)authentic Viking past can be a lucrative and sometimes controversial business. For twenty-one years, the Vikings football mascot was Ragnar, who would ride out on a motorbike with his horned helmet, long hair, tattoos, and a fetching fur gilet. In 2015, he was ousted with reports that he had demanded $20,000 a game and a ten-year contract. The following year he became a turncoat, trading in his Minnesota horned helmet for a Wisconsin cheese head to become mascot for Wisconsin's Green Bay Packers.[36]

In 2016, the football team moved to a new home: the U.S. Bank Stadium. This was an opportunity to begin a new Viking legacy, and create several new "ancient" traditions. They commissioned a new "Gjallarhorn" to be blown before the start of every match, a giant horn based on Norse mythology (the last one shattered into pieces during a cold snap before a game against the Seattle Seahawks).[37] At the start of every season, the opening ceremonies are Viking-kitsch spectacles of epic proportions: players and cheerleaders disgorged from longships, dragonheads with glowing purple eyes and flaming nostrils. Furthermore, drawing on the "Viking War Chant" that became so popular with supporters of the Icelandic football team during Euro 2016, the Minnesota Vikings decided to adopt their own. The official Vikings website ran a promotional video designed to encourage this new tradition amongst fans, with the caption "Another chapter is being added to Vikings lore."[38] Accompanied by war drums and suitably dramatic music, Aron Gunnarsson (captain of the Icelandic soccer team) and Hafþór Júlíus Björnsson (the actor who played "The Mountain" in HBO's *Game of Thrones*) appeared in the video to tell Vikings fans:

> In Iceland, we have the Vikings War Chant, uniting the people of the nation. It's a battle cry for all Vikings, striking fear into our enemies. We share this tradition with you, our brothers and sisters, the Vikings of Minnesota. From one Viking to another, it's time to come together. From one Viking to another, SKÅL! #VikingsChant[39]

The language of the promotional video is telling, focusing on the martial qualities of the Vikings ("a battle cry for all Vikings") and a shared cultural heritage between Icelanders and Minnesotans going back to the Viking Age ("our brothers and sisters," "from one Viking to another"). Ironically, the Icelandic war chant wasn't even Nordic in origin: it turns out Icelandic football fans were introduced to the "slow clap" technique during a Europa League game against the Scottish team Motherwell.[40] Ultimately this is unimportant, since the Minnesota Vikings' adoption of this new tradition had little to do with connecting to an authentic medieval past. It was more about tapping into a collective modern Viking identity. This is no longer a case of faking evidence to back up a desired version of historical reality, real or imagined. After all, the evidence is there, not only in the Vínland sagas but also in L'Anse aux Meadows and possibly Baffin Island and Point Rosee. The marketing strategy of the Minnesota Vikings is an extreme example of how new Viking-American identities continue to be constructed. They can be playful, kitsch, or tongue-in-cheek, but they are as much – or more – about ties to modern Nordic cultural heritage as they are about an authentic Norse past.

It only remains to place this modern construction of identity within its broader national context. A glance at the range of weird and wonderful Viking-branded institutions and products from the U.S. suggests that this largely faux history continues to occupy an unusually prominent place in the national consciousness, certainly when compared to the modern appropriation of the Viking image by other nations. Some draw on the associations between Vikings and their northern homelands, such as the "Viking Ice" manufacturers of synthetic skating rinks based in Wilsonville, Oregon, and "Viking Craft Ice" based in Houston, Texas, which is part of "The Hospitable Viking Group." But the branding and language used on their website indicate the deeper significance of the Viking image in the U.S. cultural consciousness. Viking Ice describes how they are "riding the crest of [the] wave" of cost-efficient alternatives to traditional ice rinks,[41] while the website of The Hospitable Viking Group describes the company with two adjectives: "frontiering and intrepid."[42] The Vikings, like the founders of the U.S.A., are seafaring, pioneering people: a flattering historical mirror that the American nation can hold up to itself.

This may also explain why a surprising number of the insignias for junior officer training corps in high schools across the U.S. incorporate a stereotypical, usually horned-helmeted Viking. What is more remarkable is that this is not confined to parts of the country with a strong Scandinavian heritage. The accompanying information on the school websites indicates exactly what the Viking image has come to represent for U.S. culture. For instance, the insignia of North Salem High School in Salem, Oregon, features a red-headed Viking with horned helmet and shield, and a longship. According to the school website, "The Viking represents a sense of adventure and boldness," while "the Viking ship in full sail describes the voyage of education."[43] Also on the West Coast, the insignia of the James Monroe High School in North Hills, California, features a warlike, heavily bearded Viking with horned helmet and shield. This time, according to the website, "The Viking and the Viking's shield represent the school's strength and how the cadets can succeed when all pull together to excel."[44] Meanwhile, the insignia of Blair High School in Pasadena, California, sports a Viking that is "symbolic of military preparedness and strength,"[45] while over on the other side of the country in Spartanburg High School, South Carolina, "The Viking is the school's mascot and conveys fierceness, power, and protection. The students identify with their mascot in their pursuit of academic as well as athletic endeavors."[46] The Viking image is a talisman that invokes strength – both physical and mental prowess – adventure, courage, and cooperation. Such talismans travel further than the Norse themselves could have ever imagined: the high school insignia of Hilo, Hawaii, features a typically bearded, horned-helmeted Viking and the motto "Viking Pride." According to the official website, this "alludes to the seafaring people of the locale."[47] From an outsider's perspective, it may seem remarkable that the image of a Viking would be considered a more appropriate representation of Hawaii's seafaring history – and source of pride – rather than the region's actual historical inhabitants. Such is the potency of the Viking image across the United States of America.

History has always been as much – if not more – about the present as about the past. In his seminal work, *What Is History*, E. H. Carr argues that "facts of history cannot be purely objective, since they become facts of history only in virtue of the significance attached to them by the historian."[48] Yet in the case of the Vikings in America, many of the so-called "facts" of history become so only because of the significance attached to them in the broader cultural consciousness. Norse explorers such as Leif the Lucky are significant not because they once visited the fringes of the North American continent and built some overwintering booths on a Newfoundland bay. They are significant because of what they represent for U.S. national identity as an intrepid, independent-minded, physically powerful people who sailed west over the ocean and reached the shores of the North American continent. In literal terms, the Norse explorers of history only visited those lands briefly before returning east to their homes in Greenland and Iceland. Yet in another sense, like the Norse deities of Neil Gaiman's *American Gods*, they never really left.

Bibliography

Barnes, Geraldine. *Viking America: The First Millennium*. Cambridge: D. S. Brewer, 2001.

Barraclough, Eleanor Rosamund. *Beyond the Northlands: Viking Voyages and the Old Norse Sagas*. Oxford: Oxford University Press, 2016.

Barry, Garrett. "Potential Viking Site Found in Newfoundland." *CBC News*, April 1, 2016. http://www.cbc.ca/news/canada/newfoundland-labrador/vikings-newfoundland-1.3515747.

Carter, W. Hodding. *A Viking Voyage: In Which an Unlikely Crew of Adventurers Attempts an Epic Journey to the New World*. New York: Ballantine Books, 2000.

Cox, Steven L. "A Norse Penny from Maine." In *Vikings: The North Atlantic Saga*, edited by William W. Fitzhugh and Elisabeth I. Ward, pp. 206–7. Washington, DC: Smithsonian Books, 2000.

Davis, Callum. "Revealed: The Origin of Iceland's 'Viking Thunder Clap' Celebration." *The Telegraph*, July 8, 2016. http://www.telegraph.co.uk/football/2016/07/08/revealed-the-origin-of-icelands-viking-thunderclap-celebration/.

Farand, Chloe. "Discovery of 1,000-Year Old Viking Site in Canada Could Rewrite History." *The Independent*, April 3, 2016. http://www.independent.co.uk/news/world/world-history/discovery-vikings-newfoundland-canada-history-norse-point-rosee-l-anse-aux-meadows-a6965126.html.

Fox Sports. "Minnesota Vikings Install Enormous New Gjallarhorn at New Stadium." http://www.foxsports.com/nfl/story/minnesota-vikings-install-enormous-new-gjallarhorn-at-new-stadium-072116.

Gaiman, Neil. *American Gods*. Chatham: Headline Book Publishing, 2001, repr. 2015.

Gísli Sigurðsson. "The Quest for Vinland in Saga Scholarship." In *Vikings: The North Atlantic Saga*, edited by William W. Fitzhugh and Elisabeth I. Ward, pp. 232–37. Washington, DC: Smithsonian Books, 2000.

Gísli Sigurðsson. "The Sagas and the Truth." In *The Medieval Icelandic Saga and Oral Tradition: A Discourse on Method*, edited by Gísli Sigurðsson, pp. 253–302. Cambridge, MA: Harvard University Press, 2004.

Goessling, Ben. "Switching Sides?" *ESPN*, January 3, 2016. http://www.espn.com/blog/minnesota-vikings/post/_/id/17480/switching-sides-ragnar-trades-viking-helmet-for-cheesehead.

Hallett Carr, Edward. *What Is History?* London: Penguin, 1961.

Hertz, Johannes. "The Newport Tower." In *Vikings: The North Atlantic Saga*, edited by William W. Fitzhugh and Elisabeth I. Ward, p. 376. Washington, DC: Smithsonian Books, 2000.

The Hospitable Viking. "Homepage." http://hospitableviking.com.

Minnesota Vikings Football. "Vikings SKOL Chant Stirs Emotion in Locker Room & Iceland." http://www.vikings.com/news/article-1/Vikings-SKOL-Chant-Stirs-Emotion-in-Locker-Room—Iceland/0fce1603-3440-4c21-b80c-0aed84343f15.

Rafn, Carl Christian. *Antiquitates Americanae, sive scriptores septentionales rerum ante Columbianarum in America*. Copenhagen: Typis Officinae Schultzianae, 1837.

Riordan, Rick. *Magnus Chase and the Sword of Summer*. St. Ives: Random House, 2015.

"Runestone Museum." https://www.roadsideamerica.com/story/2607.

Samuel, Joseph Bunford and Einar Jónsson. *The Icelander Thorfinn Karlsefni Who Visited the Western Hemisphere in 1007. Private distribution, 1922.*

Seaver, Kirsten. *Maps, Myths, and Men: The Story of the Vinland Map*. Palo Alto, CA: Stanford University Press, 2004.

Sotheby's. "Important Work by Norwegian Artist Christian Krohg of *Leif Eriksson Discovering America* to Be Offered in Sotheby's June 2010 London Sale of 19th Century European Paintings." http://files.shareholder.com/downloads/BID/5287816312x0x362490/AE7B789E-4D56-4CF7-A557-0476B2A051BE/362490.pdf.

Storm, Gustav. *Islandske Annaler Indtil 1578*. Christiania (Oslo): Grøndahl & Søns Bogtrykkeri, 1888.

Strauss, Mark. "Discovery Could Rewrite History of Vikings in New World." *National Geographic*, March 31, 2016. http://news.nationalgeographic.com/2016/03/160331-vi king-discovery-north-america-canada-archaeology/.

Sutherland, Patricia D., Peter H. Thompson and Patricia A. Hunt. "Evidence of Early Metalworking in Arctic Canada." *Geoarchaeology* 30 (2015): 74–78.

Viking Ice. "Homepage." http://www.vikingice.com.

Wahlgren, Erik. "Viking Hoaxes." In *Medieval Scandinavia: An Encyclopaedia*, edited by Philip Pulsiano and Kirsten Wolf, pp. 700–701. New York: Garland, 1993.

Wahlgren, Erik. "Vinland Map." In *Medieval Scandinavia: An Encyclopaedia*, edited by Philip Pulsiano and Kirsten Wolf, pp. 703–4. New York: Garland, 1993.

Wallace, Birgitta Linderoth. "Viking Hoaxes." In *Vikings in the West: Papers Presented at a Symposium Sponsored by the Archaeological Institute of America, Chicago Society, and the Museum of Science and Industry of Chicago at the Museum of Science and Industry on April 3, 1982*, edited by Eleanor Guralnick, pp. 53–76. New York: Archaeological Institute of America, 1982.

Wallace, Birgitta Linderoth. "Vikings at L'Anse aux Meadows." In *Vikings: The North Atlantic Saga*, edited by William W. Fitzhugh and Elisabeth I. Ward, pp. 208–16. Washington, DC: Smithsonian Books, 2000.

Wallace, Birgitta Linderoth. "The Norse in Newfoundland: L'Anse aux Meadows and Vinland." *Newfoundland and Labrador Studies* 19, no. 1 (2003): 5–43.

Wallace, Birgitta Linderoth and William W. Fitzhugh, "Stumbles and Pitfalls in the Search for Viking America." In *Vikings: The North Atlantic Saga*, edited by William W. Fitzhugh and Elisabeth I. Ward, pp. 374–84. Washington, DC: Smithsonian Books, 2000.

Ward, Elisabeth I. "Vikings in American Culture." In *Vikings: The North Atlantic Saga*, edited by William W. Fitzhugh and Elisabeth I. Ward, pp. 365–73. Washington, DC: Smithsonian Books, 2000.

The White House: President Barack Obama. "Presidential Proclamation – Leif Erikson Day, 2015." https://obamawhitehouse.archives.gov/the-press-office/2015/10/08/presiden tial-proclamation-leif-erikson-day-2015.

The White House: President Barack Obama. "Presidential Proclamation – Leif Erikson Day, 2016." https://obamawhitehouse.archives.gov/the-press-office/2016/10/07/presiden tial-proclamation-leif-erikson-day-2016.

Williams, Henrik. "The Kensington Runestone: Fact and Fiction." *The Swedish-American Historical Quarterly* 63, no. 1 (2012): 3–20.

Williams, Stephen. "Westwards to Vinland: The Vikings Are Coming." In *Fantastic Archaeology: Wild Side of North American History*, edited by Stephen Williams, pp. 189–223. Philadelphia: University of Pennsylvania Press, 1991.

The World-Tree Project. http://www.worldtreeproject.org.

Notes

1. Neil Gaiman, *American Gods* (Chatham: Headline Book Publishing, 2001, repr. 2015), p. 75.
2. Ibid., 78.
3. Rick Riordan, *Magnus Chase and the Sword of Summer* (St. Ives: Random House, 2015), p. 29.
4. W. Hodding Carter, *A Viking Voyage: In Which an Unlikely Crew of Adventurers Attempts an Epic Journey to the New World* (New York: Ballantine Books, 2000), pp. 3–5.
5. Elisabeth I. Ward, "Vikings in American Culture," in *Vikings: The North Atlantic Saga*, ed. William W. Fitzhugh and Elisabeth I. Ward (Washington, DC: Smithsonian Books, 2000), pp. 365–73 at p. 366.
6. Sotheby's, "Important Work by Norwegian Artist Christian Krohg of *Leif Eriksson Discovering America* to Be Offered in Sotheby's June 2010 London Sale of 19th Century European Paintings," http://files.shareholder.com/downloads/BID/5287816312x0x362490/AE7B789E-4D56-4CF7-A557-0476B2A051BE/362490.pdf.
7. Joseph Bunford Samuel and Einar Jónsson, *The Icelander Thorfinn Karlsefni Who Visited the Western Hemisphere in 1007* (private distribution, 1922), p. 9.
8. The White House: President Barack Obama, "Presidential Proclamation – Leif Erikson Day, 2015," https://obamawhitehouse.archives.gov/the-press-office/2015/10/08/presidential-proclamation-leif-erikson-day-2015.
9. The White House: President Barack Obama, "Presidential Proclamation – Leif Erikson Day, 2016," https://obamawhitehouse.archives.gov/the-press-office/2016/10/07/presidential-proclamation-leif-erikson-day-2016.
10. Birgitta Linderoth Wallace, "Vikings at L'Anse aux Meadows," in *Vikings: The North Atlantic Saga*, ed. Fitzhugh and Ward, pp. 208–16 at p. 213.
11. See Steven L. Cox, "A Norse Penny from Maine," in *Vikings: The North Atlantic Saga*, ed. Fitzhugh and Ward, pp. 206–7.
12. "Þa kom ok skip af Grænlandi minna at vexti enn sma Islandz fór ... Þat var akkeris laust. Þar voru á .xvii. menn ok hófðu farit til Marklandz enn siðan vordit hingat hafreka." Gustav Storm, ed., *Islandske Annaler Indtil 1578* (Christiania (Oslo): Grøndahl & Søns Bogtrykkeri, 1888), p. 213.
13. See Eleanor Rosamund Barraclough, *Beyond the Northlands: Viking Voyages and the Old Norse Sagas* (Oxford: Oxford University Press, 2016), pp. 146–48.
14. Patricia D. Sutherland, Peter H. Thompson and Patricia A. Hunt, "Evidence of Early Metalworking in Arctic Canada," *Geoarchaeology* 30 (2015): 74–78.
15. See for example, Garrett Barry, "Potential Viking Site Found in Newfoundland," *CBC News*, April 1, 2016, http://www.cbc.ca/news/canada/newfoundland-labrador/vikings-newfoundland-1.3515747.

16. Mark Strauss, "Discovery Could Rewrite History of Vikings in New World," *National Geographic*, March 31, 2016, http://news.nationalgeographic.com/2016/03/160331-vi king-discovery-north-america-canada-archaeology/; and Chloe Farand, "Discovery of 1,000-Year Old Viking Site in Canada Could Rewrite History," *The Independent*, April 3, 2016, http://www.independent.co.uk/news/world/world-history/discovery-vikings-new foundland-canada-history-norse-point-rosee-l-anse-aux-meadows-a6965126.html.
17. Birgitta Linderoth Wallace, "The Norse in Newfoundland: L'Anse aux Meadows and Vinland," *Newfoundland and Labrador Studies* 19, no. 1 (2003): 5–43 at 26–27.
18. See Geraldine Barnes, *Viking America: The First Millennium* (Cambridge: D. S. Brewer, 2001), pp. 37–44.
19. Ibid., p. 37.
20. Gísli Sigurðsson has written extensively on the "mental maps" of the Vínland sagas: see Gísli Sigurðsson, "The Quest for Vinland in Saga Scholarship," in *Vikings: The North Atlantic Saga*, ed. Fitzhugh and Ward, pp. 232–37; Gísli Sigurðsson, "The Sagas and the Truth," in *The Medieval Icelandic Saga and Oral Tradition: A Discourse on Method*, ed. Gísli Sigurðsson (Cambridge, MA: Harvard University Press, 2004), pp. 253–302.
21. Carl Christian Rafn, *Antiquitates Americanae, sive scriptores septentionales rerum ante Columbianarum in America* (Copenhagen: Typis Officinae Schultzianae, 1837), p. 358.
22. Ibid., pp. 378–82.
23. Johannes Hertz, "The Newport Tower," in *Vikings: The North Atlantic Saga*, ed. Fitzhugh and Ward, p. 376.
24. This is discussed in detail by Barnes, *Viking America*, pp. 37–59.
25. See Birgitta Linderoth Wallace and William W. Fitzhugh, "Stumbles and Pitfalls in the Search for Viking America," in *Vikings: The North Atlantic Saga*, ed. Fitzhugh and Ward, pp. 374–84.
26. Barnes, *Viking America*, p. 68.
27. Riordan, *Magnus Chase*, p. 13.
28. Ibid., p. 23.
29. The full range of fakes and forgeries has been discussed elsewhere, and here I will only focus on a few examples. See for example, Wallace and Fitzhugh, "Stumbles and Pitfalls," p. 384; Erik Wahlgren, "Viking Hoaxes," in *Medieval Scandinavia: An Encyclopaedia*, ed. Philip Pulsiano and Kirsten Wolf (New York: Garland, 1993), pp. 700–701; Erik Wahlgren, "Vinland Map," in *Medieval Scandinavia*, pp. 703–4; Birgitta Linderoth Wallace, "Viking Hoaxes," in *Vikings in the West: Papers Presented at a Symposium Sponsored by the Archaeological Institute of America, Chicago Society, and the Museum of Science and Industry of Chicago at the Museum of Science and Industry on April 3, 1982*, ed. Eleanor Guralnick (New York: Archaeological Institute of America, 1982), pp. 53–76; Stephen Williams, "Westwards to Vinland: The Vikings Are Coming," in *Fantastic Archaeology: Wild Side of North American History*, ed. Stephen Williams (Philadelphia: University of Pennsylvania Press, 1991), pp. 189–223; Kirsten Seaver, *Maps, Myths, and Men: The Story of the Vinland Map* (Palo Alto, CA: Stanford University Press, 2004).
30. Wallace and Fitzhugh, "Stumbles and Pitfalls," p. 381.
31. Ibid., p. 382.
32. Ibid., p. 384.
33. Williams, "Westwards to Vinland," p. 206.

34. Henrik Williams, "The Kensington Runestone: Fact and Fiction," *The Swedish-American Historical Quarterly* 63, no. 1 (2012): 3–20 at 20.
35. "Runestone Museum," https://www.roadsideamerica.com/story/2607.
36. Ben Goessling, "Switching Sides?," *ESPN*, January 3, 2016, http://www.espn.com/blog/minnesota-vikings/post/_/id/17480/switching-sides-ragnar-trades-viking-helmet-for-cheesehead.
37. Fox Sports, "Minnesota Vikings Install Enormous New Gjallarhorn at New Stadium," http://www.foxsports.com/nfl/story/minnesota-vikings-install-enormous-new-gjallar horn-at-new-stadium-072116.
38. Minnesota Vikings Football, "Vikings SKOL Chant Stirs Emotion in Locker Room & Iceland," http://www.vikings.com/news/article-1/Vikings-SKOL-Chant-Stirs-Emotion-in-Locker-Room–Iceland/0fce1603-3440-4c21-b80c-0aed84343f15.
39. Ibid.
40. Callum Davis, "Revealed: The Origin of Iceland's 'Viking Thunder Clap' Celebration," *The Telegraph*, July 8, 2016, http://www.telegraph.co.uk/football/2016/07/08/revealed-the-origin-of-icelands-viking-thunderclap-celebration/.
41. Viking Ice, "Homepage," http://www.vikingice.com.
42. The Hospitable Viking, "Homepage," http://hospitableviking.com.
43. Archived in the World-Tree Project online database, "Item 1214: Insignia of North Salem High School, Salem, Oregon," http://www.worldtreeproject.org/document/1214.
44. "Item 1206: Insignia of James Monroe High School, North Hills, CA," http://www.world treeproject.org/document/1206.
45. "Item 1204: Insignia of Blair High School, Pasadena, CA," http://www.worldtreeproject.org/document/1204.
46. "Item 1213: Insignia of Spartanburg High School, Spartanburg, SC," http://www.worldtreeproject.org/document/1213.
47. "Item 1215: Insignia of Hilo High School, Hilo, HI," http://www.worldtreeproject.org/document/1215.
48. Edward Hallett Carr, *What Is History?* (London: Penguin, 1961), p. 120.

Kevin Crossley-Holland
Afterword: Tell These Stories Yourself

After polishing off a bowl of porridge enhanced by Irish whiskey – no, not pickled herring or *gjetost* or *gamalost*, but fortifying nonetheless – and then marching into the first session of the *Rediscovering the Vikings* conference, I was aware of a shared sense of excitement, and even daring: a sense that in bringing together people with such diverse training and interests in the Vikings, the conference organizers were breaking risky new ground, and that the ice might not hold.

As neither an academic nor one involved in heritage entertainment, but rather as a kind of go-between, I can report that it did. It most certainly did! And while one or two academics may have narrowed their eyes at digital games and reenactment, and one or two gamesters and reenactors were little impressed by literary niceties, the center of "reception, recovery, and engagement" held completely firm.

Whilst translating Anglo-Saxon poetry during my twenties (all around me, my peers were singing along with the Beatles), I was of course continuously aware of the Vikings offstage and onstage. The martyrdom of King Edmund, and the terrifying report of the battle at Maldon, both in my own East Anglia, upset me then, and have haunted me ever since, but my first deeper engagement was a direct result of meetings with W. H. Auden during which we discussed the Elder Edda, and he counseled me to "look north." He could scarcely have had a more willing disciple. I resigned from my position as editorial director of a London publishing house, engaged with the Eddaic poems, and the sagas, and, with my two sons, headed for Iceland.

The upshot of all this was my retelling of the *Norse Myths*[1] first published in 1982 – three years in the making – now published by Penguin Books; and rereading my long introduction and notes, I can quickly see how my understanding of the Vikings has evolved after almost forty years. Let me briefly suggest some of the reasons why, and how.

First, some points of ignition: speaking at the University of Reykjavík on the riddle tradition common to Anglo-Saxon and Old Norse literature; several times meeting Vigdís Finnbogadóttir while she was President of Iceland; arguing with Halldór Laxness, Alan Boucher, Magnus Magnusson, and a brew of young Icelandic and American academics; teaching as a Fulbright DVP for twelve months at Saint Olaf College in Minnesota, and then for four years with an endowed chair at the University of Saint Thomas in St. Paul (some 30 percent of Minnesotans are of Scandinavian origin); and not least, visiting my wife Linda's cousins, descendants of many generations of fishermen, in and around

https://doi.org/10.1515/9781501513886-016

Trondheim. All this, and speaking at dozens of schools and colleges about Viking culture, now and at last firmly ensconced as not only vital in its own right, but part of the story of our own islands, and all the while reading and reading: sources, papers, and interpretations.

I think I have come to understand more about the psychology of the Vikings: what they were actually like as women, men, and children. I have seen on the ground, as it were, the land-hunger that drove many of them over-seas. I've better understood how the dark days in the north helped to shape their view of life. I've recognized that for all their energy, imagination, and wit, their gods were not much interested in human beings and their affairs (while behaving very much like humans themselves), and interacted little with them. I've come to understand that the myths are utterly apocalyptic. Do you remem-ber Robert Lowell's words in "Waking Early Sunday Morning?"

> Pity the planet, all joy gone
> from this sweet volcanic cone;
> peace to our children when they fall
> in small war on the heels of small
> war . . .

This fatalism is, I think, the cornerstone of the appeal of the myths today. They are cosmic, ice-bright, and in tune with our own time.

I hope something of this understanding is reflected in my two Viking sagas, *Bracelet of Bones*[2] and *Scramasax*[3] and my recent retelling for children, *Norse Myths: Tales of Odin, Thor and Loki*.[4] But, of course, a novel is nothing unless such understandings are embodied in the characters. Who were they, these Vikings? What were they actually like? What were their day-to-day preoccupa-tions? What did they believe in, argue about, laugh about, come to blows about? I wanted to offer a view of them at home in Norway, and as largely peaceful traders. I wanted to show the astounding stepping-stones (such as Ladoga) on their eastern routes and migrations. I wanted to show what they thought about Byzantines and Arabs, and how Byzantines and Arabs viewed them. I wanted the polytheistic beliefs of the Norsemen to collide, but some-times coincide with Christianity and Islam. And I found in my Solveig a gutsy, questioning girl – notionally the daughter of the Halfdan who inscribed his name in runes on a parapet in Hagia Sophia – who could live alongside men, think for herself, and challenge conventional wisdom.

But while writing *Norse Myths*, and contemplating Jeffrey Alan Love's force-ful and extremely powerful illustrations, I became aware that my young edito-rial assistant at Walker Books, Daisy Jellicoe, was beginning to take a very dim view of the antics and continual enmity of the deities. I thought I could perhaps reconcile something of her and our world with that of the Vikings, and so I wrote her this poem, "The Northern Gods":

Can you hear, dear Daisy,
that rousing horn and the deer-hide drum,
those distant bells on the high pastures?
Can you see that fiddler without a fiddle,
hoicking up his baggy trousers,
singing syllables and beginning to dance?
Listen! That yoik, summoning, capturing
a loved one or a favorite animal, a secret
glade cradled between rock shoulders.

I suspect you think there's very little to be said
for the northern gods, but let me translate them
into their makers, or even into your own
acquaintance. Think of some friend like Bragi
with a gift for poetry; or someone like Frigg
who – excuse my Latin – is a *mater familias*;
some old salt accustomed to iron rations.
A corn-silk blonde? A heavy drinker?
A woman driven by her instincts and passions?

Home from the halls and highlights of Asgard,
I think you'd be smitten by the gods' readiness
to take risks and laugh at themselves,
and admire their unflinching curiosity.
Their rampant sexuality might not be to your liking
but you'd be exhilarated by their energy and wit.
Maybe their childlikeness would disarm you
and you'd mourn at how, gods as they were,
they were fatalists, trapped in time.

Not only this. Look for the lines between lines.
Black scarves swirling, sweeping over tundra,
black grit smoking and scorching boot soles,
black bears, polar bears, packs of wolves,
mountain hares zigzagging across the glaciers
while the midnight sun bounces along the horizon

but then disappears for weeks on end.
Each fire flickers in its own hearth.
Nothing is ever easy on Middle Earth.

Have you ever dreamed you were sitting in the bole
of Yggdrasill, squinting up at the skull
of the white sky, then down into the icy swirl?
Have you heard the vitriol of the dragon,
the corpse-devourer, and seen how the squirrel
whisks it up to the eagle on the topmost branch?
And if, chaste and questing, you too were able
to sip water from the spring, would you
be prepared to make some great sacrifice?

"But the Vikings," you say, wrinkling your nose,
"weren't they clannish and boastful and suspicious?"
Yes, but these are the defects of virtues.
Remember *Havamal*. "Never be the first
to strain and break the bonds of friendship . . .
Never abuse a guest, and be generous
to anyone in need . . . If you know of some evil,
ensure everyone knows about it . . . A better man
often comes off worse when swords start talking."

"What about their violence, then? Their brutality?"
(You persist so prettily). "What about the blood eagle?"
By all means compare the habits of men and women
a millennium ago with contemporary values
but be very cautious . . . Can you imagine
what the Vikings would have said about us?
Come now, Daisy. Listen to the words
of a white-haired singer. Allow Idun
to tempt you with her apples, forever young.

The Vikings continue to hold center stage in my writing life, and I have been piecing together a cycle of poems about Harald Sigurdsson (Hardrada) during the years when he served in Byzantium and Sicily as a member of the Varangian Guard – the poems of a passionate young man who is also learning the nature of leadership and power and preparing for his return to Norway. And as for my fellow children's authors: let me urge them to look north as, briefly, Rosemary

Sutcliff did, and Henry Treece did, and as I have tried to do. "Medievalism" is in full swing, and, in offering informed and imaginative readings of a profoundly influential culture, there is thrilling and valuable work to be done.

Bibliography

Crossley-Holland, Kevin. *The Norse Myths*. London: Penguin, 1982.
Crossley-Holland, Kevin. *Bracelet of Bones: Book 1 (The Viking Sagas)*. London: Quercus, 2012.
Crossley-Holland, Kevin. *Scramasax: Book 2 (The Viking Sagas)*. London: Quercus, 2013.
Crossley-Holland, Kevin. *Norse Myths: Tales of Odin, Thor and Loki*. London: Walker Studio, 2017.

Notes

1. Kevin Crossley-Holland, *The Norse Myths* (London: Penguin, 1982).
2. Kevin Crossley-Holland, *Bracelet of Bones: Book 1 (The Viking Sagas)* (London: Quercus, 2012).
3. Kevin Crossley-Holland, *Scramasax: Book 2 (The Viking Sagas)* (London: Quercus, 2013).
4. Kevin Crossley-Holland, *Norse Myths: Tales of Odin, Thor and Loki* (London: Walker Studio, 2017).

Index

Anglo-Saxon 2, 7, 32, 132, 140, 202, 212, 267

Archaeology 7, 28, 32, 42, 43, 46, 53, 55, 58, 64, 68–70, 72, 74, 82, 85, 86, 88, 166, 236, 265

Battle of Clontarf 5, 168, 236, 241, 243, 246, 249

Branding 2, 5, 12, 21, 214, 216, 217, 222–225, 228, 236–238, 260

Dublinia 4, 235, 236, 241

Etymology 1, 19, 163, 176

Film 23, 34, 39, 117, 120, 128, 167, 172, 173, 177, 179, 203, 209, 227, 229, 247
– movies 221

Game of Thrones 4, 11, 162, 173, 176, 178, 233, 242, 260

Gender 8, 31, 37, 42, 89, 92, 95, 97–99, 101, 102, 106, 163, 170, 171, 244

Gesta Danorum 11, 35, 42, 81, 170, 178, 181, 197, 200

Greenland 1, 130, 169, 250, 251, 254, 255, 262

Heritage 2, 3, 5, 6, 12–14, 57, 58, 185, 214, 220, 221, 223, 224, 233–240, 242, 252, 253, 259–261, 267

Horned Helmet 2, 103, 105, 107, 116, 194, 214–216, 218, 219, 221, 222, 225–229, 231, 232, 259, 261

Ibn Fadlan 36, 43, 46

Jewelry 33, 47, 55, 56, 70, 75, 77, 87, 166

Jómsvíkinga saga 10, 47, 51, 145, 147, 150, 151, 157, 159

Jorvik 4, 172

Kensington Runestone 3, 14, 16, 258, 264

Lindisfarne 2, 23, 34

Living History 6, 7, 13, 70, 86, 241, 242, 244

Magic 12, 76, 78, 81, 93, 96, 99, 100, 117, 203–205, 209, 210

Marvel 4, 12, 89, 219, 220

Minnesota Vikings 14, 31, 224, 259, 260, 266

Mythbusting 13, 215, 225, 226

Neil Gaiman 4, 17, 40, 250, 262

Newfoundland 4, 91, 217, 221, 251, 255, 256, 261, 264, 265

Norse Myth 3, 4, 10, 11, 14, 16–18, 118, 128–130, 134, 139, 140, 142, 144, 162, 206, 213, 215, 219, 222, 226, 231, 257, 259, 267, 268, 271

Paganism 7, 35, 77, 88, 113, 131, 183, 208, 250

Ragnarök 117, 130, 134, 138, 243

Ragnar loðbrók 20, 31, 32, 35, 36, 38, 39, 42, 92, 94, 111, 118, 152–154, 181, 182, 197

Real Vikings 7, 28, 29, 37, 38, 40, 88

Reenactment 7, 8, 57–58, 69–76, 79–82, 85–87, 241, 242, 244, 267

Rune 4, 12, 20, 46, 77, 87, 201–207, 209, 210, 212, 232, 256–258, 268

Runestone 201, 204, 206, 208–211, 213, 258, 259

Rus' 1, 46, 53, 75

Tattoos 6, 34, 36, 259

The Last Kingdom 4, 43, 172, 178, 214

Thor ix, 4, 9, 10, 12, 107, 110, 129, 130, 132–136, 138, 140, 142, 144, 215, 217, 219–222, 230, 250, 251

Tolkien 11, 162, 163, 167

https://doi.org/10.1515/9781501513886-017

Tourism 3, 4, 12, 236, 238, 239, 242
– tourist 1
TV series 2, 19, 36, 79, 88, 209, 221
– drama series 29
– TV 43
– TV documentary 258
– TV drama series 31
– TV programs 89
– TV show 162, 172, 179, 251
TV series *Vikings* 7

Valhalla 8, 101, 111, 208, 244, 250
Victorian 4, 6, 8, 9, 15, 17, 23, 30, 95, 107,
       108, 110–114, 116, 124, 126, 152, 244
Video games 3, 4, 12, 201, 202

Viking Festival 2, 4, 5, 58, 69–77, 79–82, 86,
       88, 232, 239–241, 243
Viking ship 24, 220, 221, 223, 231, 252, 261
– ships 33
Viking Studies 2, 29, 31, 32, 39, 40, 43–45,
       47, 51, 53, 55, 57, 59, 64
Viking 1, 2, 6, 13, 19, 20, 21, 22, 23, 24
Vikings 3, 4, 19, 29, 31–34, 36, 40, 79, 88,
       172, 214, 233, 242
Völva 8, 36, 77–79

Wagner 4, 105, 128, 180, 181, 193, 216
Winged helmet 8, 9, 216, 220
World-Tree Project v, 5, 6, 16–18, 40, 214–217,
       221, 222, 224, 227–231, 264, 266